Political Governance and Minority Rights

Political Governance and Minority Rights

The South and South-East Asian Scenario

Editor

LIPI GHOSH

Routledge
Taylor & Francis Group

LONDON AND NEW YORK

First published 2009 by Routledge

2 Park Square, Milton Park, Abingdon, Oxfordshire OX14 4RN
52 Vanderbilt Avenue, New York, NY 10017

Routledge is an imprint of the Taylor & Francis Group, an informa business

First issued in paperback 2019

Transferred to Digital Printing 2009

Typeset by
Star Compugraphics Private Limited
D-156, Second Floor
Sector 7, Noida 201 301

British Library Cataloguing-in-Publication Data
A catalogue record of this book is available from the British Library

ISBN: 978-0-415-55071-0 (hbk)
ISBN: 978-0-367-17641-9 (pbk)

*To my beloved mother, who
inspired me to always work hard.*

Contents

Governance, Culture and the Aspirations of Minorities

Tables, Figures and Map

Tables

Figures

Map

Foreword

Mushirul Hasan

Communities, their formation, evolution and transformation have formed the grist of academic writing for centuries. In South and South-East Asia, the question of communities — minorities, majorities, alien, indigenous — has assumed a special inflection thanks to the legacy of colonialism and the vagaries of post-colonial politics and anxieties. Not surprisingly therefore, studies and scholarship on communities have generated some of the most influential and engaging debates of political theory. The result of such deliberations has enabled a fresh look at some of the more contentious issues that nation-states continue to grapple with in the form of dissent and politics of ethnicity. At the same time, there has been a closer scrutiny of historical practices that have produced multiple and competing understandings of communities making it important to unravel the intersection of the complicities of historical knowledge with the formations of modern power. The present volume represents one such attempt to unravel the play of the past with the predicaments of the present, to provide a much-needed comparative perspective on the problems of community rights and political governance in South and South-East Asia.

Across the past decades, there has been an exhaustive investigation and interrogation of the term community and of its multiple connotations, its historical location, its production as a consequence of historical thought with its aggrandizing agenda, its relationship with the nation, the highest form of the imagined community. This investigation has facilitated a more nuanced approach to history-writing that has begun to contest categories such as culture, identity, nation and tradition and alongside that, a more careful understanding of subaltern claims to social justice and to a vast range of rights and entitlements. Second, these approaches have produced a new and visible turn in the writing of contemporary history that looks more closely at governance and governmentality, state structures and

processes of continual negotiation with stakeholders and marginalized groups, of identity politics and the politicization of religion and finally of the pressures of globalization on governance and
community rights.

The present volume straddles both these emergent tendencies and
trends in scholarship and presents us with a wide-ranging selection
of essays dealing with current scenario in South and South-East Asia.
The inclusion of South-East Asia and India's neighbouring countries,
like Nepal, Bangladesh and Sri Lanka, is important not merely because
they serve to give us empirical details and thereby help identify
the crises of governance but also because they help initiate a genuine
dialogue that advances the cause of a comparative methodology to
examine the problems and processes in post-colonial Asia. Admittedly
countries like Nepal and Thailand were not formally colonized and
therefore did not go through the process of decolonization or any
such struggle for self-definition. For both these countries, the very
question of scrapping the monarchy was important and momentous
in itself, and one that brought numerous challenges to the fore.

The crisis of governance has been acutely perceived in the regions
of South and South-East Asia, defying quite clearly the assumptions held by Immanuel Kant about the inherently peaceful nature
of democracies. The lamentable track record of violence against
Muslims, women, tribals, of the pressures of displacement and immigration in parts of India, the genocide in Sri Lanka, the extra burdens
faced by women during war, the conditions of tribals and minorities
in Bangladesh and Pakistan, the vagaries of politics in Nepal and
Thailand are telling and seem hardly a positive testimony to the successful functioning of either democracy or to the commitment and
political will of governments in Asia. Most of the countries in South
Asia are witnessing insurgency movements, all of which impede
effective government in one way or the other. It is in this context
that a volume such as the present makes a decidedly important contribution, in that it sets out in graphic detail the actual pressures that
minorities face and how in their efforts to thwart what they see as
domination and oppression by the ruling state, there is a complex
intersection of violence, criminality and marginalization. The essay
on the carnage in Gujarat that was at one level the culmination of a
hate campaign and which saw unprecedented barbarities inflicted on
the bodies of women and children tells us a chilling story, especially of
how the state became the space of anarchy and not that of regulation

as it claimed to be. Complicity of state officials and the crisis of governmentality, and narratives of victimhood force us to re-examine questions of constitutional safeguards and what it actually means to be a minority. Other essays take up the question of women's peace initiatives — an area that merits substantial investigation — while the issue of migration and displacement discussed in the context of Bangladesh and North-East India reminds us again and again how internal failures conflate into external security issues. It is well-known that persecution of minorities have immediate echoes across borders, and given the perils of the nuclear option, it is prescient that we continue to keep the dialogue going, which is the only way forward.

Whether knowledge is indeed power may be debatable, but that it can be an enabling device to oversee a common humanity, is not in doubt. Problems of governance need to be continuously examined and scrutinized in the context of voices that strain to be heard, sometimes stridently, at other times in despair. Discursive formations backing right-wing movements and articulations need to be identified, understood and battled against if we are to preserve the cherished ideals of sovereignty, secularism and democracy. These are not just words to be repeated in a function of ceremony but values that must be cultivated if we are to live with some degree of equanimity in the twenty-first century. This book edited by Lipi Ghosh is a welcome addition for all of us who wish to gain more access to the problems of developing countries in Asia and thereby to share our sense of collective rights and obligations and to try and build a public opinion for inclusion and inclusiveness in our political life.

Preface and Acknowledgments

This volume had its origin in an International Seminar organized in October 2006 by the Centre for South and Southeast Asian Studies, University of Calcutta, on Minorities, Community Rights and Political Governance, sponsored by the University Grants Commission, New Delhi.

The idea of comparing South and South-East Asia was rather appealing from the beginning. Both the regions have a common heritage of colonial administration and have experienced significant changes in the post-colonial period. The nature or pattern of changes experienced is also quite similar in each society. Given their intricate nature and the historical interrelationships between state governance and the many religious and ethnic minorities that constitute these societies, a comparative analysis based on case studies by different scholars from the various relevant disciplines seemed highly desirable.

I am grateful to all those who contributed their articles to this volume. In addition to the participants of the original seminar, others who have been invited to contribute papers are Dr Maneesha Tikekar, Dr Anasua Basu Ray Chaudhury, Prof Aris Mundayat, Dr Mandy Sadan, Dr Amnuayvit Thitibordin, Dr Mala Rajo Sathian and Prof Sunil Kukreja.

I express my sincere gratitude to Prof Mushirul Hasan and Dr Asghar Ali Engineer for having consented to write respectively the Foreword and the Afterword, which will no doubt enrich our understanding of the subject.

I am also thankful to Prof P.S. Ghosh and Prof Bhaskar Chakraborty, as well as to two of my young colleagues, Dr Paula Banerjee and Dr Anasua Basu Ray Chaudhury, for their invaluable feedback and comments.

Introduction

Alchemy of Community Divides: A Historical Overview

The present generation of scholars have interpreted the term 'community' in different ways, with meanings varying from an archaic horizontal type of simplicity, to several modern-day understandings that are complex and intricate. When we look back to the use of the word 200 years ago, it generally referred to an association of people conglomerated for a single purpose or under one ideology. Gradually, however, we have become more conscious about using the term and in the modern context, the term 'community' allows us to define a more varied mosaic or conglomeration of people. Thus, a community today refers to a social group of organisms who share the same environment and normally share the same interests as well. In addition, attitudes, resources, preferences, needs, risks and a number of other conditions may be present and common to the community as a whole, affecting the identity of its members and the degree of cohesiveness between them. In my opinion, a community is a social unit comprised of a population and settlement that is based on a shared political, economic and cultural landscape. And to that extent, it has played an important role in both social integration and cultural interaction since the ancient past and right up to the present day.

Etymologically speaking, the word community is derived from the Latin word *communitas* (meaning 'the same'), which is in turn derived from *communis*, which means 'common, public, general, shared by all or many'.[1] *Communis* itself comes from a combination of the Latin prefix *com-* ('together') and the word *munis* (which has to do with performing services).

It was German sociologist Ferdinand Tönnies who presented a concise differentiation between the terms 'community' (*Gemeinschaft*) and 'society' (*Gesellschaft*). In his 1887 work, *Gemeinschaft und Gesellschaft,* Tönnies argued that 'community' is perceived to be a tighter and more cohesive social entity within the context of the larger society due to the presence of 'unity of will'.[2] He added that family and kinship were perfect expressions of the community, but other shared characteristics — such as place or belief — could also result in a *gemeinschaft.*

A number of ways of categorizing the types of community have been proposed. One such division is communities of culture, which range from the local clique, subculture, ethnic and/or religious groups in a multicultural society, to the global community cultures of today.

The question of community is often considered within the parameters of minority vs majority relations. Any given political space can be ruled only by a power that has the support of the majority — linguistic, religious, ethnic, cultural and geographical. These majorities are also represented in the instruments of power, be it the government, political parties, judiciary, army, bureaucracy, academia, media, etc. The majorities *create* community-based minorities, who then assemble in their own geographical, cultural, social, economic and political spaces. Ruler–ruled relationships between such majorities and minorities can take on different patterns, including opposition, accommodation, appropriation, conflict, coalition, negotiation, etc. In other words, minorities mobilize themselves in the form of a 'community', framed on the basis of common or shared signs, such as language, ethnicity, culture, religion, region, etc. Minority communities negotiate with the majorities on the basis of their rights, thus shaping and strengthening community/minority rights. Communities understand the need and importance of rights, they frame the elements of these rights, demand them, take up a political course of action to get the rights accepted by the powers that be and assert their rights. The understanding and practical exercise of community rights, however, is dependent on the form and the nature of governance that exists in that particular state. The nature of governance, therefore, determines the effective influence of community rights thus won by the minorities.

Historically speaking, at the time that nation-states were emerging from the fragmenting empires of continental Europe, European nations were busy consolidating their global empires. Thus, colonial expansions were taking place across Asia and in course of time different European powers were able to establish their control on different parts of South and South-East Asia — societies that were home to a bewilderingly diverse mix of states and communities. The colonial powers had the occasion to create large consolidated polities out of these multiple and diverse communities. To be sure, none of the pre-colonial states in Asia could be described as 'nation-states' in the European sense. To Clive Christie, 'they could be accurately described as "ethnic empires" where a dominant ethnic group governed a wide range of minorities,... (and) no serious attempt was made to integrate them into a common national identity'.[3] Christie, however, should be read with some reservation because, to some extent, the case of Thailand remained distinct, as will be discussed in the following pages.

Benedict Anderson, while expounding on his concept of an 'imagined nation', defines the nation 'as a *community*, because, regardless of the actual inequality and exploitation that may prevail in each, the nation is always conceived as a deep, horizontal comrade-ship. Ultimately, it is this fraternity that makes it possible, over the past two centuries, for so many millions of people, not so much to kill, as willingly to die for such limited imaginings.'[4] His rather insightful opinion is re-established when he writes: 'The nation is imagined as *limited* because even the largest of them, encompassing perhaps a billion living human beings, has finite, if elastic boundaries, beyond which lie other nations. No nation imagines itself coterminous with mankind. The most messianic nationalists do not dream of a day when all the members of the human race will join their nation in the way that it was possible, in certain epochs, for, say, Christians to dream of a wholly Christian planet.'[5]

Thus, Anderson draws our attention to majoritarian attitudes towards minority groups. He writes, 'Europeans were ... the first to think in these majority–minority terms'.[6] In the context of Asia, they actually had the opportunity to apply this. In both, South Asia and South-East Asia, the story of colonial constructions of community is very interesting. There was a time when the people referred to themselves by using various local names (endo-ethnonyms) based on the concept of man, religion and ancestral worship or place names. Contact with the outside world brought in exo-ethnic terms like 'primitive people', 'noble savage' or 'savage noble'. Later on, they graduated to terms like 'aborigines', 'backward communities' or 'tribes' and 'castes' even.[7] The civilizing mission of the colonial rulers sometimes tried to integrate these communities, while on many other instances, for their administrative needs, they followed a policy of exterminating certain communities. The census was a big tool in the hands of the colonial rulers, used in this process of constructing a community identity. In the context of India, Gerald Barrier observes that essentially initiated for informational purposes in the mid-nineteenth century, the census was subsequently regularized and thus evolved into an institution in its own right. They were a systematic guide for the colonial government to many social, economic and political issues.[8] Truly speaking, it was the census policy of the colonial rulers which resulted in the leaving out or exclusion of many ethnic groups/communities from the existing ethnic mosaic. To quote Anderson once again, 'Many ethnic groups disappeared from successive censuses as European imaginings changed, but almost certainly existed first and foremost in the minds of the Europeans. Precisely for this reason, the Europeans sought quite early to build "majority coalitions" around themselves, against groups they feared could seriously compete with them in majority terms.'[9] One pertinent example is that of colonial policy with regard to the Ahoms of Assam, whom the British colonial state feared most as having been the traditional ruling class, settled in the region for nearly 600 years. One of the essays in this volume narrates that story in great detail.

On the question of colonial constructions of the community in the South and South-East Asian context, an elaborate study was produced by French sociologist Louis Dumont. In the Indian content, his efforts took the shape of the journal *Contributions to Indian Sociology*. The journal puts caste at the centre of Hindu social life, as the basis on which different social groups were graded.[10] Caste was the instrument used by colonial rulers to delve into the multiple stratified layers of Indian society. This type of community can be described as being 'organic', a concept propounded by Christie.[11] In contrast to this organic community, there was another 'acquired' community, which had been created as a consequence of deliberate thought and organization from above; in most cases it was a colonial construct. Sekhar Bandyopadhyay's work *Caste, Politics and the Raj* (1990) also throws important light on this subject. To quote Bandyopadhyay, 'As a divisive force in Indian society, the potentiality of caste along with religion was being gradually perceived by the colonial government since the Revolt of 1857'.[12] The British colonial rulers needed to know the inner social divisions of the ruled, so that one group could be played off against the other.[13] During the late nineteenth and early twentieth centuries, caste was thus undergoing a process of politicization that was conditioned primarily by the colonial context. The colonial ethnographers studied the caste system and discovered in it a central dichotomy, with privileged higher castes located at one end and deprived lower castes at the other.

In a recent work, Anthony Reid discusses this phenomenon of nationalism growing into a nation-state. He writes, 'the world-system of competitive, theoretically equal sovereign states, inadequately labelled, the "Westphalia system" had been carried into Asia over several centuries under the "organized hypocrisy" of imperialism', an idea that Reid borrows from Stephen D. Krasner. Under the new system, it was held that only 'civilised states' could be full members of the sovereign equality club. Reid writes:

> After 1945, that exclusivist hypocrisy was replaced by a more optimistic one, which held that every corner of the planet should be divided into theoretically equal sovereign states. Some imperial constructs decolonised and democratised in a series of asymmetric federal compromises which left the outer shell of empire still able to act in the world as a nation state with the same borders as the old. India is the classic case, but in Southeast Asia the example was followed more cautiously in Malaysia. Others reacted against their humiliating pasts through the heroically ambitious path of revolution. This demanded immediately an ideal model of the modern nation state, with complete legal equality between citizens who had to forget all past loyalties, yet within the messy imperial borders.[14]

He goes on to pose a crucial question regarding the borders in Asia:

> It was the task of nationalism to perform the alchemy of Asia. The base metal of empire had to be transmuted into the gold of nationhood. The revolutionary alchemist was the most daring. His gold comprised the sovereignty of the people, the equality of all citizens under a unified and centralised state, and a complete break with past loyalties. To achieve such a transmutation from the immense variety and antiquity of political and civilizations forms in Asia would require more powerful alchemy than any that Europeans had needed in their own transitions from empires to nations. To achieve it without fragmenting the leviathans of imperial construction would require a true magic.

Could we imagine democratic nationalisms in Europe within borders created by the Hapsburgs, Romanovs and Ottomans, as we do in Asia for the empires of British, Dutch, French and Manchus?[15]

In the Asian context, the decade of the 1940s saw the idea of Pan-Asianism gain prominence in countries then under Western imperial dominance and colonial rule. As a general term 'Pan-Asianism' refers to a wide range of ideas and movements in the late nineteenth and early twentieth centuries calling for the solidarity of Asian peoples to counter Western influences. In Japan, where Pan-Asianism had a decisive influence on the course of the country's modern history and also served as an ideological justification for military expansionism through 1945, it is referred to as 'Asianism' or 'Greater Asianism'. In other words, Pan-Asianism is the ideology that Asian countries and peoples share similar values and histories and should therefore be politically and culturally united. Pan-Asian thought began to develop in Japan in the late nineteenth century and was spurred on following the defeat of Russia in the Russo-Japanese War (1904–05). It was a concept created and promulgated by the government and military of the Empire of Japan, and represented the desire to create a self-sufficient bloc of Asian nations led by the Japanese and free of Western powers. Across Asia, there developed a new civilizational discourse with a tint of Japanese imperialism, which Prasenjit Duara refers to as the 'theory of redemptive societies'.[16] Although Asian societies ultimately rejected Japan's Pan-Asianism, it did help them imbibe the new spirit of nationalism in their state system and civil society. As it happened, Asian nationalism could not forge any new alternative model, instead it remained confined within the old colonial paradigm and gave birth to a 'colonial hangover' identity.

In the context of decolonization and the resultant independence, this 'new nationalism' clearly shows that colonial powers, in the course of their dealings with the various respective nationalist units, grossly neglected the rights of many communities and failed to provide a political structure which could protect their rights and interests, first as a community and then as a minority. These communities rapidly became aware of their marginal position. Several peripheral regions and ethnic minorities felt that their interests were being ignored. It is not surprising then that the crucial phase of decolonization — between 1945 and 1954 — saw a series of community uprisings take place across South and South-East Asia.

Benedict Anderson has rightly remarked, 'The politics of ethnicity/ communitarian movements have their roots in modern times, not ancient history and their shape has been largely determined by colonial policy'.[17]

This statement can be proved with instances from South-East Asia. In the era of decolonization, which followed the Second World War, parallel events in South-East Asia encouraged the formation of a number of separatist and semi-separatist movements by different communities. The patterns traced by these movements, however, differed from place to place. The Patani Malays sought to break away from the Thai state, while the Acehnese rebels wished to gain grounds within the existing Republic of Indonesia. However, there were two factors that were common to all these movements: they shared the same historical antecedents and at the root of their separatist struggles lay the issue of identity. The era of nationalism and the ensuing period of decolonization thus helped create a new consciousness of identity and the entire process gave birth to much turmoil which continues even today.

It will be interesting to take up for consideration a few examples of colonial policy with respect to South-East Asian states. In four centuries of colonial rule, from the early 1500s to the post-Second World War era, the British conquered the areas now known as Malaysia, Brunei, Singapore and Burma, while the French controlled present-day Laos, Cambodia and Vietnam. Indonesia was incorporated into the Indies and the Philippines was colonized first by Spain and then by the United States. The Portuguese were the first colonists to conquer parts of South-East Asia. Thailand was the only country that escaped formal colonization.

Despite the various different manifestations of colonial rule in South-East Asia, many elements can be identified which were common to colonial policies vis-à-vis minority communities. Everywhere in South-East Asia colonial rule resulted in the formation of separate nation-states with viable boundaries. These boundaries often cut across community/ethnic groups, isolating the non-integrated ethnic minority groups. The inhabitants of north-east Thailand were Lao, the southernmost provinces were populated by Malay Muslims, the northern provinces were home to the Shans, Karens and other hill tribes. The British and French designed their policies in such a way that they did not have to bother about the community/ethnic mosaic of the region and so as to fulfill only colonial calculations.

Dutch rule in Indonesia disrupted the established social patterns of the villages, giving way to communitarian tension between the aristocratic *Prejajis* and the mass peasantry. In Vietnam too, colonial rule produced a parasitic economic structure that resulted in social conflict between two communities — the Mandarins and the nationalists. One important characteristic of South-East Asia is that these nations have been politically dominated by majority ethnic groups of the plains and deltas, while urban economic life has been dominated by ethnic minority groups, such as the Chinese. Problems in Myanmar today also have their roots in the colonial period. The Burmese state appears to comprise more distinct ethnic groups than any other mainland South-East Asian state, as well as reportedly the largest percentage of territory not occupied by the main ethnic group of the country, i.e., the Bamars or Burman people. There are no reliable census figures for this, but estimates of non-ethnic populations vary from 30–40 per cent of the total, occupying up to 60 per cent of the land. The ground realities for these demographics are, of course, far more complicated than this, but this ethnic jigsaw has been configured into a simplified state structure: Myanmar is comprised of seven States constituted on the basis of ethnicity. While it was the British colonial administration that sowed the seeds of ethnic divides in the land, in the post-colonial period the country's state structure and administrative set-up has followed the same logic and pattern. This often produces ethnicity-based communitarian strife in the present-day context.

This takes us to another aspect of the tussle among communities, namely the conflict between *alien* and *indigenous* identity, which is also a fruit of colonial administration. In order to serve their administrative and economic machineries, the colonial rulers brought with them various alien communities to lands which were completely unfamiliar to them, and in course of time these people superseded, and to some extent displaced, the indigenous communities. This naturally produced some outrage among the original inhabitants of the land, and the 'sons of the soil', feeling alienated in their own homeland, often attacked immigrants, who exploited them as the comprador class of the British administration. The 'Sons of the Soil' theory, as propounded by Myron Weiner,[18] evidently holds true in the case of Malaysia, where colonial rule established a 'fruitful coalition' with the alien Chinese and Indian settlers. To quote Anderson again,

'Chinese are now overwhelmingly concentrated in urban centers and the more advanced sectors of local economies, their futures are intricately tied to capitalism and capitalist society's class structure. In the Catholic Philippines and Buddhist Siam they have made the necessary cultural adaptations to form a completely integrated element of their societies' upper and middle classes.... This integration is much less complete in Indonesia and Malaysia, but in both the countries the Chinese are absolutely essential to the functioning of the existing politico-economic order and continue to hold economic power.'[19] In the post-colonial content, this aggravated the indigenous communities and produced many instances of communitarian tension. The situation in Indonesia and the Philippines is similar, which they too have inherited as a colonial legacy. The Chinese in the Philippines or alien minorities in the context of Suharto's policy of *'negara kuwat'* (strong country) vs *'kawulane suyud'* (subdued people) are nothing but re-interpretations of the colonial policy of alignment with alien powers using the policy of subjugation. Mandy Sadan summarizes the situation accurately:

> There are many ethnically diverse nations in Southeast Asia and, there-fore, regionally, a variety of ways in which assertions of non-national ethnic loyalties have been incorporated, assimilated, oppressed, respected or homogenised by states: the weight of 'ethnic' numbers in any classificatory model need not in itself produce such apparently endemic, conflictual social fissures. Second, the appearance and asser-tion of such diversity owes itself also to the historical development of systems, structures and political processes that fractured the idea of the nation through sets of ethnic sub-groups.[20]

The unfortunate part of the entire story is that none of the post-colonial South-East Asian states could do away with these colonial structures.

A similar situation exists in South Asia, which suffers once again from a 'colonial hangover'. To reiterate my earlier contention, though anti-colonial struggles successfully brought an end to the physical presence of colonizers in South Asia, they did not have the necessary ideological and institutional wherewithal to emerge fully liberated, with no colonial hangover.[21] In South Asia, both ethnicity and religion have important roles to play in constituting the sociopolitical fabric of the nation, and to that extent, state governance in the countries of this region continue to function within the colonial paradigm.

The question of community also brings us to the problem of identity. To quote Sudipta Kaviraj, 'Identities which were formerly mandatory, seem to become optional, matters of choice ... choosing to have different spaces or areas and people who were earlier part of "us" would now become part of "them", with the attendant process of readjustment of relations'.[22] The modern understanding of identity is expressed through nationalism, which leads to the formation of a nation and sometimes a nation-state. The phenomenon of nationalism, therefore, springs from a dynamic contact between ethnic consciousness and the concept of popular sovereignty. John Stuart Mill in his analysis of popular sovereignty pointed out that it is a fundamental right, within the limits of feasibility, for a community within that state to decide whether it wishes to share a state with others or form a state of its own.[23] Christie echoes Mill by saying that 'National consciousness could be said to come into being when ethnic consciousness crystallizes into a desire to create a state based on that ethnic consciousness: the prize at the end of this process of national "self-determination" is the modern nation state'.[24] The phenomenon of nationalism and the question of 'national selfness' creates an ethnic consciousness and, on a parallel track, an important dynamic for nationalism may have been the assertion of ethnic identity and the demand for community rights.

With regard to 'ethnic' communities, if we were to undertake a comparative appraisal of the dynamics of community identities and movements in the region, we would need to study the formation of different communities and explain the challenges they pose to any attempt at uniform nation-building. To Urmila Phadnis, the 'South Asian region — a congeries of multi ethnic societies — is a challenging field ... over the decades, most of the South Asian countries have been experiencing intermittent ethnic cleavages and conflicts of different magnitudes'.[25]

The history of South Asia provides innumerable examples of ethnic conglomerations. Before the advent of the Western powers, there had been several waves of migration that had enriched the cultural domains of the region. The colonial era, however, introduced some fundamental changes in the institutional as well as ideological parameters that defined the region. Colonial governance was shaped by imperial imperatives, and while there were many positive outcomes of colonial rule, the most deleterious negative impact lay in the different layers of social cleavage that resulted from their theory of nation-based rule. Thus, the notion of a 'nation-state' brought along with it some deeply negative variations in multiethnic South Asia. India, Pakistan, Sri Lanka and Bangladesh, along with the smaller states of Nepal and Bhutan, have seen the production and reproduction of many communitarian challenges to the state, and the 'minority' attribute of these communitarian expressions must be kept in mind. Throughout the region we come across various racial/ethnic, religious, linguistic and regional minorities. The point to remember is that these ethnic minorities have different social syndromes and there is no one uniform cultural marker, and no ethnic homogeneity can therefore be seen or identified.

Religion is another component of community identity which produces the communitarian syndrome of conflict in the context of majority vs minority relations. Like many South-East Asian nations, in South Asia too, colonial legacies determine the form of relations between the state and society's religious minorities. Religion, in fact, has been playing a very crucial role in the South Asian scenario. There is often seen a politicization of religion in order to gain and retain power. No doubt, a pluralistic religious situation contributed decisively to sharpening the question of minorities and state governance. The impact of the situation has been neatly summarized by Paul Brass and Achin Vanaik: 'in what used to be called the third world before the "second world" collapsed, religious fundamentalism and religious nationalism have mounted a direct challenge to the state usually seeking to command it. India, for all the vibrancy of its democratic political system has not been immune to this assault.'[26]

The fact is, in South Asia, no religion is homogeneous. Rather, each religion, be it Hinduism, Buddhism, Islam or Christianity, has remarkable internal diversity. Each of these religions have numerous sects and sub-sects that result in much heterogeneity. And each religious minority in any given South Asian state has its problems vis-à-vis state governance that is under the domination of the majoritarian powers. Till today no South Asian state has been able to successfully overthrow the colonial legacy of communalism. In several instances, the forces of secularism have in fact failed against communal zeal. Whether a democracy or a military dictatorship or an Islamic republic, we come across many similar instances of majority domination and violence against minority communities.[27]

In the Indian context, the majoritarian Hindu state structure, under the veil of democracy, often silences the voices of the many religious minorities. Sometimes, the very identity of a minority community gets shrouded by a fiery state machinery that operates on the basis of dominance and oppression. This book narrates, for example, the story of the Gujarat violence of 2002, where communal riots were a state-sponsored phenomenon intended to extinguish Muslim presence in the state. A similar situation can be found in other South Asian states, like Bangladesh, Pakistan and Nepal, where the state uses religion as a tool against minority religious groups.[28] Bonita Aleaz has rightly opined that 'the majority/minority relationship is essentially that of power and during each successive phase of defining the nation, the dimensions of power exhibit themselves in the reconfiguration of power — the goal remains that of an ultimate amalgamation'.[29]

Ali Banuazizi and Myron Weiner have vividly described the religious minority profiles of Pakistan. To them, the ethno-linguistic problems of Pakistan are somehow a response on part of the Ulema towards the state machinery. To quote Banuazizi and Weiner 'the politicization of religion is considered a form of hypocracy in the "Liberal" West but it has a quite different sense among believing Muslims.... politicization of religion, far from being taken as an abuse of religion or of the naïve faith of the masses, is the central demand of the fundamentalists and it has been adopted by many of the traditional *Ulema*'.[30] Sugata Bose and Ayesha Jalal put forward a similar view when they write, 'maulanas, maulavis and mullahs touted Islam in the bazaars and mohallas of Muslim India'.[31] Bangladesh's situation is no less different; religion is often politicized and orthodox fundamentalists often assert themselves as realpolitik nationalists. This obviously damages national unity by opening several new vistas of conflict and therefore also weakens the state machinery. Salauddin Ahmed in his latest writing re-articulates the precarious situation when he writes, 'backward looking fundamentalist religious movements had greatly retarded the progress of the Muslim community ... the resurgence of fundamentalists and militant Islam in recent years poses a serious threat to the age old tolerant, syncretistic and humanist cultural tradition of the Bengali muslims.'[32]

One common characteristic manifested by all post-colonial situations is that the role of the state is hyperactive and, in fact, there is a governance crisis. The ubiquitous role of the state has made deep inroads into most people's lives in South and South-East Asia. To Rajesh Tandon and Ranjita Mohanty, 'this has spawned a centralized and anemic culture and most state institutions have become hotbeds of corruption, crime, intrigue and nepotism ... this intrusive and interventionist role of the state has not only undermined individual initiative, it has also hampered social harmony and growth.'[33] This has spurred on the process of self-assertion by minority communities within a society and has added to their nationalist sentiments.

Thus, most social scientists believe that in the post-colonial context, ethno-linguistic and religious identities explain the forces of nationalism that can be seen in South Asian and in South-East Asian societies. Constructs like a 'national identity', as propounded by the state, contributed to the ideological discourse used by the ruling class to justify and implement their policies and practices, and community-based identities have thus often been subordinated to the interests of the hegemonic class. The idea of a national identity thus reflects a majoritarian identity and this naturally results in the building up areas of resistance by the subordinated or marginalized communities. There emerged thus, a number of grass-roots movements based on identity, seeking to reach out to their own history and construct a proper space or a clear manifestation of their new identity.

In the recent past, forces of globalization have also had something to do with the question of governance and community rights. The last two decades have seen the phenomenon of globalization acquire much importance, and this importance is being reasserted in its interaction with nation-states. The flow of ideas related to globalization gathers momentum when the question of political governance is also added to reality of ethnic minorities. Governance includes key issues such as the development of democratic institutions, civil society, the participation of citizens, etc. The idea of liberal democratic governance is today globally triumphant. All the countries, with democratic/non-democratic forms of government, whether totalitarian, monarchical or dictatorships, are now gradually moving in the direction of a liberal democracy. This receptibility of a liberal democracy has been referred to as 'global homogenization' at the end of the bipolar Cold War. Francis Fukuyama, the chief exponent of globalization, believes that liberal democracy is the only suitable form of governance that can accommodate rapid economic and social changes in all types of societies.[34] A very important question in today's world is whether global governance and a global community is in fact possible. Amitai Etzioni in his recent work has carefully discussed this question. He offers a more positive take on the subject by arguing that, 'It is possible to imagine some kind of a de facto global government, limited in scope and authority ... but the notion that we have a global community truly challenges the imagination'. Etzioni quotes Lawrence Lessig's views on the characteristics of the development of a global community, the growing personal ties across national borders, as well as a rapid increase in transnational citizenship. Lessig imagined a global authority and a global civil society.[35]

What emerges from the larger study is that whether in the phase of decolonization or nationalism, or in the era of globalization, the force of human aspirations seeking to assert their identities is a phenomenon that is a common element, moving forward from one generation to the other. This aspiration often takes on a communitarian shape and form. Although historians and social scientists have attempted to see this as a force of nationalism, the basic tenet is perhaps the community's self-perception regarding their status in society in the midst of majoritarian control. So, at times ethnicity, at times religion, caste or linguistic identities come to the forefront, and, above all, it is the responsibility of state governance as well as of civil society to forge a proper system through which all their aspirations can be channelized. Thus, what emerged out of the historical situation has had a profound impact on post-colonial independent South and South-East Asia. Following independence, various community leaders raised their voice, demanding proper recognition for their community identities. Many minority communities were thus catapulted from relative isolation into a whirlpool of competitive politics and economics. As a whole, the result was that the familiarization of these communities with new ideas, coupled with independence and the democratization of the state, has taken them into the modern world with tremendous strength and vigour. It is also the result of the absence of any specific 'safety valve' to accommodate streams of community aspirations. In the present-day scenario, we Asians lack the kind of culturally homogeneous, national assertiveness that broke up the colonial empires of Europe and the America in Asia. 'Can the new forces of globalization and "cyber nationalism" bring about change?' is a crucial question today. The reply will perhaps be negative, as the forces of globalization are today giving birth to forces of localization, adding greater force to the notion of a 'fragmented nation'. Perhaps history does not have a solution that will be able to bring an end to the process of destabilization. Therein lies the pathos of history.

While studying the question of political governance, it thus becomes imperative to study aspects like the federal principle/decentralization, political representation of minorities, the issue of minority rights, as well as the cultural aspirations of the communities that make up a society. The question of minority rights, of course, has been widely discussed in several national and international forums.[36]

This book is divided into three sections. The first section, with four cases studies from South Asia, deals with issues like community grievances taking the shape of crime, insurgencies and separatism. This section shows how often political governance and state-constructed minority politics inspire a community to take to violence. The second section presents five case-studies from different South and South-East Asian countries where we have compelling evidence of a majoritarian state policy of 'divide and rule' towards the minorities. The last article in this section looks at the important question of minority rights and provides an overall picture of minority rights across the two regions under review. The final section, with four article on South-East Asia, not only provides us more case-studies of majority–minority divides, it also talks about minority representation as can be seen in a country's literature and culture.

Governance, Insurgency, Crime and Separatism

Partha S. Ghosh's article is a case-study that deals with north-east India. During the past one-and-a-half centuries, the map of India's north-east has undergone several changes. Consequently, yesterday's internal migration has today become international migration. Even inter-district migrations have taken on politically sensitive ethnic, religious and linguistic connotations. Well-intentioned federal experiments too have, at times, further complicated the controversies surrounding these immigrations. The problem of governance, as underlined by the 130-odd incidents of insurgency that have dotted the region directly or indirectly, owes its explanation to this phenomenon. Massive central aid to the region has contributed to the nexus created between politics, insurgency and crime. This article unravels these complexities from a historical perspective.

Lipi Ghosh's article observes that ethnicity and minority questions taken together become an important subject when the subject of political governance is added to the phenomenon of ethnic minorities.

The specific and prominent feature of the South Asian situation is that all the states here have had a protracted history of direct or indirect colonial rule, and minority community-related problems share common origins that can be traced to the nation's colonial legacy. In the post-colonial scenario, South Asian states must accommodate processes of ethnic negotiation. More specifically about the Indian situation, governance under a vibrant democracy and constitutionally guaranteed free speech rights encourages the active participation of ethnic groups in politics. The present article, from the perspective of the above-mentioned notional presentation of the subject, talks about the question of political governance as it applies to the Ahoms, one of the larger ethnic minority communities of Assam. It shows how the construction of colonial policy resulted in the wiping out of the existence of the Ahoms and discusses the con-tinuation of the same policy under post-colonial regimes as well.

Anasua Basu Ray Chaudhury takes up the case of the Gujarat violence of 2002, which has come to be known as one of the worst violations of human rights in the history of independent India. During those turbulent days, the Gujarat government chose to remain a mute spectator as vandals uninhibitedly destroyed the life and property of thousands of people belonging to a religious mi-nority. That being the role of government, the question arises as to how other components of the state acted? Chaudhury demonstrates the careful stand taken by the state machinery and the government.

Paula Banerjee's article deals more specifically with minority women's rights. Any exercise concerned with minority rights and protection will need to pay special attention to women, whereas the Indian state has traditionally viewed women less as individuals and more as members of their respective communities. In this article, Banerjee discusses not merely the victimization of minority women but also speaks of the various forms of resistance they have organized in order to keep from becoming permanent exceptions to citizenship. She takes up the question from the perspective of two important border areas in South Asia. Borders demarcate those gray areas where the jurisdiction of one state ends and the other begins, and in the case of South Asia, these borders, or more precisely borderlands, are peopled by groups that have had, and continue to have, links with states on both sides of the borders. Yet, in its attempt to emphasize a national identity, state sovereignty demands the severance of all ties that 'encourage difference', leading to the conscious exclusion of the recalcitrant from all privileges being granted. This results in conflicts, as in the case of the Tamils settled in the borderlands of Sri Lanka and Nagas in the north-eastern borderlands of India. Hence, borders of democratic states, such as the kind found in South Asia, often emerge as zones of conflict. Paula Banerjee's article deals specifically with women from these two 'borderland' communities.

Majoritarian State Governance vs Minority Divides: The Issue of Community Rights

Lok Raj Baral's article looks at the situation in Nepal. He begins with a complex question: what will be the scenario in a country that has no majority–minority divides, where community rights suffer from lack of expression through legitimate channels and governance does not have proper shape and structure? The majority–minority divide in Nepal has not been conceptualized numerically, for no caste or community is in majority. Yet, there does exist a distinct religious divide, with 81 per cent of the population constituted by Hindus, who clearly dominate the country, and Buddhists making up 10 per cent of the population. Baral talks about the nature of regime change in Nepal, which, in his opinion, did not bring about any qualitative difference in the situation, and explains how and to what extent the democratic governance that Nepal intermittently witnessed, could not disentangle itself from the social and regional disparities afflicting the region. Of course, changes that are today underway in Nepal are of a fundamental nature and will have far-reaching consequences. Never in the history of Nepal have people involved themselves in such a transformation. Minorities are now vehemently calling for power-sharing and shared control over resources as well as greater representation in the various organs of the state, so much so that political parties that fail to make democracy inclusive will no doubt eventually be sidelined by the people.

Atiur Rahman's article looks at the Adivasis of Bangladesh and the larger question of minority community rights. Bangladesh accommodates a variety of ethnic, linguistic and religious identities, some of which have been historically conflicting and others that are by-products of a myopic approach to nation-building. The consti-tution of Bangladesh initially adopted the principles of nationalism, democracy, secularism and socialism. All this was aimed at building an inclusive national identity and territorial boundaries (Bengali nationalism), a political sphere (democracy) that would put an end to the politicization of communal identities (secularism), and economic opportunities for all (socialism). However, Bangladesh has not been able to successfully work towards the above ideals. Most of these ideals are now eroded, resulting in a fragmented Bangladeshi society. The worst victims of this divisive experience have been the Adivasis, along with other ethnic minorities. They have been unable to protect themselves from processes which have served essentially to worsen their social, political and economic position. They thus face a very real threat of losing their social identity along with their traditional sources of income. Their very survival as a community is at stake. Rahman's article thus looks into the role of the government vis-á-vis other forces of governance in a society which have failed to accord a proper identity and place in society to the Adivasis.

Maneesha Tikekar's article is a study of minority communities in Pakistan. While she is writing primarily on religious minorities she also attempts to look at the larger political context within which they live. The contextual framework for this is provided by the way the Pakistani state has historically envisioned itself. She observes that the Constitutions of Pakistan, though they do guarantee minority rights, have made a distinction 'between Muslims and non-Muslims not so much in defining their rights but in terms of what the state is enjoined to do for them .... [T]he state ... is enjoined to do particular things for the Muslims, whereas its role vis-à-vis others is that of a facilitator and law enforcer.' This makes the situation for minorities difficult despite all the constitutional provisions. Her concluding observation is that governance, in the true sense of the term, has failed to work here.

Mandy Sadan takes up the case of Myanmar, which has been plagued by an endemic ethnic conflict ever since attaining independence from British colonial rule in 1948. The roots of this conflict are to be found in the country's colonial past, but the post-colonial state too has failed to convince the numerous ethnic minorities that make up 30 per cent of its current population of their secure standing in the Burmese state. The various systems of governance instituted after independence consider protecting minority community rights as an important facet of state-building. Yet, so complex is the jigsaw of ethnicities and minority communities in Myanmar that this dichotomous representation of the conflict fails to adequately capture the nature of the minority dilemma: often, minority communities themselves are fractured entities, with homogeneity being imposed on them by majoritarian nationalist elites.

Amnuayvit Thitibordin's article deals with the historical development of the community rights discourse in Northern Thailand, leading up to its current state today. Thitibordin focuses on four distinctly demarcated periods from the early 1960s down to the Thaksin era in 2006, in order to understand how discourses on community rights have been constructed and have become established in Northern Thailand specifically and in Thailand in general. Initially, following the outbreak of the Indochina War, Thailand was classified as a high-risk country, based on the Domino Theory. The second period saw many historic student and intellectual-based democratic movements. The third period witnessed movements popularizing the notion of community rights, and finally, in the fourth period, revolutionary changes took place both in approaches to and discourses about local community development. His essay focuses on Chiang Mai and discusses research that has been undertaken by various Thai scholars on the question of community rights and village communities. He refers to the romantic notions prevalent in Thailand regarding 'community villages' and 'community rights', first introduced by Marxian scholars in the 1970s, which have enjoyed enduring popularity amongst Thai academics, the media and the urban middle class for the last thirty years.

The final article in this section is by Samir Kumar Das, who reviews the recent rise in concern for minority rights across South and South-East Asia. While this concern involves a certain subordination of minorities and their rights to the imperatives of governance, the assertion of minority rights in recent years points to the articulation of a new political space that is located beyond the established order of nation-states. Minority rights today are contingent on the remapping of this space and Das's essay is a preliminary study of this remapped political space in which minority rights have become relevant. He takes up the question of popular sovereignty and minority issues, the concept of nation-building in a democracy and the neo-liberal agenda of governance, concluding with a plea for the recognition of minority rights.

Governance, Culture and the Aspirations of Minorities

Mala Rajo Sathian's article looks at the Muslim minorities of southern Thailand. The south-eastern end of the country, bordering Malaysia to the south, is home to a majority of Thailand's ethnic Malays. Sathian's article tells us the causes for contestation with re-gard to ethnic minority rights, and by extension, for the articulation of ethnic identity. Also, while the state is seen as contesting the primordial rights of the minority communities (e.g., land, resources and cultural norms) and their place in the nation-state, for their part, the minorities simultaneously contest demands made on the people by the state and its encroachment in what is seen as a 'minority preserve' (i.e., Islam as a religion, its institutions and its laws). As the identity (and rights) of minorities thus 'excluded' by the nation-state is contested, their sense of 'national consciousness' also appears ambiguous, especially when we consider the contrast between the two distinct perspectives being compared, namely, from the standpoint of their traditional, historicocultural roots and that of their more recent nationality/citizenship.

Sunil Kukreja's article looks at the recent trends in Malaysian politics. His work challenges the prevailing orthodoxy on Malaysia's apparent success at forging a highly manageable form of ethnic pluralism. He argues that despite possessing all the trappings of 'co-existence', 'accommodation' and relative racial harmony, the post-*merdeka* (independence) compromise — a moderate but arguably inadequate accommodation (largely) between the Malays and Chinese Malaysians (and, to a lesser extent, Indian Malaysians) — was radically altered in the early 1970s with the introduction of the New Economic Policy (NEP). This dramatic shift in the national agenda, aimed primarily at explicitly and aggressively redistributing wealth among the Malays and widely supported by hardline Malay nationalists, carved the path for a very precarious ethnicity-based programme of institutionalized discrimination, one that has fostered greater socio-economic fragmentation, amplified cultural divides be-tween the dominant ethnic groups and resulted in new ethno-religious challenges.

The last two articles in the volume are interesting studies of re-gional literature as a reflection of people's opinion against majoritarian governance. Aris Arif Mundayat offers an analysis of minority and dominant group relationships in the urban areas of Indonesia through an understanding of their nationalist imagination. This allows us to focus on the nature of contestation between texts produced by poor people (as an economic minority) and those produced by state apparatuses (as the dominant group). These texts reflect the minority group's nationalist imagination of Indonesia at the turn of the twenty-first century, as well as their discontent vis-à-vis the state-sanctioned nationalist project. Important contradictions emerge from the construction of a state-sponsored nationalist discourse that can also be observed in the power relations between a minority group and the dominant one, which are active in the specific arenas of these encounters.

Philippine politics has always been tainted with the 'politics of perception', a phrase coined by Lily Rose Tope to describe a situation where people take political decisions based on 'perception'. Her article explains the perceptions that underlie the situation with regard to Chinese Filipinos. Most of the texts cited relate to literature and films, media that combine both empirical truth and subjective renditions. As a means of creating, receiving and disseminating perceptions, these artistic media are just as responsible for the tribulations of the Chinese Filipinos as are the media of redress.

The overarching aim of the book is to understand the nature of relationships between minority communities and political governance across different states of South and South-East Asia. It is important to note that in the South and South-East Asian contexts there has been a shift from 'government' to 'governance'. This leads us to the hypothesis that a society cannot be left only to the goodwill of the state, it must include other actors, such as people, whose unified force can ensure good governance. In a broader sense, it embraces the wider concerns of a society. There are bilateral and multilateral aid agencies/forces which associate civil society with good governance. Reciprocally, to achieve good governance, a society embraces a highly bureaucratic administrative machinery and public institutions.

Relationships between society, state, governance and minorities are not simple and straightforward. On the contrary, they are complex, dynamic and dialectical. Within a society, the state assumes complete responsibility for the fulfillment of the political, social and economic aspirations of its people and to that extent it is assumed that minority aspirations are also accommodated in a civil society, and that in due course there will emerge a proper and optimal status quo through a rhythmic yet balanced understanding between the different forces at play.

With this hypothesis in mind the book is intended as a study of minority-related issues in the context of South and South-East Asia, from which there has emerged a fascinating though undefined as well as a hitherto unknown picture. There are numerous instances where we see marginalized sections of society get alienated from the process of governance, and, as fallout, the state machinery loses its stability and legitimacy.

Here emerges the question of civil society's intermediary relations with governance, which, as a social force, ought to be located within both the state and in wider society. Civil society, therefore, must remain content with the state and with society, and problems of governance will need to be addressed in relation to both.

The present volume demonstrates the weaknesses of state governance in the different countries of South and South-East Asia. The various essays making up this volume discuss the contemporary situation vis-à-vis minorities, community rights and governance in these countries. As a carrier of the colonial administrative legacy, how South Asia has done in the post-colonial period as well as in the present era of globalization is a crucial question that has been attempted to be answered. In South Asia, Pakistan, Bangladesh and Sri Lanka are the three big powers, second to India, where 'majority vs. minority' relations take on different shapes in different contexts. Community rights obviously bring up questions regarding changes in the context of Islamic republics, democratic set-ups and authoritarian rule. In South-East Asia, on the other hand, we find diverse forms of nation-states. Thus while Thailand still carries a state system of royalty, Myanmar bears the creed of military governance and the Philippines represent a more or less mixed form of democratic government. Indonesia and Malaysia too struggle with the question of minority rights and political governance.

This collection of essays by a group of erudite anthropologists, historians and political scientists, is one of the first attempts to look at the question of community rights and state governance from a comparative as well as historical perspective. However, the selection of essays does not lay any claim to being exhaustive. It simply attempts to present a wide selection of case-studies in order to try and analyze a few major problems. The contributors have thus presented different case-studies from South and South-East Asia, also putting forward the historical background of the community they refer to. Taken together, the articles have one common characteristic — they dwell on the question of the identity of a minority community with reference to their rights within the country under consideration. The articles take note of the form and type of governance practiced by a particular government and discuss how the state controls articulation by minority communities and also controls their rights. This is followed by a discussion of the position, role and identity of that particular community in contemporary society. The articles also highlight the political, constitutional, administrative, economic and sociocultural questions facing these minority communities.

The book shows, on a comparative basis, how Indian democracy has failed to provide adequate protection to minority communities in Gujarat, Assam and the north-east, how the changing forms of democratic governance in Nepal have failed to address the problems of the minorities, and how Bangladeshi governance, whether under pronounced militarist control or under Islamic secularism, has supported the polarization of the minority community. The picture is in no way different from the repressive nature of military governance seen in Myanmar or the subordination of minorities as per the Thaization policy of the monarchical government in Thailand. Malaysian politics too, although quite vocal about successfully juggling several theories of co-existence, accommodation and harmony, in practice, amplified the cultural divide that exists between ethnic groups. Similarly, the Constitution of Pakistan guarantees minority rights in legal terms, but in real terms, has produced no effective political solutions to bridge minority divides.

This brings us finally to the debate on theories regarding control of administrative/state mechanisms in the context of minority relations. That a democratic state mechanism and private/corporate involvement is more protective of minority rights is the contention, which goes against arguments favouring public control and direct state involvement. Proponents of corporate governance favour a regulatory shift and advocate greater people's participation in governance. The opposition, on the other hand, apprehends some dangers in extending and sharing power with the minorities. They believe that majoritarian control is required for the effective functioning of good governance.

Thus arises, within the framework of this debate, the question of minority rights and the protection offered to minority communities. The present work, however, instead of dilating its focus across this new domain of minority rights and theories on the subject, confines itself simply to depicting the existing situation vis-à-vis minority divides in post-colonial South and South-East Asia.

As scholars and academicians from different parts of South and South-East Asia share experiences of their own countries, we get an insider's view of the issues being discussed — enriching our understanding of the subject and perhaps prompting us to think in new directions.

Notes and References

1. Douglas Harper, *Online Etymology Dictionary*, 2001, http://www.etymonline.com/index.php?search=community&searchmode=or (accessed 24 June 2007).
2. Ferdinand Tönnies, *Community and Society* (East Lansing: Michigan State University Press, [1887] 1957), p. 22.
3. Clive J. Christie, *A Modern History of Southeast Asia* (London and New York: I.B. Taurus, 2000), p. 8.
4. Benedict Anderson, *Imagined Communities: Reflections on the Origin and Spread of Nationalism* (Revised edition; London, New York: Verso, 1991), pp. 5–7.
5. Ibid.
6. Benedict Anderson, *The Spectre of Comparisons: Nationalism, Southeast Asia and the World* (London and New York: Verso, 1998), p. 320.
7. Barrister Pakem, *Prologue*, in Girin Phukon and N.L. Dutta (eds), *Politics of Identity and Nation Building in Northeast India* (New Delhi: South Asian Publishers, 1997), p. 4.
8. N. Gerald Barrier, *The Census in British India: New Perspectives* (New Delhi: Manohar, 1981), p. v.
9. Anderson, *Spectre of Comparisons,* p. 320.
10. For details see Louis Dumont and David Pocock, 'For a Sociology of India' and 'Village Studies', *Contributions in Indian Sociology* 1, 1957, pp. 7–22, and Louis Dumont and David Pocock, 'Village Studies', *Contributions in Indian Sociology* 1, 1957, pp. 23–42.
11. Christie, *Modern History,* p. 2.
12. Sekhar Bandyopadhyay, *Caste Politics and the Raj: Bengal 1872–1937,* (Kolkata: K.P. Bagchi, 1990), p. 29.

13. Ibid., p. 202.
14. Anthony Reid, *Imperial Alchemy: Understanding (Southeast) Asian Nationalisms* (unpublished text given to the author).
15. Ibid.
16. Prasenjit Duara, 'The Discourse of Civilization and Pan-Asianism', *Journal of World History* 12(1), 2001, pp. 99–130.
17. Anderson, *Spectre of Comparisons*, p. 328.
18. For details on the 'Sons of the Soil' theory, see Myron Weiner, *Sons of the Soil: Migration and Ethnic Conflict in India* (Princeton, NJ: Princeton University Press, 1978).
19. Anderson, *Spectre of Comparisons*, p. 328.
20. Mandy Sadan, 'Minorities and Political Governance: The Myanmar Situation' (present volume).
21. Monirul Hussain and Lipi Ghosh, *Religious Minorities in South Asia: Selected Essays on Post-Colonial Situation* (New Delhi: Manak Publications, 2002), p. 1.
22. Sudipta Kaviraj (ed.), *Politics in India: Oxford in India Readings in Sociology and Social Anthropology* (New York: Oxford University Press, 1997), p. 28.
23. J.S. Mill, *On Liberty and Considerations of Representative Governments*, edited by R.B. McCallum (Oxford: Basil Blackwell, 1948), p. 292.
24. Christie, *Modern History of Southeast Asia*, p. 4.
25. Urmila Phadnis, *Ethnicity and Nation-building in South Asia* (New Delhi: Sage Publications, 1989), p. 12.
26. Paul Brass and Achin Vanaik (eds), *Competing Nationalisms in South Asia* (Bangalore: Orient Longman, 2002), p. 1.
27. For details of case studies see, Hasan and Ghosh, *Religious Minorities*, Vols I and II.
28. More details in Hasan and Ghosh, *Religious Minorities*, Vol. I. See also, Ali Banuazizi and Myron Weiner, *The State, Religion and Ethnic Politics: Pakistan, Iran and Afghanistan* (Lahore: Vanguard, 1987), p. 263.
29. Bonita Aleaz, Lipi Ghosh and Achintrya Kumar Dutta, *Ethnicity, Nations and Minorities: The South Asian Scenario* (New Delhi: Manak Publications, 2003), p. xiii.
30. Ali Banuazizi and Myron Weiner, *The State, Religion and Ethnic Politics: Pakistan, Iran and Afghanistan* (Lahore: Vanguard, 1987), p. 263.
31. Sugata Bose and Ayesha Jalal, *Modern South Asia: History, Culture, Political Economy* (New Delhi: Oxford University Press, 1998), p. 178.
32. A.F. Salauddin Ahmad, *History and Heritage: Reflections on Society Politics and Culture of South Asia* (Dhaka: University Press Ltd., 2007), pp. 58, 69.

33. Rajesh Tandon and Ranjita Mohanty (eds), *Does Civil Society Matter? Governance in Contemporary India* (New Delhi: Sage Publications, 2003), p. 84.
34. See, Francis Fukuyama, *The End of History and the Last Man* (New York: Free Press, 1992).
35. Amitai Etzioni, *From Empire to Community: New Approach to International Relations* (New York: Palgrave Macmillan, 2004), pp. 197–98.
36. For a detailed discussion on minority rights, see James Massey, *Minorities and Religious Freedom in a Democracy* (New Delhi: Centre for Dalit and Subaltern Studies and Manohar, 2003), pp. 17–26.

Governance, Insurgency, Crime and Separatism

1

Politics of Competing Ethnicity and Violence: The Experience of India's North-East

Partha S. Ghosh

Introduction

In historical literature one does not come across the term 'north-east' the way it appears now. It was as late as 1970, when the Indian parliament passed the North-Eastern Council (NEC) Act, leading to the establishment of the NEC, that the term was used for the first time, and, ever since, North-East India (hereafter INE) has become a common expression. Till 2003, the term denoted seven Indian states, namely, Arunachal Pradesh, Assam, Manipur, Meghalaya, Mizoram, Nagaland and Tripura. Later, Sikkim was added to the list. But, regardless of whether or not the term was specifically used in strategic and economic matters, the region has received considerable importance in the reckoning of the Indian state, right from the days of the East India Company when Assam was annexed (it then comprised almost all of present-day INE) in 1826, and the fledgling Raj, as the British Indian empire came to be known subsequently.

Between 1826 and 1974, the political map of the North-East changed a number of times, indicating not only the compulsions and interests that prompted these changes but also their sociopolitical implications, which have resulted in conflicts of all kinds. One of the essential features of these changes, both as a cause and as a consequence, was the movement of people in search of greener pastures and also, at times, in search of security of life and property. If one, therefore, characterizes the history of India's North-East during the past 200 years as the history of the movements of people into INE, it would not be inappropriate. However, what makes the phenomena complex are the frequent changes in the characterization of these movements — from intra-state to inter-state, and vice versa — with their attendant political and security-related ramifications. Given the theme of the present volume, I will concentrate on those ramifications that have structural linkages with population movements and politics on the one hand, and population movements and violence on the other, both of which are intimately connected with the issue of ethnicity and identity.

One may note that we have so far meticulously avoided the word 'migration' and instead have used the phrase 'population movement'. The choice is dictated by the fact that for a large portion of the period under review, Assam was part of the province of Bengal and all the people who came and settled in Assam were from other parts of the same province. Hence, strictly speaking, none was a migrant if we were to go by the classical definition of the term. Migration is generally defined as 'a permanent change in place of residence by the crossing of specified administrative or political boundaries. The persons who fulfil these two criteria are regarded as migrants.'[1] Even if we broaden the definition of the term, in Assam's context, the problem persists. For example, the United Nations' Multilingual Demographic Dictionary suggests that the expressions 'move' and 'migration' on the one hand and 'internal migration' and 'international migration' on the other, should be distinguished. 'A move is a change of residence within the same political or administrative boundary. Migration is a change of residence and also a crossing of the political or administrative boundary. While internal migration is a change in the place of residence from one administrative boundary to another within the same country, international migration is a move over a national boundary.'[2]

But whatever may be the definitional strictures, the political, economic and cultural history of INE has been influenced so much by people coming into the region that we have to make concessions to characterize them as migrants, otherwise we would perpetually get bogged down by this conceptual controversy without making any headway in understanding the phenomenon. For our purposes here, therefore, migration would connote: a permanent change in place of residence by settling in historically understood ethnic, religious or cultural spaces in a geographical sense. The persons who fulfill this criterion are to be regarded as migrants.

The subject 'crime' has been subsumed within the discussion on violence, unless in some specific cases mentioning criminal acts has become necessary. It may be underlined that most of the references to crime in relation to ethnicity or migratory movements in INE get obfuscated as politics assumes primacy over everything else. As a result, violent human acts like murder, arson and rape, which should ordinarily be seen as penal offences, pass off as more 'respectable' and virtually unpunishable phenomena such as human rights violations by both state and non-state actors, insurgency or militant adventurism, and so on. At yet another level, but falling within the same logic of argument, corruption in the police, army or civilian state authorities in general, together with acts of extortion by militant and insurgent outfits are seen as social maladies, not to be confused with normal criminal offences. The plethora of acts passed by the Indian state in order to deal with terrorism, militancy and insurgency give credence to the fact that murder and rape do not remain merely murder and rape as the Indian Penal Code understands them if they are committed by insurgents, terrorists or people in uniform, or even by ordinary citizens in ethnic or communal riot situations. When the Karbis and Dimashas kill each other in the name of ethnic justice or the United Liberation Front of Assam (ULFA) opens fire indiscriminately in a Dhemaji school, killing several children from its own community under the pretext of teaching the Indian state a lesson for its crime of celebrating Republic Day, the perpetrators of the crime are not viewed as murderers even though innocent lives have been lost at their hands. The question, therefore, that needs to be addressed is whether it is advisable to view 'crime' in the conventional sense or does it call for a wider definition given the changing realities of the world.

Present INE Profile

Situated between 21.57°N and 29.30°N latitude and 89.46°E and 97.30°E longitude, INE embraces a total area of 255,000 square kilometres, which accounts for 7.8 per cent of the total land area of India. The terrain is largely hilly, accounting for 70 per cent of the region. The seven (plus one) states that comprise the region are already mentioned in the first paragraph.

The partition of India in 1947, which came along with Independence, broke the region's natural and traditional linkages with the rest of the country and virtually cut off this land-locked region from the other Indian states. Only a narrow corridor in north Bengal, popularly known as the 'Chicken's neck' or the 'Siliguri neck', having an approximate width of 33 km on the eastern side and 21 km on the western side, connects the two parts. INE has a considerably long international boundary with China in the north, Bangladesh in the south and south-west, Bhutan in the north-west and Myanmar in the east. The MacMahon Line, drawn during colonial times, separates the region from Tibet, now an autonomous region of China.

There is almost eight months of rain in the region. Water logging is frequent in the plains, especially in Assam, making communications and transport difficult. Rivers such as Brahmaputra and Barak flow through the plains. At certain places the Brahmaputra is so wide that it resembles an ocean. It could be as much as 14 km wide in certain places. In terms of its water-carrying capacity, it is probably the biggest river after the Ganga. Most of the other rivers flow through the hills where their flow is too fast to be navigable. The plains of INE are chronically flood-prone. Almost every year the Brahmaputra causes devastating floods in Assam.

Changing Maps

INE originally comprised of composite Assam or the old Kamrupa kingdom and the two native states of Manipur and Tripura. The long history of Assam begins with Ahom rule in the thirteenth century, which continued till the Burmese replaced them in 1819, who were replaced by the British in 1826. During the heydays of the Ahoms, even the Mughals could not effectively penetrate the region although their governor in Bengal, Mir Jumlah, made several attempts to do so. All that the latter was able to extract from the Ahom king Jayadhvaj Singh through a treaty signed on 9 January 1663 was the king's daughter for the imperial harem, the country west of Bharali river on the north bank of the Brahmaputra and the Kallang in the south, along with some elephants, gold and silver. During the reign of Gadadhar Singh (1681–96), Mughal forces were pushed out of Gauhati (present-day Guwahati) and chased all the way to up to Monas. Henceforth, both sides accepted Monas as the boundary.[3]

During British rule, the administrative map of INE changed several times, which needs to be kept in mind for the purpose that we mentioned while clarifying the definition of migration. After its conquest, Assam was incorporated into the province of Bengal. This situation continued till 6 February 1874, when it was reconstituted into a Chief Commissioner's Province. Although large in area, it still had a population of only 2,443,000 and was economically weak. To make it economically viable, in September 1874, the populous Bengali-speaking district of Sylhet with a population of 1,720,000, which was an integral part of Bengal, was added to Assam. With the incorporation of Sylhet the population of Assam increased substantially but it was still only half as populous as the Central Provinces, which was then India's next least populous province.[4]

The province of Assam as it stood in 1874 was a combination of four disparate regions: (*i*) pre-literate hill districts speaking different dialects, (*ii*) the five Assamese-speaking districts of the Brahmaputra Valley, (*iii*) Goalpara district in the Brahmaputra Valley where Bengali and Assamese cultures overlapped, and (*iv*) the two Bengali-speaking districts of the Surma Valley, namely, Sylhet and Cachar. In the 1890s Assam became a 'self-contained state responsible directly to the viceroy'.[5] In 1905, when the Bengal province was partitioned between Muslim-majority East Bengal and Hindu-majority West Bengal, the former incorporated Assam. The Bengali Hindus and Assamese Hindus resented the partition for different reasons, former for the division of Bengal, while the latter resented their inclusion into Muslim-majority East Bengal. Though originally conceived primarily as an administrative measure, the partition was expected to serve the political purpose of weakening the fledgling nationalist movement, the hub of which was Calcutta, the centre of Hindu-dominated political activity in the huge province of Bengal.[6] It was due to the vehement opposition of Bengali Hindus that the partition was eventually annulled in 1912. With this Assam reverted back to the status of Chief Commissioner's Province with its old geography that included the Bengali-Muslim district of Sylhet and the Bengali-Hindu district of Cachar. This situation continued till 1947. Pre-partition Assam thus consisted of the Brahmaputra Valley, the Surma Valley, the Garo, Khasi and Jaintia Hills, the Naga Hills, Mizo Hills and Mikir Hills, as well as the North East Frontier Tracts (NEFT).

At the time of India's Independence in 1947, INE was meant to have comprised Assam, the two princely states of Manipur and Tripura, and Sikkim, a protectorate of the British Indian Government. Present-day Meghalaya, Mizoram, Nagaland and Arunachal Pradesh (then known as NEFT) were parts of Assam. Immediately after Independence, NEFT was separated from Assam and placed under the central administration. In 1954, it was renamed as the North Eastern Frontier Agency (NEFA). So far as Sylhet was concerned, it opted to join East Pakistan following a referendum held in July 1947.

Insofar as the tribal areas were concerned, the British policy was to treat them as 'backward tracts' and keep them isolated from the rest of the country. It was done primarily keeping in mind British commercial interests in the region. Thus, when in 1873, Inner Line Regulations and Inner Line Permits were introduced, the purpose was not only to isolate the hill people from the plains, but also to bring 'under more stringent control the commercial relations of British subjects with the frontier tribes'. For example, in Lakhimpur, the operations of speculators in unvulcanized natural rubber had led to serious complications, and the spread of tea gardens beyond the fiscal limits of the settled territories of the day had involved the government in many conflicts with the tribes. The Inner Line Regulations, therefore, provided that no British subject or foreign resident could pass beyond a certain point without a licence. It also laid down rules concerning trade and the possession of land beyond the Line.[7] The Government of India Act of 1935 provided for delimitation of Excluded and Partially Excluded Areas, which were under direct administrative control of the Governor. The 'excluded areas' included present-day Nagaland, Mizoram and North Cachar Hills, whereas the 'partially excluded areas' included the two districts of Garo Hills and Khasi–Jaintia Hills, and the Mikir Hills area (Karbi Anglong district of Assam).[8]

In the aftermath of Independence, many of the tribes of INE started demanding either autonomy or independent statehood within the Indian Union or independent nationhood. The Indian state sought to deal with the situation using political, constitutional and military means. Thus, in 1963, the state of Nagaland was formed covering the Naga Hill District of Assam and the Tuensang Frontier Division of NEFA. In 1972, the state of Meghalaya was formed. In the same year, the Lushai Hills became a Union Territory by the name of Mizoram. In 1987, it became a full-fledged state in the Indian Union, after a prolonged armed struggle launched by the Mizos under the leadership of Laldenga. In 1972, NEFA was renamed as Arunachal Pradesh, which became a full-fledged state in 1987. Sikkim, which was independent to start with, became a part of the Indian Union in 1974.

The princely states of Manipur and Tripura, which had been ruled by their kings continuously for almost 1300 years, were incorporated into the Indian Union in 1949 as Part C states. (Part C states included both former princely states and provinces. Chief Commissioners governed them.) In 1963, they acquired the status of Union Territory and in 1972 became full-fledged states.

Demography, Migration and Politics

The nineteenth-century French philosopher Auguste Comte had said: 'Demography is destiny.' The rise and fall in the growth rate of population along with changes in the relative share of various groups within the population due to in-migration or out-migration has an important impact on the peace, prosperity and security of a nation. Migration, therefore, is always a political issue. Four points may be relevant to remember in this connection. First, migrants put pressure on the resources available to the host regions, causing tension between them and the locals. Second, migrants influence the politics of the state or locality because politics deals with human problems leading to the articulation of interests and the emergence of leadership. Third, there is a strong underpinning of communal and ethnic sentiments with any large-scale migration. And fourth, since some migrants, bring with them their connections with militant groups from the places of their origin, their presence in the receiving areas leads to violent politics in the latter.[9] All these factors are relevant in INE too, albeit at different points of time.

At the time of the British occupation of Assam, the population of the Brahmaputra Valley was about 1 million. By the 1870s, it had become 1.5 million, which was still quite less. The increase in population was largely on account of immigration from Bengal, which accounted for 65 per cent of the immigrants, those from the United Provinces 14 per cent, and those from the Central Provinces 10.8 per cent. Besides, there were Marwaris, an entrepreneurial community from Rajasthan, and Nepalis who were settled in the low-lying hills around the Brahmaputra Valley. Since Bengal then included the present-day Bihar, Jharkhand, Orissa and West Bengal as well as Bangladesh, the immigrants to Assam from Bengal actually refers to plantation labourers from present-day Jharkhand and Orissa, mainly the Santhals, Oraons and Mundas, as well as Bengalis who came to man government posts and to fulfill the need for professional doctors, lawyers, teachers, etc. The latter process started particularly after

April 1831, when Bengali language replaced Persian as the court language of Assam. The Bengali–Muslim immigration as farmers was a twentieth-century phenomenon. In short, therefore, nineteenth-century Assam witnessed immigrant Bengali–Hindus, tribals from the Chhotanagpur region, Marwaris, Hindi-speakers and Nepalis, while in the twentieth century it was mostly the immigration of Bengali Muslims. These two different patterns influenced Assamese politics differently.

Assamese–Bengali Cleavage: The Cultural Factor

As mentioned above, after the colonial annexation of Assam in 1826, a large number of Bengalis, the so-called Bengali *baboos,* migrated to the region in search of white-collar jobs. But even earlier, during Ahom rule, there had been diplomatic contacts with the neighbouring Bengali kingdoms of Cachar, Darrang and, Tripura notwithstanding the fact that the Ahom Kings wanted to keep their kingdom isolated from the rest of India. Rudra Sinha (1696–1740) and Siva Sinha (1741–44), in particular, had patronized Bengali culture. Bengali priests were invited and they contributed to the Sanskritization of the population.

Compared to the Assamese, Bengali Hindus had the advantage of being introduced to English education first, as the colonization of Bengal had preceded that of Assam. As a result, the Bengali middle class had a headstart over the Assamese middle class. It was this Bengali middle class which came to Assam to man the colonial bureaucracy. Bengalis soon started dominating the cultural and intellectual life of the province, thus becoming the role models for many Assamese aristocrats and intellectuals. Relations between the two communities, however, started deteriorating after Bengali was introduced as the official language of Assam in 1837. Most Assamese scholars believed that the British did so under the influence of Bengali officials working in Assam. But the fact of the matter was that since Bengali was already being used in Bengal for administrative and judicial purposes it was easy for the British to introduce it in Assam as well, where a new administrative system was being constituted on the lines of Bengal and, in any case, Assamese and Bengali were sister languages.[10]

Against this background arrived the American Baptist missionaries. They did not have much success in converting people to Christianity but contributed significantly to the popularization of Assamese language. In 1846, they published the first Assamese magazine, *Aroonaday*, from Sibsagar, and an Assamese grammar book. In 1867, Miles Bronson compiled an English–Assamese dictionary. Due to this missionary intervention, the British gradually began to change their language policy and in 1873, Assamese replaced Bengali as the language of schools and courts in all districts of the Brahmaputra Valley except Goalpara. An Assamese middle class, which was already in the making, now competed with the Bengalis for jobs and other benefits, resulting in ethnic rivalry between them.[11]

Assamese–Muslim Cleavage: The Communal Factor

The Muslims of Assam possess a multiplicity of ethnic identities. At one level they are Assamese, at another Bengali and at yet another just Muslim, depending upon the nature of the discourse and its political implications. To fine-tune the distinction, as one political sociologist has done, Assamese Muslims can be broadly classified into four categories, namely, Assamese Muslims, new-Assamese Muslims, Muslims of the Barak Valley, and North-Indian Muslims living in Assam. This categorization is necessary to comprehend contemporary social, economic, political and cultural questions related to the community.[12]

Assamese Muslims are also known as *Thalua Musalman*, meaning the local Muslims, and *Goria*. They speak Assamese at home. They are the descendants of Muslim prisoners of war exiled to Assam, medieval Muslim technicians, artisans and preachers and local converts. The Turko-Afghans and Mughals tried to capture Assam a number of times but failed not only during the Ahom kingdom, from late fifteenth century to 1819, but even earlier. The spread of Islam in Assam took place primarily under the influence of the mystic Azan Faqeer in around 1630. The colonization of Assam by the British in 1826 ended the relative isolation of the area from the Indian subcontinent, an important result of which was migration of all kinds of groups to Assam. The migrants who came from East Bengal (present-day Bangladesh), mainly from the beginning of the twentieth century from the districts of Rangpur, Mymenshingh and Pabna, are the ones whom we now call the new-Assamese (*Na-Asamiya*) Muslims. These migrants arrived looking for an escape from feudal oppression and poverty on the one hand and more land available for cultivation on the other. Viewed purely from an economic perspective it was a welcome development, but since the linguistic and religious composition of the two regions differed, societal conflicts were inherent in the circumstances. It was not an easy task for the British rulers to reconcile these two opposite poles without appearing to be partial. One idea that was mooted to contain the inherent tension was the Line System, which after a few years of discussion was introduced in 1920.

The Line System

Under this system a line was drawn in those districts where immigrant pressure was greater, allowing settlements only up to the line. The system, however, did not serve the purpose as expected. Being more industrious and prolific compared to the local Assamese people, these Bengali Muslims lured the former to sell off their lands, in which both Marwari and Assamese moneylenders played a contributory role. As the matter started assuming political colour, some measures were taken to assuage Assamese sentiments. Villages in wastelands were classified into three categories: (*i*) those exclusively available to immigrants, (*ii*) those exclusively available to local people, and (*iii*) those available to both categories. There were also some ceilings imposed on land transfer and restrictions imposed on hiring immigrants as agricultural labour. But these policies too had limited efficacy, partly because of corruption among revenue officials and partly because of unabated encroachment by immigrants into areas earmarked for the local Assamese people.[13]

The British had a stake in immigration because it yielded more crops and hence more revenue, yet at the same time the political implications of the process could not be ignored either. Between 1928 and 1936, some steps were taken to regulate colonization, but the local (Assamese) versus outsider (East Bengali) political conflict could not be prevented from growing. This conflict had several dimensions. On the one hand, it was linguistic, between Assamese-speaking people, which included Assamese Hindus and Assamese Muslims, and Bengali-speaking people who included Bengali Hindu settlers in Assam from the previous century and Bengali Muslims from East Bengal who had been constantly pouring in. On the other hand, it was a religious conflict between Assamese Hindus and Bengali Hindus on the one side and Assamese Muslims and Bengali Muslims on the other. But in respect of the latter, it must be qualified that while Assamese Muslims were substantially integrated into Assamese culture, the connection between Assamese and Bengali Muslims was at best superficial.[14]

The Muslim Question

The essential thrust of Assam politics was thus the conflict between Assamese Hindus and East Bengali Muslims. During the 1930s and 1940s, as Assamese nationalism and Muslim separatism grew, the conflict intensified. It was in this conflict that the controversy over 'Grow More Food' or 'Grow More Muslims' got entrapped. There was no doubt that the pull factors in favour of Muslim migration included the patronage it received from the Muslim League, which ruled Bengal in the late 1930s and early 1940s.[15] The Assamese Hindus were apprehensive of the systematic growth of the Muslim population in Assam. They articulated their grievances through the Congress forum as well as the Asam Sangrakhani Sabha and the Jatiya Mahasabha. Dr Rajendra Prasad, a leading congressman who subsequently became the first President of the Indian Republic, sought a solution to the problem by encouraging Hindu peasants from his own district Chhapra, in Bihar, to migrate in large numbers to offset Muslim growth. The phenomenon of Muslim population growth was so prominent that one British census officer remarked in 1931 that eventually the Assamese race would be found only in Sibsagar district. He, of course, was using this politically loaded statement to drive a wedge between the Hindus and Muslims of Assam.[16]

Post-Partition Blues: A Binary Conflict

Two types of conflicts emerged during the period 1826–1947, one linguistic, between Assamese speakers and Bengali speakers, and the other religious, between Assamese Hindus and Bengali Muslims, and continued even after Independence. The first conflict found its most widespread expression in the early 1970s while the second became prominent in the late 1970s. So far as the first was concerned, besides immigration from other districts of Assam into the Brahmaputra Valley, there was also the issue of Bengali Hindu refugees from East Pakistan. In respect of the second, it was alleged that there was a constant flow of illegal migrants into Assam from neighbouring East Pakistan/Bangladesh, which had the potential of upsetting the precarious demographic balance of Assam in favour of Bangladeshi Muslims.

Assamese vs Bengali

For as long as Sylhet was part of Assam and, therefore part of India as well, many Bengali Hindus migrated to the Brahmaputra Valley in search of jobs and then settled there. The process was transformed into an exodus once Sylhet became part of East Pakistan. Sylhet's Hindu Bengalis had all along resented the district's incorporation into Assam and agitated for its reunion with Bengal. But when the choice was between joining East Pakistan and Assam, they opted for the latter. Understandably, many left Sylhet for different districts of Assam after the referendum. There was also a constant flow of Bengalis into Brahmaputra Valley from the Bengali-majority Cachar district, which had been a part of Assam since the partition of Bengal in 1905. In 1961, 1 million of the 7 million people living in Brahmaputra Valley were Bengalis, concentrated mostly in the urban centres. Amongst the urban dwellers, Bengalis outnumbered the Assamese. The latter being predominantly a rural people, only 5 per cent of them lived in urban areas, whereas 40 per cent of the valley's Bengalis lived in those very areas. In some towns in Goalpara, Darrang and Nowgong districts, Bengalis constituted over 40 per cent of the population.[17] In post-Independence Assam, of course, the Bengalis also included refugees from East Pakistan (Table 1.1).

Table 1.1: Hindu Refugee Population in Assam, 1951–71

Year	Hindu refugee population
1951	274,455
1958	487,000
1961	600,000
1968	1,068,455
1971	1,500,000 (estimated)*

Source: Sajal Nag, *Roots of Ethnic Conflict: Nationality Question in North-East India* (New Delhi: Manohar, 1990), p. 170.

Note: *During the Bangladesh War 1971–72, the number of Hindu and Muslim refugees entering Assam and West Bengal totalled 10 million. Although after the war this population returned, yet it is assumed that a chunk of this population did not go back and settled in those provinces. Therefore, considering this population and the natural increase of the earlier refugee entrants, the Hindu population in Assam would not be less than 1.5 million by 1971–72.

The Assamese-dominated Congress party, which ruled Assam after Independence, was more concerned about the uplift of the Assamese community than about the state in general. Massive funds were allocated for the education of the community resulting in a surplus availability of educated youth for jobs, pitting them against the Bengali community. Preference started being given to Assamese in job selection, certain sectors of which witnessed rapid expansion. Against this background, the language policy became the bone of contention between the Assamese and Bengalis. The Assamese wanted their language to be the sole medium of instruction in schools, whereas Bengalis wanted both Assamese and Bengali to be used. The Assamese wanted the Bengalis to acknowledge Assamese cultural symbols like the Bihu festivals, historic events, heroes, etc., which the Bengalis resented. Weiner has explained how this dichotomy got increasingly conflictual and by the early 1970s it culminated in anti-Bengali riots, which saw widespread arson damaging Bengali properties throughout the Brahmaputra Valley.[18]

Assamese vs Bengali Muslims

Hardly had the dust of the anti-Bengali riots settled that Assam was once again in flames towards the end of 1970s and this time the targets were the outsiders, i.e., the unauthorized settlers from Bangladesh. It was argued that these settlers from East Pakistan/ Bangladesh were such a large number that a situation could soon arise where the Assamese people would become a minority in their own state. We need not go into the details of this subject, for many scholars have already discussed it. It may, however, be relevant here to refer to the Illegal Migrants (Determination by Tribunal) Act of 1983 (popularly known as the IMDT Act), which was recently nullified by the Supreme Court of India, resulting in an amended version of it being issued by the central government.

The IMDT Act was introduced two years before the Assam Accord of 1985. At the height of the Assam Movement it was quite common for someone to report to the police that such and such Muslim was an unauthorized national, which often led to his harassment by the local police under the Foreigners Act. Even such Muslims who had been residents of Assam for many decades and had earned a respectable reputation in Assamese society were sometimes not spared. The police even harassed the widow of Moidul Islam Bora, a former president of the Asom Sahitya Sabha, Syed Abdul Malik, a noted writer and former president of the Asom Sahitya Sabha, and Nurul Amin, a noted sports personality. These people ultimately prevailed upon Hiteshwar Saikia, erstwhile chief minister of Assam, who, with the help of Law Minister Abdul Munib Mazumdar, got the IMDT Act approved by the Government of India.[19] Mercifully for the latter, when the bill was tabled in the parliament all the MPs from Assam were on a boycott of the house. When the Assam Accord was signed in 1985 its Clause 5.9 simply said: 'The Government will give due consideration to certain difficulties expressed by the AASU/AAGSP regarding the implementation of the Illegal Migrants (Determination by Tribunals) Act, 1983.'

The subject remained controversial and in July 2005, in response to a writ petition filed by Asom Gana Parishad MP Sarbananda Sonowal, the Supreme Court ruled the IMDT Act unconstitutional. The ruling produced mixed reactions in Assam. While caste Hindus were jubilant, Muslims in general were apprehensive, particularly because assembly elections were due within a year. Other communities were by and large indifferent. In actual terms, however, the scrapping of the IMDT Act has no meaning. In any case, whether it is the IMDT Act or the Foreigners Act, it involves judicial processes of one form or the other. When the Indian judicial system is already virtually collapsing under the burden of millions of pending cases, it is most unlikely that the implementation of the Foreigners Act in Assam to detect and deport illegal migrants will have any real effect. The whole discourse, therefore, has only a political and hence electoral significance, which the Assam assembly elections results of May 2006 demonstrated. For the first time in Assam's history, an 'immigrant' Muslim party, Assam United Democratic Front (AUDF), won as many as ten seats, all from the Muslim-majority areas of Lower Assam.

Conflicts Without Much Violence

Considering the fact that Assam has witnessed two major types of societal conflicts, one between the Assamese and Bengalis and the other between the Assamese and Bengali Muslims for more than a hundred years, the eruption of violence emanating from these conflicts has been rather infrequent, particularly when compared to other parts of India. Even in the wake of the partition, when extremely violent Hindu–Muslim riots rocked Kolkata, Noakhali, Tarapur in

Bihar and Punjab, Assam escaped the fury.[20] But in the aftermath
of the passage of the Immigrants' (Expulsion from Assam) Act on
13 February 1950 by the Indian parliament, riots broke out in Lower
Assam, leading to about 100,000 immigrant Muslims leaving for East
Pakistan. It was Assam's first big riot against a minority community.[21]
The subsequent instances of violence were the anti-Bengali riots
of 1972, the Nelli massacre of Muslims in February 1982, and the
murder of Muslims in Barpeta, Kokrajhar and Bongaigaon in 1994.
Although there can be several sociological reasons explaining these
anti-Muslim riots, the communalization of the Assam Movement
was at least one important reason. The movement was controlled
essentially by upper-caste Hindus. In response there was the sectarian
movement of the Bodos. In between were crushed the unorganized
Muslim peasants. To add to their woes was the role played by the
regional press, dominated by the Assamese high castes, which consciously bundled the new-Assamese Muslims together with the outsiders, Bangladeshis, foreigners, etc. In keeping with its own class
interest, the press sometimes campaigned tacitly, sometimes blatantly,
against the Muslims of Assam. Monirul Hussain laments: 'Such political socialization in a situation wherein the state has failed to resolve the complex nationality/ethnic question and massive popular
discontent, the Muslims have become the most vulnerable social
group of repeated violence. Therefore, it would be erroneous to blame
the Bodo leaders alone — because wider issues and processes have
conjoined in the Barpeta massacre.'[22]

Competing Ethnicities

While the Assamese–Bengali and Assamese–Muslim conflicts persisted
even after the partition, both of which had a direct relationship with
immigration, as Independence neared, a new dimension was added
to the politics of the state. The tribal communities of Assam, which
the British had kept at a safe distance from their mainstream politics,
could not be kept like that forever. With the 1935 Government of
India Act a beginning was made in terms of their inclusion into the
national polity. Barring the Nagas, who steadfastly opposed incorporation into the Indian Union, other tribal communities had virtually
reconciled themselves to a future in the Indian state. How much autonomy and political power they could extract from the latter was
the issue. Though the process had nothing to do with the immigration

question, as an indirect connection with the phenomenon, it drew its sustenance from the fact that Assam was a state without any clear dominant community, which was a result of immigrations into the Brahmaputra Valley taking place ever since the British had arrived. In this process, whoever had the wherewithal could extract their pound of flesh at the cost of the territorial integrity of the state. Thus, if linguistic and religious conflicts were the dominant themes of pre-Independence Assam politics and which continued even thereafter, ethnicity-based tribal demands for autonomy, statehood within the Indian Union or complete independence became the dominant themes of post-Independence Assam as well as other parts of INE. The circumstances were favourable for such a situation. Geographically, most of these tribes were located at the periphery of India; strategically, they were close to India's neighbours with whom India had unfriendly, or, at least tense, relations ([East] Pakistan and China); culturally, they were strangers not just to Indians in general, but even to the Brahmaputra and Barak Valley Assamese, Bengali and Muslim population; politically, they were of least significance, and economically speaking they were underdeveloped. The Indian state, therefore, had the task of ensuring that these tribes were integrated into the national polity, otherwise they could be a geo-strategic liability. The tribal leaderships understood this predicament of the Indian state and extracted all that they could in terms of political autonomy and financial benefits.

The structural link between the demand for tribal autonomy and the centre's compulsion to pump more and more financial aid into the region took its toll, with the region becoming one of the most violent and disturbed in India. The multiplicity of ethnicity in the INE and their respective demands for more and more autonomy on the one hand and, on the other, the Indian state's willingness to listen to them only when they take up arms has created a nexus between the insurgency, central aid, corruption and extortion syndromes, in which every party seems to have developed a stake. It is not easy to document this nexus but in Tables 1.2 and 1.3 we have tried to underline the magnitude of the potential intellectual confusion that an analyst would be vulnerable to. These tables warrant rigorous methodologically sound scrutiny which is not possible as part of this article. For the moment, it may suffice to highlight the following three points. One, the process of reorganizing states in INE is still on and the region may end up with more states than the existing seven

Table 1.2: Ethnic and Linguistic Profile of the North-East (District-wise), 2001

S. No.	District	Population	Major ethnic and linguistic groups (in most cases they coincide)	Conflict scene (insurgent groups)**	Remarks
1.	Changlang	124,422	Adi, Galo, Chakma, Lisu, Nocte, Tase, Tutsa, Singpho	NSCN–IM, NSCN–K	Arunachal Pradesh is by and large a peaceful state. It is only recently that the NSCN has made inroads, using it as their base and seeking shelter there.
2.	Dibang Valley	57,720	Idu Mishmi, Adi, Galo, Digaru Mishmi		
3.	East Kameng	57,179	Hruso, Sajalong		
4.	East Siang	87,397	Adi, Padams		
5.	Lohit	143,527	Adi, Galo, Chakma, Digaru Mishmi, Khamti, Miji Mishmi	EILF	EILF is an indigenous organization.
6.	Lower Subansiri	98,244	Apatani, Miri		
7.	Papum Pare	122,003	Karbi		
8.	Tawang	38,924	Membas, Khambas		
9.	Tirap	100,326	Chakma	NSCN–IM, NSCN–K	
10.	Upper Siang	33,363	Khamti		
11.	Upper Subansiri	55,346	Adi, Galo, Apatani		
12.	West Kameng	74,599	Bugun, Hruso, Moinba, Sajalong		
13.	West Siang	103,918	Khamti		
14.	Borpeta	1,647,201	Assamese	MULTA	

(Table 1.2 continued)

(*Table 1.2 continued*)

S. No.	District	Population	Major ethnic and linguistic groups (in most cases they coincide)	Conflict scene (insurgent groups)**	Remarks
15.	Bongaingaon	904,835	Assamese	BLTF, ULFA, RNSF	
16.	Cachar	1,444,921	Assamese	MULTA	
17.	Darrang	1,504,320	Assamese	ULFA	
18.	Dhemaji	571,944	Assamese	ULFA	
19.	Dhuburi	1,637,344	Assamese	ULFA, RNSF	
20.	Dibrugarh	1,185,072	Assamese	ULFA	
21.	Goalpara	822,035	Assamese	ULFA, RNSF	
22.	Golaghat	946,279	Assamese	ULFA	
23.	Hailakandi	542,872	Assamese	MULTA	
24.	Jorhat	999,221	Assamese	ULFA	
25.	Kamrup	2,522,324	Assamese	ULFA	
26.	Karbi Anglong	813,311	Karbi, Kuki, Dimasa, Assamese	KLNLF, KLA, KNF, DHD (Black Widow faction and Dilip Nunisa faction), UPDS	
27.	Karimganj	1,007,976	Assamese, Bengali	—	
28.	Kokrajhar	905,764	Assamese, Bodo	BLTF, ULFA	
29.	Lakhimpur	889,010	Assamese	ULFA	
30.	Marigaon	776,256	Assamese	ULFA	
31.	Nagaon	2,314,629	Assamese	ULFA, TNRF	
32.	Nalbari	1,148,824	Assamese	ULFA	

33.	North Cachar Hills	188,079	Dimasa, Hmar, Beitei, Jemi Naga, Kuki, Karbi, Nepali, Bengali, Assamese.	DHD (Black Widow faction and Dilip Nunisa faction), HPC (D), NSCN–IM, KNF, UPDS
34.	Sibsagar	1,051,736	Assamese	ULFA
35.	Sonitpur	1,681,513	Assamese	ULFA
36.	Tinsukia	1,150,062	Assamese	ULFA
37.	East Garo Hills	250,582	Garo	AMLA, ANVC, GNC
38.	East Khasi Hills	660,923	Khasi	HNLC
39.	Jaintia Hills	299,108	Jaintia, Khasi	—
40.	Ri Bhoi	192,790	Khasi	—
41.	South Garo Hills	100,980	Garo	—
42.	West Garo Hills	518,390	Garo	—
43.	West Khasi Hills	296,049	Garo	—
44.	Dimapur	309,024	Angami, Cachari, Lotha	NSCN–IM
45.	Kohima	310,084	Angami, Kachari, Northern Rengma, Sakechap	NSCN–IM
46.	Mokochung	232,085	Ao	NSCN–K
47.	Mon	260,652	Mao, Konyak, Nocte	NSCN–K
48.	Phek	148,195	Chakesang, Khezha	NSCN–K, NCSN–IM
49.	Tuensang	414,818	Khiamniungan, Konyak, Phom	NSCN–K, NSCN–IM
50.	Wokha	161,223	Lotha	NSCN–IM
51.	Zunheboto	153,955	Sema	NSCN–IM
52.	Peren		Zeliangrong	NSCN–IM
53.	Longleng		Samtang	NSCN–IM

(Table 1.2 continued)

(Table 1.2 continued)

S. No.	District	Population	Major Ethnic and Linguistic Groups (in Most Cases they Coincide)	Conflict Scene (Insurgent Groups)**	Remarks
54.	Kiphire		Phom	NSCN–IM	
55.	Bishnupur	208,368	Chiru, Koireng		
56.	Chandel	118,327	Aimol, Anal, Beitei, Koireng, Khoibu, Moyon, Purum	NSCN–IM, KNF	
57.	Churachandpur	227,905	Aimol, Paite, Chiru, Gangte, Hmar, Simte	HPC (D), KNF	
58.	Imphal East	394,876	Manipuri	PREPAK, PLA, KCP, PULF, NEMF, INF, IRF, UILA	
59.	Imphal West	444,382	Manipuri	PREPAK, PLA, KCP, PULF, NEMF, INF, IRF, UILA	
60.	Senapati	283,621	Aimol, Koireng, Maram, Purum	NSCN–IM, KNF	
61.	Tamenglang	111,499	Chiru, Zeme Naga	NSCN–IM, PREPAK, KNF	
62.	Thoubal	364,140	Chiru	PRA, PULF, NEMF, INF	
63.	Ukhrul	140,778	Tangkhul	NSCN–IM, KNF	
64.	Aizawl	325,676	Hmar, Kuki, Bru, Reangs, Chakma	ZRA, HPC (D), BNLF	
65.	Champai	108,392	Hmar, Kuki	ZRA	
66.	Kolasib	65,960	Hmar, Kuki		
67.	Lawngtlai	73,620	Hmar, Kuki		
68.	Lunglei	137,223	Hmar, Kuki		
69.	Mamit	62,785	Hmar, Kuki		
70.	Saiha	61,056	Hmar, Kuki		

71.	Serchhip	53,861	Hmar, Kuki	
72.	Dhalai	307,686	Thado, Bengali, Kok Borok	NLFT (NB), NLFT (MK), TNV, BNCT TRA, UNBLF, TPDF
73.	North Tripura	590,913	Thado, Bengali, Kok Borok	
74.	South Tripura	767,440	Thado, Bengali, Kok Borok	
75.	West Tripura	1,532,982	Thado, Bengali, Kok Borok	

*Note: *Nos 1 to 13–Arunachal Pradesh (1,097,968); 14 to 36–Assam (26,655,528); 37 to 43–Megahalya (2,318,822); 44 to 54–Nagaland (1,990,036); 55 to 63–Manipur (2,293,896); 64 to 71–Mizoram (885,573); 72 to 75–Tripura (3,199,203). Total population of North East–38,441,026 (excluding Sikkim).
**For abbreviations see pp. 29–30.

Table 1.3: Grants-in-Aid to INE states, 2005–10 (INR mn.)

States	Transfer of central taxes	Transfer of total grants	Total transfer	Grants as % of total transfers	Annual per capita grants to states (INR)
Arunachal Pradesh	17,673.4	17,582.2	35,255.6	49.87	3,223
Assam	198,506.9	44,787.1	243,294.0	18.40	336
Manipur	22,214.4	46,487.6	68,702.0	67.66	3,891
Meghalaya	22,766.1	20,911.6	43,677.7	47.87	1,813
Mizoram	14,665.2	31,943.9	46,609.1	68.53	7,170
Nagaland	16,136.7	58,397.4	74,534.1	78.35	5,872
Tripura	26,260.9	57,909.1	84,170.0	68.80	2,471
India	**6,131,120.2**	**1,426,396.0**	**7,557,516.2**	**18.87**	**277**

Source: Government of India, Ministry of Finance, Report of the Twelfth Finance, Commission (2005–10), cited in, Left Behind: A Case Study of Assam (New Delhi: Centre for Policy Alternatives [CPAS], 2005), p. 16.

with further bifurcation not only of Assam but also some other states like Arunachal Pradesh, Manipur and Meghalaya. Two, Assam's 'North-East' tag does it little service and sooner it sheds the tag the better it will be, a point I have made elsewhere.[23] Three, India's federal experiment operates only in name in INE — in practice, it is a unitary system managed through the complex mechanism of central assistance, with the governor functioning essentially as the 'watchdog of central interest'.

Migration, Ethnicity and Crime

There is not enough evidences with respect to the crime scene in INE in the conventional sense, particularly in relation to immigration. It was noted, however, that after the British annexation of Assam there was a perceptible increase in the incidence of violent crimes like highway robberies, murders and dacoities, involving the loss of lives. This was attributed to the abolition of the earlier system of delivering justice, which was extremely harsh and punishments were often not confined merely to the convicts but would extend to their family members, including their parents, spouses, children and siblings. Capital punishments were quite common.[24] Gradually, the British system of justice became more popular because, on the one hand, it made the punishments more humane and, on the other, it was based on a uniform code of penal laws that did not distinguish between the rich and the poor, high and low.[25]

In recent times, complaints of petty crimes have become common in border areas where it is alleged that the cross-border cattle lifting and theft are routine matters. During the author's field trips to such border areas in Assam's Dhuburi district, which is adjacent to Bangladesh, the phenomenon of *goru churi* (cow lifting) was noticed as being the subject of much discussion. In other parts of the border areas there have been cases of cross-border armed robberies. In many of the tribal areas of Arunachal Pradesh and Meghalaya, local people complain that after the emergence of immigrant settlements, petty crimes increased manifold, which were earlier virtually non-existent.[26]

In the context of ethnicity and crime, it may be noted that the matter has to be discussed from two different perspectives — crime and non-tribal populations, and crime and tribal populations. So far as the first is concerned, one does not come across the so-called

Hindu caste panchayats that are quite common in parts of North India and which come in the way of a uniform criminal justice system. Vasudha Dhagamwar notes that the existence of community-based personal laws in many parts of India has not only created an unjust social situation but has also intruded into the realm of criminal justice, thereby making a mockery of criminal law in the rural areas. As a result, not only does bigamy take place, by circumventing the law or even the wider ambit of law by taking recourse to incomplete marriage rituals, even crimes as defined by the IPC are perpetrated in the name of personal and customary laws. When a young Scheduled Caste man and his wife were beheaded in UP by their caste members. Mahendra Singh Tikait, leader of a powerful agricultural lobby of north India, justified the killings on the grounds that anyone violating caste norms deserved to be punished. The state did not contradict him. The line demarcating personal law from criminal law, or for that matter even constitutional law, thus often gets blurred, making it difficult to ascertain where one ends and the other starts.[27]

Insofar as the tribals of INE are concerned, they have all along resisted the imposition of laws by non-tribal groups, right from the days of the British, who were the first to try and impose a uniform criminal legal system. Although in 1916 the Indian Penal Code was introduced in the tribal areas it was meant to deal only with serious criminal offences. The promulgation of the Assam Frontier (Administration of Justice) Regulation of 1945 ensured that most disputes and cases in these areas would be adjudicated by tribal customary laws and practices.

This hiatus continued even after the British left. After Independence, the tribal INE was brought under the purview of the Sixth Schedule of the Constitution and certain categories of criminal offences and civil disputes were to now be adjudicated through the mechanism of Autonomous District Councils. According to Clause 5(3) of the Sixth Schedule 'the Code of Civil Procedure [C.P.C.], 1908, and the Code of Criminal Procedure [Cr.P.C.], 1898, shall not apply to the trial of any suits, cases or offences in an autonomous district or in any autonomous region to which the provisions of this paragraph apply'.[28] Arunachal Pradesh and Nagaland are outside the purview of the Sixth Schedule, but that does not mean that the laws operative in the rest of India operate here. In Arunachal Pradesh, the Rules for Administration of Justice promulgated during the British period are still in force, while in Nagaland, the traditional village councils administer justice. The hill tribes of Manipur are governed by the Manipur Hill Areas Village Authorities Act of 1956 and ever since 1979, the Tripura Tribal Areas Autonomous District Council has been administering justice in the areas under its jurisdiction.

In short, the so-called 'rule of law' has little meaning for tribespeople who, writes Dhagamwar, 'have long since concluded that the law was not for them. It was difficult to understand, it was expensive and time consuming. Law was meant to exploit and oppress them. At all costs, one should avoid the law. It worked only for the rich and the powerful'.[29]

Conclusion

Whatever may be said in criticism of the British policy of segregating the tribal regions of Assam into 'excluded' and 'partially excluded' areas, viewed from the perspective of immigration drastically changing demographic profiles in the rest of the province as well as in Tripura and to some extent in Manipur, it may be concluded that it was probably a foresightful policy and for the same reason the Government of India, after Independence, did not do away with the system of Inner Line Passes and Restricted Area Permits. Immigrations have caused a great deal of societal tension in Assam, which still requires a solution. In Tripura, the immigration of Bengali Hindus from neighbouring East Pakistan/Bangladesh has diametrically altered the population balance against the locals. Even in Manipur, the latest figures indicate that the indigenous community of Meities has become a minority because of the growing number of people from outside the state. All these, however, make one wonder whether historical processes, of which immigration/emigration are just one manifestation, can ever be prevented or is the only solution available to work out strategies and find ways of addressing ever-changing human problems by making the best use of historical experiences wherever possible.

Notes and References

1. A.K.M. Nurun Nabi and P. Krishnan, 'Some Approaches to the Study of Human Migration', in Kuttan Mahadevan and Paarameswara Krishnan (eds), *Methodology for Population Studies and Development* (New Delhi and London: Sage Publications, 1993), p. 83.

2. Ibid., p. 85.
3. Sir Edward Gait, *A History of Assam* (Fifth edition, Guwahati: Lawyer's Book Stall, 1992), pp. 100–184.
4. Amalendu Guha, *Planter Raj to Swaraj: Freedom Struggle and Electoral Politics in Assam 1826–1947* (New Delhi: Tulika Books, [1977] 2006), p. 24. See also, Sajal Nag, *Roots of Ethnic Conflict: Nationality Question in North-East India* (New Delhi: Manohar, 1990), pp. 59–60.
5. Myron Weiner, *Sons of the Soil: Migration and Ethnic Conflict in India* (New Delhi: Oxford University Press, 1978), p. 84.
6. S. Gopal, *British Policy in India 1858–1905* (London: Cambridge University Press, 1965), pp. 268–69; Abu Nasar Saied Ahmed, *Nationality Question in Assam: The EPW 1980–81 Debate* (Guwahati: OKDISCD; New Delhi: Akansha, 2006).
7. Verrier Elwin, *A Philosophy for NEFA (Arunachal Pradesh)* (Itanagar: Directorate of Research, Government of Arunachal Pradesh, [1957] 1999), p. 66. Also, Arun Chandra Bhuyan, *Facets of Assam History* (Guwahati: Jaya Prakashan, 2003), pp. 13–18.
8. Guha, *Planter Raj to Swaraj*, pp. 263, n. 4.
9. Partha S. Ghosh, *Unwanted and Uprooted: A Political Study of Migrants, Refugees, Stateless and Displaced of South Asia* (New Delhi: Samskriti, 2004), pp. 63–64.
10. Monirul Hussain, *The Assam Movement: Class, Ideology and Identity* (New Delhi: Manak Publications and Har-Anand Publications, 1993), pp. 229–32; Weiner, *Sons of the Soil*, pp. 92–93, n. 5.
11. Guha, *Planter Raj to Swaraj*, pp. 46–52, n. 4; Hiren Gohain, 'Origins of the Assamese Middle Class', *Social Scientist* 2 (August), 1973, Thiruvananthapuram, pp. 11–26.
12. Hussain, *The Assam Movement*, p. 197, n. 10.
13. Amalendu Guha, 'East Bengal Immigrants and Bhasani in Assam Politics: 1928–47', in Indian History Congress, *Proceedings of the Thirty-fifth Session* (Calcutta: Jadavpur University, 1974), pp. 348–65.
14. The cultural integration of Assamese Muslims can be seen in their participation in the Bihu festivals, and some of them are, in fact, worshippers of Goddess Kali (*Kali sadhaks*). Often it becomes difficult to identify Assamese Muslims, but for their names. Muslim chronicler Shihabuddin Talish, who accompanied Nawab Mirjumla in his Assam expeditions (1662–63), in his *Taraikh-i-Assam* and *Fathiiyya-i-Ibriyya*, provides an elaborate account of Assam and its people in the latter half of the seventeenth century. Talish found amongst the Assamese Muslims 'nothing of Islam except the name; their hearts are inclined more towards mixing with the Assamese than towards association with the Muslims'. J.N. Sarkar, *Translation of Fathiyya-i-Ibriyya, Journal of the Bihar and Orissa Research Society*, 1915, p. 193, quoted in M. Sujaud Doullah, *Immigration of East Bengal Farm Settlers and Agricultural development*

of the Assam Valley, 1901–1947 (New Delhi: Institute of Objective Studies, 2003), p. 10.

15. Hussain, *The Assam Movement*, p. 201–4, n. 10.
16. Ibid., pp. 204–07.
17. Weiner, *Sons of the Soil*, pp. 94–95, n. 5,
18. Ibid., pp. 111–30.
19. Abu Nasar Saied Ahmed and Adil-ul-Yasin, 'Problems of Identity, Assimilation and Nation Building: A Case Study of the Muslims of Assam', in Girin Phukon and N.L. Dutta (eds), *Politics of Identity and Nation Building in Northeast India* (New Delhi: South Asian Publishers, 1997), p. 148.
20. Guha, *Planter Raj to Swaraj*, p. 252, n. 4.
21. Ibid., p. 271.
22. Monirul Hussain, 'Understanding Barpeta Massacre 1994: Ethnicity, Communalism and State', in Asghar Ali Engineer (ed.), *Towards Secular India* (Bombay: Centre for Study of Society and Secularism, 1994), p. 43.
23. Partha S. Ghosh, 'Challenges of Peace building in India's Northeast: A Holistic Perspective', in Wasbir Hussain (ed.), *Order in Chaos: Essays on Conflict in India's Northeast and the Road to Peace in South Asia* (Guwahati and New Delhi: Spectrum Publications, 2006), pp. 92–93.
24. H.K. Barpujari, *Assam in the Days of the Company (1826–1858)* (Shillong: North Eastern Hill University, 1996), p. 34.
25. Ibid., pp. 214–15.
26. Sengjirang N. Sangma, *Bangladeshi Immigrants in Meghalaya: Causes of Human Movement and Impact on Garo Hills* (Delhi: Anshah, 2005), pp. 92–93.
27. Vasudha Dhagamwar, 'Invasion of Criminal Law by Religion, Custom and Family Law', *Economic and Political Weekly* 38(15), Mumbai, 12 April 2003, pp. 1483–92.
28. *The Constitution of India* (New Delhi: Universal Law Company, 2007), pp. 341–61.
29. Vasudha Dhagamwar, *Role and Image of Law in India: The Tribal Experience* (New Delhi: Sage Publications, 2006), p. 352.

Abbreviations

AMLA	: Achik Matgrik Liberation Army
ANVC	: Achik National Volunteer Council
ASF	: Adivasi Security Force
BLTF	: Bodo Liberation Tiger Force
BNCT	: Borok National Council of Tripura

BNLF	:	Bru National Liberation Front
DHD	:	Dima Halam Daogah (Black Widow faction and Dilip Nunisa faction)
EILF	:	East India Liberation Front
GNC	:	Garo National Council
HNLC	:	Hynniewtrep National Liberation Council
HPC (D)	:	Hmar People's Council (Democratic)
INF	:	Islamic National Front
IRF	:	Islamic Revolutionary Front
KCP	:	Kangleipak Communist Party
KLNLF	:	Karbi Longri National Liberation Front
KLO	:	Kamatapur Liberation Organization
KNF	:	Kuki National Front
MULTA	:	Minority United Liberation Tigers of Assam
NEMF	:	North East Minority Front
NLFT (MK)	:	National Liberation Front of Tripura (Montu Koloi faction)
NLFT (NB)	:	National Liberation Front of Tripura (Nayan Bashi faction)
NSCN–IM	:	National Socialist Council of Nagaland–Isak Muivah
NSCN–K	:	National Socialist Council of Nagaland–Konyak
PLA	:	People's Liberation Army
PREPAK	:	People's Revolutionary Party of Kangleipak
PULF	:	People's United Liberation Force
RNSF	:	Rabha National Security Force
TNRF	:	Tiwa National Revolutionary Force
TNV	:	Tripura National Volunteers
TPDF	:	Tripura People's Democratic Front
TRA	:	Tripura Resurrection Army
UILA	:	United Islamic Liberation Army
ULFA	:	United Liberation Front of Assam
UNBLF	:	United National Bengali Liberation Front
UPDS	:	United Progressive Democratic Solidarity
ZRA	:	Zomi Revolutionary Army

2

Ethnic Minority and Political Governance: The Tai-Ahoms in Colonial and Post-Colonial Assam

Lipi Ghosh

Introduction

'Ethnicity' is a term used by people to identify themselves from other groups in terms of race, kinship, language, customary modes of livelihood, culture, religion, etc. Academic discourses on ethnicity are a late twentieth century phenomena, even though ethnic groups have asserted their identity since time immemorial. Moreover, it is the eastern world that has seen more intensive and turbulent growth of ethnicity, although it is the western world that popularized academic debate on it.

Just as ethnicity is an important concept, so is the phenomenon of minorities. In every nation of the world, there exists one or more groups of minorities. The relation between ethnicity and minorities is thus a complimentary one. The kaleidoscopic nature of ethnicity-related issues is exhibited by the plethora of writings that have appeared on the subject, especially when we turn to South Asia. Often, in the perception of minorities, the state appears to employ more than one, in fact many different policies towards the minorities. In the constitution of the majority–minority problem, the state then appears as an anarchic space. To put it differently, minorities see realm of the state as one of anarchy, force and power.

All post-colonial states face agitation by minority groups in which ethnic minorities form powerful blocs. Sometimes, as in the case of South Asia, these agitations are strong enough to create new nation-states in which the ethnic minorities are able to convert themselves into a majority. The study of ethnic minorities has thus become a fascinating area of research.

Its importance grows when the question of political governance is added to the phenomenon of ethnic minorities. Governance includes a few key issues such as the development of democratic institutions, civil society, participation of citizens, etc. The idea of liberal democratic governance is today globally triumphant. All countries, with democratic/non-democratic forms of governance, whether totalitarian states, monarchies or dictatorships, are now gradually turning towards the structure of a liberal democracy. This receptivity to liberal democracy has been called 'global homogenization', coming at the end of the bipolar Cold War. Francis Fukuyama, chief exponent of globalization, believes that a liberal democracy is the only suitable form of governance that can accommodate rapid economic and social changes in all types of societies. To study the question of political governance it thus becomes imperative to study features like the federal principle/decentralization, political representation of minorities and legal pluralism.

An especially outstanding feature of the South Asian situation is that all South Asian nation-states have a protracted history of direct or indirect colonial rule and, therefore, minority problems (either ethnic or religious) here have common origins, rooted in the colonial legacy. In the post-colonial scenario, South Asian states are home to processes of ethnic negotiation. In the Indian situation, governance under a vibrant democracy and free speech provisions encourage the active participation of ethnic groups in politics.

This article discusses the question of political governance amongst the Ahoms, a large and important ethnic minority community in Assam. Assam is one of seven states in north-eastern India, geographically referred to as being placed at the cartographic periphery, although strategically it holds a very important location, being situated on the border between South and South-East Asia on the one hand and between India and China on the other.

Ahoms in Assam: Political Governance in Colonial and Post-Colonial India

The Ahom community ruled Assam for almost 600 years since their arrival in the region in AD 1228. Initially, a Shan tribe of northern Burma, this Mongoloid group of people established their kingdom in the plains of Assam, which, in course of time, comprised the whole of the Brahmaputra Valley. They were an offshoot of the great Tai race, which inhabits many regions of South-East Asia.[1]

It was under British political supremacy that the Ahoms were finally defeated and Assam was conquered in 1826. In course of history, British policy-makers attempted to exterminate the political identity of this ruling-class minority community. It was not just in the bureaucracy, legislation, judiciary, education and policy-making arena that the colonial powers gradually placed the Ahoms in a second-grade position, but, alter effectively sapping the vitality of their community representation, the very name 'Ahom' was dropped from the census of 1931.[2] This policy of deprivation practised by the British ultimately resulted in the inauguration of the Ahom nationalist movement for the re-establishment of their ethnic identity.

During colonial rule, the Ahoms were constantly fighting to re-gain their independent status. As the traditional ruling elite, they objected to colonial rule and gradually initiated movements against the British. As a result, the British did not recruit Ahoms to positions of responsibility in the government. They considered the Ahoms to be remnants of the past. Dalton (1872) and Risley (1891) concluded that the present-day Ahoms had degenerated into superstitious, backward and apathetic Assamese. The colonial census-makers deemed the Ahoms a 'semi-Hinduised aboriginal group of Assamese'.[3] Increasingly, in British administrative circles, Ahom and Assamese were used as synonymous or interchangeable categories, and in 1931 the label 'Ahom' was finally dropped from census records. As a result the Ahoms were discriminated against in matters of employment and deprived of various economic benefits. In the social sphere too, the British cultivated a new and privileged middle class, comprising caste-Hindu Assamese. Their recruitment to the bureaucracy adversely affected the Ahoms.[4] Thus the Ahom did not benefit from British rule, rather they were driven into backwardness. Meanwhile, the non-Ahom Assamese upper-caste elite occupied dominant positions in the government, and competition developed between the Ahoms and the Assamese.

The restrictive and discriminatory nature of colonial governance gave birth to a new protest movement among the Ahoms. Conscious-ness about their distinct identity developed from the late nineteenth century onwards, when the Ahoms first began political mobilization with the formation of the All Assam Ahom Association (AAAA). From 1893 till the year of national independence, i.e., 1947, the Ahom movement progressed on a track parallel to that of the Indian National Congress within Assam, which came to be characterized entirely as a majoritarian caste-Hindu Assamese-dominated organization. AAAA stood for the preservation of Ahom ethnic identity and gradually became involved in wider politics, demanding reservation of seats in the legislature for Ahoms, recognition of their minority status, a separate electorate, etc. Thus, parallel to the national movement there existed a community movement which implied nothing but of minority mobilization against majoritarian political governance. Ahom leaders characterized the Congress as an enemy of the Ahoms and asked all Ahoms to boycott the 'Assamiya'.[5] As President of the Ahom Association, Surendranath Buragohain asserted the separate identity of the Ahoms:

> It is a great fortune on the part of Indian Union that the great Tai family people have been within India. The Indian government can utilise this force as a medium to establish friendship between India and Eastern Asia. We hope that the Government of India will understand this point and will attempt to resolve different issues raised by the Ahom Association relating to Ahom people's problems.[6]

Two other Tai-Ahom members of the Assam Legislative Assembly, Jogesh Chandra Gohain and Rai Sahib Daulat Chandra Gohain, repeatedly asserted that Ahoms were an inseparable part of the larger Assamese society and that the upliftment of the Ahoms would serve the interest of Assamese society. To maintain a distinct identity and build on the prosperity of the Ahoms, they demanded the recognition of Ahoms as a minority community. The Tenth Annual Conference of the AAAA (5–6 April 1941) demanded a separate electorate for the community.[7] In view of the aspirations of the Ahoms, on 20 November 1943, the Assam Legislative Assembly adopted a resolution:

> The Assembly was of opinion that the Ahom Community of this province be included among the recognised Minorities for the future Indian constitution and that the Government of India and Her Maiesty's Government for consideration and acceptance of the Community as a minority.[8]

Here again Surendranath's active participation was important. Before raising the proposal, in the House he declared:

> I rise to discharge a highly important task of asking the House on behalf of the Ahom community of this province, to which I have the privilege to belong along with two other members of this House, Mr. Jogesh Chandra Gohain and Rai Sahib Daulat Ch. Gohain, to accept the plea of the community to be recognised as a minority in the future free India Constitution.[9]

The executive committee meeting of the North Bank District Ahom Association (28 September 1944) at Lakhimpur resolved that in the event of India being divided into Hindustan and Pakistan, Assam should be separated from India and constituted as a dominion on the basis of history, culture and ethnic identity. The Ahom elite felt that they had a legitimate claim to dominance in Assam.

The AAAA also demanded a sovereign, independent state for all the tribes and races of Assam. They maintained that all the tribespeople (both in the hills and the plains) felt close to each other as they all belonged to the Mongoloid and Tibeto-Burman ethnic groups, distinct from the Aryans. The All-Assam Tribes and Races Federation was formed at Shillong in 1944, with representatives of the Ahoms, Kacharis, Miris, Deoris, Garos, Nagas, Lushais, Mikirs, Chutiyas and others.[10] In its first Convocation (21–23 March 1945), this Federation unanimously resolved that

> Historically, Assam proper was never a part or province of India (so) this convention emphatically opposes to Assam proper with its hills, being included into any proposed division of India Pakistan or Hindustan and demands that it should be constituted into a separate free state into which the hill districts bordering Assam be incorporated.[11]

Thus, by the late 1940s, the Ahoms were demanding a separate state for the Mongoloid communities, free from caste-Hindu domination. This poses a contradiction to the view of a few scholars who believe that the Ahom leaders represented themselves as a part and parcel of Assamese society and requested the 'Mongolia' groups — the Kacharis, Muttacks, Deuris — to come together against the Hindus.[12]

The AAAA was followed by a number of similar associations in different districts of the state, including North Lakhimpur (1893), Tejpur (1902), Jorhat (1909) and Nowgang (1910).[13] Initially these bodies functioned independently, but in 1910 they merged with the AAAA.

Initially, the AAAA had no formal structure or constitution, but a set of rules was adopted in and amended in 1941 and 1944. These rules prescribed a three-tier organizational structure. At the apex was the Central Unit with an Executive Committee and Action Committee; below this came the District Units, which were authorized to constitute Primary Units in the *mauza* or regional areas. The Central Executive Committee could affiliate with or incorporate other Ahom organizations with similar aims and objectives.[14]

The AAAA initially achieved many of its political goals. The Acts of 1909 and 1919 conceded minority status to the Ahoms.[15] However, the Act of 1935 reversed this ruling. In 1944, Ahom youths decided to form a separate student wing of the AAAA, called the All-Assam Ahom Student Federation (AAASF). But after merely two meetings (at Sibsagar and Dibrugarh), it lapsed into inactivity and then completely disappeared.[16]

That being the situation under colonial rule, the question arises — did the Ahoms regain their identity in post-colonial India? In other words, how did governance in independent India deal with the Ahoms? The truth is that even after 62 years of independence, the situation today is the same as it was under the British. There has been no change in policy formulations regarding this minority community. After Independence, the Ahom elites mobilized the community with renewed vigour to ensure that their political demands were met. However, under the newly drafted Indian Constitution, neither central nor state policy formulations gave them Scheduled Tribe (ST) status which would have ensured special privileges for them, and it was a sheer repetition of colonial policy when, in 1968, the Mehta Commission ruled that the Ahoms were 'Assamese' rather than tribal, thus marking a new assault on the identity of the Ahoms. Gopinath Bordoloi, an Assamese Brahmin who formed the Congress ministry in the state, declared the Ahoms a 'backward group'.[17]

In the late 1960s, the Ahom elite complained that they had been deprived of a 'legitimate share' of political power and privileges. Between 1947 and 1967, there had not been a single Ahom in the state cabinet. One group within the Ahom elite demanded an autonomous state consisting of two districts of Upper Assam — Sibsagar and Lakhimpur. The community as a whole, however, resolved to become more united and, in 1965, the faction ridden AAAA was dissolved and replaced by the All-Assam Tai Sabha (AATS).[18]

On 13 January 1967, the central government in New Delhi announced plans to re-organize Assam into plain and hill districts. Following the advice of tribal leaders, an Ahom conference was convened in Sibsagar, under the presidentship of Padmeshwar Gogoi, to demand an autonomous Ahom unit in Upper Assam.[19] The AATS, renamed the Ahom Tai Rajya Parishad, demanded the 'creation of a separate centrally administered unit in which Ahom-Tai and the various other tribes would enjoy social recognition and all political rights.'[20]

Several new Ahom organizations were thus formed, including the Gauhati University Tai Students Association, Mongoloid National Front, Ahom Tai Rajya Parishad and the Ahom Sabha. In October 1967, all these organizations were brought under one political umbrella called the Ahom Tai Mongolia Rajya Parishad (ATMRP) with Siva Burgohain as its General Secretary. Their demand was for the formation of a separate Mongolian state in Upper Assam.[21] However, on 13 January 1968, the Mehta Commission ruled that the Ahom were Assamese rather than 'tribal', and that, therefore, a separate state was inappropriate.[22]

Following this setback, the Ahoms tried to make their strength felt through the ballot box. On the eve of the mid-term elections in 1971, the ATMRP was renamed as the more secular-sounding Ujoni Asom Rajya Parishad (UARP), with the objective of improving the socio-economic condition of the people of Upper Assam through the creation of a separate state or an autonomous unit.[23] The UARP, however, failed because of the actions (or inactions) of their party leaders; many joined the Congress. Siva Buragohain became a minister under the Congress banner and Khagendra Nath Saikia was given the coveted post of Judge in the Gauhati High Court.

These defections provoked a change of direction. Many now felt that the Ahom issue was being exploited for the personal ambitions of a few leaders. At this juncture, as Yasmin Saikia remarks, 'the label Ahom now entered the realms of mass appeal although it continued as a luxury item accessible to the few politically powerful members'.[24] The struggle to maintain an Ahom identity within a larger Assamese society now focused itself on Ahom language, literature and cultural heritage. Scholarly studies of ethnicity had begun to emerge on a wider scale. A new generation of Western scholars carried out research on different types of Tai races. In 1968, George Coedes formulated his theory of Tai migration from Nanchao, and described the Ahoms as the westernmost Tai settlers.[25] B.J. Terwiel published a two-volume study of Ahom rituals which also bolstered the claims of the Ahoms to be identified as the Tai.[26]

The reconstruction of a Tai-Ahom identity gathered momentum when Ahom representatives met Thai scholars at the International Conference on Thai Studies held in 1981 in New Delhi. One articulate section of the Ahom elite formed a sociocultural association named the Ban Ok Pup Lik Moung Tai (BOPLMT).[27] Details of their activities do not fall within the scope of this article, but the main objective of the BOPLMT was to preserve the racial existence of the Tai-Ahoms by developing and preserving their culture.

In 1985, the Asom Gana Parishad (AGP) came to power in the state. A section of the Ahoms increasingly believed that the Assamese upper castes dominated the key positions in the state and would not protect the interests of the Ahoms. The Tai-Ahom Yuva Sangathan was formed in 1987, and the All-Tai Ahom Students Union in 1988.[28] Ahoms were also an important part of the United Liberation Front of Assam (ULFA), especially in Sibsagar and Dibrugarh districts, the former being the original home of Ahom politics. They continued with their demand for an independent state in Upper Assam with the name Ahomia or *Mioung Dun Sun Kham* — the old name of the Ahom kingdom.

From 1991 to 1996, the government of Assam under Hiteswar Saikia encouraged the Tai-Ahom revival movement. Different measures were taken to highlight past Ahom glories and to emphasize the link with the Tais. Many new leaders emerged. While most were working for an Ahom sociocultural revival, a few also wanted political power. The BOPLMT spearheaded the movement to create a separate political unit in Upper Assam, and revived the demand for Scheduled Tribe status for the Ahoms. Ahom leaders wanted to be recognized as a valley-dwelling tribal community with a royal heritage.[29] Scheduled Tribe status would open up various avenues of employment in administrative, professional and technical fields. Politically, it would also ensure that certain electoral constituencies would be dominated by the Ahoms.

Hiteswar Saikia's government came to an end on 22 April 1996 and a fresh election brought the AGP back to power. Suddenly, all attempts to reconstruct a Tai-Ahom identity ceased. The future looked a bit uncertain.

The present Chief Minister, Tarun Gogoi, who also belongs to the 35-lakh strong Ahom community, was once accused of having links with ULFA (comprising some ultra-Ahoms). Denying and challenging the authenticity of the allegations made against him, Gogoi said 'Prove my links with ULFA, I would quit politics.'[30]

It is important to review the Gogoi government's stand regarding the centre's decision to reject the demand for ST status made by six ethnic communities in Assam, which landed the Congress government in a soup. The six communities that were promised ST status by the Congress before the last assembly election in the state have now threatened to resort to agitation against the government's rejection of their demand by Union Tribal Affairs Minister P.R. Kyndiah in the Lok Sabha. Gogoi, who finds himself in a fix over Kyndiah's action, has vowed to take up the matter with the UPA government in New Delhi. 'I am definitely going to press the centre to review its decision to reject the demand for ST status for Koch Rajbongshi, Tai Ahom, Moran, Motok, Chutia and Tea Tribe communities',[31] Gogoi said. The powerful Ahom lobby that used to take pride in one of their own being at the helm of affairs in Dispur today distances itself from both chief minister Gogoi and his Congress party. Threatening to float a separate political party as a 'fitting reply to betrayal of the community'[32] by the ruling party, the Sodou Asom Ahom Sabha signalled its intent by declaring a 12-hour Upper Assam bandh on 6 August 2005. The primary grievance is the government's failure to ensure ST status to the community. There was great apprehension that Tarun Gogoi would lose his seat in the forthcoming Assam Assembly Election of 2006. Gogoi, however, retained his Titabar seat as before and was reinstalled as the new Chief Minister of Assam.

In sum, there has been continuous tussle between the caste-Hindu Assamese and the Ahoms. Assamese society is a casteist society, based on Aryan culture and Assamese language. The Ahoms, on the other hand, who trace their origin to the Mongol tribes, and are considered to be of a lower caste. The Tai-Ahom leaders tried to mobilize the community by fostering and building a consciousness of 'Tainess' and old Mongoloid traditions in opposition to Aryanized caste-Hindu domination. But Ahom mobilization should not be characterized as merely a sociocultural affair; it was also very much political. Many political organizations were formed from time to time as the Ahoms felt deprived of a legitimate share of political and other powers under the domination of caste-Hindu Assamese society. But these organizations were usually weak and shortlived. Some Ahom leaders appeared to be exploiting the movement for personal benefit. Above all, the Ahoms had fallen prey to the strategy of assimilation, completely giving up their own language, dress and culture.

Even so, the consciousness of an Ahom identity has been the focus of political mobilization at different levels of society. The Ahoms are a minority group who have been an important factor in Assam politics. At present, they understand well the need to revive their traditional culture. At the second Ahom Round Table Conference, which began on 7 May 2005 in Sivasagar district, historian Jogendra Nath Phukan, stressed the need to form a strong committee comprising of members from different Ahom organizations and eminent personalities from the community under a strong and determined leadership so that the problems faced by the Ahom community could be addressed or resolved.[33]

In a recent communiqué, Tai-Ahom leaders agreed that the community has been marginalized since the days of British rule in Assam and identified the broader reasons in support of their claim:

- The British did not take Tai-Ahom nobles into confidence while ruling Assam, which was natural for a colonial power.
- In order to rule Assam, the British promoted members of other higher castes which seem to have lacked the wisdom of administering a multiethnic society. This has led to the formation of an 'elite' Assamese class which assumed cultural and political leadership and gave birth to a chauvinistic Assamese nationality. These elite Assamese nationalists still represent Assamese culture and control the media.
- Due to the influence of a chauvinistic Assamese nationalism, a majority of the Tai-Ahom youths did not take Western education seriously and were left illiterate in the process. Some of them have taken up arms to safeguard this Assamese nationalism, which is foolish in the present global context. They are simply becoming henchmen of these Assamese nationalists.
- Tai-Ahom people in general lost touch with the Ahom value system, which their forefathers had practised and were thus

able to win the confidence of most of the ethnic groups of Assam. They also feel that, 'In the present scenario, the Tai Ahom community should take a few important steps like —

1. Education should be the top priority of Tai Ahom youths. TANCA can think of an Educational Fund for helping poor Ahom students.
2. Never practice 'Chauvinistic Assamese Nationalism'. Ahom values which our great leader Chaufa Siu Ka Pha introduced should be again followed.
3. Asserting our rights with arms should be avoided. Intelligence is more important in todays globalized scenario.
4. There should be efforts to encourage business entrepreneurship so that the community becomes economically very strong. Follow the Parsees for example.
5. Encourage a liberal Assamese culture, which should have ingredients from all the ethnic groups. Ahoms should take the leadership in this respect.
6. Ahom youths should involve the media (TV, newspapers, etc.).
7. Cohesiveness among Tai Ahom is very important. All the Tai Ahom intellectuals should be brought to the same platform by networking.[34]

Conclusion

In the foregoing section I have discussed on the one hand, the history of political governance by the central authorities vis-à-vis the Ahoms and, on the other hand, the parameters of political governance as understood by the Ahom minority community itself. In other words, the article presented two histories: a history of domination by the central authorities and a sense of deprivation as felt by the minorities, which gives birth to another history — of the struggle to assert ethnic identities. The article explains the position of the Ahoms in both colonial and post-colonial structures, and narrates the story of their interaction with the ruling authorities.

What becomes evident is that Ahom mobilization should not be characterized as merely a sociocultural affair. It is political to a large extent. The Ahoms felt deprived of their legitimate share of political and other powers under the domination of caste-Hindu Assamese society. But these political organizations were weak and shortlived. Some leaders appeared to be exploiting the movement for personal benefit. Above all, the Ahoms had fallen prey to assimilation. They had completely given up their own language, dress and culture. Even so, the consciousness of an Ahom identity has been a focal point for political mobilization at different levels of society. The Ahoms are a minority group who have been, and still are, a forceful factor in Assam politics.

If we consider governance a tool for resolving Ahom identity assertion, it is sad that post-colonial government policies still continue with the colonial policy structure. Instead of accommodating this minority group, attempts are still being made to crush them and assimilate them into the mainstream politico-cultural pattern of the majoritarian society.

Notes and References

1. E.A. Gait, *A History of Assam* (Guwahati: Surjeet Publications, 1926). The British colonial rulers considered the Ahoms to be a proud race of the Shans but also saw them as being backward and apathetic like the Assamese.
2. Girin Phukon, 'Search for Ahom Identity in Assam', *Proceedings of the Northeast Indian History Association*, XI Session, 1990, p. 305.
3. Nirala Buragohain, 'Socio Economic Bases of Identity Assertion of the Ahoms: A Historical Perspective', paper presented at the Seminar on Politics of Identity, Conflict and Nation Building in Northeast India, Political Science Department, Dibrugarh University, 6–7 November 1995, pp. 2–4.
4. Ibid., pp. 5–6.
5. Phukon, 'Search for Ahom Identity in Assam', p. 306.
6. Surendranath Buragohain's speech as quoted by Umesh Chutia in Assamese in an article published in *Lik Tai Khwam Tai* in 1990, made available to the author by Tharuram Gogoi.
7. *Assam Tribune*, 25 April 1941.
8. Umesh Chutia, 'Tai Ahoms and Surendranath Buragohain' (Tai Ahom Jati aru Surendranath Buragohain), *Lik Tai Khwn Tai*, Souvenir, Eighth Annual Congress, 17–18 February 1990.
9. Ibid.
10. Phukon, 'Search for Ahom Identity in Assam', p. 208.
11. *Assam Tribune*, 28 March 1945.

12. S. Yasmin Saikia, a scholar from the University of Wisconsin Madison, is of the view that by the 1940s the Ahoms liquidated their identity as Ahom and under Congress influence came to be seen as Assamese.

13. Padmanath Gohain Barua, 'Sadou Asom Association Sanmilon', in *Gohain Barua Rachanavali* (Gauhati, 1987), pp. 935–36.

14. Nirala Buragohain, 'Identity Consciousness of the Ahoms', MPhil Dissertation, Dibrugarh University, 1992, p. 49.

15. Ibid., pp. 49–50.

16. Ibid., p. 50.

17. S. Yasmin Saikia, 'Twentieth Century Biographers of a Community: Brokering the Tai-Ahoms', *Proceedings of the Sixth International Conference on Tai Studies*, Theme IV, Vol. II, Chiangmai, 14–17 October 1996, p. 17.

18. However, a group of AAAA members claimed the organization continued to exist. Buragohain, 'Identity Consciousness of the Ahoms', p. 58.

19. *Assam Tribune*, 7 August 1962.

20. *Assam Tribune*, 8 June 1967.

21. *Assam Tribune*, 3 June and 5 October 1967.

22. Saikia, 'Twentieth Century Biographers', p. 478.

23. Buragohain, 'Identity Consciousness of the Ahoms', p. 60 and Saikia, 'Twentieth Century Biographers', p. 478.

24. Saikia, 'Twentieth Century Biographers', p. 478.

25. George Coedes, *The Indianized States of Southeast Asia*, ed. Walter F. Vella and trans. Susan Brown Cowing (Honolulu: East-West Center Press, 1968).

26. B.J. Terwiel, *The Tai of Assam and Ancient Tai Ritual*, Vols I and II (Gaya: Centre for Southeast Studies, 1981).

27. For details regarding their activities, see Saikia, 'Twentieth Century Biographers', p. 479.

28. Buragohain, 'Identity Consciousness of the Ahoms', pp. 62–63.

29. Saikia, 'Twentieth Century Biographers', p. 480–83.

30. *Pratyush*, 21 August 2007, New Delhi, http://pratyush.instablogs.com/entry/prove-my-links-with-ulfa-i-would-quit-politics-tarun-gogoi/ (accessed 6 February 2008).

31. *The Tribune*, Sunday, 19 August 2007.

32. *The Telegraph*, 30 July 2005.

33. http://assam2007.blogspot.com/2008/01/education-related-news-from-assam-in.html (accessed 6 February 2008).

34. Email from Jayanta Borgohain, Dignoi to Dr Hemanta Kumar Gogoi, Simaluguri, dated 6 February 2008.

3

Violence, Victimhood and Minority Women: The Gujarat Violence of 2002*

Anasua Basu Ray Chaudhury

Introduction

I first heard about the tragic story of Ruksana[1] (name changed to protect her identity) and her family from the Aman Pathiks (social workers) of Aman Samudaya, a non-governmental organization (NGO) and a sister concern of the ActionAid India. They had met Ruksana and her family at the Halol relief camp in the aftermath of the violence in Gujarat in 2002. Like many other social workers, the Aman Pathiks too had helped the displaced people by supplying relief materials to the camp at Halol.

Reaching Ruksana was not easy. After several days of searching, I met her at the Kashimabag Housing Society, a newly-built colony for the rehabilitation of displaced people. The society was located just behind the Gayatri *mandir* (temple), near the Kalol bus stop. Earlier, this place was a vacant piece of land. After the violence in 2002, the Islamic Relief Committee, an NGO, converted it into a residential colony for the rehabilitation of displaced people. The English signboard outside the colony indicated that the society was established in June 2002 and was home to 175 households. All the houses in the society looked similar and were attached to one another in a continuous manner, under the same roof. Each house had one big room, which was in most cases partitioned into two sections, along with a small bathroom.

When I first met Ruksana in Kashimabag, it was half past twelve in the afternoon. She was preoccupied with her household activities.

I sat on her bed and waited for her to finish her work. Within half-an-hour she was free to talk to me. She was about twenty-seven or twenty-eight, short, thin and dark, and was wearing a pink *salwar kameez*. When I stated the purpose of my visit, after a brief pause she agreed to talk to me. She started by telling me that she had lost her husband in the violence of 2002. In her own words:

> *Mera Sauhar to shahid hua (*my husband has become a martyr*). Aur bhi bidhva hain is colony me jiska sauhar ko mar dia gaya usi time pe* (There are other widows in this colony who lost their spouses during that time). Like other widows living in this society, I as a family member of my dead husband received only one-third portion of a total of Rs 150000 in cash and the rest in the form of certificate of government bonds. That was the only help I received from the government. We are now getting Rs 500 each on the basis of a monthly income scheme against these government bonds. We are altogether twelve *bidhva* (widows) staying here. Didi, how we are surviving, we only know. What can we do with only Rs 500? If we have some work to do, we can at least earn something. Didi this *dhamaal* (turbulence) has changed our lives totally.... When I got married to Feroz Rasul Sheikh, I was very young. Our Delol village was situated on the Godhra road. We had our own house and lived in a joint family. We did not have our own cultivable land. My husband was a rickshaw-puller. We were not rich but we were happy. This *dhamaal* has snatched happiness from our lives in every sense. After losing my husband I am all alone now. I don't know how to survive the rest of my life. A fear of *dhamaal* has become a part of our lives. We have a fear for the future — for ourselves, for our family members as well as for our community. Not only that didi, we are worried about the effects of the uncertainty and dislocation on our children. Look at Faizan, my little boy. He saw everything with his own eyes that happened to me. Can you imagine what kind of effect it can have on his mind? ... Shall we ever get justice, didi?

I did not have any answers to her questions. However, Ruksana's take on the changes in her life in the wake of the violence of 2002[2] encouraged me to go deeper into understanding, the traumatic experiences of these hapless, displaced minority women in a conflict situation.

In fact, the question of minority rights and protection in general, and of women in particular, became critical once again following the Gujarat violence of 2002. The incident begged for an immediate reassessment of the constitutionally guaranteed rights for minorities in India and their implementation through policies of the state. Minority communities in the country were defined by the framers of the Constitution of India primarily on the basis of their religious identity. No doubt, the Constitution refers to linguistic and cultural minorities as well, but in actual terms, very little attention was paid to them. Therefore, in popular parlance in India 'minority' refers to Muslims in particular, and other religious minorities in general. However, the principle of the equality of different communities encouraged the Constitution to support the idea of pluralism by discouraging the politics of 'majoritarianism' and 'minorityism'[3] (although state practices over the years indicate otherwise). Many instances of violence against minorities in India after 1947 reveal the disturbing gap between the 'ideal' and the 'actual.'[4] The dreadful violence in Gujarat against Muslims has raised the point once again.

I propose to explore the perception of Muslim women regarding their victimhood and re-examine the rights that minority women enjoy, in practice, against this backdrop. Ruksana's story, therefore, prompts us to ask several questions: to what extent did these women face a double jeopardy — of being women as well as of being members of a religious minority — when they were displaced and rendered destitute in a situation of communal unrest? Have the identities of these women changed in any way in the wake of the violence and displacement? If so, how did this change take place and what kind of impact did it leave on the victims? Keeping Ruksana in mind, like many other widows who lost their husbands and other family members in the Gujarat violence of 2002, in this article I would like to focus on the victims' understanding of their sufferings.

For the sake of this study, I shall retell some of the experiences narrated by my respondents, who live in the Kashimabag Housing Society of Kalol in Godhra district (earlier a part of Panchmahal district, which has since been divided into Dahod and Godhra), and in Faizal Park of Vatva in Ahmedabad. Kashimabag Society is now home to a large number of women displaced from the village of Delol, who lost their husbands and other family members in the violence there, whereas Faizal Park is a huge Muslim ghetto where a large number of displaced women from Naroda Patiya, the place that witnessed the worst kind of brutalities against women, have been rehabilitated.

Mapping the Violence

In her well-known essay 'On Violence', Hannah Arendt stressed on the instrumental character of violence by arguing that violence appears whenever power is in jeopardy.[5] The gruesome massacres that took place in different parts of Gujarat after the burning of the S6 Sleeper Coach of the Sabarmati Express near Godhra railway station on 27 February 2002, probably certify the logic of violence in the context of the larger matrix of sociopolitical power as posed by Arendt.

Central Gujarat, comprising Ahmedabad, Vadodara, Sabarkanta and Panchmahal districts — the epicentre of the violence — was the most adversely affected region by this pogrom (see Map 3.1). Saurashtra, Kutch and southern Gujarat remained relatively peaceful. It was mainly in the villages of north and central Gujarat, where the Congress party had a larger presence, that Muslims were targeted. One may recall that the Congress party had swept the district and taluka panchayat elections in 2000 and had started gaining in strength in north and central Gujarat as well. Under these circumstances, the Bharatiya Janata Party (BJP), the ruling party of Gujarat and a part of the Sangh Parivar became desperate to recover its eroding social base in these regions with a 'carefully crafted and subtly executed politics of hatred'.[6] BJP's landslide victory in the Legislative Assembly elections of 2002 is testimony to the trend of manipulating communal violence as a political weapon to polarize an already divided society for the consolidation of the Hindu vote. In this way, communal violence got legitimized as an election strategy of the BJP and further strengthened the process of 'spatial purification' aimed at creating a Hindu national identity in Gujarat.[7]

The Gujarat violence of 2002 is a testimony of one of the worst violations of human rights in contemporary India. The Gujarat government, led by the BJP, remained a mute spectator while angry mobs killed and maimed, and vandals destroyed the property of thousands of people belonging to a religious minority in a manner that was almost surgical. This uninterrupted violence not only claimed more than a thousand lives but also displaced thousands of men, women and children.

The violence of February–May 2002 targeting Muslims assumed ominous proportions in its reach and intensity. Women were the

Map 3.1: Mapping the Violence of 2002 in Gujarat

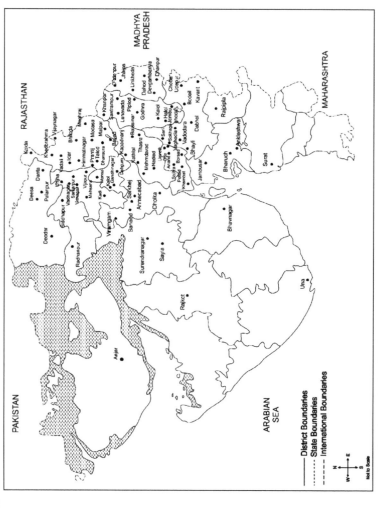

Source: Achyut Yagnik and Suchitra Sheth, *The Shaping of Modern Gujarat: Plurality, Hindutva and Beyond* (New Delhi: Penguin, 2005), p. 280.

worst affected by this pogrom. In many cases, they were brutally tortured and raped. Even children were not spared and were burnt alive. The means of living and livelihood of the Muslims were systematically destroyed. The shrines and places of worship of the community were desecrated and destroyed. Social and economic boycott of the community was encouraged. Muslim commercial and residential establishments and individual houses were carefully selected and targetted at the time of violence, mostly in parts of the cities that were cosmopolitan in nature. Prior to February 2002, systematic propaganda by the Sangh Parivar included dissemination of venomous literature and conducting household surveys with malafide intentions. In most places, especially in the *chawls* (slums) of Ahmedabad and Vadodara, Hindu houses were marked by saffron flags or with pictures of Ram or Hanuman, in order to distinguish them from Muslim ones. On the eve of the attack, members of the Muslim households were interviewed by government representatives in the name of a BPL (Below Poverty Line) survey. Many affected families are convinced that, in the name of the BPL survey, these so-called government representatives gathered information about the socio-economic conditions of the Muslim households in order to come up with a combative strategy for the future.[8] One of the principle intentions was not to allow the minority community to accumulate wealth. Through this kind of exclusion of the Muslims, the followers of Hindutva tried to ensure some kind of communal monopoly over local business.[9]

The violence continued for three months, at the end of which approximately 2000 people were believed to have been killed, although the official figure was only 762.[10] According to one estimate, initially, 150,000(the government's figure was much less) persons were displaced, of which approximately 100,000 were displaced in Ahmedabad itself, and took shelter in 121 makeshift relief camps in and around affected areas, all over Gujarat.[11] Even after the loss of life and displacement of that many people, the Gujarat government refused to provide any assistance. In short, the basic humanitarian needs of these displaced persons were completely ignored.

After six years of such ghastly crimes against humanity being commited, the victims are still too scared to recall those days of violence. The camps for displaced persons may not exist any more, but the people displaced in semi-urban areas and district towns have not yet been able to return to their original homes. For instance, in Faizal Park, a Muslim ghetto in Vatva, the inhabitants are still unable to come to terms with the loss of their homes and belongings. Moreover, it is still impossible for most of them to accept the loss of their near and dear ones.

Faizal Park is a place where a large number of displaced Muslims arrived from Naroda Patiya in order to resettle themselves. Naroda Patiya was one of the worst affected areas of loot, arson and mass destruction. Before the 2002 incident, the total population of Naroda Patiya was between 12,000 and 15,000. The Muslims numbered only about 1,000, were mostly poor, daily-wage earners, and a large number of them were migrants from Karnataka and Maharashtra.[12] This locality witnessed the worst forms of sexual violence against women and young girls, many were even burnt alive. Officially, 91 people were killed. Unofficial estimates, however, suggest that as many as 200 may have died in the Naroda Patiya violence.

After their displacement, these people took shelter in the makeshift camps of Vatva, set up by community organizations and NGOs. The Government of Gujarat neither set up a single relief camp nor took any concrete steps to rehabilitate these people. Rather, very soon the government directed the camps to be shut down. This frightened women like Safia Bibi (age 32)[13] (name changed), as she shuddered at the thought of returning to her home. She said:

> Jab hum ghar vapas gaye na didi, kuch dino ke bad, tab wahan kuchh nahin tha, bilkul khetan jaise tha. Upar se un logone dhamki di thi — agar hum wapas aye to is se jada buri halat hoga.
> (When we went back home after a couple of days, there was nothing left, it was flat like a field. Moreover, these people threatened us not to return again — and that if did things would be even worse).

According to Safia, when a few Muslim families tried to return home following the closure of their camps, they expected to be able to gradually restart their traditional petty trades of tailoring or grocery. But, they soon realized that their Hindu neighbours were absolutely unwilling to allow them to do so. After all, Naroda Patiya faced the worst sort of brutality and destruction despite there being a camp of the State Reserve Police (SRP) nearby. In Safia's words:

> The tola (crowd) arrived, armed with trishuls and swords wearing khaki pants, white shirts and saffron fettis (headscarves) shouting — 'Miya ne maro, Miya neo kato!' (beat the Muslims, kill the Muslims!).

Some of them started pelting stones. We were about 50 helpless people and they were a few thousand. As we were running helter-skelter, the police blocked our road, chasing us back toward the riotous mob. '*Chalo maar do saalo ko*' (kill the bastards), they shouted. For the first time, we faced this kind of situation in our locality. We used to stay at *Chetan das ki chawl* (Chetan Das's shanty), where the Muslims and Hindus used to stay side by side. Our Hindu neighbours had never disturbed us. But when the Bajrang Dal started having training camps in the temple of the locality, many of these Hindus started joining them. My husband, like many other males in the locality had got scared and feared that they could generate animosity toward us as they had been projecting us as enemies.

The memories of those days of violence and destruction came to her mind off and on:

We only had stones. So, we tried to protect ourselves with those stones. But, the police opened fire at us that took lives of three innocent young Muslim boys and seriously hurt two others. The telephone lines were snapped, water and electricity supplies were cut. They were also throwing petrol and kerosene-filled tyres at us. The entire back portion of the Gangotri Society was set on fire. I could clearly hear the screams of people, 'save me'!

After some time, I saw my neighbour's daughter, Kausar, who was pregnant, lying on the road. The men stabbed her in her stomach with a sword and cut open her womb. They took out the foetus and then put both the mother and the foetus into fire. After seeing this, my brain stopped working… They killed my husband too. He was a rickshaw-puller. My brother was shot in his leg when he tried to save my husband. The police threw tear-gas shells on us while the attackers continued to destroy our houses forcing us to leave our place.

Safia Bibi had to flee with her sons, Rafiq and Asfaq, and daughters Tahera and Hena, and they were resettled in Faizal Park with the help of an NGO. Like Safia, Rajia Bibi (28), Zarina Bibi (40) and Roshan Bibi (42),[14] the residents of Kharkar in Faizal Park, narrated their own experiences with louder voices. All of them left the Qutb-e-Alam Dargah Relief Camp with the surviving members of their respective families to take shelter in Faizal Park. They recounted the events of the afternoon of 1 March in a manner almost identical to Safia. All of them lost their husbands in violence. They also specified that the Hindu residents of the Gangotri and Gopinath Society were fully aware, well in advance, that the *dhamaal* (violence) would take place on 1 March, and so they had locked their houses and left in advance. According to these women, at the mass grave dug on 6 March, of 96 bodies retrieved from Naroda Patiya, 46 belonged to women.

Initially, Ruksana had a hesitation in sharing her painful experiences with me in Kashimabag. She took time to open up and then she began:

> On the morning of 28 February 2002, they attacked our mosque and soon our house was also attacked by the mob. They painted their face black and were wearing vests and shorts. We were altogether thirty-three in our family at that time. We all ran and hid in the fields. Along with our children, we spent the entire day and night there. The next morning we all made our way to a lime orchard near the village. We found many Muslim neighbours of our village hiding inside that orchard. In the afternoon, a tribal woman known to us brought some *rotis* (bread) for us. We gave it to our children who had not eaten anything for more than 24 hours.
>
> In the afternoon, the mob returned. We saw a huge crowd approaching the field shouting '*Maro, Kato*' (beat them, kill them). We all ran back towards the village. We became very terrified when we heard that another group of fanatics were approaching us from the opposite direction (from Khadi village). We realized that we were trapped. Our only escape route was to climb into the milk van and leave the place as soon as possible. About forty of us got in one such van and Feroze drove the tempo towards the Kalol bus stand, which is about 7 kilometres away from that place. Just before the tempo was to reach Kalol town, a Maruti car came and blocked the road near Lal Darwaza of Ambica Society. A mob gathered. Feroze tried to take a turn but he lost control of the vehicle. We were forced to get off. We were all screaming with fear; the children were yelling and crying. Old men were begging for mercy. We heard the screams of family members, who were being attacked with sticks and swords. They threw kerosene and started burning people. We could hear the mob screaming: 'Take off their clothes, and let them go naked on the streets.'
>
> A few children fell at the feet of the mob begging to be spared. My husband Feroze Bhai, his brother Razzak Bhai, my sisters-in-law Mumtaz Ben and Amina Ben and her daughter Rozina Ben, Ayub Bhai — all were with me. But they burnt all the men alive, including my husband, while women ran in different directions towards the fields to save their lives.
>
> In this turbulence, my daughter and I got separated. My son Faizan was in my arms and I fell behind. Some people started chasing us and

one of the men held me by my hair. I struggled with all my strength to get myself free, but was soon overpowered by them. They dragged me to the riverbed, which was dry and pulled me down. Faizan fell from my arms and started crying. My clothes were torn and I was stark naked. One by one, the men raped me. All the while, I could hear my son crying. They then hit my foot with a sharp weapon and left me in that state there. I lay unconscious for sometime...When I regained my senses I saw that my son was sitting near my head and crying. I picked up my son and started searching for my clothes. He was then only four years old. I could only find my top. I pulled it on and ran with my son along the river towards Delol. I didn't go towards Kalol, since I didn't know the place well. Just as the day was fading, I reached the lime orchard again where we had hidden the previous day and hid there with my son. I spent the entire night in a daze, and didn't move from there for the next two days. On the third day, Parvat bhai, a neighbour saw me. I requested him to bring me a pyjama as I had left some clothes in his house when they attacked our house. On Sunday night, I finally started walking through the fields towards Kalol. I reached Lal Darwaza, Nava bazaar, in the morning. I collapsed on the street and asked a man in a shop to help reach me Kasba. He called the police and they dropped me to the camp where I was united with my daughter later...

Later, Ruksana filed a complaint, but no FIR (First Information Report) was admitted. She could not recognize any of her perpetrators, but she believes that she can still identify them.

Farida was in her early thirties when I met her in Kashimabag.[15] She was there with her two sons, Farzan (14) and Ashfaq (9) and two daughters, Tasleema (8) and Rashida (5). She lost her husband and elder daughter Shabana (then 11) in 2002:

I used to live in a joint family. My father-in-law was a retired school-master and my husband, a driver in the State Transport Service. There were approximately forty-five Muslim houses in our locality. On 28 February, we came to know that riot had broken out nearby. We had to leave the village immediately and went to Kalol where there was a larger Muslim community. My father-in-law believed that, as he was a respected man in the village, an old inhabitant of that locality, no one could physically assault them. So while almost all other Muslim families left for Kalol that day, we stayed put....After some time, a huge mob surrounded our house and started stoning and abusing us. As the tension escalated, thirteen members of our family, including Mehboob Bhai and a relative from Eral village, who had sought refuge with them, left the house and hid in the fields. My in-laws were in an empty house belonging to the Thakurs. For two days and nights they kept changing places. My in-laws were asked to vacate the house on Saturday morning. The house-owners were apprehensive that their house too would be set on fire, as people already came to know that these people were taking refuge there. Chhaganbhai, who had given them food and water for two days, himself had given them this information!

On Saturday, 1 March , at around five in the afternoon, a mob of 400–500 men, armed with sharp weapons, petrol and kerosene first looted and then burnt down the houses of Muslims. That night no one gave them refuge. They were afraid of being attacked if they were seen helping the Muslims.

On Sunday morning, we all decided to hide in a labourer's hut in the field of Adam Punja. At around one in the afternoon, the mob attacked the hut. Having nowhere else to go, we ran helter-skelter and hid in the maize field. We tried not to make any sound. But the mob started searching the field and they found us and started attacking. I could hear many members of my family screaming and begging for mercy as they were attacked. I recognized two persons in the mob — Gano Baria and Sunil — of our village pulling my elder daughter, Shabana, who was then only eleven years old and my niece Suhana. Both the girls were screaming and asking the men to get off them. The screams of Shabana and Suhana begging for their *izzat* could be heard clearly from even a distance. My youngest daughter and I were hiding nearby and from there we could see these girls being gang-raped. Then they cut off their breasts and burnt their bodies in front of our eyes...

Farida paused for a while. She closed her eyes and then said:

Didi, my daughter was like a flower, yet to experience life....Why did they do this to her? What kind of men were they?

Breaking the Silence

Communal violence was not new in Gujarat. After India's partition in 1947, the country's first major riot broke out in Ahmedabad in 1969. After that Gujarat witnessed riots in 1981, 1985, 1986, 1990–1991 and again in 1992 (following the demolition of the Babri Masjid.[16] But, 2002 was completely different in many ways. On this occasion, rapes, especially gang-rapes were used as a means of humiliating the minority community. After all sexual violence against women signifies a simultaneous humiliation of the patriarchy of the attacked community, by dishonouring their women.[17] The torture of men is a subject of empathy and solidarity among the targeted community, while the sexualized torture of women is particularly destructive to patriarchal notions of female honour.[18] A fact-finding team found that sharp objects had been inserted into the private parts of the women in many cases. Pregnant and young women were specifically targeted. A majority of rape victims were burnt alive. Before they were finally killed, some were beaten up with rods and pipes.[19] A pattern of unprecedented cruelty against women became part of the violence. First of all, a woman's body became a site of almost in-exhaustible violence, with infinitely plural and innovative forms of torture. Second, their sexual and reproductive organs were attacked with special savagery. Finally, their children — born and unborn — shared the attacks and were killed in front of their eyes.[20] These left a permanent scar on the psyche of the victims in such a way that they are still traumatized. Usually, incidents of molestation or rape of women are not discussed in public. But 2002 probably changed the situation altogether. The survivors have no hesitation in discussing the atrocities they had to suffer.[21] Yet, behind every woman speaking out, there could be many more silently suffering.

According to a report published by International Initiatives for Justice in Gujarat (IIJG) 'the silencing has been in multiple ways, as it usually is in the case of sexual assault. Some women have chosen silence because it is shameful to proclaim sexual violence on one's body in a traditional ethos. In the patriarchal family structure and system of values, the violation of women's body integrity becomes a source of shame not only for the women as individuals but for them as members/symbols of the family and community. In many cases support and acceptance from male members (fathers/husbands) has been lacking.... In Gujarat, when the attacks were meant to dishonour the community, the silence came from the community as well.'[22] In the Gujarat carnage, the violation of the bodies of Muslim women was used as a political strategy. Women are the biological reproducers of a community, and the Hindu perpetrators wanted to destroy the sources of reproduction by targetting and attacking the female reproductive organ.

Threatened Existence

After being dislocated from their homes, most of these widows had no choice but to take shelter in the makeshift camps set up by the community organizations and NGOs. The only refuge available was in camps set up by the Muslim-dominated panchayats and/or by Muslim religious trusts, which took upon themselves the task of providing protection to the victims, feeding them and housing them. The Government of Gujarat did not set up a single relief camp. The displaced too did not expect the state to provide shelter either, especially after its alleged tacit support in the riots. There were 171 camps altogether, set up throughout Gujarat. Of these, forty-five were located in Ahmedabad (as on 16 March 2002). Later, the number of the camps increased further.

On 6 March, in its policy resolution the Government of Gujarat stated that, the district administration would provide assistance up to 31 May only to those camps that satisfied a number of conditions. These stipulated that the organizers of the camps had to be a registered society or a trust. If unregistered bodies were already running such camps, they would require special permission from the government. Each camp was to have at least 100 inmates.[23] It had to be located in a clean area, with toilet facilities, medical care, drinking water, a clean kitchen, and the camp organizers were supposed to maintain a daily register recording the details of all inmates, including losses and injuries suffered, their time of arrival, departure and destination. Violation of any of these conditions could lead to the closure of the camp. Consequently, many camps were de-recognized as they did not meet the stipulated requirements. In camps recognized by the government, the inmates could have a weekly ration comprising 500 grams of cereals and 50 grams each of pulses, edible oil, sugar and milk and a cash dole of Rs 5 per person, per day.[24] However, the quality of the food received in the camps from the government was too poor to eat. Basic amenities such as potable water, medical and sanitation facilities were completely absent in almost all the camps, especially in the rural areas. As a result, most displaced persons suffered from diseases such as measles, typhoid and gastroenteritis.

There was hardly any privacy for the women inmates. Non-provision of proper sanitation and the use of outdoor toilets endangered the health of inmates especially women and girls as it led to outbreak of diseases. Lack of sufficient lady doctors, gynaecologists and paediatricians further complicated the situation. At the time of delivery by a pregnant woman, other woman inmates of the camp, acted as *dais*(midwives).[25] In fact, in most cases, there were no toilets for the inmates in the camps. Moreover, the National Commission for Women observed, there were no facilities for women and girls who had been widowed or orphaned to get any special training that would allow them to be able to earn their own livelihood. No efforts were made to even make these women aware of the compensations that had been promised to them.[26]

It has been observed that in the early phase of their displacement the survivors were hesitant to come forward and register cases against their perpetrators, as the latter, in many instances, had strong political connections. In some cases, the police had intimidated the victims into withdrawing their cases. There were hardly any arrangements in the relief camps for the victims to register their claims for compensation for deaths of their family members or for destruction of their property. Many were also too terrified to return to their homes and file cases for claims regarding destruction of property and theft or loot.

After the winding up of the camps, the government hardly took any concrete steps to resettle and rehabilitate the displaced persons. NGOs like ActionAid, Islamic Relief Committee, Aman Samudaya, Gujarat Relief Committee, Jan Vikas Sanstha, Anandi, Jagruti and SEWA, played a significant role in trying to rehabilitate them in newly-built colonies and also offered them assistance for their livelihood. Under tremendous pressure from civil society, human rights groups and the media, the government, at a later stage, announced a number of measures of 'aid, assistance and relief'. The types of relief assistance announced by the government were:

1. House construction aid of up to Rs 50,000 to riot-affected families and an ex-gratia relief in case of the damage to the earning assets of miscellaneous business up to Rs 10,000.
2. Cash dole and household effect aid of up to Rs 3,000.
3. Ex-gratia relief of Rs 3,000–10,000 to the small traders for the damage of their earning assets.
4. Relief of Rs 2,000–10,000 to the persons who became disabled as a result of violence.

5. Relief of up to Rs 150,000 to the families that had lost its members during violence.[27]

However, the amount offered by the government in the name of compensation was shocking in its paltriness. While some of the victims received Rs 1,250–2,500 as monetary support to rebuild their houses, many did not receive any assistance at all. Even those who received government help felt that it was too little too late. There were other bottlenecks as well. While the compensation for deaths was to be released on production of relevant death certificates, many displaced did not have such certificates in their possession as they had to flee their home and neighbourhood all of a sudden. Therefore, many riot victims did not receive any death compensation from the government at all. In such a situation, having lost their male partners, widows were compelled to live in ghettoized clusters for their own security. They perceived their vulnerability as being greater when in physical isolation from one's own community. Indeed, many survivors pointed out that they would prefer to settle in more secure places with a predominantly Muslim population. Even after the winding up of camps, many chose to stay in places next to the dismantled camps instead of returning to their original places of residence, which are in areas with a mixed population.[28] As many law-keepers turned into law-breakers, they felt more vulnerable in living with the 'enemies'. Muslim ghettos were not uncommon in urban Gujarat. But 2002 brought ghettos to rural and semi-urban areas as well.

Vulnerability Persists

Safia, Razia, Zarina or Roshan Bibi have now shifted to Faizal Park, where they feel less threatened. But living in ghettos does not ensure economic security. As their husbands were mostly *chuttak mazdoor* (daily casual labour), they belong to the poorest strata of society. After the loss of their husbands and having moved to these ghettos, these women are, in a way, facing more economic hardship. It has become very difficult for them to earn a daily wage in an alien locality. Some of them are now working as domestic helps in nearby households, although some have received sewing machines from the Islamic Relief Committee. But even these recipients are facing difficulties in buying raw materials for stitching because they do not have enough money. Neither do they feel safe in outside alone. However many feel that a sewing machine for each family could have helped them a lot. After all, Rs 500 per month is too little for survival in these new colonies. SEWA, a prominent NGO working in the region, took initiatives for the education of their children. It arranged for their school fees, uniforms, pencils and notebooks. But, much remains to be done still.

Violence has also created many female-headed households, as in many cases all the male members of the family were lost their lives during the riots. The women, under such circumstances, had to embark on an unknown journey. Displacement completely changed their attitude to life. Violence transformed the housewife of yesteryears — the wife of a rickshaw-puller or a daily-wage earner or a small shopkeeper. Before 2002, these women used to live in a private space, behind veils and were largely ignorant of the world outside. All of a sudden, violence has brought them out on the streets, in the public domain. In spite of living in male-dominated households, these women were secure from outside interventions before the violence of 2002. All hell broke loose during the pogrom. Violence brought them out of their private worlds. As the patriarchs felt insecure, women also perceived themselves as being unsafe. New insecurities and uncertainties engulfed their lives when they lost their male partners. The self-appointed male guardians were no longer around to play the role of the protector. As these women began to reconstruct their lives in an alien place, the division between public and private became blurred.[29] Violence reshaped their identities and forced them to change their priorities in life; it required them to step out of their homes to earn their own livelihood.

Conclusion

Gujarat 2002 helps us to examine interactions between violence, memory and the cognition of such events in women's lives. It is believed that only through an explication of the combination of the experience and the memory of the carnage can one possibly arrive at the lingering effects of that traumatic period, and understand how it continues to shape the victim's present outlook. Memory is the engine and chassis of all narratives.[30] The memories of these women are objects that spontaneously tumble out of their minds and link their present state of loss with the past. A traumatic memory has a narrative structure that works on a principle opposite to that of any historical narrative.[31] A historical narrative, after all, concentrates on an event, explaining its causes and the timing. However, sometimethe voices of subject belonging to the 'marginalia of history' may remain unheard in the procers. Perhaps this is why Rabindranath Tagore wrote:

> ...it is very difficult to distinguish the truth and lies. The words flow like a dynamic entity. They transform through passage of time and through the interpretation of the people....This is why we have different versions of the same incident from different persons....The state of the past cannot be determined by a few incidents alone. It is also important to note how the people perceived those incidents. Therefore, memories along with the interpretations of different incidents, together constitute a historical truth.[32]

Narratives are always related to some sense of self and are told from someone's own perspective perhaps in an attempt 'to take control of the frightening diversity and formlessness of the world'.[33] Through the narrative, the self finds a home, or perhaps it would 'describe the process better if we say that around a particular home they try to paint a picture of some kind of an ordered, intelligible, humane and habitable world'.[34] The self tells the story to an audience — in this case the author — and thereby creates a kind of relationship with the listener.[35] In the process, 'the historical self configures memories differently from the way the ahistorical self does'.[36]

But can memory really capture the truth of violence? One could ponder over this question while exploring the psyche and memories of survivors who have tried to save their own lives and their children's lives from the violence of 2002. The truth may elude a person more when she/he delves deep into the minds and memories of women who had a tryst with the violence and trauma associated with that violence. The way Ruksana, Farida, Safia and all other respondents narrated their tales of dispossession — of their 'self' and the loss of their husbands, sons or daughters and their basic dignity — may appear to some as 'exaggerations' or 'excesses', as an attempt to try and sensationalize their losses for a possible reconstruction of their lives. But, do not contested momories also bring us closer to the truth, even if they fail to capture the sufferance of the narrator?

Their deep-seated detestation of the 'other' (Hindu fanatics) is still intense, primarily because of personal experiences but also because of the state's deliberate reluctance to provide relief to them and rehabilitate them. Not only these widows but also Faizan, the small boy of Ruksana and many other children in Gujarat are still suffering from psychological trauma as they recall the horrific violence that they witnessed at a very tender age.[37] To conclude, I would like to share a conversation between Faizan and me to make it understandable to the reader how intense his hatred was against the 'other'. That day, Faizan was staring at me with his inquisitive eyes. I asked him 'What do you want to become when you grow up?' He replied promptly, 'Police'. I asked again, 'Why police, and not a doctor or a teacher?'

He smiled and said, '*Un logo ko sabak sikhana ha,.*' (I have to teach those people a lesson).

I asked, '*O log kaun the?*' (Who were those people?)

'*Hindu the*' (They were Hindus).

'*Aap kya yeh jante hai ke main bhi ek Hindu hoon?*' (Do you know that I am also a Hindu?)

He nodded and said, '*Nahin, aap kaise Hindu ho sakti hai? Aap jo hamara gharka banaya hua khana kha liya, paani bhi pi liya, aap Hindu ho nahi sakti. Hindu to o log the jo mera abba ko mar dala mera mammi ka upar hamla kiya... Maine sab dekhi thi...*' (How can you be a Hindu? You have taken food cooked at our home. You have drunk water in our house. You cannot be a Hindu. Hindus were those who killed my father, who tortured my mother... I saw everything...)[38]

Notes and References

* The author sincerely acknowledges her debt to CSDS, ICSSR, Delhi and CRG, Kolkata for their assistance which enabled the completion of this study. She is also grateful to Ashis Nandy and Ranabir Samaddar for their valuable comments.

1. Ruksana was interviewed on 21 September 2005.
2. In this essay, words like 'pogrom' and 'carnage' have been used instead of 'riots', because in a riot people usually get involved spontaneously, whereas in Gujarat it was systematically organized state-sponsored violence in 2002.

3. In this context, see D.L. Sheth and Gurpreet Mahajan (eds), *Minority Identities and the Nation-State* (New Delhi: Oxford University Press, 1999); Samir Kumar Das, Paula Banerjee and Sabyasachi Basu Ray Chaudhury (eds), *Towards a New Consideration: Justice for the Minorities* (Mahanirban Calcutta Research group [CRG], Kolkata, 2007).

4. Monirul Hussain and Lipi Ghosh (eds), *Religious Minorities in South Asia: Selected Essays on Post-Colonial Situations*, Vol. II (New Delhi: Manak Publications, 2002), p. xi.

5. Hannah Arendt, 'On Violence', in Nancy Scheper-Hughes and Philipe Bourgois (eds), *Violence in War and Peace: An Anthology* (Oxford: Blackwell Publishing, 2004).

6. Yogendra Yadav, 'The Patterns and Lessons', *Frontline*, 3 January 2003, pp. 10–16. See also Dionne Bunsha, 'Hindutva's Triumph', *Frontline*, 3 January 2003, pp. 4–8.

7. See Ravinder Kaur (ed.), *Religion, Violence and Political Mobilization in South Asia* (New Delhi: Sage Publications, 2005); Anasua Basu Ray Chaudhury, 'Sabarmati: Creating a New Divide?', *Economic and Political Weekly* 42(8), 24 February–2 March 2007, pp. 697–703.

8. On my visit to places like Gomtipur, Kalurur, Jamalpur in Ahmedabad, I met many violence-affected families who had taken shelter at the Shah Alam Dargah. These hapless people had been interviewed as part of the BPL survey.

9. V.D. Savarkar defined a Hindu as 'a person who regards his land of Bharatvarsha from the Indus to the seas, as his Fatherland as well as the holy land' (cited in Ashis Nandy, Shikha Trivedy, Shail Mayaram, Achyut Yagnik, *Creating a Nationality: The Ramjanmabhumi Movement and Fear of the Self* [New Delhi: OUP, 1995], p. 67.) Thus, Savarkar gave the concept of Hindu a predominantly territorial component. Ashis Nandy has indicated that, in this context, a concept of holy land was introduced in a fashion 'that would create a stratarchy of Indians'(ibid.) In fact, the Hindutva philosophy was institutionalized by the Rashtriya Swayamsevak Sangh (RSS), formed in 1925. Since its inception, the RSS has been the intellectual and ideological motor for a multitude of organizations that work in the political, cultural, religious and social spheres of India, propagating the Hindutva philosophy. This family of affiliated organizations is together known as the Sangh Parivar. The Sangh Parivar includes the BJP, RSS, Vishwa Hindu Parishad (VHP) and the Bajrang Dal.

10. 'Genocide Gujarat 2002', *Communalism Combat*, March–April 2002, pp. 77–78.

11. Estimates calculated by Citizen's Initiative, an organization involved in relief work after the violence.

12. Siddharth Varadarajan (ed.), *Gujarat: The Making of a Tragedy* (New Delhi: Penguin India, 2002), p. 136.
13. Safia was interviewed on 18 September 2005.
14. Rajia Bibi, Zarina Bibi and Roshan Bibi were interviewed on 19 September 2005.
15. Farida was interviewed on 22 September 2005.
16. Ashutosh Varshney, *Ethnic Conflict and Civic Life: Hindus and Muslims in India* (New Delhi: Oxford University Press, 2002).
17. Ritu Menon and Kamla Bhasin, *Borders and Boundaries: Women in India's Partition*, New Delhi: Kali for Women, 1998), p. 41.
18. *Threatened Existence: A Feminist Analysis of the Genocide in Gujarat*, Report by the International Initiative for Justice (IJI), Bombay, December 2003, pp. 33–45.
19. See Syeda Hameed, Ruth Manorama, Malini Ghose, Sheba George, Farah Naqvi and Mari Thekaekara, *How Has The Gujarat Massacre Affected Minority Women?: The Survivors Speak*, Fact-finding by a Women's Panel, sponsored by Citizen's Initiative Ahmedabad, 16 April 2002.
20. Tanika Sarkar, 'Semiotics of Terror: Muslim Women and Children in Hindu Rashtra', *Economic and Political Weekly* 37 (28), 13 July 2002, pp. 2872–76.
21. The Gujarat violence of 2002 took place in an India with cable televisions. This could have also changed the mindset of the victims. The large-scale involvement of many NGOs too could have encouraged the victims to break their silence in hope of having justice.
22. Infra, n. 17.
23. See People's Union for Democratic Rights (PUDR), 'Little Relief, No Rehabilitation', in Siddharth Varadarajan (ed.), *Gujarat: The Making of a Tragedy* (New Delhi: Penguin Books, 2002), pp. 307–30.
24. Ibid.
25. See Vasudha Dhagamwar, 'The Women in Gujarat Camps — I', *The Hindu*, 22 May 2002, available at http://www.hinduonnet.com/hindu/2002/05/22/stories/2002052200351.htm (accessed 25 April 2003). See also *Gujarat Carnage: Women's Perspectives on the Violence in Gujarat*, Report by PUCL Vadodara and Shanti Abhiyaan, Vadodara, 27 February–26 March 2002, Vadodara.
26. 'Report of the Committee Constituted by the National Commission for Women to Assess the Status and Situation of Women and Girl Children in the Wake of Communal Disturbance', in *The Gujarat Pogrom: Indian Democracy in Danger* (New Delhi: Indian Social Institute, June 2002), pp. 48–56.
27. *Rebuilding from the Ruins: Listening to the Voice from Gujarat and Restoring People's Right to Housing, Livelihood and Life* (New Delhi:

Habitat International Coalition [HIC], Delhi and Youth for Unity and Voluntary Action [YUVA], Mumbai, sponsored by the Citizen's Initiatives, Ahmedabad, August 2002), pp. 102–05.

28. See Neera Chandhok, Praveen Priyadarshi, Silky Tyagi, and Neha Khanna, 'The Displaced of Ahmedabad', *Economic and Political Weekly* 42(43), 27 October–2 November 2007, pp. 10–14.

29. Rachel Weber, 'Re(Creating) the Home: Women's Role in the Development of Refugee Colonies in South Calcutta', in Jasodhara Bagchi and Subhoranjan Dasgupta (eds), *The Trauma and Triumph: Gender and Partition in Eastern India* (Kolkata: Stree, 2003), pp. 59–79; Patricia Uberoi, 'Feminism and the Public–Private Distinction', in Gurpreet Mahajan and Helmut Reifeld (eds), *The Public and the Private: Issues of Democratic Citizenship* (New Delhi: Sage Publications, 2003), pp. 205–29.

30. Indrajit Hazra, 'A Time to Remember', *The Hindustan Times*, Kolkata, 22 November 2000.

31. Dipesh Chakrabarty, 'Remembered Villages: Representation of Hindu-Bengali Memories in the Aftermath of the Partition', *Economic and Political Weekly* 31(32), 1996, p. 2143.

32. Rabindranath Tagore, 'Itihash (Appendix 2)', in *Rabindra Rachanabali*, Birth Centenary edition, No. 13 (Calcutta: West Bengal Government, 1961), p. 470.

33. Sudipta Kaviraj, 'The Imaginary Institution of India', *Subaltern Studies*, Vol. VII (New Delhi: Oxford University Press, 1993), pp. 1–39.

34. Ibid.

35. Ibid., p. 33.

36. Ashis Nandy, 'State History and Exile in South Asian Politics: Modernity and the Landscape of Clandestine and Incommunicable Selves', in Ashis Nandy, *The Romance of the State: And the Fate of Dissent in the Tropics* (New Delhi: Oxford University Press, 2003), pp. 117–18.

37. In this connection see Kavita Panjabi, Krishna Bandopadhyay and Bolan Gangopadhyay, *The Next Generation: In the Wake of Genocide, A Report on the Impact of Gujarat Pogrom on Children and the Young* (Citizen's Initiative, Ahmedabad and ActionAid India, Kolkata, 2002).

38. Faizan was interviewed on 21 September 2005.

4

Negotiations with a Difference: Minority Women in the Borderlands of Sri Lanka and India

Paula Banerjee

Two hundred years back Emmanuel Kant had presumed that democracies are inherently more peaceful. Although prophetic in many ways, this particular assumption of Kant has proved to be seriously wrong. South Asian experiments in democratic state formations have neither led to social justice for all nor has it facilitated conditions of peace. In fact it has shown that in a multiethnic and multicultural state, democracy may lead to the reinforcement of traditional cleavages based on religion, language, ethnicity, caste and gender, and transform them into newer inequities. In such democracies there is a continuous effort to create a homogenized understanding of citizenship that supports the central role of the ruling elite. Such an identity is forged through the state's privileging of majoritarian, patriarchal, monolithic cultural values. According to one observer of South Asian democracies, a monolithic state ideology is designed primarily to legitimise control over diversities, both local and regional.[1] This control is further validated through liberal and democratic discourses of state formation that camouflage the political will which consciously decides who belongs and who does not.[2]

Borders become the site where this contest over inclusion and exclusion is played out. They demarcate the inside from the outside, sovereignty from anarchy and the singular from a pluralistic space. They construct 'the space of agency, the mode of participation in which we act as citizens in the multilayered polities to which we belong'.[3] Hence, borders are not merely lines, they are zones that situate the gray areas where the jurisdiction of one state ends and the other begins. They are the common ground between two or more states that not only share them but also interpret its meanings 'in very different ways to its citizens in their national narratives, history writing and collective spatialized memories'.[4] In the case of South Asia, these borders, or more precisely borderlands, are peopled by groups that have link with both sides of the borders. Yet, in its efforts to emphasize a national identity, state sovereignty demands a severance of all such ties that 'encourage difference', leading to the conscious exclusion of the recalcitrant from privileges. This results in conflicts, as in the case of Tamils in the borderlands of Sri Lanka and Nagas in the borderlands of India. Hence, borders of democratic states, such as the kind found in South Asia, often emerge as conflict zones. My article deals with women living in these borderlands that Edward Said calls 'the perilous territory of not-belonging',and discusses how they negotiate their differences with a state, albeit democratic, which denies space to difference based either on ethnicity or gender.[5]

A legitimate question to ask at this juncture is why privilege women's experiences? This is because women, who are the subject of this article, not only belong to these perilous territories or borderlands but also constitute them. According to Yuval-Davis, the universalistic nature of citizenship that emanates from traditional liberal and social–democratic discourses is extremely deceptive as it conceals the exclusion of women from national identities of citizenship.[6] Thus, the ideological constructions of the state is weighted against women, who remain on the borders of democracy. Yet, in moments of conflict, at times they assume centrality. This is because in times of civil conflict, men withdraw from civic life for compulsions of war and self defence. In such a situation, the public sphere retreats into the private and women constitute civil societies. They assume roles that are completely new to them and, confront and negotiate with the awesome power of the state machinery in their everyday lives. Further, as transmitters of cultural value, women constitute the differences that shape the future of democracy. This is reflected in the roles assumed by women in the border regions of Sri Lanka and India; particularly by Tamil and Naga women. Yet the narratives of borderlands given to us are male narratives that privilege male modes of discourse and power-related compulsions. There is hardly any work that engages with women's issues in the borderlands. This article is meant to fill this lacuna in the existing literature. It deals with women from these two major conflict zones and discusses their negotiation with a state that has traditionally privileged values that are perhaps alien to them. I analyze how, through their engagements, these women transform the traditional definitions of democracy, nationalism and resistance.

Tamil Women in Sri Lanka

Sri Lanka is a multiethnic island state sharing the southern maritime borders of India that are inhabited by Tamils. In Sri Lanka at present, the Sinhalese form 74 per cent of the population and Sri Lankan Tamils make up about 13 per cent of the population. According to one observer, 'At the time of independence spokespersons for the 69 per cent Sinhalese majority, the 11 per cent indigenous Tamil minority, and the 6 per cent Moorish minority shaped a constitutional bargain that provided for a democratic parliamentary system with substantial safeguards for the rights of the minorities.'[7] But ever since Independence, the relative political and cultural standing of the Tamils and the Sinhalese has been a source of contention and conflict. As the Sinhalese saw it in the early 1950s, although they constituted the overwhelming majority, 40 per cent of all clerics and one-third of all university graduates were Tamil. The Tamils on the other hand argued that the majority Sinhalese community systematically undercut their opportunities over the years and reduced them to a state of second-class citizenship. From 1956 onwards, the Tamils began to feel that their personal security was under threat. Discussions on the Sinhala Only Act made them all the more nervous for it threatened to cut them off from further government services, which were coveted by the Tamils.

From 1956 onwards, there developed an action–reaction dynamic between the Tamils and the Sinhalese. The Sinhalese favoured the kind of unitary and centralized state that they inherited from the British. The Tamils wanted decentralization and the liberty to manage their own affairs in the north and the east. The Sinhalese protested against any motions in favour of decentralization being discussed between the government and the Tamil spokespersons. Neither the Sinhalese nor the Tamils were homogeneous communities and there was enormous difference of opinion within each of these communities. From 1956 onwards, the educational policy of the country set the Tamil and Sinhalese youth on different and divergent tracks, with each of them being educated in their respective languages. By 1977, differences between the two communities became so acute that the Tamils started demanding their own *Eelam* or nation. Although J.R. Jayawardene, who came to power in 1977, gave the Tamil language a substantially higher constitutional standing than before and tried to negotiate with the members of the Tamil United Liberation Front (TULF), the situation did not improve, in fact it continued to deteriorate.

Sri Lanka has been the site of a brutal ethnic conflict since the 1980s. By 1990, about 10 per cent of the Sri Lankan population had been internally displaced.[8] The situation stabilized in the early 1990s with some displaced people being repatriated, but worsened once again in October 1995, as the Sri Lankan armed forces launched an operation to wrest Jaffna from the control of the Liberation Tigers of Tamil Eelam (LTTE). Almost 90 per cent of the people living in these areas came to be displaced. In 2000, LTTE launched a counter-offensive to regain control of Jaffna, followed by a similar government offensive in 2001. In this protracted conflict, civilian life was tremendously affected. According to estimates of the United Nations High Commissioner for Refugees (UNHCR) and Refugees International by 2001 almost 800,000 people had been displaced. In February 2002, for the first time in seven years, the Sri Lankan government and the LTTE signed a formal bilateral cease-fire. On 2 January 2008, the Sri Lankan government took a policy decision to abrogate the 2002 ceasefire agreement with LTTE, but that is a different matter.[9] At this juncture, the important question for us is the condition of Tamil women caught in the conflict.

In terms of social indicators, the status of women in Sri Lanka was considered a marvel of South Asia before the ethnic conflict began. Even today, Sri Lanka has the highest literacy rates among women in South Asia. Female literacy rates are as high as 83 per cent and their average life expectancy is 72 years. Maternal mortality is as low as 39.8 per 100,000 live births. Sri Lanka also has the distinction of having elected the first woman Prime Minister in the world. Sri Lankan women have enjoyed adult franchise since 1931 and the country has ratified a series of international pro-women treaties. In 1981, it ratified the Convention on the Elimination of Discrimination against Women (CEDAW) without any reservation. It has also ratified the International Covenants of Civil and Political Rights and Economic, Social and Cultural Rights, the Convention on the Rights of the Child and the UN Convention against Torture and Other Cruel, Inhuman or Degrading Treatment or Punishment. However, it has not ratified the key ILO Conventions regulating standards for women workers. As for internal mechanisms, the Penal Code (Amendment) Act Nos 22 of 1995 and 29 of 1998, the Code of Criminal Procedure (Amendment) Act No. 28 of 1998 and the Judicature (Amendment) Act No. 27 of 1998, are laws that have created a legal framework for more effective prosecution of alleged rapists. Among the latest changes in the Penal Code was the inclusion of a new provision recognizing the phenomena of rape while in police custody. However, even after ratifying all these international instruments and creating pro-women legal mechanisms it is important for us to note the plight of Sri Lankan Tamil women and children, who form the vast majority of those affected by the war.

The war in Sri Lanka has affected Tamil women in many different ways. One obvious way was how the war came to women and how they became participants. In *Women Fighters of Liberation Tigers*, Adele Ann, the Australian wife of LTTE theorist Anton Balasingham, wrote that as cadres, women were for the first time being treated as equal to men. She discussed the military training received by LTTE women cadres and emphasized its rigour. According to her, the roles expected of women combatants are no different from that of male combatants — death makes martyrs of both of them. The women are able to transcend patriarchal notions of feminized ideals and participate in public activities. She felt that the LTTE brought a radical transformation to Tamil women's roles. Adele Ann stressed that the decision to join, in most cases, is an act that marks a clear departure for Tamil women. 'Normally young women remain under the control of the father and the brother. Male control follows them throughout their lives. The decision to break out of this cycle of suffocating control is a refreshing expression and articulation of their new aspirations and Independence.'[10] Their joining LTTE tells society that they are not satisfied with their social status and are capable of defying authority. To Adele Ann, by entering into the military programme, these young women made it known that they were willing to accept the social challenge for the cause of a national struggle.

It is true that the war gave minority Tamil women many new roles to play, but it remains debatable whether all of them were empowering or not. Minority Tamil women were caught in the conflict in ways more direct than their Sinhalese counterparts. Adele Ann celebrates this direct involvement of Tamil women in the conflict. But there are others who have found that the roles that these Tamil women played were not all that agentive. Neloufer De Mel, in her essay 'Agent or Victim?', makes a similar point. Regarding the case of women members of the United Liberation Front of Assam (ULFA) and the women cadres of National Socialist Council of Nagalim (NSCN) I have made similar arguments elsewhere.[11] De Mel argues that from being controlled by the father these women's lives are now controlled by the LTTE. They have never been free of institutional control and the LTTE is also a great authoritarian patriarchal structure and there were no ways of escaping it. This is proved by the fate of Rajani Tirangama and her sister Nirmala Nityanandan. After they left LTTE there was a vicious campaign of shaming and denigrating them. In fact, De Mel calls the LTTE a feudal organization. She says that at its crux is the personality cult of Prabhakaran. He is often invested with the 'aura of a deity'.[12] He is the man who creates a space for the women and plays the role of a midwife or usher, thereby establishing a hierarchy in which women would remain perpetually reliant on men. Also, the women's wing of the LTTE is not much concerned with the issue of gender hierarchy. They raise the question of liberation from only one kind of bondage. Moreover, within the organization there is control of ones sexuality and so relations established is overall considered familial. Compatriots are brothers or sisters, and any other relationship is seen as being transgressive. According to observers such as De Mel, women's roles in the LTTE are still supportive in nature and hence the lack of women leaders in the front ranks. In the final analysis then, for the Tamil women of Sri Lanka militarism is at best an ambiguous move towards liberation. Even for those not involved in direct combat, the situation is extremely difficult.

As early as 1995, Francis Deng, the Special Representative of the United Nations Secretary-General on Internally Displaced Persons reported that some women had been raped prior to their displacement.[13] Human Rights observers from Amnesty International repeatedly reported that security forces in conflict areas in Sri Lanka were raping women and obviously mostly Tamil women were the victims of such rape. In one such report it was stated that 'Two Tamil women who were taken into custody in the northwestern Mannar district by naval personnel were allegedly gang-raped by them on March 19. Tamil politicians and the Catholic bishop of Mannar protested strongly and took the matter up with the authorities.'[14] In another report it was stated that two soldiers raped a 70-year-old internally displaced widow.[15] This is, in fact, not exceptional but a typical report. Amnesty International also reports that the figures documenting the rapes committed by security forces also include 'many internally displaced women.'[16] In another comprehensive report it is stated that the 'risk of sexual violence for displaced women dramatically increases in the conditions immediately prior to, during and post flight.'[17] From such reports and other incidents of rape, it is apparent that in Sri Lanka rape has been used to displace Tamil women and among those who are displaced many have been victims of rape. Sadly, when instruments of the state, such as members of the armed forces, perpetrate rape they are hardly ever prosecuted.[18]

Tamil women from north and north-east Sri Lanka are perhaps the worst affected by the political conflict. Among the vast majority of displaced Tamil families were a number of matriarchal households. Although 89 per cent women in Sri Lanka are literate, due to two decades of armed conflict women from the north and the north-east have lower levels of education, with one in four women being illiterate. A report based on research carried out in Mannar district observes that among the 190,000 internally displaced persons (IDPs) women often find it impossible to generate an income adequate for buying food for the entire family. In Illupakkadavai, all thirty-six women heads of such households stated that they rely on dry rations for approximately 90 per cent of their nutritional requirements and that the children are most vulnerable to exploitation. Not surprisingly then, in Sri Lanka, suicide rates for women have doubled in the last two decades.[19]

The conflict in Sri Lanka has resulted in the collapse of community and family structures. Many women have had to leave their homes without any community support. This has rendered them more vulnerable to sexual violence. A large majority of the IDPs stayed with people known to them. However, even while living with friends, women are expected to shoulder responsibilities for which they are often unprepared. In a recent CEDAW committee report it was stated that almost half of the female-headed households are run by elderly women, many of whom are illiterate and devoid of adequate sources of income.[20] This has taken a heavy toll on women's mental and physical health. Moreover, according to the UN Special Rapporteur on

Violence Against Women, internally displaced women often lack easy access to healthcare facilities.[21] As for women's mental health, this has not been considered an issue at all. In areas of conflict, one of the principle reasons why healthcare is such a problematic issue is that even though a range of international, national and local aid agencies provide assistance to the internally displaced, the government restricts the flow of many relief supplies, including medical provisions.

Among the Tamil IDPs who live in government-run camps, as reported in 2001, the condition of women is extremely serious. Often, old *saris* and other pieces of rag are all that separate families from each other. There is a severe lack of privacy in these camps.[22] These camps, known as welfare centres, are heavily guarded and entry and exit is restricted. In such a situation, young women are particularly vulnerable and according to one social worker, there has been an alarming increase in the incidence of pregnancy among teenage girls in these camps.[23] It has been pointed out by one observer that the 'Sri Lankan experience shows that displaced women are more likely to seek work or engage in economic activity than men'.[24] The restriction of entrance and exit into camps affects these women, who work outside of the camps. Also, Sri Lanka's non-ratification of the ILO Conventions regulating standards for women workers has adversely affected women IDPs, who are now forced to take up jobs in the unorganized sectors. Further, according to reports of the Jesuit Refugee Service, these camps are recruiting grounds for agents who send these women to different countries to work as maids. Often they are victims of sexual abuse, but because of the difficulty of finding employment in these camps IDP women are forced to take up oversees assignments, which then drive them into abusive and coercive situations.

A failed nationalization project in Sri Lanka has encouraged the government to segregate those women who are considered threatening. They are displaced from their homes and ghettoized in camps. Most are then transferred from one camp to another, which discourages them from establishing any kind of social or political connections. Their involvement in any kind of political activities, even if peaceful, is considered threatening. Many of these women are not only displaced and but also pushed beyond the country's borders. Countries in which they seek asylum often consider them as being threatening as well. As for Sri Lankan Tamil women in India, Rajiv Gandhi's death convinced the state that these women are of little use to India's nationalizing and nation-building project. From being asylum-seekers, they were hereby reduced to the status of hostages, who were deemed so dangerous that they had to be segregated. Thus, when agents of human trafficking arrived the state turned a blind eye. This was one easy way of getting rid of women who were considered problematic.

When women return from other places of refuge abuse seems to follow them. There is the well-known case of Ida Carmelita. She had returned to Sri Lanka from India in 1994 and was brutally raped and killed by the security forces in 1999. This is not an isolated incident. There are other women, such as Thambipillai Thanalakshmi, who were brutally raped after they returned to Sri Lanka.[25] Women are always the first to be repatriated because there is a fear that if men return they may be lured by the rebel groups or apprehended by security forces. In such a situation, it is best to involve women's groups to explore whether it is safe for women to return to high security zones. The strip-searching of a Sinhalese woman in broad daylight on the suspicion that she was a Tamil suicide bomber shows that the situation for IDP women is precarious.[26]

Apart from being women combatants in the LTTE and IDPs, the other role that Tamil women play is that of peacemakers. In the South Asian scenario, one of the few ways that women enter public discourses in times of conflict is through the institution of motherhood. As mothers it is considered legitimate for women to criticize and protest against violence. In most of South Asia motherhood is valourized. The relationship between the state and its citizens is seen as that between a mother and her sons. The nation is often described as *deshmatrika,* and the citizens are sons protecting the honour of the mother. However, motherhood has little to say about high politics. Its realm is that of mass politics. That is why the elite custodians of the state are often ambivalent about mothers' movements. Yet, people's politics encourages the formation of mothers' movements. The Tamils in Sri Lanka are no exception to this rule and have seen the creation and demise of a number of Mothers Fronts (MFs). One of the first MFs was created in 1984. They urged the mothers of Jaffna to come to the army with their children and their identity cards. This was a time of numerous instances of disappearance. The mothers, thinking that this would help protect their young ones, took their children to the army headquarters in large numbers. The army segregated the boys from the girls and took the boys away.

Many were tortured and some were killed. Village after village was surrounded and demands were made for the Tamil families to give up their boys.

At this time, the MF was still organizing itself. The mothers whose sons were arrested joined the movement in large numbers. On one occasion 630 boys were arrested, following which their mothers joined the movement en masse. Many of the boys who were released were left traumatized, and this experience of witnessing the arrest and torture of their sons encouraged the mothers to join MF. In June 1984, the MF organized a march with nearly 10,000 women and confronted the Government Agent of Jaffna, asking him to release their sons. No amount of persuasion by the Agent could dispel the women, who made it amply known that they meant business. Notably, the mothers clearly distinguished themselves from other liberty seekers as citizens of Sri Lanka. Dissatisfied with the response of the government, who released only a few boys, the MF organized another march on 24 August 1984, calling for the release of the 500 other young men who were innocent and had been arbitrarily arrested. This time nearly 2,000 women stormed the Agent's office, demanding the release of their sons. According to Selvy Thiruchandran, 'The protest march yielded only partial and momentary results but left a permanent impact on the activities of the state which slowed down arbitrary arrests and began to use some discretion in the arrests of youths'.[27]

The MF did not last very long, losing much of its significance soon after the event mentioned above. But motherhood continues to be a contentious issue both for the state and for the rebels. The LTTE publication entitled *Women and Revolution: The Role of Women in Tamil Elam National Revolution* (1983) carried a photograph of a Palestinian woman holding a gun in one hand and a baby in the other. So motherhood remained an ideal for the LTTE, but mothers in politics were a different issue altogether. The MF received covert support while it lasted but when it refused to be subsumed within the movement for *Eelam* it lost much of its support.[28] The LTTE reserved the right to tell these women when to take up arms and when to go tending to babies — just as the state does. That the movement tried to contain women's sexuality was revealed by the bizarre incident of the '10 commandments for women', listed in a poster that was found pasted on the walls of Jaffna in late 1984. The commandments included that women wear the traditional dress or the *sari*, keep their hair long, not go out in housecoats etc. Women who refused to abide by these commandments were threatened with being whipped. Although the LTTE denied any responsibility for the poster, the ideas presented there were very much in keeping with the views of some of its leaders. A statement by LTTE that appeared in *Mukamoodikal Kilihinrana* two years later declared that: 'It is important for women to take care in their dress, in their pottu and make-up. It doesn't mean that we are enslaved if we dress according to tradition. Some married women says it is expensive to wear saris. This is not acceptable.'[29]

Apart from the LTTE, even the state is unwilling to accept Tamil women as major players in the peace process. Perhaps this is one of the reasons why MF did not last very long. There were other MF's in the east still, but they were not very successful either. One reason for this is that women's politics is much influenced by society itself. If society does not support their politics women find it very difficult to sustain their movements. Let us now turn to another community in South Asia that provides us with a successful example of a MF. This is the Naga community in north-east India.

Naga Women in India

The Nagas are composed of forty tribes (of which sixteen are major tribes) living between the Chindwin and Brahmaputra plains. Part of the land came under British rule in 1879 and the term Naga was also first used by the British. The state of Nagaland was the sixteenth state of India. Each tribe is distinct in character, with its own customs, language, dress and culture. It is also a land of folklore passed down through the generations by word of mouth. But this beautiful land is also the theatre of the longest civil war in India. From 1953, the Government of India introduced a plethora of laws which have curbed everything from the resources available to the state to human rights, failing only to curb insurgency. Naga women have one of the worst sex ratios even by north-east Indian standards but the second-best literacy rate. The sex ratio is 890 and the literacy rate is about 55.72 per cent. The sex ratio for women in rural areas is 912 and in urban areas it is 789.[30] This shows that greater out-migration of men from villages and the ongoing conflict is the main reason for that. Although there were some outstanding women political leaders in Nagaland, such as Rano Shaiza, they were only exceptions and not the rule. In the recent Lok Sabha elections even Nagaland failed to send any women parliamentarians. Among the forty-one senior officers of the Nagaland Secretariat only two are women.[31] Such statistics may suggest that women are completely marginalized in Naga political life but that is not true. Women participate in large numbers, both in war and in peace. All Naga insurgent groups have women's wings. But the decision-making authority lies in the hands of men. For this reason, here we will privilege narratives of peace. An outstanding feature of Naga women's interventions in conflict is the multiplicity of the peace movements that they have initiated. The best known among these organizations for peace is the Naga Mother's Association (NMA). The head office of the NMA is in the largely Angami city of Kohima. It came into existence on 14 February 1984, with a preamble that stated, 'Naga mothers of Nagaland shall express the need of conscientizing citizens toward more responsible living and human development through the voluntary organisation of the Naga Mother's Association.'[32] Membership of NMA is open to any adult Naga woman, irrespective of whether she is married or single. Members are free to join through the women's organizations of their own tribes as well. The organization encourages human development through education and seeks to eradicate social evils and economic exploitation, and work towards peace and progress.

The NMA has rendered valuable service for the cause of peace. It mediated between the Government of Nagaland and the Naga Student's Federation over the question of maximum age limit for jobs and came to an equitable settlement. An other achievement of the NMA is the formation of the Peace Team in October 1994 in order to confront the deteriorating political situation. Their slogan was 'Shed No More Blood'. The NMA spoke against killings not only by the army but also by the militants. In a pamphlet released on 25 May 1995, representatives of the NMA wrote, 'the way in which our society is being run, whether by the overground government or the underground government, have become simply intolerable'. The NMA celebrates 12 May each year as Mother's Day and renews their appeal for peace.

Apart from peace initiatives, the NMA has also worked for social regeneration. In Nagaland there is rampant alcohol and drug abuse. The NMA provides facilities for de-addiction. They collaborate with the other foundations for the rehabilitation of drug users. The NMA has also started anonymous HIV testing. They are probably the first women's organization in the north-east to test pregnant women for HIV. The NMA is providing pioneering service by providing care to patients afflicted with AIDS. An im-portant concern that is pre-occupying the doctors of NMA is the increase in HIV-positive cases among pregnant women. One NMA spokesperson was of the opinion that conflict in Nagaland is the result of chronic underdevelopment, which is why the NMA believes that without addressing develop-mental issues there cannot be any peace in Nagaland.[33]

NMA's greatest achievement is that almost all the Naga women's organizations are its collaborators. Members of the NMA also collab-orate with the Naga Women's Union of Manipur. Rallies organized by the NMA are always well attended by other Naga women's organizations. The NMA work very closely with the Naga Hohos (apex bodies of Naga tribes). That the NMA has assumed enormous influence in Naga politics is borne out by the fact that they are the only women's group in South Asia that has participated in a cease-fire negotiation. In 1997, they mediated between the Government of India and the NSCN–IM (Isak Muivah) faction and facilitated a cease-fire.

The NMA, however, is not the only women's group. There are a number of others, of which one important organization is the Watsu Mongdung. An extraordinary case catapulted the Watsu Mongdung to fame. The incident took place on 27 December 1994, in Mokokchung town. Ten members of the Assam Rifles entered the town and carried out indiscriminate rape and arson. Innumerable women were raped. The Naga Human Rights Commission entrusted to Watsu Mongdung the job of investigating and identifying the victims. The Watsu Mongdung formed a special committee and in-vestigated the matter. They identified eight victims and reconstructed the incident after a thorough discussion with them. None of the other social organizations wanted to take up this matter, so members of the Watsu Mongdung decided to litigate on behalf of the rape victims. The case is still pending. Although the Watsu Mongdung is largely an Ao organization, they have participated in protest marches organized by the Lothas and such other tribes.[34] However, they are one of the few women's organizations that do not collaborate with the NMA. This may be because of traditional Ao and Angami antagonisms.[35]

The Watsu Mongdung is not the only group that provides such services. There are other women's groups, such as the Tangkhul Shanao Long (TSL), which operate both in Nagaland and Manipur. In July 1997, after an ambush by the NSCN–IM, the Assam Rifles went on a rampage in Ukhrul town, beating up the men, including schoolteachers. People were so traumatized that life in Ukhrul town came to a complete standstill. The TSL not only spoke to the army and convinced them to release over forty civilians but also tried to instill confidence among the people of the town and its adjoining villages. They helped the people of the area to return to a normal life by requesting the shopkeepers to keep their shops open. They also appealed to the stranded people to go back home, which brought back some semblance of normalcy to the town.

In recent years, groups such as the NMA, the Watsu Mongdung and the TSL have gained recognition as serious actors in the peace process. Their organized campaigns and rallies have facilitated the cease-fire. They continue working with other Naga organizations to reduce the violence and brutalization of the Naga society. They actively participate in discussions on peace and human rights. Through their negotiations for peace they have created a niche for themselves in the public sphere.

State Policies, Minorities and Gender

Nira Yuval-Davis once said that women have a dualistic relationship with the state: on the one hand women are always included, at least to some extent, in the general body of citizens of the state and its social, political and legal policies; on the other, there is always, at least to a certain extent, a separate body of legislation which relates to them specifically as women.[36]

In the case of the borderlands of India and Sri Lanka this dualistic nature of women's engagements with the national and ethnic collectivities leads to further discrimination against them. This becomes problematic because social attitudes over time get transformed into legal provisions. Therefore, women have to live not only under draconian national laws, by virtue of their geographical location, but also suffer other discriminatory traditions and practices because of their minority status and gender.

Women's initiatives are not just determined by but also determine wider social movements. In Sri Lanka, active opposition to women's initiatives might have alienated women from institutional politics but they have channelled their energy into many other movements that they consider empowering. They have sporadically organized mothers' fronts, participated in ceasefire negotiations and fashioned a number of protest movements. There is a logic behind their sporadic movements. These are the types of movements that majoritarian political power structures tolerate. Hence the constant recurrence of such movements. These sporadic movements occur at regular intervals and this is how they negotiate with the state and with ethnic collectivities.

The Naga women have been successful in creating an independent space in politics. They were able to convince all the parties involved in the peace process that they are not governed by any specific faction. Most Naga women continue to retain their belief in the community's cause, but their actions show that they are on the side of peace. They want to achieve their goals through political actions and not through a brutalization of society. Their politics of peace have helped them to gain space even in formal statist politics. They have become an important and necessary component of the Naga Hohos. Yet, even the state machinery is not averse to using them for purposes of peace. There are a number of reasons for the success attained by Naga women. Naga women have been able to situate their political manoeuvrings within their traditional roles. Peace to them is not just a political phenomena it is also economic and social necessity. They have in fact coined a term which means 'just peace' or peace with equity. They believe that without development there cannot be peace and this is where they differ from the majoritarian attitude towards peace. They equate peace with progress. They entered the political space through peace activism, now they are making an effort to alter the character of that space.

Taken collectively, these women's movements lead to the democratization of society. If by democratization we are referring only the space appropriated by formal and elitist political activities such as representational politics, then some of these women have been unsuccessful at it. However, if we were to privilege informal and populist activities, then the women have excelled. If democracy can be equated with peace and social justice, then the women have certainly made inroads there. Even when the sphere of public activity underwent a process of masculanization, as in the case of Tamil women in Sri Lanka, women did not always passively acquiesce.

They adopted various strategies in order to maintain their involvent in/with the public space. With their grievances they entered the non-governmental sector and created a niche for themselves in public charity organizations. They transformed their societies by constantly engaging with state politics and other male-oriented politics, albeit through the mode of protest. But even protest is a legitimate mode of engagement. In places where women could carve out an independent space they had greater flexibility and room to make a mark. In Nagaland, by creating their own independent and collective space, they engaged successfully with other collectivities and successfully entered the space of 'high' politics. In Sri Lanka too, Tamil women created a space for themselves in ceasefire negotiations. But when the entire ceasefire failed, women had very few avenues open to them to make a difference to the peace process.

Thus, the experiences of women from the borderlands of Sri Lanka and India suggest that in places where women have appropriated peacemaking as their realm of activity, they have been more success-ful. I, however, make no essentialist plea here. Peacemaking is often recognized by a male-dominated society as women's own work. The majoritarian leadership therefore fails to recognize the political nature of the work of peacemaking. The experiences of Nagaland and Sri Lanka show that through peacemaking, women are able to negotiate spaces in the public sphere. This recognition subsequently helps them in other negotiations such as in their reworking of other rights.

Notes and References

1. Ayesha Jalal, *Democracy and Authoritarianism in South Asia: A Comparative and Historical Perspective* (New Delhi: Cambridge University Press, 1996), p. 245.
2. See Etienne Balibar, 'The Nation Form — History and Ideology', *New Left Review* 13(3), 1990, pp. 329–61.
3. Nira Yuval-Davis, 'Gender and Nation', in R. Wilfred and R. Miller (eds), *Women, Ethnicity and Nationalism: The Politics of Transition* (London and New York: Routledge, 1998), p. 17.
4. Anssi Passi, 'Space Boundaries and the Social Construction of Territorial Identities', unpublished paper presented at the conference 'Rethinking Boundaries: Geopolitics, Identities and Sustainability', 21–24 February 2000, Chandigarh.
5. Edward Said, 'Mind in Winter: Reflections on Life in Exile', *Harper's* 269, September 1984, p. 51.

6. Yuval-Davis, 'Gender and Nation', p. 26.

7. Howard Wriggins, 'Sri Lanka: Negotiations in a Secessionist Conflict', in I. William Zartman (ed.), *Elusive Peace: Negotiating an End to Civil Wars* (Washington, D.C.: Brookings Institution, 1995), p. 36.

8. This figure has been quoted in Kumudini Samuel, 'Foregrounding Women's Human Rights', *Women in Action* 2, 30 June 1997, p. 23.

9. This article was written prior to the ending of the ceasefire and the Sri Lankan army's offensive against the LTTE that is currently underway.

10. Adele Ann, *Women Fighters of Liberation Tigers* (Jaffna: LTTE Publication Section, 1993), p. 8.

11. Paula Banerjee, 'Between Two Armed Patriarchies', in Rita Manchanda (ed.), *Women, War and Peace in South Asia: Beyond Victimhood to Agency* (New Delhi: Sage Publications, 2001).

12. Neloufer De Mel, *Women and the Nation's Narrative: Gender and Nationalism in Twentieth Century Sri Lanka* (New Delhi: Kali for Women, in association with the Book Review Literary Trust, 2001), p. 221.

13. Francis M. Deng, *Internally Displaced Persons,* Report of the Representative of the UN Secretary General on Internally Displaced Persons, UN Document E/CN.4/1995/50, 2 February 1995, para. 30, Brookings Institution Library, Washington.

14. Amnesty International Report, quoted in Christine Jayasinghe, 'Amnesty alleges security forces getting away with rape', *India Abroad* 31 (28), p. 12.

15. 'Sri Lanka: Rape in Custody', *Amnesty International*, AI Index: ASA 37/001/2002, 28 January 2002, p. 6, http://www.amnesty.org/en/library/info/ASA37/001/2002/en (accessed 28 April 2008).

16. *Amnesty International*, AI Index: ASA 37/001/2002, 28 January 2002.

17. Sophia Elek, *Choosing Rice over Risk: Rights, Resettlement and Displaced Women* (Colombo: Centre for the Study of Human Rights, 2003).

18. *Amnesty International*, AI Index: ASA 37/001/2002, 28 January 2002, pp. 8–9, http://www.amnesty.org/en/library/info/ASA37/001/2002/en (accessed 28 April 2008).

19. Paula Banerjee, 'Agonies and Ironies of War', *Refugee Watch* 2, April 1998, Kolkata, p. 21.

20. CEDAW, 26th Session, CEDAW/C/2002/I/CRP.3/ADD.5, 30 January 2002, para. 41, Brookings Institution Library, Washington.

21. *Preliminary report submitted by the Special Rapporteur on violence against women, its causes and consequences, Ms. Radhika Coomaraswamy, in accordance with Commission on Human Rights resolution 1994/45, E/CN.4/1995/42, 22 November 1994,*

http://www.unhchr.ch/Huridocda/Huridoca.nsf/TestFrame/75ccfd797b0712d08025670b005c9a7d?Opendocument (accessed 29 April 2008).

22. Mario Gomez, 'National Human Rights Commission and Internally Displaced Persons: Illustrated by the Sri Lankan Experience', Occasional Paper, The Brookings — SAIS Project on Internal Displacement, July 2002, p. 12.

23. A social worker (who prefers to stay anonymous) interviewed by the author on 25 January 2000 in Trincomalee.

24. Gomez, 'National Human Rights Commission', p. 12.

25. *Amnesty International*, AI Index: ASA 37/001/2002, 28 January 2002, p. 7, http://www.amnesty.org/en/library/info/ASA37/001/2002/en (accessed 28 April 2008).

26. Case reported in 'Women's Rights Watch Year Report 1999', cited in 'In Search of a Haven: The Tamil Women in Sri Lanka', *Refugee Watch*, March 2000, p. 27.

27. Selvy Thiruchandran, *The Politics of Gender and Women's Agency in Post-Colonial Sri Lanka* (Colombo: Women's Education and Research Centre, 1997), pp. 42–43.

28. I am indebted to Shanthi Sachidananda who shared with me her views on the MF during our journey from Colombo to Trincomalee in the year 2000.

29. Quoted in De Mel, *Women and the Nation's Narrative*, p. 217.

30. S.R. Luhadia, *Census of India 1991*, Series 18, Supplement 6, Paper 1 of 1991 (New Delhi: Controller of Publications).

31. *The Statistical Handbook of Nagaland* (Directorate of Economics and Statistics, Government of Nagaland, Kohima, 1997), p. 23.

32. Constitution of the Naga Mothers' Association (Reprinted in Kohima, 1992).

33. Interview with Ms Kheseli, Former President of NMA, 27 January 1999, Kohima and 10 October 1999, Kolkata.

34. Watsu Mongdangi Inyaka Aruba Report, 5 May 1995 (Mokokchung, Nagaland: unpublished).

35. Interview with Merenla Jamir, member of Watsu Mongdung, 26 January 1999, Dimapur.

36. Yuval-Davis, 'Gender and Nation', p. 27.

State Governance
and Community Rights

5

Inclusive Democracy and Governance in 'New' Nepal

Lok Raj Baral

State Structure and the Politics of Discrimination

The rulers of Nepal had always been guided by the idea that the assimilation of all minorities and social groups into a broader Gorkhali culture would be the bedrock of the modern Nepali state. Indeed, the conquest of Nepal valley by the Gorkha kings laid the foundations for uniculturalism (monoculturalism) and the absorption of all other cultural and social groupings into the so-called unified nation-state. Thus, the integration model established under the Shah and later under the Rana regimes differed from the 'bourgeois' models of nation building emerging during the same period in the Western world in one fundamental respect: under the Shahs and the Ranas sovereignty remained *de jure* with powerful individuals and factions able to manipulate and/or represent the monarch. From the point of view of the rulers, the plurality of the Nepalese [Nepali] society was conceived within a uniform socio-political framework; diverse castes and ethnic groups were incorporated into a holistic framework of a national caste hierarchy'.[1] Assimilation thus fit into the Gorkhali agenda of domination by one group of people over the other, insofar as the attitude of the modern Nepali state was concerned.

Thus, as opposed to integration, which 'provides for the coexistence of minority cultures with the majority culture; assimilation requires the absorption of minority cultures into the majority culture. The aim of assimilation is a monocultural, even a monofaith society; the aim of integration is a multicultural, pluralist society.'[2] In the opinion of Leo R. Rose, 'a syncretic form of Hinduism, encompassing much that is Buddhist or "animist" in derivation, therefore, is the dominant religious and cultural form throughout much of Nepal.'³ Yet, a controversy persists between the Hindus and non-Hindus, with the latter opposing the imposition of Brahminic Hindu values on the rest. Since the people were subjugated by a predatory state, their resentment against such an imposition was mute, but the process cannot be considered 'painless'.

Such an approach to the process of nation-building lasted for 240 years, and a unitary state structure was taken as the model for keeping the ethnic mosaic intact. However, the discriminatory attitude of the unifier (by force) of the country was manifested when he selectively employed a few caste and ethnic groups in his army. While groups such as the Newar and people from Tarai were isolated from being included in the army, the ethnic hill groups or *jan jatis* were disproportionately recruited into various state services. As Mahesh Regmi states: 'The standing army of the Gorkhali rulers had a narrow social and territorial base. The subject populations of the Empire were divided into two categories, only one of which was eligible for recruitment. King Prithvi Narayan Shah had instructed his successors to restrict recruitment only to four communities, namely, Khas, Magar, Gurung and Thakuri. The list does not mention such other communities as Khawas, Khatri and Chhetri, who gained entry into the army in subsequent years.'⁴

It is interesting to note that inspite of the numerous changes made in the administrative and political sectors, the discriminatory policy put in place by the Gorkha and Rana rulers did not show any radical departures from the past. Although Nepal did experience a sudden break with the past with the demise of the Rana oligarchy in 1951, the change resulted in nothing more than the restoration of absolute monarchy 104 years after the Ranas had thrown it into political oblivion after the coup of 1846. Taking revenge against the Rana's usurpation of power, the Nepali monarchy, by allying with the forces of revolution, was able to reincarnate itself in the post-revolution period because of the gradual weakening of political parties. It was also proved that the Nepalis had ended Rana rule, but the subject political culture of the past continued, allowing the Nepali kings to pursue policies of 'divide and rule' in order to consolidate Shah ascendancy. All the revolutionaries started looking at the Palace as their safest constituency, forgetting the basics of democratic governance. Personal allegiance to the ruler, the same old discriminatory policies, albeit employed in more refined manner and patronage routes to power and privilege, etc., became the basis of the political system. So when King Mahendra staged a coup against the first-ever elected government in 1960, it was the innate spirit of palace intrigues and conspiracies that prevailed once again. As Bhuwan Joshi and Leo Rose remark:

> Historically, the nearest parallel to king Mahendra's action was the arrest of Prime Minister Bhimsen Thapa in 1836 by King Rajendra on specious charges, later recanted by the King himself, of disloyalty to the royal family. Those were the days of conspiratorial politics, and vicissitudes in political fortunes were sometimes expressed through poisonings, hired assassins, bloody massacres, and dark dungeons. In 1960 the participants were different, and the political methods and vocabulary were modern, but the basic spirit and idiom of Nepali politics remained unchanged.[5]

There was a change in 1990, brought about by the mass movement, but was not qualitatively different in the arena of institution-building. Yet, whatever exercises Nepal went through during the 1990s and in early 2006, made Nepalis more agile and politically conscious. Such exercises also prompted Nepali intellectuals, political leaders and others in favour of a paradigm shift for an inclusive democracy. There were many discourses that could impress upon the political parties and others the need to keep pace with the new temporal context and depart from the traditional mindset and from caste, region and clan-based prejudices. The Maoist People's War had been especially responsible for sensitizing the underprivileged sections of society to the fact that access to power and the resources of the country had been denied to them.

The Jan Andolan of 2006 added some new features to the socio-political dynamics of Nepal. The ten-year-old Maoist insurgency movement or the People's War and the various new discourses generated by political parties, civil society groups, professionals and intellectuals have greatly enlivened the debate. A broad coalition of forces that has been able to set common goals — popular sovereignty, a federal republic, an inclusive democratic system, social justice and the emancipation of Dalits, ethnic groups, women and other deprived sections of society — could transcend such issues that were otherwise expected to be divisive for the country. The movement of 2006 had been able to forge a broad alliance of political forces, ethnic groups and others, hoping that the future order would not only be a formal democracy but it would also be transformative or revolutionary in nature. Being a controlled movement, it prevented the country from falling into the abyss of civil war. So, unlike Sri Lanka, where ethno-political conflict does not show any sign of abatement despite intermittent ceasefires and negotiations, the Nepali crisis is now over due to a variety of factors. Uyangoda has aptly summarized the difference between Nepal and Sri Lanka in these words:

> In conflicts where issues of social justice, economic redistribution or democratic reforms are central to the struggle, the popular imagination is fired by social-transformative impulses. In such conflicts, people find political bonding across class, caste, regional, and ethnic differentiations...Ethnic conflicts often mobilise people for war and violence, not for issues of social justice, political change and democratic transformation, but for goals defined by feelings of ethnic exclusivity and group separateness.[6]

Nepal's struggle for democracy was basically targeted against the exploitative nature of the state, whose power structure had forever remained unchanged. This does not mean that the upsurge of ethnic, Dalit, women's and regional agendas did not influence the people's movement. But these aspirations have now become a common cause for all parties and groups, as if for the first time in its history, Nepal has embraced integrationist trends. Ethnicity and regional aspirations are thus placed within the framework of the political agenda of a democratic Nepal. What is more significant is that given the heterogeneity of Nepal's ethnic population and its distribution, and the strong tendency of the people of Madhesh to assert their rights within the boundaries of the Nepali state, separatism in the Sri Lankan sense does not exist in Nepal. Some however argue that any concessions given to the greater ethnic and regional demands for transforming Nepal into a federal state will trigger secessionist trends. Presenting Madhesh as a flashpoint for disintegration, it is sometimes suggested that Madhesh might be created reconstituted a separate state or it may opt in favour of becoming a part of northern India. But such an assumption is preposterous given the strong Madheshi sentiment affirming national unity within the framework of diversity. The manner in which the main Madhesi parties took part in the election to the Constituent Assembly held in April 2008 and established themselves as a force to reckond with in the country has demonstrated the trends of power sharing, or what Arend Lijphart calls 'consociational democracy' in a divided society.[7]

Moreover, although Nepal's social and regional diversity does not clash with the agenda of greater democratization, all the minorities who constitute 'Nepalis' in terms of a broad national identity want to mitigate the roots of discrimination in the Nepali state. And it has now been realized by most political parties and by members of civil society, that without breaking Nepal's centralized power structure and opening up the processes of social and political inclusion, the structural discriminatory character of the state will not change.

Nepal is unique with respect to majority–minority divides, it does not mirror other South Asian countries. All the groups that constitute the state are minorities, except in terms of religion, with about 81 per cent of the population being Hindu. Buddhists constitute 10 per cent of the population, but the Hindus consider Buddhism to be an offshoot of Hinduism. Religious tolerance and syncretic cultural traditions have never allowed Nepal to become a country known for religious bigotry. It is because of this that even as Nepal became a secular state, the people in general accepted it without being swayed by a small section of society bent on whipping up religious fervour. However, the ethnic hill groups of Tibeto-Burman origin, now known as Jan Jatis, do oppose the distorted Hinduism which had been used by the Hindu rulers for the last 240 years. The Shah and Rana rulers reinforced the caste system, which enabled the Brahmins and Chhetris to be become the dominant caste groups with the passage of time, while other communities and the people of Tarai, the Madheshis became the underprivileged sections.

Nepal is a country of ethnic groups writ large because, as mentioned earlier, there is no single majority community. The National Foundation for Development of Indigenous Nationalities (NFDIN) has described Nepal as 'a multiethnic, multilingual, multicultural and multireligious country'. The Constitution of the Kingdom of Nepal, 1990 had accepted this kind of diversity. According to the Task Force on indigenous people, people who do not belong to the caste hierarchy and have no definite role in modern politics and governance but do possess a distinct cultural identity, along with their own language, culture, religion, customs, and who refer to themselves as *janjatis*, belong to the category of *janjati*. Newar was initially listed as a *janjati*, but leaders of this community opted out of this system, for

Newar is one of the more enterprising communities and its members are better placed in different professions.

There are 101 ethnic and tribal groups in Nepal, and Brahmins and Chhetris, who are now a major target of the deprived sections of society, especially the ethnic communities of the hills, for their continuous domination and discrimination, constitute only 30.89 per cent of the total population, while the other Madheshi and hill ethnic groups and Muslims constitute the remaining 70 per cent. The hill Dalit group, which is divided on the basis of occupation, forms 7.11 per cent. Like other hill caste groups, the dalits are also divided according to *gotra* and *thar*. Ethnic communities that belong to the Mongoloid group, including the 5.48 per cent Newar popular have a 28 per cent share in the total national population. The Madhese group, comprised of thirty smaller groups, makes up 15.24 per cent of the population. The Madheshi Dalits constitute eleven communities and are 3.98 per cent of the population. The Tarai (Madhesh) caste group has fifteen communities and constitutes 12.38 per cent of the national population. Among the various ethnic groups, the Muslims are 4.27 per cent of the population. In terms of gender, women constitute 50.04 per cent of the population.[8]

The pattern of representation in the various national legislatures and local bodies shows the domination of the same hill caste groups in politics as well. The composition of the lower houses of parliament in 1991, 1994 and 1999 reveals the unchanging picture of Brahmin–Chhetri domination (see Table 5.1).[9]

In 1991, the hill caste groups had 114 representatives or 55.61 per cent of the entire strength in a house of 205, followed by 34 representatives from the Kirat/Mongol ethnic groups who made up 16.59 per cent of the House, and the Madhese caste groups. How different communities that are minorities from a national demographic perspective are dispersed across the country is an interesting point that needs to be discussed. Of the 75 districts in Nepal, the Chhetris are in greater number in nine districts, and the Magars, Tharus, Tamangs, Newars and Gurungs are majority communities in fourteen districts. The hill castes and ethnic groups, are in majority in twenty-eight districts each, while the Madhese communities in eight and the Janjatis in one district are in a majority. Among the remaining ten districts, the hill and Madhese communities are in majority in three districts each and in four districts no hill and Madhese communties are in

Table 5.1: Representation of Caste/Ethnic Groups and Genders in Nepal's House of Representatives (1991, 1994 and 1999)

Caste/ethnic groups	Population	Percentage of total population	1991 No. of elected representatives and their percentage share	1994 No. of elected representatives and their percentage share	1999 No. of elected representatives and their percentage share
Hill caste groups	702,320	30.89	114 (55.61%)	129 (62.93%)	122 (59.51%)
Dalit	1,692	7.11	1 (0.48%)	–	–
Kirat/Mongol Ethnic Groups	501,131	22.04	34 (16.59%)	24 (11.71%)	28 (13.66%)
Newar	124,532	5.58	14 (6.83%)	12 (5.85%)	14 (6.83%)
Ethnic Groups of Inner Madhesh (inner Tarai)	251,117	1.11	1 (0.48%)	–	–
Madhese Castes	3,464,249	15.24	18 (8.71%)	22 (10.73%)	29 (14.15%)
Madhese Dalit	904,924	3.99	–	–	–
Madhese Ethnic Groups	2,814,927	8.11	18 (8.78%)	14 (6.83%)	10 (4.88%)
Muslim	971,056	4.27	5 (2.43%)	4 (1.59%)	2 (0.97%)
Female	11,377,556	50.04	7 (3.41%)	7 (3.41%)	12 (5.85%)
Male	11,359,378	49.96	198 (96.6%)	198 (96.6%)	193 (94.15%)

Source: Lok Raj Baral, Krishna Hachhethu and Hari Sharma, *Leadership in Nepal* (New Delhi: Adroit Publishers, 2001).

a majority.[10] As has been pointed out earlier said that 'ethnic activists in Nepal increasingly point out that a minority is running a multiethnic nation'.[11]

Nepal, however, had never felt the pressure of ethnic heterogeneity on political structures until quite recently. The country's underdevelopment, lack of political consciousness and the fear of retribution from the state might have made most of them docile. Moreover, the resurgence of the Nepalization process, through the imposition of Nepali language, dress and a political culture, that was essentially *durbari* or feudal, injected fear. And those who tried to ventilate the feeling of deprivation were misunderstood as 'communalists'. During the 1950 anti-Rana movement, and later in 1979–80 during the period of Referendum (ordered by the late King Birendra to choose between a multiparty or panchayat system [partyless] with reforms) had brought to the fore some pent up feelings of the hill ethnic groups. However, the freedom enjoyed by the people soon faded, following the result of the referendum which went against the multiparty system.

That freedom makes people fearless and allows them to spontaneously articulate their interests has been proved by two events. The Jan Andolan of 2006 not only broadened the aspirations of ethnic groups but the issue of regional disparity also came to dominate the political agenda of the country. Given that Nepal is a country of minorities, all outstanding issues concerning them constitute the core of issues related to development and democratic sustenance. The relevance of political institutions to ethnic heterogeneity and 'the effects of ethnic heterogeneity on political structures and behaviour' have led political parties, civil society and others to adopt the agenda of restructuring the Nepali state in order to bring about a qualitative change in democratic governance in the future. Therefore, the very agenda of democratization or democratic governance has been influenced by the agendas of an inclusive democracy and the empowerment of people. More the country modernizes along with a broadening of political opportunities, greater would be the scope of ethnic mobilization. However, in the given context, an ethnic agenda, if not intensified conflict, is the outcome of a regime of structural disparity perpetuated by the Nepali state.

The dynamics of modernization tend to become disintegrationist only when the state continues to rely on its coercive mechanisms, which are monopolized by the dominant castes and classes. Therefore, 'it is the failure of the dominant classes and the governments to lead the process of change towards integration on an egalitarian basis which brings about separatist reactions'.[12] Nepali power and its political elites too remained indifferent to the aspirations of the deprived sections of society till such people became assertive with the freedoms they came to enjoy in the post-1990 period. So it was not only the imperial elites of the Gorkha variety who enforced caste politics based on a patron–client relationship, the rulers and other agents of change also turned out to be embedded in the same traditional palace culture. This palace-centric psychology, however, changed with the unprecedented popular upsurge against monarchical rule as imposed by King Gyanendra on 1 February 2005. However, due credit must be given to the democratic exercises conducted during the 1991–2002 period, using which the people put up some resistance to the monarchy. Now the political parties were under pressure not to ignore the minorities and deprived sections of society. A strong demand for the empowerment of people has become the common agenda. The Maoists, who have all along been demanding the setting up of Constituent Assemblies (CA) and a republican system, are no less responsible for protecting the interests of minorities as well as for bringing about a qualitative change in the overall structure of the Nepali state. Now that all the political parties and civil society and intellectuals have also adopted this agenda, democracy is being redefined with a view to contextualizing it in keeping with Nepal's contemporary situation. Restructuring Nepal and introducing a republican order is a popular agenda. So is the empowerment of people with the drafting of a new democratic constitution by the CA.

Restructuring the State: A Comprehensive Agenda

The agenda of restructuring the state is incomprehensible to some who wonder how a country can be restructured when four elements of the state are already so well-defined. To others, it is merely the physical form against which some structures have to be adjusted in keeping with the changed context. In my opinion, the concept and spirit of this restructuring go much beyond such a narrow perspective, as this agenda embraces both new structures and the spirit of democracy. Democracy, as has been borrowed from places outside Nepal has certain universal features, however, many of the changes that need to be made to make democracy inclusive, people-centric and just, are based on Nepal's own ground realities, with which foreigners might not be completely familiar.[13]

The structural plan aims at creating a new geographically determined administrative division within the country on the basis of ethnicity, region, population distribution, etc. Different organizations and individuals have suggested various models for a carving out autonomous regions for a federal system. The Maoist model proposed nine ethnic and two territorial divisions and three sub-divisions in the Tarai, creating autonomous regions along ethnic and territorial lines. The regional autonomous units proposed by the Maoists are Kirat, Limbuwan, Kochila, Tamsaling, Newar, Tamuwan, Magarat, Tharuwan, Madhesh (with Mithila, Bhojpuri and Awadhi as sub-regions), Bheri-Karnali and Seti-Mahakali Autonomous Regions. The last two regions have a homogeneous caste make-up, thus making them non-ethnic regions. Other models have also been offered, but which of these will be practicable is not yet decided.

The distribution of the population of Nepal does not, however, fit neatly within the framework of ethnic divisions, because migrations from one place to another have resulted in a universe of diverse ethnic, caste and other types of groups. The Maoist model lacks adequate homework and the creation of ethnic and territorial regions (which refer to the Western and Far Western regions that have no significant ethnic composition) has been suggested on arbitrary grounds. In the beginning, the creation of a Kirat region was not acceptable to the Limbus because the Kiratis have numerous sub-groups or divisions while the Limbus are a more or less homogeneous community of the Far Eastern hill districts. Now, the Maoist model considers Limbuwan as a separate federal entity, while the three districts, Jhapa, Morang and Sunsari, now form the Kochila Autonomous Region. Common language, common territory, similar economic activities and a shared psychology are considered to be the rationale behind Maoist divisions. 'Caste group, on the other hand, denotes a social group that is classified by status and hierarchy (*Jat*)...ethnic groups are horizontally distributed in space while caste groups are vertically stratified by ritual status.'[14]

In the present context, restructuring implies a transformation of the feudal order that has existed in the country for the last 240 years. The CA's declaration in May 2008 of Nepal having become a republic ended the monarchy and feudalism associated with it, but many more serious actions need to be taken in the direction of making Nepal truly democratic. This would require physical re-designing, an attitudinal change among the elites and people freeing themselves from their traditional inherited mindsets, indoctrination in a participatory political culture, economic and social emancipation of the people, access for all sections of society to resources and power. This will disperse power out of Kathmandu, create regional and local institutions for realizing people's aspirations and make Nepal a well governed, just and democratic country. Making each part of the country capable of providing representative governance would also mitigate feelings of regional disparity.

The two parallel election systems — majority or first-past-the post (FPTP) and proportional representation (PR) systems — adopted for CA election have changed the representation pattern in the country considerably. Now there are mandatory provisions to ensure the participation of women, Dalits, Madheshis and ethnic groups, according to the size of their population. The majority system, with a 42 per cent share and the proportional system with a 58 per cent share in representation, have introduced a major change speaking both quantitatively and qualitatively. The CA election results made a departure by not allowing a single party to be in a majority. Although the Communist Party of Nepal (Maoist) was able to establish itself as the single largest party in the CA, no major parties, like the Nepali Congress (NC) and the Communist Party of Nepal (Unified Marxist–Leninist or CPN-UML) were able to maintain their traditional hold. On the contrary, the emergence of Madheshi parties and the Maoists has changed the political landscape. What is more interesting, even small parties with only 25,000 popular votes made in to the Constituent Assembly through the proportional representation system. Tables 5.2 and 5.3 show parties' position and the social representation pattern in the CA make substantive change in making democracy inclusive.

The CA election, based as it is on parallel systems, has put a brake on the major parties, like the Maoists, the NC and the CPN (UML), from wresting a comfortable majority of 301. The Maoist party, which had bargained heavily for the whole PR system to be accepted, suffered great losses in the PR system but was able to make a 50 per cent gain from the majority system. So the CPN (Maoist) is now stuck with 220 seats in a house of 601. The smaller parties on the other hand have made substantial gains in CA elections, thus forcing the major parties to work together and ensure *sahakarya* (co-operative action) without which the functioning of government would not

Table 5.2: Party Positions in the Constituent Assembly Election Results, 2008

S. No.	Political parties	FPTP result	PR result	Total
1	CPN (Maoist)	120	100	220
2	Nepali Congress	37	73	110
3	CPN (UML)	33	70	103
4	Madheshi People's Rights Forum	30	22	52
5	Tarai-Madhesh Democratic Party	9	11	20
6	Sadbhawana Party (Mahato)	4	5	9
7	Janamorcha Nepal	2	5	7
8	Nepal Workers and Peasants' Party	2	2	4
9	Janamorcha Nepal	1	3	4
10	Independents	2	0	2
11	Rastriya Prajatantra Party	0	8	8
12	CPN (ML)	0	8	8
13	CPN (United)	0	5	5
14	Rastriya Prajatantra Party (Nepal)	0	4	4
15	Rastriya Janashakti Party	0	3	3
16	Rastriya Janamukti Party	0	2	2
17	CPN (Unified)	0	2	2
18	Nepal Sadbhawana (Anandi Devi)	0	2	2
19	Nepali Janta Dal	0	2	2
20	Federal Democratic National Fourm	0	2	2
21	Samajbadi Prajantantrik Janata Party Nepal	0	1	1
22	Dalit Janajati Party	0	1	1
23	Nepal Pariwar Dal	0	1	1
24	Nepal Rastriya Party	0	1	1
25	Nepal Loktantrik Samajbadi Dal	0	1	1
26	Chure Bhawar Rastriya Ekata Party Nepal	0	1	1
	Total	240	335	575*

Source: http://www.election.gov.np/CAResults/reportbody.php and *Constituent Assembly* Election — 2008, Comprehensive Report (Kopundole, Lalitpur: National Election Observation Committee [NEOC], 2008).

Note: *In addition to this, 26 members were nominated by the Constituent Assembly from the various sections of society to make up the full strength of the 601-member CA.

Table 5.3: Social Representation in the Constituent Assembly, 2008

Population groups	FPTP result	PR result
Janajati (hill)	59	88
Janajati (Madhesi)	18	27
Madhesi	48	76
Muslim, Churaute	7	9
Dalit (Madhesi)	2	11
Dalit (hill)	5	29
Others (hill) Brahmin, Chhetri	101	95
Total	240	335
Women	30	160

Source: http://www.election.gov.np/CAResults/reportbody.php and *Constituent Assembly Election — 2008, Comprehensive Report.*

be possible. It is this 'consociational' or power-sharing democracy, which defies the 'winners take all' approach.

Community Rights

Community rights belong to communities — including caste groups and other members of society. These can be conceptualized as yet another form of social capital where common rights are articulated only by forging trust and co-operation among the members of a community. It is both an individual assertion of various ethnic and other group interests that try to merge into the broader community interests. Although Nepali politics continues to be uncertain due to the lack of a clear roadmap for political parties, the dichotomy that existed so far seems to have gradually changed. All the people, regardless of their ethnic and regional loyalties, have now realized that unless they make a common cause of their interests, both the nation and the communities will suffer. The democratic freedoms enjoyed by them and the vicissitudes of politics have considerably changed their cognitive domain, which in turn has had an impact on political dynamics.

Governance

Nepal's main problem obstructing development is the crisis of governance. All forms of government — monarchical, authoritarian, elected, minority or majority, coalition or single party — seem to have been affected by this. During the thirty years of monarchical rule and later in the period of elected government, no distinct change could be noticed in elite attitudes and Nepalese political culture. The outstanding issues that were needed to be urgently addressed by the new elites received only passing mention in speeches and official documents. But once the Maoists started capitalizing on the issue of discrimination, more specifically on the issues of ethnicity, caste, gender and regions, the Deuba government (of the erstwhile undivided Nepali Congress) started setting up Commissions to enquire into these questions. However, no substantive policies and programmes were introduced that could develop processes of governance in which the various social and regional groups could be included.

Since governance is a process, a certain type of institutional behaviour, elite accountability, and systematic procedures are certain preconditions that are required of it. In Nepal, there has been no institutional growth in the political and administrative set-up, as well as the police and army, because all of them have been afflicted by the traditional authoritarian political culture that has prevailed in the country for the last 240 years. Governance is based essentially on the *hukumi tantra* (peremptory command) and has no coherence or procedures that have been laid down. What is even more significant is that there existed no distinction between civil and military administration because all the top-ranking military posts were automatically occupied by members of the royal family. The people were merely mute spectators, whose influence on power and access to resources was virtually non-existent. Only Brahmins and people of the other upper castes had some advisory roles to play, using which they could get closer to the rulers.

The changes introduced by the 1990 People's Movement for the restoration of democracy could not set definite trends in the art of governance. Leaders of the opposition to did nothing to help develop institutions, ensure accountability and transparency. The educational institutions were in shambles, favouritism and nepotism continued to rule the roost, the criterion of merit and achievement were never encouraged, and the universally accepted norms of democratic governance and administration were not followed. Party splits became a routine affair, leaders and workers displayed utter normlessness in governance. As a result, there was rampant corruption in governance, along with vulgar ostentatious lifestyles being led by the people's representatives. The traditional feudal political culture thus, was not replaced by a new sense of direction and a feeling of responsibility, on the contrary, democracy turned out to be a façade, dashing all hopes of being inclusive and substantive. Although the 1990 Constitution embraced the people of Nepal as being sovereign and laid down certain guiding principles to end socio-economic disparity and ensure social justice, no such policies were implemented. On the contrary, the gap widened even more after the introduction of a multiparty system in 1990. Nevertheless, the awareness created by these democratic exercises and by Maoist insurgency cannot be underestimated. Statistics show that during the decade of multiparty rule, Nepal's development record surpassed the pace of development seen during thirty years of monarchical rule.[15]

Post-1990, Nepal has witnessed the opening up of new vistas in its democratic trajectory. Feudal remnants seem to have been given a jolt at the village and district levels because of the strong Maoist presence there. Although Nepal's political roadmap is still unclear and is full of uncertainties, there has been a convergence of major parties looking to carry forward the agendas of the new Nepal. The victory of the Maoists in the CA elections and the emergence of regional parties, especially from the Tarai region, have made other parties no less conscious of their role. All of them are working together to make Nepal a republic, by restructuring the country along federal lines, making democracy more inclusive and ensuring security and peace.

Notwithstanding all this, the overall performance of the Seven Party Alliance (SPA) government is not as impressive as it could have been. It enjoys the revolutionary mandate, all the people of Nepal, including the Maoist party, were/are behind it and even the international community has shown its readiness to be supportive in matters of political and economic development, but following the CA elections, the picture has changed, with the other parties emerging as a strong force and the Maoists becoming the single largest party in CA. How well they manage to continue their co-operative partnership in the future determine both the future of the new republic and its democratic stability.

Their unchanging mindset and penchant for petty interests have made the SPA leaders prisoners of partisan politics. Conceivably, appointments to be made for numerous posts — university authorities, the Chairman and members of the Election Commission, members of the Human Rights Commission, ambassadors for more than a dozen countries — are made on the basis of political partisanship and loyalty shown towards a particular party, thus making no basic departures from past practices. The SPA has therefore has belied the expectations of the people that they would be different actors in the new Nepal.

The Maoists also harbour the suspicion that the SPA government, led by an NC leader, seems to pursue a hide-and-seek policy because of its lack of courage and clarity of thought, and fears that the Maoists will overtake them if they accept the Maoist commitment to allowing insurgents to keep arms. The Maoists, on the other hand, believe that a political solution alone can help solve the arms issue given that their entire struggle was precisely to change the discriminatory nature of the existing Nepali state.

The Federal Republic of Nepal and the Challenges it Faces

Nepal entered a new phase of historical development on 28 May 2008. The much awaited formalization of the federal republican agenda by the first session of the newly elected CA ended the 240-year-old monarchical system. The drafting of a new democratic constitution by the CA and the abolition of monarchy effectively put an end to the leftovers of history. The dramatic turn of events that led to all this provide a lot of insights and information to us as well as to those who are directly involved. The background against which these developments are taking place confirm that any ruler who fails to read the barometer of popular opinion and continues to resist it will face consequences similar to those experienced by King Gyanendra. Full of mystery and drama, and replete with instances perfidy, treachery, deceit and sexual extravaganza, monarchy in Nepal is now history.

The rise and fall of all monarchies share certain common features despite being country-specific and contextual. Monarchies are by nature regressive in outlook and orientation. Monarchy and democracy could not go together in Nepal due to some of these factors. First, the political leaders of Nepal were novices who did not understand the ethos of palace's political culture. Nor could they read the minds of the Shah Dynasty, whose primary mission was to take back power under any pretext. King Tribhuvan, who was declared the father of nation (*Rashtrapita*) after he joined the anti-Rana movement, in a couple of years, himself turned out to be an autocrat. For their part, the leaders of political parties provided a ladder of support to the ambitious monarchs by undermining the very foundations of the democracy.

Second, regime change did not prove to be conducive to institutionalizing democratic processes in the country. All movements and changes introduced were only cosmetic, thus continuing with old practices and norms. Finally, the failure of politicians to project a good image drove the army to be closer to the King, who proved to be a better wielder of power than the politicians. Such a traditional context is now transformed, with the army switching its loyalty to become representatives of the people.

Thus, Nepali politics has undergone a sea change after Jan Andolan II (2006). How we are going to consolidate these fundamental gains is of course a different matter. Whatever the reasons, the new republic of Nepal will have to pass through yet another turbulent phase which may not necessarily be good for democratic stability if the political forces were to fail to abide by the spirit of the movement. Moreover, if the political leaders once again revert to the old game of numbers (simple and two-thirds majority) with the sole intention of upsetting the party in power, regressive forces shall raise their heads and spoil the gains made by the movement. The latest manoeuvres and counter-manoeuvres displayed by the key political players of Nepal often leave the people feeling despondent over the prospects of a successful republican order.

Yet, there is no denying that a new republic is born and it can be safely said that despite the ambivalent positions taken by some politicians in the past, events and the mood of the people have dictated them to be steady in the course of implementation. So, with the monarchy gone, what new forms and substance democracy will take in Nepal is anxiously being watched by the Nepali people as well as by the international community. Any institution, like an individual, outlives its utility if it fails to renew itself. Institutions become outdated because of their failure to be flexible, performance-oriented and dynamic. Political parties in Nepal will face the same challenges if they fail to be inclusive and democratic in their organizations. Thus, any success or failure of this new Nepal will depend on cooperation and mutual understanding among key political players. If they repeat past mistakes by falling apart and failing to stay united, Nepal may once again slip into a political abyss.

Changes that are underway in Nepal today are of a fundamental nature and will have far-reaching consequences. Never in the history of Nepal, have people involved themselves in such transformations. Minorities have staked a claim on power sharing and control over resources, as well as representation in the various organs of the state, so much so that political parties that fail to make democracy inclusive are likely to be sidelined by the people. The composition of the new CA, formed on the basis of a mixed electoral system, has made it more representative in character if not in quality, thus becoming a major departure from past patterns of representation. However, making Nepal a federal state is a process that is likely to encounter a lot of challenges, not least because of heterogeneity in the country's settlement patterns. Serious homework needs to be done to arrive at a solution acceptable to all the concerned groups of the country.

Federalism is a fait accompli in the context of today's politics, but making it practicable is going to be the major task of the Nepali Constituent Assembly.

Notes and References

1. Borrowing Andras Hofer's ideas from his book, *The Caste Hierarchy and the State in Nepal* (1979), Joanna Pfaff-Czarnecka discusses this in her article 'Debating the State of the Nation: Ethnicization of Politics in Nepal — A Position Paper', in Joanna-Czarnecka *et al.* (eds), *Ethnic Futures: The State and Identity Politics in Asia* (Delhi: Sage Publications, 1999), p. 52.

2. Sivanandan, 'Integration vs. Forced Assimilation', *The Hindu*, Delhi edition, 14 September 2006.

3. Leo E. Rose, *Nepal: Strategy for Survival* (Mumbai: Oxford University Press, 1971), p. 8.

4. See Mahesh Chandra Regmi, *Imperial Gorkha: An Account of Gorkhali Rule in Kumaun (1791–1815)* (Delhi: Adroit Publishers,1999), p. 69. This information was taken by Regmi from the Royal Nepal Army Headquarters (RNAH). On Prithvi Narayan's favouritism towards certain castes and communities (Pandes, Basnayat, Pantha, Thakuri and Magars) see Mahesh Chandra Regmi, *Kings and Political Leaders of the Gorkhali Empire 1768–1814* (Patna, 1995), p. 38.

5. Bhuwan L. Joshi and Leo E. Rose, *Democratic Innovations in Nepal: A Case Study of Political Acculturation* (Berkeley: University of California Press, 1966), p. 392.

6. Jayadeva Uyangoda, 'Dialogue among Ethnic-Nationalists?', *Economic and Political Weekly* 41(27 and 28), Mumbai, July 2006, p. 2962.

7. See Arend Lijphart, *Thinking About Democracy* (London and New York: Routledge, 2008).

8. See Shanker Pokhrel, 'Rajyako Punarsamrachana ra Jantako Sahabhagita Sawal' (Restructuring of the State and the Question of People's Participation), 10th Series of Contemporary Essays, Nepal Centre for Contemporary Studies (NCCS), July 2004.

9. For a detailed description of the pattern of representation, see Lok Raj Baral, Krishna Hachhethu, Hari Sharma and NCCS, *Leadership in Nepal: A Pilot Study* (Delhi: Adroit Publishers, 2001).

10. Krishna Khanal, *Rajyako Punarsamrachana — Ek Prastav* (Kathmandu: Nepal Centre for Contemporary Studies, May 2004), p. 6.

11. Joanna Pfaff-Czarnecka, 'Debating the State of the Nation', p. 49.

12. Manoranjan Mohanty, 'Introduction: Towards a Creative Theory of Social Transformation', in Manoranjan Mohanty, Partha Nath Mukherji

with Olle Tornquist (eds) *People's Rights, Social Movements and the State in the Third World* (Delhi: Sage Publications, 1998), p. 15.

13. See Lok Raj Baral, 'The Way Ahead: State Restructuring as an Agenda', *Himalayan Times*, Kathmandu, 23 August 2006.

14. The Task Force on the development of indigenous ethnic groups defined the various ethnic communities (*janjatis*) as those who do not fall within the caste hierarchy, have a distinct language, culture, tradition, or share a common cultural identity and location. See the interview of Om Gurung, Secretary General of Jan Jati Maha Sangh in the *Annapurna Post*, 1 September 2006. See also, Harka Gurung, Yogendra Gurung and Chhabi Lal Chidi, *Nepal Atlas of Ethnic & Caste Groups* (Kathmandu: National Foundation for Development of Indigenous Nationalities [NFDIN], 2006), p. 1.

15. See Ram Sharan Mahat, *In Defence of Democracy: Dynamics and Fault Lines of Nepal's Political Economy* (Delhi: Adroit Publishers, 2006).

6

Fighting Exclusion: Towards Understanding the Predicament of Adivasis in Bangladesh

Atiur Rahman

Introduction

Amartya Sen's *Identity and Violence: The Illusion of Destiny* (2006) brings into sharp focus the illusion of a unique identity which serves only to divide people and breed violence. Be it religious, civilizational or community-based, this 'unique identity' challenges the cherished vision of a 'shared humanity', ignoring the multiple identities around which the lives of most people are constructed and revolve. 'The uniquely partitioned world is much more divisive than the universe of plural and diverse categories that shape the world in which we live'.[1] An appreciation of the pluralities of human identity, cutting across and through each other, is at the heart of our desire for a harmonious world, which is of course, missing right now. If we are to construct a more inclusive society and avoid the ongoing violence and injustice, we also have to appreciate the mosaic of people who connect with each other through a network of relationships that compel them, irrespective of their creed, community, gender and political persuasion, to live in harmony.[2] These identities 'involve competition over resources or power, and thereby intrude into the political domain, which are likely to generate conflict'.[3]

Bangladesh also accommodates a variety of identities, some of which have been historically conflicting while others have been by-products of a myopic approach to nation-building. 'Indeed the over-emphasis on our religious identity led to the separation from the body politic of India and from West Bengal, and our association with the state of Pakistan. The second conflict, associated with our political, linguistic and cultural identity, culminated in the division of Pakistan and the creation of Bangladesh'.[4]

Given this divisive past, our founding fathers attempted to build 'a genuinely inclusive society which could democratise opportunities for the poor and dispossessed, as well as religious and ethnic minorities, who could participate equitably in the political process and share in the benefits of development'.[5] The Constitution of Bangladesh initially adopted the principles of nationalism, democracy, secularism and socialism. All this was aimed at achieving an inclusive national identity and territorial boundaries (Bengali nationalism), a political sphere (democracy), ending the politicization of communal identities (secularism) and ensuring economic opportunities for all (socialism). However, we have not been able to live up to the above ideals. Most of them have been gradually eroded, culminating in a fragmented society. Today's Bangladesh is divided along the lines of politics, gender, ethnicity and, of course, communal identities. The worst victims of this divisive experience have been the Adivasis or ethnic minorities, who have genuine reason to feel excluded from the so-called Bangladeshi identity. Besides the historical omission made by the founding fathers who provided them with a special status in the Constitution in recognition of their special concerns, earlier events, such as constructing the Kaptai Dam in the 1950s, which displaced a large number of them, the subsequent settlement of a huge number of plain-land people in the hills and the continuous dispossession of land from the Adivasis (who believe in the right to common property) have alienated them from the mainstream population of Bangladesh. The 1997 Chittagong Hill Tracts (CHT) Peace Accord, though a step in the right direction, has not been earnestly implemented. Similarly, the Adivasis of the Garo Hills and north-west Bangladesh have been further marginalized as they constitute much smaller numbers. Most of their customary land rights have been violated. The Santhals of Rajshahi division, who were at the heart of the Tebhaga Andolon, seeking protection of their traditional land rights, were brutally suppressed by the Pakistani state and were mostly forced out of erstwhile East Pakistan. Even today, the indigenous people of Bangladesh find themselves in a rather vulnerable environment, particularly with regard to their livelihood. This is recognized in public documents as well, e.g., the Poverty Reduction Strategy Papers (PRSP), chapter 5.3, indicates that the measures being taken to protect these people from insecurity, fear and dispossession are not well anchored.[6] Moreover, they are also unable to protect themselves from the processes that are worsening their social, political and economic position. They therefore face a real threat of losing their language, culture, customs, and art forms, in addition to their traditional means of livelihood. Their very survival as a community is at stake. This calls for some concrete actions on the part of the government of the day to address the specific injustices being imposed on the Adivasis. At the very least, specific measures should be taken to protect the property rights of the Adivasis and effective policies should be introduced to give them a stake in the developing economy.

The Exclusionary State: Historical Experiences

Bangladesh unfortunately has inherited the legacy of the largely ex-clusionary state of Pakistan, where identity conflicts were proactively built into the very nature of the state. Pakistan always overlooked the multiple identities of its citizens who that really make up the state. Instead, it opted for the simplistic identification of religion as the basis of its national identity. 'The emphasis on religious identity in determining the composition of the two states that emerged from imperial India placed the fate of the religious minorities left within the boundaries of the partitioned states as the first major problem to confront the two states....The political obligation to accommo-date sizeable religious minorities on both sides of the divide should have compelled both India and Pakistan to build a secular and inclusive state where religious identity was no longer part of the instru-mental dynamic of political life.'[7] The tragedy of Pakistan, and to a lesser extent of India, was their 'failure to transcend the divisive brand of inheritance of communalised politics'.[8] The impact of this divisive brand of politics was felt on the eve of the Partition of India, on both sides of the border, in the form of the first instance of ethnic cleansing in the post-War period. The massacre of religious minorities in East and West Punjab exceeded the scale of brutality witnessed in contemporary cleansing episodes in Bosnia, Ruanda and more recently, in Darfur. Minorities were forced to flee from their ances-tral homes in Punjab. A similar flow of refugees entered West Pakistan from East Punjab. Muslims from Uttar Pradesh and Bihar also joined the flow. Many of the Bihari Muslims ended up in East

Bengal. Although the two Bengals were spared the kind of large-scale ethnic cleansing that was seen in Punjab, there were nevertheless some episodes of communal violence, particularly in Kolkata and Noakhali. This once again encouraged a comparatively smaller exodus of Muslims from India and Hindus from East Bengal. Yet, in absolute terms, the dislocations were massive.

Pakistan could never come out of this religious tension and did not even make an attempt to establish a plural and inclusive society. On the contrary, its body politic thrived on this divide. However, East Pakistan, which accounted for 54 per cent of the country's population, did not cleanse itself of its religious minorities (28 per cent of its population being Hindu and 1 per cent accounted for by Buddhists and Christians during Partition).

Yet, because of the unholy alliance between the feudal elites of West Pakistan, the armed forces and the bureaucracy, which controlled power at the centre, Bengalis as a whole were excluded from Pakistan's mainstream decision-making and development processes. In addition, because of the overriding emphasis on religious identities, religious minorities, including Hindus and Christians, and various types of Adivasis were discriminated against even more. This exclusionary state of Pakistan resorted to a political process which was anti-democratic, centralized and inegalitarian for its own survival. The state never cared for popular legitimacy and opted instead for military power, coercing its citizens to accept such an exclusionary order. It also received enough external support in the form of both military assistance and development aid. The Pakistani elites plundered resources from East Bengal, monopolized external aid and suppressed democracy using the larger, shared religious identity as a facade to conceal the elitist and Punjab-centric Pakistani state. Bengalis in general and the other ethnic minorities of Pakistan thus joined hands to attain self-rule for the people of Bangladesh, passing through various phases of struggle, focusing on democracy, regional autonomy, social justice, secularism and, finally, a nationalist struggle. The exclusionary nature of the Pakistani state, built solely on the basis of religious identity, was perceived to be doomed from its very birth. The Pakistani elites emphasized religious identity in order to undermine the cultural rights of the Bengalis, and proclaiming Urdu as the state language, inspired the historic Bengali language movement of 1952. Simultaneously, they were attempting to divert attention from the assault taking place on the democratic rights of the Bengalis and their exclusion from economic opportunities.[9] The final chapter of Pakistani rule came to an end with the genocide of 1971.

The Bangladeshi state was born with a commitment to correct the injustices done to its people during Pakistani rule. It committed itself to the principles of democracy, secularism and social justice, needed to ensure that it retained its distinct national identity and its territorial integrity. However, thirty-five years of its existence as an independent state has not yet led to the desired correction of the injustices and inequalities witnessed during the Pakistani period. Instead, the people of Bangladesh have been witnessing a progressive erosion of the commitment which our founding fathers made to the nation and to the rest of the world. Bangladesh can no longer wholeheartedly claim that it has been able to build an inclusive state that democratizes opportunities for all communities and also accommodates the concerns of the socially dispossessed and the marginalized ethnic groups. 'The marginalization of our religious and ethnic minorities from all aspects of public life and economic opportunity has remained relentless over the last three decades of our national existence'.[10] Given this historical context, in what follows, we will document the vulnerabilities of the Adivasis in the exclusionary state of Bangladesh.

The Vulnerable Adivasis

The Adivasis or the so-called tribespeople of Bangladesh constitute a vulnerable community facing multiple risks and uncertainties, and finding it very difficult to sustain their distinctive ethnic identity and traditional lifestyle. Their vulnerabilities are being accentuated by the imposed modernization taking place in the guise of development (for example, the construction of eco-parks in some of the forest areas dominated by ethnic minority groups). The social discrimination suffered by them has also been phenomenal. Public documents, like the PRSP prepared by the government, also recognize this. For example, Chapter 5.3 of the document states that Adivasis have been made to 'experience a strong sense of social, political and economic exclusion, lack of recognition, fear and insecurity, loss of cultural identity and social oppression'.[11] Mainstream development efforts have mostly either ignored their concerns or had a negative impact on them.

In Bangladesh, there are at least 2.5 million people who belong to various indigenous communities or ethnic minority groups. They are commonly referred to as 'Adivasis', while the Government of Bangladesh often refers to them as 'tribals'. The latter connotation makes Adivasis feel inferior to the mainstream Bengali population. In Bangladesh there are about 49 different Adivasi communities, some living in the plains lands and some in hilly areas. They are: 1. Garo, 2. Khiang, 3. Mro/Murong, 4. Bom, 5. Chakma, 6. Chak, 7. Pankhu/Pankhua, 8. Lusai, 9. Marma/Mog, 10. Tripura, 11. Tonchonga, 12. Rakhain, 13. Khashia, 14. Monipuri, 15. Kuki, 16. Ushai, 17. Lauua, 18. Khumi, 19. Hajong, 20. Banai, 21. Koch, 22. Dalu, 23. Shantal, 24. Paharia, 25. Munda, 26. Mahato, 27. Shing, 28. Kharia, 29. Khondo, 30. Gorkha/Gurkha, 31. Pahan, 32. Rajuyar, 33. Mushar, 34. Hodi, 35. Palia, 36. Mikir, 37. Rai, 38. Bedia/Bede, 39. Bogdi, 40. Kol, 41. Rajbongshi, 42. Patro, 43. Muriar, 44. Turi, 45. Mahali, 46. Malo, 47. Khatria Barman, 48. Gondo, 49. Kachhari. Of these, 43.7 per cent were estimated to be Buddhist, 24.1 per cent were Hindu, 13.2 per cent were Christian and 19 per cent made up the miscellaneous category 'other'. However, the government maintains a record of only thirty groups, with number 30 standing for the 'others'.[12]

While the Bangladesh Adivasi Forum estimates the ethnic minority population to be 3 million, the above-mentioned PRSP document claims it is 2 million. Both sources, however, agree that Bangladesh has about forty-five Adivasi communities, living in the hill regions as well as in the plains. The largest concentration is in the Chittagong Hill Tracts. The other areas where they live include Chittagong, greater Mymensingh, greater Rajshahi, greater Sylhet, Patuakhali and Barguna.

There are significant differences in the social, political, cultural and economic status of the Chakmas, Santals and Garos, the three most important Adivasi groups. The Chakma Hill Tracts (CHT) is the only region in Bangladesh with a majority indigenous population, and the Chakmas have therefore been able to establish an extensive semi-autonomous administrative structure that has no parallel in other parts of Bangladesh. Several laws that apply to the rest of Bangladesh do not apply to the CHT, and vice versa. The indigenous people of the CHT are often referred to as the 'Jummas', and are comprised of eleven different Adivasi groups, of whom the Chakmas are the most numerous. The Garos, sometimes referred to as 'Mandis,' have been able to gain acceptance from the majority population of Bangladesh because of being better educated and organized. But they still face a number of forms of negative discrimination from the state as well as from society. Thus, to quote Inger Niemi:

[The Santhals are worst off in all aspects of education, employment and land, and are one of the poorest and most vulnerable indigenous people in Bangladesh. Santhals face discrimination from the majority community and the government of Bangladesh in the form of land grabbing, unemployment, lack of education and social insecurity.

The Santhals are the second largest indigenous group in Bangladesh and estimates of the numbers of them in Bangladesh range from 200,000 to 500,000. The government has a record of 200,000, while the NGOs and the Santhals themselves consider that number to be a gross underestimation, and believe that they are at least 450,000.[13]

Major Problems Faced by Adivasis

Of all the problems faced by the Adivasis, the dispossession of their land is certainly the most acute. While the problem is common to all the Adivasis of the country, the process of land dispossession varies from place to place. In CHT, Kaptai Dam and a number of forest projects were the key reasons for land dispossession. They also lost their lands to the fraudulent and coercive tactics of the settlers (sponsored by the Bangladesh government in 1979–80). In accordance with the 1997 CHT Peace Accord, a Land Commission has been established to provide justice in land disputes in an expeditious manner, but the Commission is yet to start its work. It cannot start because the CHT Land Commission Law of 2001 was not passed in accordance with the CHT Peace Accord of 1997. This law, therefore, needs to be amended immediately, if the Commission is to start its work in keeping with the Accord.

Panchagarh is one of the north-western districts of Bangladesh. Adivasi Santhals from the plains are scattered all over the district. Responsible for having turned vast expenses of fallow land cultivable with sheer physical labour, they now have no right to their own land simply because they are Adivasis. They have been rendered landless with indirect and direct 'help' from the administration, from influential persons and political leaders. They now get only the worst kind of jobs and the lowest wages. Mainstream Bengalis are acquiring land and other valuable assets by resorting to fraudulent means.

Santhals are learning their traditional jobs (e.g., fishing, hunting, farming, cottage industries, etc.), that had been practiced by their fathers and grandfathers. The reasons are manifold. Rivers have lost navigability and, ponds and lakes are void of fish. So they have given up fishing and now pull rickshaws and sell their physical labour on daily basis.[14]

Land dispossession in the plains is perhaps most acute in north-western Bangladesh. In numerous cases, land-grabbing was accompanied by acts of arson and murder on the part of the non-Tribal Peoples (TPs). In the same region, people have unscrupulous used the Vested Property Act[15] to seize Adivasi lands. Land-grabbing has also taken place in the southern and south-eastern coastal plains, forcing the Rakhaine people to petition the Prime Minister on several occasions to enforce the 1950 Act that restricts transfer of aboriginal lands to others. A land commission like the one set up for CHT could resolve land-related disputes in the plains as well. The government also needs to consider taking other legal measures to return illegally acquired land belonged to TPs but is now occupied by non-TPs. Such laws have been passed in states of Tripura and Kerala. Unless such measures are taken, financial difficulties, lack of confidence in court procedures and delays in litigation will continue to haunt TPs and other small landholders for many more years to come. A relevant report in this regard states:

> Patuakhali is the southern-most district of Bangladesh. Most of the Rakhaine Adivasis live in this district. Land grabbers, locally influential persons and political leaders are acquiring their land. Krasi Rakhaine (70) of Kalapara upazila reported with grief, 'You will not find any Rakhaine family who did not face problem with its land. A Rakhaine family whose neighbour is a Bangali lose some amount of land every year. Beside cultivable land Rakhaines are also deprived of their religious land of Pagoda.'[16]

Besides land dispossession, the Adivasis also have fewer opportunities in education and skill development. Illiteracy rates are very high among these communities. Since they are located in remote and dispersed areas, existing government rules regarding the setting up of schools do not address their special needs. A lack of job-related skills constrains them from entering the job market. They hardly have any access to capital, entrepreneurship and marketing facilities.

They also lack access to information and new technology. The three districts of CHT do not have mobile phone connectivity, as the necessary towers could not be built due to security concerns. This has not only denied the Adivasis day-to-day connectivity but has also constrained the growth of trade and commerce. The lack of information, in fact, has also condemned these communities to retain many prejudice, suffer ill-health, adverse nutritional conditions and bad hygiene. All this is resulting in a great degree of marginalization and also corroding the Adivasi social fabric.

For long, they have suffered serious violations of human rights, in the form of wanton killings, threats, forced migrations, population transfers, evictions and general insecurity. The government does not have any policy for the protection and development of Adivasi people and their culture. As minority groups they face endless discrimination and harassment. Their land and forests, where they lived for generations, have been taken away without their consent to build national parks, eco-parks, dams, protected areas, reserve forests, tourism, etc.[17]

The Bangladesh government plans to establish an eco-park in Moulvibazar district (near Sylhet), which will take up more than 1,500 acres of ancestral Adivasi land. This plan was initiated by the government in July 2000 without any consent from the Adivasis. In fact, the government did not even mention the Khasi and Garo villages in their project proposal. Seven hill villages will be affected by this project. Approximately 1,000 Khasi and Garo families face eviction from the lands they have been living in for thousands of years. The government has still not cancelled the eco-park project. On 3 January 2004, thousands of Garos participated in a peaceful protest rally against the eco-park project undertaken by the government in the Madhupur forest (near Mymensingh). At Jalabada, a remote village in the forest, a Garo man Piren Snal was shot dead on the spot and bullets wounded and injured twenty-five other Adivasis, including women and children, when the police and forest guards opened fire. Utpol Nokrek, a student of class ten, was shot in the leg and it is feared that he will never be able to walk again. The Garos got no justice and still face serious threats of eviction from their ancestral land.

In the name of aforestation, a project funded by the Asian Development Bank (ADB) has resulted in the planting of foreign varieties of trees in 0.3 million acres of land in different forest areas of

Bangladesh, which has caused the elimination of a wide variety of local flora and fauna. The establishment of such eco-parks is a clear threat to natural environment of Bangladesh and to the livelihoods of thousands of poor Adivasi families. However, although the government promised to provide 3–4 acres of land to each household as compensation, nobody has received that land as yet. Another report confirms this fact:

> Rani Sangma (70), a childless widow, is a resident of Telungia village in Netorkona district. She was widowed eight years back. Her husband was a day-laborer. She does not have land other than her small dwelling house. Nobody takes care of her. She produces *haria* (a kind of wine made of fermented rice) at her house and sells it at the makeshift shop in the local rural market. This is her only means of living.
>
> As she is very old , she cannot produce *haria* everyday. So, she starves very often. Rani requested the UP (local government) leaders to provide her an old-age allowance card. But she did not get it just because she is an Adivasi.[18]

The situation among Adivasi women varies from community to community and from region to region. Compared to women from the majority Bengali community, Adivasi women face fewer social restrictions. However, their inheritance laws tend to discriminate against women. Notable exceptions exist in the case of the Khasi and Mandi (Garo) people, and to a lesser extent, the Marmas. Politically speaking, most Adivasi women are quite marginalized, even among the matrilineal Khasi and Mandi groups. The literacy rates for women are far lower than men in all parts of the country. Although no separate estimates are available for the Adivasis, the 1991 Census suggests that literacy rates among women are lower even in areas with a significant Adivasi population.

Poverty is a formidable barrier for most Adivasi groups, which makes it difficult for them to improve their socio-economic status. One reason for their poverty is the very high rates of unemployment prevalent among them. As they belong to a minority community, they find it difficult to compete with the Bengali population in the job market. The population growth rate in Bangladesh is high and Adivasis are fast being pushed out of the employment market or are being engaged mostly in lowly jobs.

Lack of education is prevalent among most of the Adivasis. Without proper education, they are unable to advance in the employment market and enhance their quality of life. The major impediments in the education of the Santhals are language problems, discrimination and financial constraints. For example, only 12–14 per cent of the Santhals are literate, against 65 per cent adult literacy for the rest of the country.[19]

Government Policy towards Adivasis

While PRSP recognizes the problem and suggests various actions to correct the injustices done to the Adivasis, the Government of Bangladesh has not yet developed a comprehensive policy to uplift their condition. The Constitution of Bangladesh outlaws discrimination on grounds of race, religion and place of birth (Article 28) and provides scope for affirmative action ('positive discrimination') in favour of the 'backward section of citizens' (Articles 28 and 29). Following these provisions, a small percentage of public sector jobs and seats in a number of state-run educational institutions have been reserved for Adivasis. In addition, there are some specific laws that contain references to Adivasis. In the plains, the only such law is Section 97 of the East Bengal State Acquisition and Tenancy Act, 1950, which forbids the transfer of lands owned by 'aboriginals' to non-aboriginal persons without the expressed consent of the government's district officer. The CHT, in contrast, has a far larger body of laws that refer sdirectly to Adivasi people. Some of these laws recognize Adivasi people's customs regarding the ownership and use of land and other natural resources. The most important of these laws is the CHT Regulation of 1900. Other laws include the Hill District Council Acts of 1989 and the CHT Regional Council Act of 1998. The last two laws mentioned were passed after the signing of the 'peace' accord of 1997, which ended more than twenty years of armed conflict and provided a framework for the recognition and strengthening of the CHT self-government system. However, many provisions of the accord are yet to be implemented, especially with regard to the transfer of powers to the regional and district councils, resolution of land disputes by a Commission on Land, demilitarization of the region, holding of elections to district and regional councils with permanent resident voters, rehabilitation of refugees and internally displaced people, etc.

From 1919 to 1964, the special administrative status of the CHT was constitutionally recognized, but an amendment to the Constitution in 1964 repealed the 'tribal area' status of the CHT, and it has not been revived since then, despite repeated demands from the region's leaders. Various parts of the Mandi-inhabited Mymensingh district were also regarded as specially administered, 'partially excluded' areas up to 1962. This status too has not been revived. In 1972, the late M.N. Larma demanded constitutional recognition for the Adivasis of the country. His demands are still being strongly echoed by Adivasi groups and progressive sections of Bengali civil society. However, most of these demands are yet to be fulfilled despite the signing of the Peace Accord.

As the Adivasis of CHT struggle for justice, the Bangladeshi government is under pressure to withdraw security forces from the region, end the culture of impunity, return lands to the indigenous people, assure indigenous people access to the full spectrum of human rights, and deliver on the promises of the 1997 Peace Accord.

In 1972, Bangladesh signed the International Labour Organization (ILO) Convention on Indigenous and Tribal Populations, 1957 (no. 107), which is the first international law concerning the protection and integration of indigenous and other tribal and semi-tribal populations in independent countries. The law recognizes the rights of ownership — collective or individual — over lands which the populations concerned have traditionally occupied. However, this law is not being implemented in Bangladesh and the government has also failed to sign the successor to ILO Convention No. 107, which is ILO Convention No. 169. This clearly demonstrates the lack of interest and consideration for the Adivasi population on the part of the government. The Government of Bangladesh often does not understand the fact that the Adivasis have a traditional right to the land; consequently, they are indirectly taking part in the land alienation process by not enforcing the laws and protecting the Adivasis.

Budgetary Policies and Programmes

Most of the Adivasi groups in the country are indeed poor. They do not have even a formal record of their own lands. Influential local Bengalis force them to transfer their land. Those who purchase their land offer them lower prices. The size of the Adivasi population provided in the Population Census of 1991 is also controversial. According to the Census, the population of the twenty-nine listed Adivasi groups has been estimated to have a strength of only around 1.2 million. However, Adivasis are not satisfied with this figure. They claim that the number of small ethnic groups is in fact thirty-nine and by the year 2005 their numbers had reached 3 million. The Population Census of 2001 does not even provide the numbers of the Adivasi population. This is one way of ignoring them from budgetary policies and initiating any pragmatic policies and programmes directed towards alleviating their miseries.

Budgetary allocations have been too meagre to address Adivasi needs and aspirations. Only a negligible number of projects have been initiated over the last five years that have had a direct impact on reducing poverty. The other projects are concerned with establishing cultural institutions for them and are not directed at addressing their overwhelming financial miseries. Lack of employment opportunities, conerns regarding safety and security, the absence of roads and other social infrastructure are some of the many problems that have emerged over the years and are causing them to remain increasingly vulnerable.

Budgetary allocations for Adivasis are been increasing, but without any substantive change in quality and quantity. Per capita allocation hovered between 1 and 3 US dollars since the fiscal year of 2002. But without reducing the pervasive poverty prevalent among the Adivasis the overall poverty reduction strategy will remain overambitious. The special needs of marginalized Adivasis in terms of poverty alleviation, fulfilling the fundamental human rights guarantees and attaining social progress will have to be addressed as a special priority by the state. Immediate attention has to be given to the following areas:[20]

- Creating adequate and appropriate employment opportunities for Adivasis.
- Constructing roads and bridges for transport in all seasons.
- Initiating land administration reform measures to maintain an appropriate record of their lands.
- Establishing health centres/hospitals in the vicinity of their houses and adequate presence physicians and medicines.
- Allocating *khas* (government) land and sanctioning housing loans for those who do not have their own houses.
- Widening of credit facilities.

Conclusions

Adivasis add to the interesting diversity of Bangaldeshi's plural national identity. If we do not want to fall into the trap of Pakistan's single identity based only on religion, then there is an imperative to invest more in these ethnic minorities. In order to improve their condition, there has to be an effective recognition of these communities and the government must address their special needs. The lands taken away from the Adivasis must be returned to them. Full implementation of the CHT Peace Accord must be made effective without any further delay. The government must commit itself to action for the protection of the rights of Adivasis, particularly their rights to land and forests. The 'Land Disputes Regulation Commission' and 'CHT Refugees Task Force' should immediately be made fully operational. Representatives from the Adivasi community should be included in all development activities that affect their lives and livelihoods. Special efforts should be made to provide them with education, develop their skills, provide health-care and IT connectivity, encourage NGO involvement, ensure environmental protection, human rights protection, electrification, telecommunications, etc. The useful lessons already learned from the experiences of accommodation of Adivasis, for example, in China, India, Denmark, Norway, New Zealand, and Australia should be put to use in Bangladesh after making the necessary changes to suite this context.

We must work hard to retain our multiple identities and create a sociopolitical and economic environment where, 'a Hindu, Christan, Chakma or Santhal woman from a working-class background should be able to aspire to become a High Court Judge, Foreign or Finance secretary, president of FBCCI, rise to leadership positions in major political parties, be elected to parliament from constituencies dominated by Muslim votes and aspire to a senior position if her party wins the election'.[21]

To address this issue, NGOs and other civil society organizations must work on building awareness and include Adivasis in their decision-making bodies, while the Government of Bangladesh must adopt a pro-indigenous policy. However, these steps will not be completely effective until the Adivasis themselves become united and organized.

The Constitution of Bangladesh has a number of provisions looking to enhance the rights of Adivasis and ensure equality of all groups of people. Article 27 of the Constitution states, 'All citizens are equal before law and are entitled to equal protection of law'. Moreover, Article 28 (1) states, 'The State shall not discriminate against any citizen on grounds only of religion, race, caste, sex or place of birth'; (2) 'Women shall have equal rights with men in all spheres of the State and of Public life'; (3) 'No citizen shall, on grounds only of religion, race, caste, sex or place of birth be subjected to any disability, liability, restriction or condition with regard to access to any place of public entertainment or resort, or admission to any educational institution'; and (4) 'Nothing in this article shall prevent the State from making special provision in favour of women or children or for the advancement of any backward section of citizens'. On the other hand, Article 29 (1) states, 'There shall be equality of opportunity for all citizens in respect of employment or office in the service of the Republic'and (2) 'No citizen shall, on grounds only of religion, race, caste, sex or place of birth, be ineligible for, or discriminated against in respect of, any employment or office in the service of Republic'. The Government of Bangladesh must carry out its constitutional obligations towards all people, without discrimination, for the socio-economic advancement of backward groups and uphold the right of Adivasis to live as human beings and as citizens of the country.

The degree of success met in improving the living conditions of the Adivasis depends on the extent to which they are involved in the formulation and implementation of the programmes. If they were to be directly involved in all the processes of development, it would certainly have the desired impact. Finally, the Government of Bangladesh has to come forward and end the many injustices committed towards Adivasis. In order for their socio-economic status to improve, the government must adopt a pro-Adivasi policy, educate them and formally recognize them in the Constitution of the republic. Moreover, all other provisions regarding equality and non-discrimination already given in the Constitution should be implemented so that Adivasis too have their rightful demands fulfilled.

Notes and References

1. Amartya Sen, *Identity and Violence: The Illusion of Destiny* (London: Allen Lane, 2006), p. xiv.
2. Rehman Sobhan, 'Identity and Inclusion in the Construction of a Democratic Society in Bangladesh', *Barrister Syed Ishtiaq Ahmed Memorial Lecture 2006*, organized by the Asiatic Society of Bangladesh, Dhaka, 12 July 2006, p. 5.
3. Ibid.
4. Ibid.
5. Ibid., p. 6.
6. General Economic Division, *Unlocking the Potential: National Strategy for Accelerated Poverty Reduction* (Dhaka: Planning Commission, Govt. of Bangladesh, October 2005).
7. Sobhan, 'Identity and Inclusion', pp. 7–9.
8. Ibid.
9. See Atiur Rahman and Mahfuz Kabir, ' State, Language and Culture Modern Period', in E. Ahmed and H. Rashid (eds), *State and Culture*, Cultural Survey of Bangladesh Series — 3 (Dhaka: Asiatic Society of Bangladesh), pp. 220–37.
10. Ibid., p. 16.
11. General Economic Division, *Unlocking the Potential*, p. 152.
12. Inger Lise Niemi, *Improving the Status of the Santals in Bangladesh* (Dhaka: American International School, 2005).
13. 'Santhals get worst jobs, lowest wages', *Prantaswar (Voice of the Marginalized)* 3 (1), Shamunnay, Dhaka, February 2007.
14. Ibid.
15. The Vested Property Act was a controversial law in Bangladesh that allowed the government to confiscate property from individuals deemed to be enemies of the state. Before Independence, it was known as the Enemy Property Act, and is still referred to as such in common parlance. The act has been criticized for being a tool used for appropriating the lands of the minority populations. In 2001, erstwhile Prime Minister Sheikh Hasina and the ruling Awami League succeeded in their drive to repeal this act. In its place, the Vested Properties Return Act (2001) was implemented, in an effort to make amends for the confiscated property.
16. 'Bengali neighbours grab land every year', *Prantaswar (Voice of the Marginalized)* 3 (1), Shamunnay, Dhaka, February 2007.
17. Atiur Rahman and Dilruba Yasmin Chowdhury, *Need for Budget of the Marginalised towards Attaining the MDGs* (Dhaka: Shamunnay, 2005).

18. 'Rani wants an old-age allowance card', *Prantaswar (Voice of the Marginalized)* 3 (1), Shamunnay, Dhaka, February 2007.
19. Niemi, *Improving the Status of the Santals in Bangladesh*.
20. Ibid.
21. Sobhan, 'Identity and Inclusion', p. 27.

7

Non-Muslims in an Islamic Republic: Religious Minorities in Pakistan

Maneesha Tikekar

Minorities are groups of people who share common ethnic, racial or religious backgrounds and constitute a comparatively small proportion of a given population. They often have fewer rights and less power than majority groups. In a heterogeneous or plural society, cultural and class differences between various groups of population can become more pronounced, causing inequalities among groups, that are strengthened through policies of overt or subtle discrimination. Majorities and minorities clash throughout the world over myriad issues like language and cultural rights, religious freedom, political representation, power sharing and even interpretation of history. In extreme cases, minorities become 'self-determining' and even seek to redraw state boundaries, as in the case of Kurds living in Iran, Iraq and Turkey or Sri Lankan Tamils or Kashmiris in the vale of Kashmir. Minority status of a group is not necessarily determined by its numerical disadvantage alone. An undersized group may not inevitably experience political, social economic or even cultural discrimination say like the Jews in America or the Parsis in India, while a sizable minority may continuously feel threatened; and of course there are majorities who suffer from an imaginary, perceived or real persecution complex and acquire a 'siege' mentality like the *Hindutvavadis* in India. What is crucial in the constitution of a minority is the self-perception of the group as a minority vis-à-vis other groups in society. A minority consciousness develops when a group experiences disadvantages and continuously suffers from discriminatory or antagonistic treatment. In this context the role of the nation-state becomes quite vital and central.

A community of people begins to perceive itself as a minority when it feels disadvantaged in the context of the nation-state; and the claim for minority rights gets strengthened when a case of discrimination is convincingly made. It has been generally observed that nation-states tend to acquire a majoritarian character irrespective of their underlying philosophies or constitutional provisions. Persecution of minorities stems from a belief that the nation-state should be homogeneous. Every deviation from 'that' ideal homogeneous nation is considered an interpolation that has to be removed by all means. The Nazis epitomized this thinking to an extreme. The formation of the minority through such a process is integral to politics and the exercise of power, regardless of the system in which it is practised. Minorities in this sense are a political construct.

Minority groups have acquired political significance in the contemporary world because of their status and political actions. Their political significance is determined by the following two criteria. The group collectively suffers from systematic discriminatory treatment vis-à-vis other groups in the society, which becomes the basis for political mobilization and collective action in defence or promotion of its self-defined interests. Minority groups are therefore identity groups, and the possible bases of identity include shared language, religion, national or racial origin, common cultural practices, and attachment to a particular territory. Most communal identity groups also share a common history, or myths of shared experiences, which often include their victimization by others. However, none of these is essential to group identity. Fundamentally what matters is the belief by people who share some common traits that these traits set them apart from others in ways that justify their separate status and treatment.

Though minorities are constituted in the context of a nation-state, their struggles for protection of rights and self-esteem have international ramifications. Kofi Annan, former Secretary-General of the United Nations, while presenting his Millennium Report[1] on 3 April 2000, acknowledged the growing interest in tackling issues affecting minorities worldwide. He spoke of this growing awareness and in doing so conceded that the principles of the United Nations Charter may be strengthened by meeting the legitimate interests of national or ethnic, religious and linguistic groups and emphasized that minority rights were being increasingly recognized as integral to the United Nations' work for the promotion and protection of human rights, sustainable human development, peace and security.

The growing international concern about rights of minorities was evident in the adoption of the Declaration on the Rights of Persons Belonging to National or Ethnic, Religious and Linguistic Minorities by the UN General Assembly in 1992, and in the establishment of the United Nations Working Group on Minorities in 1995. But even before that, the International Covenant on Civil and Political Rights adopted in 1966 had laid down that in those states where there exist ethnic, religious or linguistic minorities, persons belonging to such minorities shall not be denied the right, in community with the other members of their group, to enjoy their own culture, to profess and practice their own religion, or to use their own language; and a UN report had insisted on the need for adoption of special measures to protect minority cultures as a fundamental human right.[2]

Resolving disputes between minorities and majorities, which have been rampant in Eastern Europe and in developing countries, has been one of the greatest challenges faced by contemporary democracies. In the West, disputes have raged over the rights of immigrants, indigenous people and other cultural minorities. Yet, for long political theory remained indifferent to the treatment of these issues, until only recently, observes Kymlicka.[3] In recent years though, the growing academic concern about minorities and their status worldwide is well represented by the mega project Minorities At Risk (MAR) undertaken by the Center for International Development and Conflict Management, University of Maryland, founded by Ted Gurr.[4] The Project monitors and analyzes the status and conflicts of politically-active communal groups in all countries with a population of at least 500,000. It is interested in monitoring the persecution and mobilization of ethnic groups worldwide and maintains data on 284 politically-active ethnic groups.

While the 1960s witnessed a debate on identity politics beginning in the US with the emergence of political movements such as feminism, black civil rights, and the American–Indian movement based on claims about injustice done to certain social groups, its genesis could be traced back to the development of a 'general intellectual tendency' towards pluralism in the 1920s which rejected the notion of 'cultural homogeneity' in American politics.[5] Britain entered into the debate on identity politics in the context of immigration and multiculturalism; developing countries or the new nation-states were confronting the issue of the status of minorities. The works of John Rawls in the early 1970s[6] and on the liberal–communitarian controversy of later years, in which the argument focused on 'how to accommodate cultural and ethnic claims into broadly liberal political theory', sharpened the ongoing debates. They involved discussions on Western liberal values in relation to non-Western traditions, minorities and immigrants.

In political theory, these debates have tended to concentrate on the socio-political implications of such concerns for liberal democratic nation-states. Recent developments in political theory have been preoccupied with discussions on the actual and potential consequences of religion-based, ethnic and ethno-national claims for modern nation-states. These discussions have ranged from orthodox defences of liberalism and liberal democracy, to alternative communitarian, consociational, conceptions of the nation-state. Questions of ethnicity, nationalism and identity politics have been explored in relation to basic normative concepts such as equality, liberty, democracy and justice.[7] Liberal political theory for long had concentrated on the individual and the state, and the relationship between the two. Vernon Van Dyke finds this 'individualistic paradigm' with its excessive concentration on individual rights as 'inadequate' and advocates the adoption of more 'complex paradigm of individual and group rights, both legal and moral, to exist side by side'.[8] Walzer makes an insightful comment about liberalism: liberal writers acknowledged plurality of interests, not plurality of cultures. Thus, contemporary political theory fiercely debates notions of group rights, cultural rights of communities and community rights as moral rights.[9]

Notions of identity politics and minority rights are unacceptable to classical liberal theory and the resultant ideas of democracy and rights, as these notions betray the idea of 'universal man' and therefore universal human rights. Liberal critics believe that group-based demands celebrate the difference. 'They are not', comments Akeel Bilgrami, 'for inclusion within the fold of "universal humankind" on the basis of shared human attributes; nor is it for respect "in spite of" one's differences. Rather what is demanded is respect for oneself *as* different'.[10] In the social ontology of liberal political theory, citizens were seen as similar individuals divested of specific identities or affiliations. Their associations were expected to be in the form of interests shared voluntarily and not guided by primordialism. Therefore, the guiding principle of liberalism has been integration or assimilation, which in practice meant that the minorities would have to conform to the culture and identity of the majority. What the liberals termed 'integration' was seen by minorities as their subordination, discrimination, oppression and eventually a near extinction of their language and culture.[11]

Social theory has been dominated by a constructivist approach towards group identities, which rejects any one-dimensional and compact notion of groups, emphasizes the complex and cross-cutting identities at play in the post-modern world and articulates and explores the consequences of a more fluid politics of identity and representation. These debates also include anthropological discussions of culture and ethnicity, highlighting 'the complex, and at times constructed and contradictory interconnections' between various identity claims.[12]

Minorities broadly make three types of demands on the state: political, cultural and psychological. Political demands are about just representation, devolution of power and self-determination; then there are demands for the accommodation of the distinct variety of cultural practices in the larger state, and demands that pertain to the issue of collective esteem, which may include protection of language, sociocultural practices sanctioned by religion, and certain symbols of distinctness.[13] Identity conflicts and disputes over minority rights are difficult to resolve. Majorities often tend to view minorities as 'evil' opponents, as outsiders or foreigners, out to dismember their precious possession — the nation-state. Even apparently innocuous demands of the minorities are ignored and brushed aside in the very first go for the fear of directly or indirectly encouraging 'secession'. Plural and multicultural societies face some inherent challenges in majority– minority relationships. The most formidable one is perhaps the challenge of 'curing' the majorities' xenophobic fear of minorities. At the political level, the challenge is of implementing democratic norms and constitutional provisions; at the local administrative levels and at the social level, it exists in promoting the consciousness of minority rights, and their history and culture — as part of a larger common national history and system of values.

A reference is made above to the nation-state striving towards homogeneity. T.K. Oommen's argument about this aspect of a nation-state is worth noting. Starting with the Treaty of Westphalia, 1648, which inexorably linked nation and state, Oommen writes, 'the state is inherently uncomfortable with the notion of cultural diversity and is prone to label and count citizens; the lesser the number of social categories the more comfortable the state is. In order to be comprehended by the state the sociocultural world had to be standardised and simplified; the idea of single "uniform homogenous citizenship" had to be created. Consequently the single most important project of nation-state was, and continues to be, homogenization. In this respect, the state's tendency to homogenize minorities is particularly evident'.[14] While the orientation of the nation is against the homogenizing orientation of the state, because nation is essentially diversifying, it has a tendency to differentiate one community from the rest. Nation-states are zealous about protecting their sovereignty. Therefore, despite the growing concern about minorities and their rights, international law does little to permit intervention in the internal affairs of states on behalf of the minorities.

It is with reference to the above conceptual framework and in the context of the South Asian situation that this article will attempt to analyze the situation of religious minorities in Pakistan. The practice and protection of the rights of minorities is largely determined by the nature and quality of governance. This, in turn, is a result of the manner in which a state envisions itself and articulates state ideology, the way power is distributed in the polity and the specific policies undertaken by the state from time to time. Therefore, apart from documenting exploitation, oppression and the denial of rights to minorities in Pakistan, the present article will provide an overview of the sociopolitical milieu in which they live; will look into the manner in which state of Pakistan has been envisioned through constitutional provisions; the politics of Islam and the resultant Islamization of the country; the system of Separate Electorates which now stands revoked; and the infamous Blasphemy Laws which have together contributed to making the life of non-Muslims in Pakistan difficult.

The South Asian Backdrop

Minorities in South Asia have been for centuries, and increasingly, exploited, oppressed and in some cases even persecuted. Overt and subtle infringement of minority rights is common in the region, notwithstanding the unequivocal promises made through constitutional provisions for the protection of their rights by every state in the region. Yet, historically speaking, the notion of minorities was alien to this immensely diverse region with a great many ethnic, religious, cultural and linguistic groups. By and large, the multiplicity of cultural and religious groups existing side-by-side had a commonly shared daily life that was rooted in mutual respect and accommodation and an unconscious sharing of customs irrespective of individual religious dictates. It is common knowledge that the colonial administration through its procedures of organizing and managing this great diversity and through the manipulation of socially distinct groups, notably religious groups, created social divisions out of social diversity. Social markers got converted to identities. The census procedures counted, classified and labelled people; personal laws of religious communities were formally protected; weaker sections of the society were provided a sort of corporate identity under the categorization of scheduled castes and scheduled tribes and provided reservations in local bodies; the introduction of separate electorates embittered relations between the two major communities, Hindus and Muslims, in the Indian sub-continent.

The Partition of India, contrary to expectations, did little to improve their relations. The introduction of a democracy and the system of elections, however restricted, and the spread of education albeit slow, made social groups aware of their numerical strength; majorities and minorities were not merely political terms but also, and emphatically so, communal. This helped internal consolidation within communities which till then had been loosely structured. I.A. Rehman, Director Human Rights Commission of Pakistan, makes an apt comment about state formation in the region in his paper 'Minorities in South Asia' (2003). He observes that at the time of independence, South Asian states were considerably influenced by two international discourses; one, on self-determination and the other, on human rights. While the former had a strong appeal for majorities (communal), the minorities were swayed by the latter and became aggressive about defending their identities. He holds several factors responsible for the plight of minorities in the region. Among them are: the continuation of colonial patriarchal state structures; centralized state structures envisaged by constitutions that effectively exclude minority groups; theoretical safeguards for minorities without adequate guarantees of their enforcement; economic discrimination against minority groups that perpetuate their primary social affiliations and accentuate their feelings of hurt at real or perceived discrimination; ineffective policies of national integration; and political manipulation of religion. One more factor that impinges on minority conditions in the region, especially in the states of India, Pakistan and Bangladesh is the principle of reciprocity. It has been a dominant principle after 1947, which influenced the treatment of minorities in these states. The treatment of minorities in one country finds resonance in another.[15] The extra territorial identity attributed to the Hindus and Muslims from Bangladesh and Pakistan, and India respectively on the basis of religious belonging often leads to reprisals against minorities and their institutions.

In his book *Democracy in Plural Societies*, published in 1982, Arend Lijphart propounded the concept of 'consociational democracy' to explain the mechanisms of political stability in societies with deep social cleavages. His fundamental assumption is that the stakes of politics are usually much higher in plural societies, than in homogeneous societies; therefore a 'grand coalition' of elites is crucial for the success of democracy in such societies as against government versus opposition pattern in 'majoritarian' democracy. For him, the consociational model implies a national pact for power sharing through the empowerment of minorities. But South Asian states, which are not nation-states in the strict sense of the term but could be described as 'composite nation-states'[16] or better still 'state-nations',[17] opted for a majoritarian model with constitutional guarantees of minority rights that have not been adequate to protect their interests. Over the years, although coalition governments have become the norm in the region, coalition building has usually resulted in the creation of a minimum winning coalition, assuring the victory of a certain political party and eventually leading to the creation of a majority in the legislature.

Minorities in Pakistan

Despite the ethnic and linguistic plurality of Pakistan, its communal profile is 'over tilted'. It is communally a monolithic society, where Muslims constitute 96 per cent of the population, of which 77 per cent are Sunnis and 20 per cent Shias. Religious minorities in Pakistan are a little over 3 per cent of the population that prominently includes Christians (1.58 per cent) and Hindus (1.60 per cent). Of the Hindus, 70–75 per cent are said to be Dalits,[18] but Pakistan government's statistics shows them to be 0.25 per cent of the total population. Sikhs are a small community but important for political reasons. Ahmadis or Qadianis, or Lahoris (a newly 'created' minority) are 0.22 per cent. Other minority groups are Parsis, Buddhists and Bahais, and tribals, like the Kalash and Chitralis in the northern parts of the country. The overwhelming majority of the Muslim population and the constant projection of Pakistan's Islamic identity underplay its diversity.

The claim that religious minorities in Pakistan (anyone non-Sunni) get a fair treatment by the government and other institutions has always been highly suspect. It is also claimed that communal conflicts are so sporadic that they can even be called rare. This is true because communal riots normally take place when the minorities *qua* minorities are numerically strong. In the context of the dominant rule of a religious or ethnic majority, miniscule minorities prefer to lead an self-effacing existence.

This is more true of Hindus than Christians in Pakistan. Minorities in Pakistan suffer from physical attacks, social stigmatization, psychological insecurity and economic marginalization. Hindus are found largely in the interior of Sindh, in Karachi and Hyderabad and in the vicinity of Quetta in Baluchistan. Apart from urban Hindus who are educated and in professions like teaching and medicine, the majority of them are poor, uneducated and perform menial jobs. But, within the Hindu community, charges of discrimination and marginalization are levelled by Dalits against the upper caste Hindus who constitute a still smaller group. Dalits complain of 'many forms of untouchability, caste discrimination, human inequality and humiliation from the caste Hindus and Muslims as well', being deprived of their due share in government schemes because the benefits go to upper caste Hindus, and of their poor political representation. In village schools, Dalit students routinely face discrimination and are prohibited from using utensils that are used by other students and are often treated badly by Muslim teachers and students also.[19] Pirbhu Lal Satyani, author of *Hamey Bhi Jeeney Do: Pakistan Mai Acchoot Logon ki Suratehal* ('Let us Also Live: The Situation of the Untouchables in Pakistan') offers a vivid picture of the predicament of Dalits in Pakistan. Dalit women are often gang-raped, murdered or are forced to convert to Islam, but no action is taken against the perpetrators of such heinous crimes. 'Upper' caste Hindu landlords and businessmen in Sindh, writes Satyani, show little concern for the plight of Dalits and, instead, they are often seen as being complicit with Muslim feudal lords, in oppressing them. Due to discrimination by 'upper' caste Hindus, many Dalits have voluntarily converted to Islam or Christianity.[20] Human Rights Commission of Pakistan routinely draws attention to the kidnapping of Hindu girls and their forced conversion to Islam.[21]

Hindus are an almost non-visible community in Pakistan; they lead a low-profile life and normally, as a group, do not incur the wrath of the majority community. This is also because it is necessary for Pakistan to showcase its minority Hindus to the world. To say that the problems of Pakistani Hindus are directly related to the Indo-Pak discord due to the communalization of relations between India and Pakistan is to state the obvious. Whenever hostilities between the two countries mount or communal tensions in India escalate, Hindu women in Pakistan suffer atrocities and temples are desecrated. However, it must be noted that the communal carnage that took place in Gujarat, India, in 2002, in which hundreds of Muslims were killed, hardly provoked any anti-Hindu reaction in Pakistan.[22]

Majority of Pakistani Christians live in the Punjab and are scattered in cities like Hyderabad, Karachi, Peshawar, Rawalpindi and Quetta. Christians are a visible community as they are active in the education and health sectors. Interestingly, Pakistani Christians appear to be protesting against the revocation of the Separate Electorate System in 2002. A Memorandum on Election System and Religious Freedom issues of Christians in Pakistan presented by Pakistan Christian Congress to His Holiness Pope Benedict in 2007 argues that since 2002 the incidents of persecution of Christians have escalated. 'Priests have been shot dead, pastors have been brutally murdered, Christian women have been raped, elders have been harassed, churches have been desecrated, worshipers have been martyred, hospitals and schools have been attacked.... The construction of roads, streets walks, drainage system and electric facilities changed the shape of Christian slum areas from 1985 to 2000 during practice of separate elections in Pakistan'.[23] The Memorandum claims that Christians in Pakistan are 'second class citizens' who live below the poverty line. In rural areas, they perform farm labour under Muslim landlords and in urban areas they work mostly as sanitary workers in municipal corporations. 'The Muslim majority hates to eat and drink with Christians and treats them as untouchables.' Curiously enough, according to the Memorandum Pakistani Christians are now demanding 'Dual voting rights with

Separate Electorates'. They are demanding the revival of Separate Electorates that had invited considerable flak not only from the minorities but even from liberal elements in the majority community and had become a matter of debate at international forums as observed below. They argue that joint elections have completely silenced legislative representatives from the community. Human rights activist Hina Jillani says Hindus and Christians in Pakistan are looked down upon. 'That is why they have to take up inferior jobs; their chances of rising in any field is (sic) low.'[24]

Sikhs are found mostly in Punjab and a small number in the NWFP and tribal areas. It appears that the historical antagonism and a sharp divide between the Sikhs and Muslims since the days of partition have been firmly put behind and the Pakistani government has adopted a policy of cajoling the Sikhs. The Wagah border checkpost is opened for Indian Sikhs to cross into Pakistan for the annual Nankana Sahib pilgrimage, and the Pakistan government is interested in inviting investments from Sikhs residing in other countries.[25] Minorities in Pakistan are allowed to sit in all examinations, including the one conducted by the Inter Services Selection Board (ISSB), but neither a Hindu nor a Sikh has ever been selected for army service ever since the country's inception. Christians, however, have served in the army. In December 2005, a Sikh youth, Harcharan Singh of Nankana Sahib, became the first Pakistani Sikh in the country's 58-year history to have been commissioned in the Pakistan Army as an Officer.[26] Sikhs have been less vulnerable to a Muslim backlash compared to Christians and Hindus because, reasons Iftikhar Malik, they are not perceived as posing any social, religious or economic threat to others; and the lay Muslim's view of them being anti-Hindu allows a bit more space.

Concentrated in Karachi, but also present in Lahore, is a small community of Zoroastrians or Parsis who maintain a low profile, are well educated, and are mostly engaged in business and industry. This is also true of the Bahais, who are primarily part of the middle class and engaged intellectual professions. The well-known Parsi writer Bapsi Sidhwa, originally from Pakistan and now an American citizen, in an interview in 2002, claimed that as a community in Pakistan, 'we were not interfered with and we have prospered'.[27] This could be perhaps because of 'their strong commercial links and non evangelical nature of their faith'.[28]

According to Sidhwa's estimate presently there are about 3,500 Parsis in Pakistan. Though there are references to Parsis in Sindh from almost a thousand years ago, their influx into Karachi increased after the British takeover of Sindh in the mid-nineteenth century. Parsi contributions to Karachi could hardly be overestimated. In the twentieth century, the Parsis of Karachi continued to prosper and enrich the city with their philanthropy, by establishing schools, dispensaries and hospitals, restaurants and hotels. The community also gave Karachi one of its most distinguished icons, Jamshed Nusserwanjee Mehta, who had the unique distinction of being elected the Mayor of Karachi for twelve consecutive years in the earlier part of the century. He is fondly remembered even today as the 'Maker of Modern Karachi'.[29] A very interesting account of Parsis in Quetta, capital of Baluchistan, is available on the internet, which traces a brief history of Parsis in the city, who arrived from India as a part of the convoy of Charles Napier in the mid-nineteenth century. The anonymous author of the article writes about the 'magical life' that Quetta Parsis, who numbered 350–500 in the first decade of the twentieth century, have lived in the city. Most Parsis then worked in the various departments of the British Army, civil services and railways. In 2006, when the article was posted on the net, Quetta's Parsi Colony had precisely seven homes, with two outside it; the total Parsi population being seventeen.[30]

It is not surprising that the Jews are a forgotten and yet despised community in Pakistan. At the beginning of the twentieth century Karachi hosted a 2,500-strong community of Jews — Marathi-speaking Bene Israelis — who had migrated from the coastal regions of Bombay Presidency and were engaged in trade, crafts and civil service. There was also a Jewish community in Peshawar. The creation of Israel in 1948 proved to be a defining moment for Pakistani Jews. The synagogue in Karachi was set on fire and the Jews of the city bore the brunt of the Pakistani public's ire.The Arab–Israel wars of 1956 and 1967 resulted in further persecution of Jews, prompting large-scale immigration to India, Israel and the UK. The small Jewish community in Peshawar had ceased to exist by then. By 1968, Jews in Karachi were reduced to a small number of 250. In the 1980s, the city's growing religious intolerance and the builders', mafia brought about the demolition of Karachi's last synagogue to make way for a shopping plaza. The few remaining Jewish families preferred to pass themselves off as Parsis.[31] In 2000, one Rachel Joseph was said to be, in all probability, the last surviving Jew in Karachi.[32]

Ahmadis (Qadianis/Lahoris) are a newly-created minority.[33] Narrow Islamic prescriptions have led to the ex-communication of Ahmadis from the *ummah*. Immediately after the creation of Pakistan, the Deobandi Ulema made three demands on the government: that Ahmadis be declared non-Muslims in the Constitution; that Foreign Minister Sir Zafrullah Khan be removed from his position for being an Ahmadi; and that no Ahmadi be allowed to retain a key position in the country because Pakistan was an Islamic state. The anti-Ahmadi agitation reached its peak in 1953, when Martial Law was introduced in the province of Punjab. Interestingly, the Munir Report (1954)[34] based on the public inquiry of the anti-Ahmadi agitation concluded that there existed no consensus on the definition of a Muslim in Pakistan. As a result of a violent agitation on the status of Ahmadis in the early 1970s, that included physical attacks, harassment and persecution of Ahmadis (including the suspected ones), burning down their offices and businesses and the forcible closure of their mosques, the Zulfikar Ali Bhutto government relented to 'Muslim' pressure and declared the Ahmadi community as non-Muslim through a constitutional amendment in September 1974. The plight of Ahmadis worsened with Zia-ul-Haq's Islamic fervour, that led to the addition of two draconian sections to the Pakistani Penal Code, 298-B and 298-C, imposing stringent conditions on the community.[35]

Minorities are almost invisible in Pakistani public life. Rarely do they occupy offices of public importance or acquire name in public activity. Exceptions do exist. Alwin Robert Cornelius became the Chief Justice of Pakistan in 1960, Sir Dorab Patel a Parsi was a Supreme Court judge and Rana Bhagwandas, a Hindu Supreme Court judge was elevated as the acting Chief Justice of the Supreme Court on 22 March 2007 (following a grave judicial crisis). C. E. Gibban, the former Deputy Speaker of the National Assembly, Cecil Chaudhary, former army officer and active member of the human rights movement, Eric Siprian, noted intellectual of the left movement, Yousuf Youhana (until his conversion to Islam in 2005 and became Mohammad Yousuf) was one of the handful of Christians to play for the Pakistan cricket team, Colin David, artist, the Benjamin Sisters and Irene Parveen, reputed singers, are all Christians. Ardeshir Cowasjee, well-known journalist, M.P. Bhandara, industrialist, member of the National Legislature and freelance writer, Behram Awari, proprietor of Awari Group of hotels and Jamshed Marker, a diplomat, are all Parsis. There are hardly any prominent Hindus in Pakistan. Years ago, Ms. Mangatrai was the principal of the prestigious Kinnaird College for women in Lahore, Rochiram is an advocate in Sindh and lately two fashion designers, Deepak Pherwani and Sunita Acharia have carved a niche for themselves in the world of *haute couture* in Pakistan. Still, by and large, minorities have little role to play in the decision-making process. A member or two from minority communities are offered ministerial berths merely as a formality.

Pakistan as an Ideological State

But more serious than the social ostricization and marginalization of the minorities is the number of formal, state-constructed measures through discriminatory laws and practices that have bulldozed minority rights and thwarted their integration into the mainstream, inviting more Muslim violence against them. The issue is not just of an overwhelming Muslim majority but of the blurred distinction between the state and religion, which reduces non-Muslims to a second class citizenry. Swarna Rajagopalan's work *State and Nation in South Asia* (2001), with reference to India, Sri Lanka and Pakistan, reinforces the observation made above. Rajagopalan is interested in finding out how these states envision themselves and find an answer in the scrutiny of their constitutions, for the constitutions are the 'founding documents of the state' and are used to 'reconstruct the state's self portrait'. She finds that provisions dealing with the definition of the state in the three Constitutions of Pakistan of 1956, 1962 and 1973 (including the Legal Framework Order of 2002) have remained almost unchanged. What had changed 'dramatically' were the provisions related to the structural and functional aspects of government and law enforcement. What Rajagopalan finds striking is that the state's name, the Islamic Republic of Pakistan, has remained unchanged in these constitutions; but the number of supporting provisions have tripled from seven in 1956, fifteen in 1962 to twenty in 1973.[36] The second amendment to the Constitution (1974) defines who is a non-Muslim;[37] Rajagopalan finds it striking not only because the definition is negative but that the Constitution has made a pronouncement on 'what is essentially a theological matter' is also striking.[38]

The Third Amendment Order of 1985 defined both Muslims and non-Muslims.[39] While by the Amendment of 1974 who is a Muslim was implied in negative terms, in the Third Amendment Order a Muslim was defined positively and in terms of an individual, whereas the non-Muslims were simply grouped together under community labels. Thus, Article 260 of the Constitution defines 'citizenship with reference to majoritarian Islamic parameters'. It first defines a Muslim using an exclusionary definition of Islam, then defines a non-Muslim with reference to a Muslim thus defined. What is striking about these Constitutions is, they distinguish 'between Muslims and non-Muslims not so much in their rights but in what the state is enjoined to do for them...the state...is enjoined to do particular things for the Muslims, whereas its role vis-à-vis others is that of a facilitator and law enforcer.'[40] For example, the Directive Principles of State Policy confer on the state certain specific responsibilities towards the Muslims of Pakistan. The state must take steps to enable Muslims to order their lives in accordance with the fundamental principles and basic concepts of Islam and help them understand the meaning of life according to the Quran and Sunnah (Article 31:1). The state is also enjoined to ensure the teaching and exact printing and publishing of the Quran (Article 31:2a) and to promote unity and observance of Islamic moral standards (Article 31:2b), and yet the state is also called upon to discourage 'parochial, racial, tribal, sectarian and provincial prejudices among citizens (Article 33).'

Discrimination against minorities is inbuilt in the Constitution and law. The Constitution of Pakistan is explicit about the role of Islam in the state of Pakistan. One may quote several provisions of the Constitution that elaborate this role. For example, the Preamble to the 1973 Constitution of the Islamic Republic of Pakistan invests sovereignty in 'Almighty Allah alone' and the authority of the people of Pakistan is to be exercised within the limits prescribed by Him.[41] On the issue of sovereignty, I.A. Rehman in a pointed article has argued that Pakistan has become a nation of two sovereignties.[42] The Constitution stipulates that the principles of democracy, freedom, equality, tolerance and social justice are to be implemented as enunciated in Islam (Preamble); that Right to Freedom of Speech and Expression is subject to any reasonable restriction imposed by law in the interest of the glory of Islam (Article 19); that the teaching of Holy Quran and Islamiat will be compulsory in educational institutions. It further stipulates that all existing laws ought to be brought in conformity with the injunctions of Islam as laid down in the Holy Quran and Sunnah — a Federal Shariat Court was constituted to the realization of this end — but assures that the personal laws of non-Muslims will be protected (Article 227). The President (Article 41:2) and Prime Minister (Article 91:3) of Pakistan are required to be Muslims. Pakistan is an ideological state; a state created by the ideology of Islam. Protection of this ideology is a constitutional responsibility of the highest offices of the country, the President and the Prime Minister; therefore it is necessary that both these offices are held only by Muslims and are expected to be custodians of Pakistan's ideology. The Constitution provides for an advisory body, the Council of Islamic Ideology (Article 228) to recommend and advise the executive and legislature on ways and means of formulating future legislation and bringing existing laws in conformity with the injunctions of Islam.

The Constitution of Pakistan, like any other modern constitutions does make provisions for minorities to 'profess, practise and propagate' their religions and develop cultures (Articles 20, 21 and 22); and guarantees their fundamental rights, including equality of status, of opportunity and equality before law; social, economic and political justice and freedom of thought, expression, belief and association, subject to law and public morality. But when the state envisioned through the Constitution is Islamic how far could these rights be real?[43]

Pakistan is a self-proclaimed ideological state, one based on an Islamic ideology.[44] This self-proclaimed character of the Pakistani state is affirmed through school and college textbooks and the media. Religious parties and the Ulema have been at the forefront in reiterating the ideological character of the Pakistani state although, initially, they had opposed the creation of Pakistan. Was Pakistan envisaged as an ideological state during the Pakistan movement or at its birth in 1947? Pakistani scholars are at variance on this issue. Both Hamza Alavi (2002) and Javid Iqbal[45] are of the opinion that an Islamic ideology was fostered by Pakistani rulers after the creation of Pakistan. Jinnah did not espouse the Pakistan Ideology or the Ideology of Pakistan during the Pakistan Movement. In fact, before Partition, every attempt to bring up the issue of religious ideology was firmly rejected by the Muslim League leadership. What Jinnah did emphasize though, according to Iqbal, was a 'Muslim Ideology'. The idea was that Islam would be a source of guidance for social and cultural values and would also have bearing on political processes of the country. Often attention is drawn by these scholars to a brief statement in the Objectives Resolution passed in 1949 that said 'Muslims shall be enabled to order their lives... in accordance with the teachings and requirements of Islam ...' to establish that there was no commitment to an Islamic ideology in the Objectives Resolution. This ambivalence on the role of Islam resulted from the interplay of a peculiar mix of Islamicity and ethnic consciousness in the Pakistan movement. When the leaders of the Muslims of the Indian subcontinent demanded a separate state for Muslims on the basis of a two-nation theory they were using Islam as a subterfuge for ethnicity. Muslims, they claimed, constituted a separate nation, different from the Hindus in language, culture and religion. But the creation of Pakistan changed the role of Islam. The assertion of the distinct linguistic and cultural identities of three out of the four provinces of West Pakistan and Bengal in the east, soon after the emergence of Pakistan, threw down the gauntlet at Islam. Islam was no longer paraded as a unique ethnicity, rather it was charged with the task of containing its upsurge. Pakistan was created not merely to protect the religious interests of Muslims but perhaps more importantly their political, economic and cultural interests as well. This was the vision of the founder of Pakistan, Muhammad Ali Jinnah. Going by his oft-quoted Presidential address in the Constituent Assembly on 11 August 1947,[46] it can safely be said that he visualized Pakistan as a modern, progressive and secular state. His notion of Pakistani nationalism comprised religious freedom, political equality and the state's distance from religious and sectarian realms of activity. Yet it cannot be overlooked that he repeatedly invoked the Islamic idiom. He hoped there would be a 'renaissance of Islamic culture and ideals' in Pakistan. On other occasions Jinnah spoke of creating a state of 'our own concept', of taking 'inspiration and guidance from the Holy Quran' and making Pakistan a 'bulwark of Islam'.[47] The fact that it was sought as a homeland for a religious community was bound to bring up the issue of Islam's place in the nation's polity. Iqbal states that despite Jinnah's perception of the state as 'modernist, progressive and liberal', 'against the background of Jinnah's public addresses and statements, one cannot help arriving at the conclusion that he had a definite perception of the state in Islam, although he did not specifically use the term "Islamic" state'.[48] I.A. Rehman makes a discerning observation on Jinnah's address in the Constituent Assembly: 'Those who bank on this address ignore the fact that a single address could not persuade the people to purge their minds of ideas and arguments thrown up not only during the communal confrontation in the subcontinent but which had been fertilising in the Muslim mind across the globe for a much longer time'.[49]

Pakistani political scientist Hasan Askari Rizvi is somewhat reluctant to label Pakistan as an ideological state. He makes a distinction between an 'ideological state' and a 'state with an ideology' and argues that 'the emphasis on Islam in the constitutional, legal and political structures of Pakistan does not make it an ideological state.'[50] At best it is state with an ideology. An ideological state, he contends, is a political concept which is 'doctrinaire' and 'self righteous' in nature and therefore inevitably 'dogmatic', 'rigid' 'authoritarian' or 'totalitarian'. Ideology overrides all other considerations. Husain Haqquani has a different take on the Objectives Resolution. 'The first formal step towards transforming Pakistan into an Islamic ideological state was taken in March 1949 when the country's first Prime Minister, Liaquat Ali Khan, presented the "Objectives Resolution" in the Constituent Assembly. The resolution laid out the main principles of a future Pakistani constitution. It provided for democracy, freedom, equality and social justice "as enunciated by Islam", opening the door for future controversies about what Islam required of a state', comments Haqquani.[51]

There exists a general consensus that Pakistan acquired the robes of an ideological state after its creation. Even Askari admits that the fine yet rather hazy distinction he made between an ideological state and a state with an ideology eventually got blurred. Islamic symbolism or the rhetoric of Ayub Khan's regime was turned into Islamic populism by the next Pakistani ruler, Zulfikar Ali Bhutto. General Zia-ul-Haq's regime consciously cultivated orthodox Islamic elements and used the state apparatus and the state-run media to promote 'an orthodox Islamic ideological state'. His regime made serious attempts to Islamize all aspects of polity and society through the introduction of sweeping changes. The revenue system, banking, the legal system, laws dealing with various crimes, education, culture, democratic freedoms — every possible thing in Pakistan was brought under the sweep of Islamization. Zia's rule saw the proliferation of laws and ordinances, new institutions and new ideas purportedly introduced to make the Islamic Republic of Pakistan more Islamic. An Islamic economic system was brought into operation; separate electorates were introduced for non-Muslims; a parallel system of judiciary was introduced with the establishment of Sharia Courts in 1980 to ascertain the validity of any law or legal provision with reference to Islamic injunctions laid down in Sunnah and the Quran. The reconstituted Council of Islamic Ideology became a conduit to Zia's large scale programme of Islamization. Zia attempted to convert Pakistan into an ideological state, but the contours of this ideology were never spelt out clearly; the implication, however, was that Pakistan was not just a geographical entity but also an ideology that was reflected in its unique culture.

The Politics of Islam

The politics of Islam in Pakistan, which worst affected the minorities, was manifested in two of Zia-ul-Haq's creations: one, the system of Separate Eletorates, and two, the Blasphemy Laws.[52] The worst case of institutionalized separatism for minorities was the Separate Electorates System (SES) introduced by Zia in 1979 through an amendment of the Peoples Representation Act. Ultimately, SES became a part of the Constitution through a Revival of the Constitution of 1973 Order, 1985. This system was abolished by Musharraf in 2002 and the General Elections of 2002 were held on the basis of joint electorates with reservation of seats for minorities, to their great relief. The amendment of 1979 had been introduced at the request of the religious-political parties that subscribe to the view that non-Muslims in Pakistan are *zimmis* or second-class citizens. The rationale for the system was provided by arguing that this provision of Pakistani law protects the rights of religious minorities. It is interesting to read Khalid Rehman's valiant defence of the system. Though he concedes that the system highlights the differences between the majority and minorities and that the latter are sidelined from mainstream politics, he disagrees with the major arguments objecting to the system and writes:

> [A] separate electorate eliminates chances of clash on religious basis in spite of the hot and provocative atmosphere of elections, and thus provides protection to the minorities. While in the case of joint electorates, chances of clash and violence increase manifold especially

in a constituency where there is a considerable number of minorities wanting to use their collective vote in favour of a particular candidate in exchange of acceptance of their agenda and demands. The debate on joint or separate electorate should bring to fore these arguments. It would become clear that minorities are entitled to several benefits because of the separate the biggest of them being their over-representation in the assembly.[53]

He found the separate electorate system as holding great benefits for the minorities, the biggest of them being their over-representation in the assembly. The system of separate electorates has the effect of denying religious minorities in the country the fundamental right of universal adult franchise.

Under the Separate Electorate System Muslim voters voted only for Muslim candidates while the non-Muslims only for the non-Muslim candidates contesting for a few reserved seats. Voters had no right to vote for candidates outside their own religious affiliation. Ten seats were reserved for minorities in the National Assembly: four each for Christians and Hindus, one for Parsis and Sikhs together and one for the Ahmadis. SES was also applicable to Provincial Assembly seats. It meant, for example, Christians from all over the country would vote to elect four representatives who might be total strangers to them. This policy of discrimination among voters on grounds of religion had cut off the non-Muslim citizens of Pakistan from mainstream national political life. Further, it had denied them the right to participate directly in national decision-making processes as well as in the framing of national economic, social and cultural policies. A joint written statement submitted by Franciscans International, the Commission of the Churches on International Affairs of the World Council of Churches and the World Alliance of Reformed Churches to the United Nations Commission on Human Rights, on the situation of religious minorities in Pakistan in 1996, heavily indicted the system of separate electorates for religious minorities and Blasphemy Laws 295-B and 295-C of the Pakistan Penal Code (PPC) for the plight of minorities in Pakistan.[54]

A review of the Blasphesmy Laws may help in gauging the extent of Islamization of Pakistan and its consequent impact on the minorities. Blasphemy Laws are a legacy of the British administration. In 1860, the British Government introduced Sections 295, 296, 297 and 298 in the Indian Penal Code to impose a two-year imprisonment and fine on those who defiled or damaged places of worship, disturbed religious rites, or uttered words intending to offend religious feelings of any community. Pakistan inherited these sections in 1947. In the early years of Pakistan these laws were rarely invoked. In the first thirty-five years there were only six blasphemy charges made under these laws. However, a demand for strengthening of the Blasphemy Laws came from certain quarters of Pakistani society, from the very beginning of the formation of Pakistan.

Prior to 1980, Section 295-A of the PPC dealt with defiling objects or places and outraging religious feelings with deliberate intent to insult the religion of any class. It carried a maximum punishment of ten years with a fine. Section 295-B stipulated life imprisonment for defiling damaging or desecrating a copy of the Holy Quran wilfully or of an extract there from or using it in any derogatory manner or for any unlawful purpose. From 1980 to 1986, the PPC was amended with great zeal to include severe punishment for blasphemy or insulting the feelings of Muslims.

The most draconian addition came in 1986, when Zia promulgated Section 295-C, stipulating fine, life imprisonment or death to whoever by word, either spoken or written or by visible representation or by imputation, innuendo, or insinuation, directly or indirectly defiles the sacred name of the holy prophet Muhammad. It defined blasphemy in such a sweeping manner that the law was bound to be misused. In 1990, Nawaz Sharif's Federal Shariat Court amended Section 295-C, eliminating life imprisonment and making the death sentence mandatory.

Blasphemy Laws of Pakistan, while purporting to protect Islam and the religious sensitivities of the Muslim majority of Pakistan, are said to be vaguely formulated and arbitrarily enforced by the police and judiciary often under religious and social pressure, resulting in the abuse, harassment and persecution of minorities, especially Ahmadis and Christians. In the last decade, approximately 1,500 Ahmadis and an equal number of Christians have been charged with blasphemy. The 1994, a case was brought before the Lahore Court under this law against three Christian youth — Manzoor, Rahmet and Salamat Masih. Salamat Masih was illiterate and twelve years of age when he was condemned to death for writing graffiti against Prophet Muhammad on a mosque. Their case received international attention and invited prompt condemnation from the world community. Later of course the Court freed the accused. In 1998 Rev. Dr John Joseph, Catholic bishop of Faisalabad and a high-profile human rights activist, shot himself dead in the corridors of a sessions court in Sahiwal in protest against the death sentence given to one Ayub Masih for blaspheming Islam. There have been attacks on Christians in Shanti Nagar, Khanewal and other towns in Punjab on accusations of blasphemy. But it is not only non-Muslims who bear the brunt of blasphemy laws, even Muslims are not spared by the Islamic extremists. There was also a call to kill noted human right activist Asma Jahangir for providing counselling to many Christians and other minorities implicated in blasphemy cases.

Blasphemy Laws have been most cruel perhaps to Ahmadis. Sections 298-B and 298-C are as if made only for Ahmadis. Section 298-B deals with the misuse of epithets, description and titles, etc., reserved for certain holy personages or places in Islam. The Ahmadis are prohibited from using epithets or names of the Prophet Muhammad for their prophet or refer to or call their place of worship a 'mosque'; they are forbidden from referring to their call to prayers as an 'Azan' which is claimed as a Muslim prerogative. Section 298-C forbids Ahmadis from professing Islam and from using Muslim practices in their worship or in the propagation of their faith, thereby keeping them from outraging the religious feelings of Muslims. In 1993, the Supreme Court ruled against the Ahmadis in a case on the constitutionality of Section 298-C. The Court held that Islamic phrases are in essence a copyright of the Islamic religion. The use of Islamic phrases by Ahmadis was deemed equivalent to copyright infringement, an offence under the Trademark Act of 1940. The judgement also reiterated that the use of certain Islamic phrases by Ahmadis was equivalent to blasphemy.[55]

Stephen Gill quotes from an article by Aziz-ud-din Ahmad from *The Nation* about the abuse of law.

> The Blasphemy Law has been applied mostly, if not always, to non-Muslims notwithstanding the fact that it is unimaginable in a society like Pakistan for a member of a religious minority to indulge in a highly provocative act of this kind. There have been cases when non-Muslims have been murdered even before being charged in a court with, or convicted for, blasphemy.... The blasphemy laws have brought only miseries to the nation of Pakistan...[56]

Powerful feudal lords who wield considerable influence on the social, religious and political life of Pakistan support these laws so as to get rid of Christian farmers and occupy their lands. These laws have been used mostly against Christians because they are more vocal than other minorities in Pakistan. They have proved to be divisive, dangerous and repressive, and are being used to legally terrorize the minorities.

In their present form, the Blasphemy Laws are said to be a source of victimization and persecution of minorities in the country. Minorities suffer all manner of humiliation through false accusations made under these laws. They have become a major tool in the hands of extremist elements used to settle personal scores against members of religious minorities. An act of blasphemy carries a mandatory death sentence in some cases. Often it is argued, in the defence of the laws, that no death sentence has been actually carried out by law until now. But this is a weak argument, for those who have been freed by the superior courts were not freed in the real sense of the term. In most cases, mobs took the law in their own hands and tried to kill the accused. Some of those who were eventually freed have sought asylum in other countries. It has also been found that the law is being manipulated by people to register false cases against adversaries and rivals. Once a person is accused of blasphemy, the stigma of the accusation, and the fact that the burden of proof lies on the accused makes the prospects of an acquittal bleak. An appalling aspect of the Blasphemy Laws is that they not only cover intentional blasphemy but also unintentional blasphemy. This element subverts the principle that a criminal act requires criminal intention. It also indicates the exceptional scope of these laws and the ease with which they can be used arbitrarily. There is one more disadvantage for women and minorities in blasphemy cases: only a Muslim male can initiate a blasphemy case against an individual, women and non-Muslims are prohibited from doing the same. The law of evidence, *Qanoon-i-shahadat,* enacted by the Zia government is prejudiced against women and non-Muslims; it equates the evidence of two women and two non-Muslims to that of one Muslim man.

Conclusion

The virtual non-existence of the non-Muslim minorities in Pakistan raises a fundamental question about Pakistani polity and society. Going by Jinnah's speech of 11 August 1947, it was envisaged that Pakistan would have a sizable population of minorities, particularly Hindus. Immediately after the partition, Pakistan, both wings together, had nearly 20 per cent Hindus. Today they are less than

2 per cent. A sizable presence of Hindus in Pakistan would have had the political effect of moderating the country's politics. Religiously mixed societies on the either side of the border would have prevented what Ishtiaq Ahmed calls 'pathological politics'[57] in both the countries. Socially, with the exodus of Hindus, Pakistani society has been left bereft of cultural plurality and social variety depriving it of an internal self-correcting mechanism. Minorities in Pakistan, says Rehman, encounter 'cultural marginalisation, discrimination, economic hardships and religious persecution'. Aurat Foundation's Nuzzhat Shirin too blames Islamic fanaticism for the ordeal suffered by Hindus and other minorities. 'It's Muslims winning by intimidation. It's Muslims overcoming a culture(s) by threatening it (them).'[58]

The Pakistani establishment moved from the politics of Islam to an official sponsorship of Jihad, which sowed the seeds of Islamic radicalism, pitting not only Muslims against non-Muslims but also Muslims against other Muslims. The Pakistani situation is a paradoxical one. Despite its overwhelming Muslim majority, a major theme that runs through Pakistan's history since its inception is a search for national identity. It faced a huge challenge in creating an entirely new national identity with a short history. One acceptable definition or manifestation of it seemed possible by rejecting everything that was Indian. To be different from India was essential to provide a rationale for the two-nation theory and for Pakistan's battle for a separate identity. It thus took recourse to Islam. It is indeed ironical that instead of minorities resorting to identity politics it was the Muslim majority community that chose to play the politics of identity and self-aggrandizement. Minorities in Pakistan — Ahmadis and Hindus in particular — are self-effacing; they have withdrawn into a shell and tend to camouflage their identities. In the Punjab, Hindus are said to have either embraced Christianity or taken Christian names. Sometimes, even the Shias are discreet about their identity. In India, Hindutva suddenly emerged as a political force with gusto; the Sinhalese of Sri Lanka are very assertive about their Sinhala Buddhist identity and are determined to prove that the island of Sri Lanka was truly a Sinhala Dweepa from time immemorial; Bangladesh has effectively juggled between its religious or linguistic identity from time to time, whichever way they toss it, it is to the advantage of Bengali Muslims; Nepali politics has been engaged in projecting the majority community of Hindus to the detriment of numerous ethnic tribes; and in Bhutan, the ethnic Bhutanese have adopted a belligerent attitude towards Bhutanese people of Nepalese origin. Majority communities brandishing their identity has perhaps become a norm in South Asian politics.

Notes and References

1. Kofi Annan, Millennium Report, *We the Peoples: The Role of the United Nations in the 21st Century*, 3 April 2000, http://www.unhchr. ch/minorities (accessed 30 April 2007).
2. Jeremy Waldron, 'Minority Cultures and Cosmopolitan Alternatives', in Will Kymlicka (ed.), *The Rights of Minority Cultures* (New York: Oxford University Press, 1995), p. 97.
3. Will Kymlicka, *Multicultural Citizenship: A Liberal Theory of Minority Rights* (Oxford: Clarendon Press, 1996), p. 1.
4. Ted Robert Gurr *et al.*, *Minorities at Risk Project* (College Park, MD: Center for International Development and Conflict Management, 2005), http://www.cidcm.umd.edu/mar/ (accessed 29 April 2007).
5. Michael Walzer, 'Pluralism: A Political Perspective', in Will Kymlicka (ed.), *The Rights of Minority Cultures* (New York: Oxford University Press, 1995), p. 144.
6. 'Justice as Reciprocity', in Samuel Gorovitz (ed.), *Utilitarianism: John Stuart Mill: With Critical Essays* (New York: Bobbs-Merrill, 1971); *A Theory of Justice* (Cambridge, Massachusetts: Harvard University Press, 1971); 'Constituitional Liberty and the Concept of Justice', in Thomas Schwartz (ed.), *Freedom and Authority: An Introduction to Social and Political Philosophy* (Encino & Belmont, California: Dickenson, 1973), p. 4; 'Distributive Justice', in Edmund S. Phelps (ed.), *Economic Justice: Selected Readings*. Penguin Modern Economics Readings. (Harmondsworth & Baltimore: Penguin Books, 1973); 'Justice as Fairness', in Richard E. Flathman (ed.), *Concepts in Social & Political Philosophy* (New York: Macmillan, 1973), p. 6; and 'Fairness to Goodness', *Philosophical Review* 84(4), October 1975, pp. 536–54.
7. Stephen May, Tariq Madood and Judith Squires (eds), *Ethnicity, Nationalism, and Minority Rights* (Cambridge: Cambridge University Press, 2004), pp. 2–4.
8. Vernon Van Dyke, 'The Individual, the State, and Ethnic Communities in Political Theory', in Will Kymlicka (ed.), *The Rights of Minority Cultures* (New York: Oxford University Press, 1995), pp. 33–37.
9. Will Kymlicka's edited volume, *The Rights of Minority Cultures* (1995), offers an excellent window into these debates.

10. Akeel Bilgrami, 'Notes Towards the Definition of "Identity"', *Daedalus: Journal of the American Academy of Arts & Sciences* 135(4), Fall 2006, pp. 5–14, http://findarticles.com/p/articles/mi_qa3671/is_200610/ai_n16840844 (accessed 2 February 2007).

11. The liberal critique of identity politics focuses on the group-based nature of demands that uses the notion of sameness to justify political mobilization. Such a politics creates a 'single axis' identity and tends to ignore the fact that even an individual is a heterogeneous self with multiple identities.

12. May *et al.*, *Ethnicity, Nationalism.*

13. Ibid., p. 4.

14. T.K. Oommen, 'New Nationalisms and Collective Rights: The Case of South Asia', in Stephen May, Tariq Madood and Judith Squires (eds), *Ethnicity, Nationalism, and Minority Rights* (Cambridge: Cambridge University Press, 2004), p. 121.

15. This was Jinnah's typically prophetic hostage theory. Talking to the British Cabinet Mission in 1946 about the protection of minorities that would be left in India and Pakistan he has said 'their best protection will be the establishment of two strong states, neither of which will dare misbehave towards each other's minorities'. If one state mistreated its minorities the other state would retaliate against its minorities. It would be tit for tat. See M.V. Kamath, http://www.hvk.org/articles/1101/238.html (accessed 26 June 2007).

16. Unlike the largely homogeneous nation-states of Europe, the post-colonial states of South Asia are heterogeneous, hence the term composite nation-states.

17. Although Athar Hussain has used the term to describe nation formation in Pakistan, it is applicable to the entire South Asian region. The inversion draws on E. Gellner's shift of focus from 'what a nation is' to 'how a nation is formed'. See Athar Hussain, 'Peregrination of Pakistani Nationalism', in Michael Letter (ed.), *Asian Nationalism* (London: Routledge, London School of Economics and Asia Research Centre, 2000), pp. 127–28. The process of the management of a national identity imparted to the South Asian states a hegemonic role in their multi-ethnic societies.

18. Surendar Valasai, founder President of the Scheduled Caste Federation of Pakistan claims the percentage of Dalit's in Pakistan's Hindu population is 70 per cent. See news report, 'Dalits in Pakistan turn to Pervez for help', *The Asian Age*, Mumbai edition, 10 May 2007, p. 1. And 75 per cent is the figure put forward in Pirbhu Lal Satyani's *Hamey Bhi Jeeney Do: Pakistan Mai Acchoot Logon ki Suratehal* (Urdu) (Lahore: ASR Resource Centre, 2005), http://www.countercurrents.org/dalit-sikand230905.htm (accessed 19 May 2007).

19. This was my observation as well. The notion of 'purity–pollution' is prevalent even at workplaces, where the same glass for water is often not shared by Dalits and non-Dalits.
20. See n. 17 *infra*.
21. See, for example, a report in *Dawn*, http://www.dawn.com/weekly/mazdak/20051203.htm (accessed 10 May 2007). On the kidnapping of Hindu girls see Irfan Hussain, 'Conversion Losses', *Dawn*, 3 December 2005, http://www.dawn.com/weekly/mazdak/20051203.htm (accessed 25 April 2007). Also see Sunny, 'The sad state of Hindus in Pakistan', *Pickled Politics*, 20 January 2006, http://www.pickledpolitics.com/archives/243 (accessed 25 April 2007).
22. News of the demolition of the last Hindu temple, Krishna Mandir, in Lahore in June 2006 to make way for a commercial complex caused anger among Hindus in India. *HAF* (Hindu American Foundation) *News* 1(2), October 2006, p. 10.
23. Memorandum signed by Dr Nazir S. Bhatti, Chief, Pakistan Christian Congress and Editor, *Pakistan Christian Post*, http://www.pakistan christianpost.com/editorialdetails.php?editorialid=86 (accessed 10 July 2007).
24. Quoted by Amir Mir, http://www.pakistanchristianpost.com/news viewsdetails.php?newsid=437 (accessed 10 July 2007). Jillani feels the system is heavily loaded against them. She cites the example of Pakistani cricketer Yousuf Youhana who converted to Islam and became Mohammad Yousuf because, in her opinion, he would otherwise have had no chance at becoming the captain of the Pakistani cricket team.
25. I am tempted to briefly narrate the story of a Pakistani film, *Tere Pyaar Mein*, that I watched in Islamabad in 2001. It is a syrupy romance between an Indian Sikh girl and a Pakistani Muslim youth. When the Pakistani boy goes to India to meet the girl, officers of the Indian Army question the girl's father about the presence of a Pakistani boy in their house. A major altercation follows and the army officers shoot the father. Before breathing his last he wonders aloud if the Sikhs had done the right thing in deciding to be part of India at the time of partition. I do not believe that I am reading too much into the latent politics of this statement.
26. *Dawn*, 20 December 2005, http://www.dawn.com/2005/12/20/nat12.htm (accessed 24 May 2007).
27. http://www.valentinammaka.net/sidhwa2.english.htm (accessed 24 May 2007).
28. Iftikhar H. Malik, *Religious Minorities in Pakistan* (Report) (London: Minority Rights Group International, 2002).
29. For a brief history of Parsis in Karachi see http://www.vohuman.org/Article/Beyond%20Compare%20—%20Parsi%20Pioneers%20of%2 0Karachi.htm (accessed 23 May 2007).

30. http://www.vohuman.org/Article/Quetta%20Calling.pdf (accessed 26 May 2007).
31. http://www.jewishvirtuallibrary.org/jsource/vjw/Pakistan.html (accessed 26 May 2007).
32. Kamal Siddiqi, 'In Pakistan's city of strife, 82-year-old fights for her community's dead', *Indian Express*, 17 December 2000, http://www.indianexpress.com/res/web/pIe/ie/daily/20001217/iin17034.html (accessed 20 May 2007).
33. The Ahmadis are followers of Mirza Ghulam Ahmad, born in 1835 in Qadian, Gurdaspur district of India, who claimed to be the *Mujaddid* (divine reformer) of the fourteenth Islamic century, the Promised Messiah ('Second Coming of Christ'), the *Mahdi* awaited by Muslims in the latter day, and a prophet.
34. For a gist of the main arguments of the Munir Report see Hamid Khan, *Constitutional and Political History of Pakistan* (Karachi: Oxford University Press, 2001), pp. 120–22.
35. See, Rasul Bakhsh Rais, 'Religious Radicalism and Minorities in Pakistan', in Satu Limaye, Mohan Malik and Robert Wirsing (eds), *Religious Radicalism and Security in South Asia* (Honolulu: Asia-Pacific Center for Security Studies, 2004), pp. 456–57.
36. Swarna Rajagopalan, *State and Nation in South Asia* (Boulder: Lynne Rinner Publishers, 2001), p. 45.
37. The following clause was added to Article 260: 'A person who does not believe in the absolute and unqualified finality of The Prophethood of MUHAMMAD (Peace be upon him), the last of the Prophets, or claims to be a Prophet, in any sense of the word or of any description whatsoever, after MUHAMMAD (Peace be upon him), or recognizes such a claimant as a Prophet or religious reformer, is not a Muslim for the purposes of the Constitution or law.'
38. Rajagopalan, *State and Nation*, p. 46.
39. The term 'Muslim' refers to a person who believes in the unity and oneness of Almighty Allah, in the absolute and unqualified finality of the Prophethood of MUHAMMAD (PBUH), the last of the Prophets, and does not believe in, or recognize as a prophet of religious reformer, any person who claimed or claims to be a prophet, in any sense of the word or of any description whatsoever, after MUHAMMAD (PBUH); and a 'non-Muslim' is a person who is not a Muslim and the category includes persons belonging to the Christian, Hindu, Sikh, Buddhist or Parsi community, a person of the Qadiani group or the Lahori group (who call themselves 'Ahmadis' or by any other name), or a Bahai, and a person belonging to any of the Scheduled Castes. See, http://www.pakistani.org/pakistan/constitution/orders/po24_1985.html (accessed 23 May 2007).

40. Rajagopalan, *State and Nation*, p. 46
41. According to Khalid Rahman, Director, Institute of Policy Studies, Islamabad, in Islam absolute sovereignty lies with Almighty Allah. Muslims cannot deviate from this position, and this is what distinguishes Muslims from non-Muslims. See Khalid Rahman, 'Electoral System and Minorities', paper presented at a conference organized in Islamabad by German think tank Friedrich Ebert-Stiftung in 2000, http://www.gdnet.org/fulltext/IPSelect.pdf (accessed 12 July 2007).
42. As per this theory of 'two sovereignties', argues Rehman, 'every Pakistani Muslim has a right and a duty to bring his fellow beings under a regime he thinks his belief prescribes even if this involves a defiance of state-made (that is, man-made) laws and rules'. Though not permitted by law [of the state], Islamists believe that apostasy invites the death penalty and any Muslim can and is supposed to act 'as the prosecutor, the judge and the executioner'. Also, even though non-Muslims cannot, technically speaking, fall within the category of apostates, such a person can be executed by a Pakistani Muslim on the charge of blasphemy. The state's inaction and silence vis-à-vis actions taken by individuals under the pretext of religious beliefs or dogma is nothing but criminal. The Lal Masjid episode, spanning over the first half of 2007, is one example of criminal inaction on the part of the Pakistani state. The state conducted Operation Silence only when it was no longer possible to remain silent and inactive. I.A. Rehman, 'A Nation of Two Sovereignties', *The Asian Age*, Mumbai edition, 11 April 2007.
43. Iftikhar H. Malik draws attention to a rather ironic inscription in the main hall of the Federal Ministry of Religious Minorities Affairs of Pakistan that says, 'Of course, Islam is the best religion in the eyes of GOD'. Iftikhar H. Malik, *Religious Minorities in Pakistan* (London: Minority Rights Group), p. 22.
44. The core of Pakistan as nation was defined by religion and equally importantly by language. The place of Urdu in the ideological state was perceived as being invincible. During the early years of the Bhasha Andolan in East Pakistan, the defense of Urdu as the national language vis-à-vis the demand for a similar status for Bengali had acquired almost heroic and moral unquestionable proportions. Jinnah once said, Urdu 'embodies the best that is in Islamic culture and Muslim tradition and is nearest to the language used in other Islamic countries'. Quoted in Philip Oldenburg, '"A Place insufficiently imagined": Language, Belief, and the Pakistan Crisis of 1971', *The Journal of Asian Studies* 44(4), August 1985, pp. 716–17.
45. Hamza Alavi, 'the unholy alliance', *Dawn*, 6 October 2002, and Javed Iqbal, *Islam and Pakistan's Identity* (Lahore: Iqbal Academy Pakistan and Vanguard Books, 2003), p. 352.

46. Jinnah had stated, 'You are free; you are free to go to your temples, you are free to go to your mosques or to any other place of worship in this State of Pakistan. You may belong to any religion, caste or creed — that has nothing to do with the business of the State.' See, Hamid Khan, *Constitutional and Political History of Pakistan* (Karachi: Oxford University Press, 2001), p. 76.

47. Anwar Syed provides a comprehensive and in-depth study of Muslim and Pakistani nationhood in the context of national identity of Pakistan. See Anwar Syed, *Islam, Politics and National Solidarity* (Lahore: Vanguard, 1984).

48. Iqbal, *Islam and Pakistan's Identity*, p. 353.

49. Rehman, 'A Nation of Two Sovereignties', *The Asian Age*, Mumbai, 11 April 2007.

50. Hasan Askari Rizvi, 'Is Pakistan an Ideological State', *Daily Times*, 9 May 2005, http://www.dailytimes.com.pk/default.asp?page=story_9-5-2005pg3_2 (accessed 17 May 2007).

51. Husain Haqquani, 'Dysfunction of an Ideological State: Pakistan's Recurrent Crises in Historic Context', received from asiapeace@yahoo.com on 24 February 2007.

52. http://www.pakistanchristianpost.com/newsviewsdetails.php?newsid=437 (accessed 4 July 2007).

53. Rahman, 'Electoral System and Minorities'.

54. http://www.unhchr.ch/Huridocda/Huridoca.nsf/0/9da54d3f22f184f1802567390039e0d6?Opendocument (accessed 13 July 2007).

55. 'Swearing by Reforms: Time to put Pakistan's Blasphemy Laws on Trial', South Asia Human Rights Documentation Centre, February 2002, http://www.hrdc.net/sahrdc/hrfeatures/HRF52.htm (accessed 9 July 2007).

56. Stephen Gill, 'Blasphemy Laws of Pakistan', http://www.authorsDen.com/stephengill and http://home.ican.net/~sgill (accessed 29 June 2003). This is a very useful, detailed and comprehensive article on blasphemy laws in Pakistan. Another useful article is Saad Anis, 'Blasphemy law: open to abuse', *Daily Times*, 24 June 2003.

57. 'The Partition of India', writes Ahmed, 'played a significant role 'in conferring legitimacy to the politics of communal and national animosities and hostilities....Partition epitomizes the politics of identity in its most negative form: when trust and understanding have been undermined and instead fear and insecurity reign supreme, generating angst at various levels of state and society. In the process, a pathological socio-political system comes into being....such a system functions within the domestic sphere as well as in India–Pakistan political interaction.' Ishtiaq Ahmed, 'The 1947 Partition of India: A Paradigm for Pathological Politics in India and Pakistan', *Asian Ethnicity* 3(1), March 2002, p. 9.

58. http://www.pakistanchristianpost.com/newsviewsdetails.php?newsid=437 (accessed 11 July 2007).

8

Minorities and Political Governance: The Myanmar Situation

Mandy Sadan

Background: A Local Context

On 29 September 2007, senior members of the Kachin Independence Organization (KIO), whose military wing, the Kachin Independence Army (KIA), had for much of Myanmar's post-colonial history been in armed conflict with the central government, attended a mass rally ostensibly in support of the military government's National Convention process. This 'process' is considered by most observers to be a highly controlled and controversial attempt by Myanmar's military regime to create a new constitution for the country and has been rejected as a sham by many of Burma's leading opposition figures including the National League for Democracy (NLD), whose figurehead is Nobel Laureate Daw Aung San Suu Kyi.[1] The attendance of Kachin representatives at this rally occurred almost at the same time as monk demonstrators in Yangon, the former capital, and other urban areas across Myanmar were protesting against the massive price rise in basic commodities, a protest which grew into a more generalized opposition to the present regime. The events which followed, including the brutal repression of the protests, placed Myanmar in the international spotlight in an unprecedented way. The obvious contrast of witnessing Kachin leaders seemingly standing in support of the regime at this time appalled many ethnic Kachin people, both inside the country and abroad. Yet, in some ways the contrast acts as a mirror to the complicated state of ethnic politics in Myanmar today. Many in the wider democratic opposition movement at times feel frustrated by the lack of coherence revealed by ethnicized political organizations, including the failure of the various armed ethnic groups and their civil and underground networks to unify towards a common objective, cutting across ethnic fractures. For non-ethnically defined Burmese opposition groups the objective is to replace the current regime at the centre with a form of democratic government that will permit a system of civic governance to develop, which will address the concerns of ethnic minorities as well as alleviate the severe social and economic pressures faced by ordinary Burmese people across the country. Many ethnic minority leaders, on the other hand, feel weighed down by a history of mistrust of Burmese politicians and feel that, in light of the huge cost in terms of lives lost and the sacrifices their respective communities have been forced to make over many decades in their demand for governmental autonomy, they must adhere to their primary goal of pursuing local transformations in governmental structures, which can be sustained beyond the vagaries of ambition historically demonstrated towards them by the Burmese state. The reluctance of the NLD until recently to openly declare itself in favour of a 'tripartite' dialogue on the country's future indicates to many ethnic minority politicians that there is still a fundamental misunderstanding of ethnic minority goals in Burmese politics at all levels, especially if the Burmese opposition persists in the belief that a unitary state has always been, or will always be, the objective of the country's principal 'National Races'. A tripartite dialogue involves constitutional discussions that would include representatives of the military regime, the democratic opposition, as well as representatives of ethnic minority communities. It was proposed in 1994 by a resolution of the UN General Assembly as a means of moving the country towards a solution of its ethnic crisis, particularly by invoking the terms of the 1947 Panglong Agreement, which is discussed below.

A recent statement by the Ethnic Nationalities Council, a Thailand-based pressure group, evokes this perception of a rupture in understanding between the claims for democracy and claims for autonomy, which lie at the heart of much Burmese–ethnic minority disagreement on the establishment of a system of governance that will be workable in the longer term:

> The Council's view is that the political crisis in Myanmar today was not just an ideological confrontation between democracy and military rule, but was rooted in a constitutional crisis, which came about because the Panglong Agreement was never fully implemented.[2]

In 1994, the KIA entered an armed ceasefire with the Burmese military government, and since then there has been a gradual transformation in the local structures of political control in the Kachin region. The current difficulty, as these structures of control become consolidated, is how to strategize within this difficult situation for any kind of semi-autonomous future given that the central regime is actually becoming more powerful in Kachin State, especially through its increasing control of the economic infrastructure and persistent extension of military power. During the decades of conflict, the central regime was to a large extent prevented from accessing Kachin State's rich mineral wealth and natural resources. Control over these resources ensured the continued funding of armed resistance by the KIA, along with the development of an opium-based economy in many areas of Kachin region. In this context, KIO attendance at the government rally is deemed a tactic, albeit one that demonstrates either the degree of entrapment that these ethnic minority leaders experience at this time, or a certain miscalculation of the national and international mood, which raises questions about their own political abilities. Subsequent events suggest the former. In October 2007, reports filtered through the international Kachin News Group network that Yup Zau Hkawng, a leading business figure in Kachin State made wealthy primarily from the State's jade mines and someone who is frequently used as a public figure by the Kachin State military administration to advertise their claims of local development, and yet who also retains a role in Kachin nationalist organizations, had gone into self-imposed exile in Japan to escape the pressures placed on him by the then Regional Military Commander, Major General Ohn Myint. Subsequently dismissed as being incorrect, this report reveals how the underlying nature of power relations in the region at present are perceived. The perception of entrapment was further consolidated following the KIO's recent refusal to agree to an already-prepared document opposing Aung San Suu Kyi's statement in favour of a tripartite dialogue, which was followed by the closing of border posts and raids on KIO offices in Myitkyina, the State capital, all of which were strategies to put pressure on the KIO/KIA. More recently, the tenth-hour announcement by the KIO that Kachin servicemen should all 'Vote Yes' in favour of the recent referendum held on the constitution seems to have been matched not by an easing of relations with the regime but a local shutdown by the Burmese military of access routes into Laiza, the base of the KIA/KIO infrastructure in its supposedly 'liberated area'. No action produces a linear response and the apparent inability to strategize beyond issue-led politics seems endemic in the local political environment.

The above account describes a discourse on the state of relations between ethnic minority claims to rights and the system of governance through which those rights might best be achieved, based on what took place in the space of a few months in just one part of the country. If one extended this exercise to other localities and times, attitudes and responses to these events in different 'ethnic' organizations, in different parts of Myanmar as well as globally, one would encounter multiple and different, local and regional tactics with regard to conflict and cease-fire, negotiation and disengagement, as well as attitudes towards the National Convention and a Tripartite Dialogue: an apparently baffling array of responses and interpretations, influenced by various local circumstances and historical experiences and practises. It is beyond the scope of this article to elucidate these aspects or even to describe the complexities of Burma's post-independence ethnic political crisis in any detail. This article, therefore, will consider some of the main constitutional issues that have arisen and which provide key historical markers in the failure to establish an effective system of governance for Myanmar's multi-ethnic state. The debate on the present constitutional proposals will not be included in detail, only some of the historical precursors that still influence much of the discourse as it is presented. In this I take my lead from the previously-quoted statement that this crisis should not be considered primarily as a bi-polar ideological one. Indeed, this article will go beyond this to argue that not only is the primary difficulty not ideological (in relation to the status of ethnic relations within the state), but that, in fact, the rather intuitive and prejudicial underpinnings of the contemporary state's attitude to ethnic issues would perhaps benefit from further elaboration at an ideological level, as a means of resolving the under-lying issues of mistrust that beleaguer inter-ethnic relations at almost every political level in contemporary Myanmar.

The State of Ethnicity in Myanmar

Most discussions on ethnicity and minority rights issues in Myanmar usually begin with two statements: first, that Myanmar is one of the most ethnically diverse countries in South-East Asia, and second, that the country has experienced some of the most endemic, ethnically-framed, post-independence conflicts not only in South-East Asia, but anywhere else in the world. The background to the former statement relates to the fact that, in terms of ethno-linguistic origins, the classification of language–culture communities and official estimates regarding the number of ethnic groups derived from these models, the Burmese state appears to contain more distinct ethnic groups (officially 135, related through 13 ethnic 'families') than any other mainland South-East Asian state, as well as reportedly the largest percentage of territory not occupied by the principal ethnic group of the country, in this case the Bamars or Burman people.[3] There are no reliable census figures but estimates of non-Burman populations vary from 30–40 per cent of the total, occupying up to 60 per cent of the land. The ground realities of these complex demographies are, of course, more complicated, but this ethnic jigsaw has been configured, nonetheless, as a simplified state structure: Myanmar is constituted of seven States[4] and seven divisions. The seven States are Mon State, Chin State, Kachin State, Kayin State, Kayah State, Shan State and Rakhine State. The names of these States reflect the principal categories of non-Burman ethnic people who are deemed 'indigenous' inhabitants of these territories today.

In relation to the second statement, concerning the apparently endemic state of ethnic conflicts, this national peculiarity has facilitated a discourse in which a multiplicity of ethnic identities is presented as an inevitable precursor of conflict. Since the time of Independence, Burma/Myanmar has suffered continuous internal conflict, at times pressing close on the doors of the former capital at Yangon (Rangoon), and for much of the independent nation's history, large areas of its territory have been held by armed insurgent groups, and indeed still continue to be so in variously configured 'Special Regions' and other zones of relative (though undeniably not ab-solute) autonomy. A baffling array of both small and large ethnic armies, in almost every region of the country, have at some point emerged, grown, declined, agglomerated, split, negotiated and, in the case of many, recently attempted this difficult objective of strategizing within armed ceasefires. The occurrence of conflict has been influenced by a host of specific local interests, such as drug economies, as well as pressures from national, regional and global concerns, particularly communism, for much of Myanmar's post-independence history. The Burma Communist Party (BCP) was a significant player in Burma's ethnic politics for much of the inter-War and post-Second World War period, and indeed, has also been a forum through which many ethnic Burman people, who formed the bulk of the BCP's armed forces, have been involved with these issues.[5]

Both statements present, to some extent, accurate accounts of the situation in post-colonial Myanmar, but their inter-relationship should be qualified somewhat: the latter (i.e., conflict) is not an inevitable consequence of the former (i.e., diversity). There are many ethnically-diverse nations in South-East Asia and, therefore, regionally speaking, a variety of ways in which assertions of non-national ethnic loyalties have been incorporated, assimilated, oppressed, respected or homogenized by the state: the weight of 'ethnic' numbers in any classificatory model need not by itself produce such apparently endemic, conflictual social fissures. Second, the appearance and assertion of such diversity owes itself also to the historical development of systems, structures and political processes, which fractured the idea of the nation through sets of ethnic sub-groups. This is not to deny the enduring and powerful reality of such identities to those expressing them, as will be delineated in this article, but their incorporation into a national discourse of social incohesion relates also to various emerging and intersecting frameworks of social classification (e.g., Burmese, colonial, their hybrids, and other influences of external origin).

Furthermore, whilst conflict has been longstanding and perpetual in the post-Independence period, it has occurred in the form of a variety of flows and counter-flows, or what Martin Smith has recently termed 'cycles of conflict'.[6] And with this, various 'ethnic' histories have at times speeded up or slowed down as the play of national politics unravelled itself and became unravelled across the nation's ethnic landscape. Endemic conflict reflects not the inevitable or the historically predetermined, but the repeated failure of developing and maintaining trust between political centres and their 'peripheries', and of developing an ear sensitive to the narratives and discourses of non-national histories and identities.[7]

Yet, despite all this emphasis on the ethnographic, Myanmar seems to have failed to develop a state ideology based on 'ethnicity' and ethnic incorporation, as previously stated, and seems to offer no solution to the prevailing understanding of ethnicity as a deep social fissure other than a vague aspiration towards a common national 'spirit', as will be discussed. Without proposing this as a model to aspire to given its many obvious failings, one might contrast, for example, the situation in Vietnam, where a distinct form of Vietnamese ethnology emerged and continues to evolve through state-sponsored structures.[8] This was originally, and inevitably, an offshoot of the Soviet school of anthropology, which modified itself over a period of decades in keeping with its own findings, but also with a view to maintaining an ideological discourse about ethnicity. Inevitably, this model has been flawed in its understandings and its applications, but it is striking when juxtaposed with Myanmar, where the ideological origins of many of its principal political elites were Marxist–Leninist, and where the global forces of political ideology seem, on the surface, to have been so significant in the interplay of national politics. That the Burmese state has not produced an ideology of ethnic integration, only a mindset relating very powerfully to the concept of 'security', relates perhaps to Mary Callahan's recent interpretation that the political life of contemporary, militarized Myanmar is not, despite the propaganda and overt statements of national goals and interests, driven by an ideological position, but by a mentality.[9] This certainly seems to be the case in terms of the understanding of ethnicity and ethnic relations promoted through the state, and only when state archives become more accessible will it be possible to determine the degree of ideological impetus there may have been in the conduct of ethnic politics emanating from central structures.

Idealizing Ethnic Relations in Burma

Attempts to develop cultural constructions of Myanmar's political life, including its ethnic politics, are often criticized, but it is difficult to explain the longevity and gravity of Burma's ethnic fissures through any straightforward model of ethnic politics that excludes an analysis of the politics of ethnicity, with its significant cultural dimensions. The search for explanations of Myanmar's ethnic crisis has, perhaps inevitably, led to the view that it was the colonial state that transformed ethnic relations, and that it did so in such a way that conflict was made inevitable. This is incontrovertibly true in some respects, but the deeper meanings of this transformation are yet to be fully understood in the case of Myanmar. It may yet be the case that the colonial state did not create the empirical and epistemological level of misunderstanding between Burman and 'minority' cultures that this model tends to infer — instead it forced a re-orientation to ethnicity as a social fissure that would no longer permit a lack of familiarity at the level of governance. The alternative view is the rather pointless perspective that there was a kind of innate ethnic harmony or empathy in pre-colonial relations when, as Thant Myint-U recently pointed out, the historical reality was that pre-colonial Burma was an expansionist, aggressive and, until the arrival of the British forces, an increasingly confident military state.[10] There was no need in the traditional Burman polity to intellectualize the experience of difference with non-Burman peoples other than through its own models.

There has been significant research on Burma's pre-colonial 'ethnic' relations, and it tends to focus on the description of social (hierachical) and political (spatial and centre/periphery) relations between the historical Burmese state and what are today defined as Myanmar's ethnic groups. Yet these were not neutral or even equal relationships, although significant degrees of autonomy were often maintained by groups in contact with the Burmese court or with its military extensions. These relationships tended to be confirmed and consolidated through certain socioritual practices in which participation indicated the integration (even if only temporarily) of one domain into the sociopolitical world of the other. Bénédicte Brac de la Perrière, for example, has described how the extension of the Burman *nat* or spirit cult, officially sanctioned by the Burmese kings, was an important part of the integration of localities, including non-Burman territories, into one political, ritual and cosmological sphere. The pantheon of the particular spirits concerned often had non-Burman origins, but Brac de la Perrière states:

> Shan identity appears emblematic of all ethnic differences in the Burmese cult. This could be linked to the fact that, in Burmese history, Shan chiefdoms have often occupied an intermediate position between Burmese kingdoms and the populations living at the margins. However, stories of nat convey an image of the superiority of the Burmese polity over the Shan political order. In other words, they are conveying Burmese conceptions of the differences between the working of Burmese society and that of neighbouring societies.[11]

One might consider here Michael Taussig's view of mimicry as a faculty, and in the politicized domains of the ritual and social, mimicry and alterity were and still are well developed political sensibilities in ethnic relations across Myanmar's sociopolitical landscape. For those on the 'power' side of the power relationship, however, there is no need for a complex reconfiguration of the meanings of social difference, which can be modelled in line with their own assumptions and prejudices. However, this political 'faculty', as Taussig would have it, also enables symbols and cultural forms to be redefined alterically, producing an inversion of power relations through local narratives of difference. It is this which enables many ethnic groups in Myanmar to feel that, despite the power of the modern state and its will to represent them according to its own models, they still have powerful intellectual weapons to contest state constructions of their societies — and this is what underpins the politics of ethnicity.

It is often inferred that the mimicking of the cultural features of Myanmar state's 'Others Within', through museum displays, parades and national rituals, is an ideologically driven and manipulative reductionism of ethnic cultural complexity, formulated as a policy within the state. It may not, however, be necessary to interpret these representations of Myanmar's 'National Races' in this way: we should not dismiss the idea that perhaps they are a more genuine reflection of the state's understanding of its Others than is sometimes assumed, once again pointing towards the non-ideological structure of ethnic relations as defined by the central regime. Especially for the 'traditional' hill-dwelling people beyond the Buddhist realm, this fissure is not perceived as an ideological dilemma but as an outcome of deep-rooted prejudices, which in turn have had implications for the development of systems of governance through which non-Burman minorities are permitted to access their community rights.

An appeal for a return to supposedly pre-colonial 'norms' in the ethnic relationships of the Burmese state, the idealized model of a 'National Spirit' to which the regime currently seems to aspire, even if it were possible, would not enable post-colonial Myanmar to confront, in substantive ways, the range of social and cultural fissures now evident within its territories, of which ethnic identities are a cause, a reflection and a component. Yet, fundamental cultural prejudices and cognitive models of Other-ness that stand somewhat outside and beyond a colonial heritage seem to have driven the rhetoric of governance towards both 'indigenous' and 'non-indigenous' groups in the territories of contemporary Myanmar. The negative experience of colonialism seems to have validated these notions and transfigured them into an extreme form, and the emphasis on security in the modern millitary state seems to have facilitated the further development of these cultural preconceptions within a larger idio-syncratic, officially-sanctioned mentality of xenophobia. It is this, combined with the lazy discourse of the 'loss' of an ethnic idyll based on an ahistorical projection of contemporary Myanmar on a range of competing geographies, that has significantly hindered the resolution of Myanmar's tragedies.

Federation, Union and the Breakdown of Trust

As stated earlier, it is frequently commented by non-Burmans of their neighbours that the fundamental difficulty, whilst its resolution must take on a political form, resides at a deeper, epistemological level, in the domain of prejudice and the discourses of discrimination.[12] There is thus a complex inter-relationship between this less tangible notion of the failure of political governance towards minority communities in Myanmar and the detailed history of its tangible political failings.

Burma gained independence from the British in January 1948. The governmental structure of the newly independent country, derived from a Constitution agreed upon in 1947, is sometimes referred to as being 'quasi-federal' but was in fact centered on a bicameral parliament, the lower house of which was the legislative Chamber of Deputies, the upper chamber being called the Chamber of Nationalities. This was the seat for representatives from the State Councils of the country's various regions, as well as some non-Burman ethnic communities residing in the heartland of the historical and contemporary Burmese state. The Chamber of Nationalities had been created in an attempt to encapsulate and resolve the increasingly forceful post-War demands of many of Burma's ethnic minority political elites, especially as independence became an imminent prospect, that the new state should not only adequately represent their distinct interests but should also include them visibly and meaningfully in the representative and legislative process at the centre of the 'federal' structure which in fact never lived up to its name. In the upper chamber 125 seats were created, of which seventy-six, including four for Anglo-Burman communities, were dedicated according to categorizations incorporating a non-Burman ethnic dimension. For 72 of these seats, the ethnic dimension was territorially grounded, 25 seats being allotted to Shan State, 12 to Kachin State, 8 seats to the Special Division of the Chins (from 1974 known as Chin State), 3 seats to Karenni State (later renamed Kayah State), 24 to ethnic Karen constituencies (the structure of a Karen

State not being confirmed at the time of independence), and 53 to all other territories, which were considered predominantly (but not exclusively) Burman.

In many respects, the 1947 Constitution resembles more a work in progress than a full-fledged system of governance, and most striking in this respect is the right the Karenni and Shan States were accorded, undoubtedly unrealistically given Burma's regional security concerns, to cede from the Union after ten years if agreed by State plebiscite. This article was adopted after the initial publication of the Constitution on 24 September 1947, and was agreed upon following a series of consultations with ethnic minority leaders, who suspected that the federal ideal was not being fully addressed by a system of State Councils and a Chamber of Nationalities and federalism could not otherwise be guaranteed as a goal of the newly independent nation. This is a point of view still expressed, for example, by the late Chao-Tzang Yawnghwe, the Shan politician and descendant of the first President of Burma, Sao Shwe Thaike, who commented that the Burman political elite of all orientations must reconsider their understanding of the Burmese term for 'Union' (as in Union of Burma), *Pyidaungzu*, as a conglomerate of equal components, and not as a structure that places the Burma 'mother state' at its gravitational centre.[13] Likewise, many ethnic leaders today object to the term 'ethnic minority' for its implication of subordinate status, preferring 'ethnic nationality' as a means of addressing what is perceived to be an endemic prejudice, embedded in central political structures, towards ethnic claims for equality of political rights, as discussed. Ultimately, this article of the Constitution led to its dysfunction. When Shan State decided to claim this right, it provoked a political crisis that ultimately led to the establishment of the military regime in 1962. In 1974, this regime introduced a new Constitution which put in place a unitary structure of government, because of which the States lost their internally autonomous administrations.

Yet, even the original 1947 Constitution was, from the outset, considered by many to be an act of compromise. Prior to this constitutional arrangement, a pact of understanding known as the Panglong Agreement had been signed on 12 February 1947 between General Aung San and leading Kachin, Chin and Shan political representatives — an event which is evoked today in the UN's call for a contemporary Tripartite Dialogue. General Aung San was a leader of the main nationalist Burmese organization, the Anti-Fascist People's Freedom

League (AFPFL), a collective of different groups with somewhat divergent goals and interests, and was also leader of the Executive Council of the Governor of Burma in the period immediately preceding Independence. In July 1947, he was assassinated along with six other members of his Cabinet and his role was then assumed by the socialist idealist, Thakin Nu, later U Nu, who was Prime Minister from 1948 to 1956, and then again in 1957–58 and 1960–62, at which point there was a coup by the army under General Ne Win, which has retained power ever since.

The Panglong Agreement itself came close on the heels of another more contentious 1st Panglong Conference held in March 1946, which Aung San did not attend because initially he had not been invited and because he refused to go when he finally was. The first Panglong Conference had been initiated as part of a cultural festival organized by the *soapha* or traditional chiefs of the Shan States, but it has long been suspected that the instigator of the event as a political forum for the discussion of the political future of the predominantly non-Burman Frontier Areas was H.N.C. Stevenson, Director of the Frontier Areas Administration and a fascinatingly controversial defender of ethnic claims for political autonomy in the years preceding Independence. A few revealing documents pertain especially to the 1946 meeting. Some of Stevenson's comments, as revealed in a Secret Report, point at a micro-level to certain core themes in the failure of governance in Burma to deal with the wider issues of ethnic minority political claims and rights. Not least is the revelation that the controversial Burmese politician U Saw, who was implicated later in Aung San's assassination, was a much more effective personality in his dealings with the ethnic minority leaders than U Nu, who, by Stevenson's account, shocked the audience with his anti-British rhetoric and failure to understand the political culture he was entering.[14] Stevenson commented that 'Saw...made the first concrete constitutional proposals ever made to the Frontier peoples by a leading Burman.' His conclusions however were that '[Saw] might have carried the day if only the Hill people had been able to feel the least confidence in Burmese promises. That was the crux of all the arguments against union.... From every side hopes were expressed that the day of union could be postponed until the peoples of the Frontier Areas had built up a federal organisation strong enough to ensure equitable treatment from Burma. In short the frontier peoples are still very uncertain and afraid about the future.'[15]

The reason why the Panglong Agreement, therefore, remains a key marker for many ethnic groups who reject the idealized workings of a latter day Union 'Spirit' and the discrepancies of the 1947 Constitution, is because it posited a definite federal administrative structure for the new state: 'Full autonomy in internal administration for the Frontier Areas is accepted in principle',[16] in which representatives from the various non-Burman majority areas would have one Counsellor and two Deputy Counsellors on the Executive Council but, crucially, this Executive Council would not interfere in the internal administration of these autonomous states. However, the reason why this Agreement was accepted, rather than a continued demand for independence within a Burma with Dominion status, is explained in the preface to the Agreement:

> A conference having been held at Panglong, attended by certain Members of the Executive Council of the Governor of Burma, all Saohpas and representatives of the Shan States, the Kachin Hills and the Chin Hills, the members of the conference, believing that freedom will be more speedily achieved by the Shans, the Kachins and the Chins by their immediate co-operation with the Interim Burmese Government, have accordingly, and without dissentients, agreed as follows: ...

The rapid progress made in the negotiations towards full independence necessitated some speedy internal agreements that would carry along a critical mass of ethnic opinion, if not all. Clearly some ethnic leaders considered this to be a necessary act of realpolitik. This also explains to some extent the acceptance of the 1947 Constitution, which seemed to be an even greater compromise or an act of faith in relation to the prospects of a federal future. Certainly, this is the interpretive account of events and their outcomes that many ethnic minority leaders adhere to today.

The Panglong Agreement was, therefore, markedly different in certain key respects to the 1947 Constitution, namely in its recognition that a federal structure should be established and in acknowledging the internal autonomy of the so-called Frontier Areas. These territories had since 1937 been administered separately from what was then known as Ministerial Burma — the Burman heartland and centre of the colonial Burmese state. The Panglong Agreement has become a key marker in any discussion of minority rights and political governance in Burma/Myanmar, as stated earlier. Although the Agreement was never realized, it was subsequently rhetorically transformed, indeed mythologized, as the more ephemeral 'Panglong Spirit' by all of Burma's civil nationalist and military regimes, as well as by the contemporary democratic opposition led by the NLD. The 'Panglong Spirit' was/is deemed to be an empathetic, mutually respectful relationship between all the ethnic communities within the modern Burmese/Myanmar state. It is the ideal *frame-of-mind* — rather than being an agreement — to work towards harmonious systems of ethnic governance, the federal nature of which remains a somewhat ambivalent goal even for the NLD, and it evokes the idealized understanding of historical relations described above. Inevitably, therefore, much of the rhetoric of this 'Spirit' is determined by historical assumptions and preconceptions rather than as an ideological framework born of interpretive models of ethnicity and meanings of difference. The transformation from 'Agreement' to 'Spirit' originated less as an ideological shift at the centre of Burma's political life than as an empirical one. The term 'Panglong Spirit' seems to have been used first in 1953, following the first Union Conference after the establishment of the new territory of Karen State. The domicile of many Karen peoples lay in the heartland of the ethnic Burman state and its delta region, and the delineation of Karen constituencies made the simple carving out of an ethnic Karen territory a difficult task in the hurried negotiations leading to independence. The initial constitutional territorial base of the Karen peoples was thus through the medium of the 'Kaw-thu-lay' (Kawthoolei) Special Region, carved out of Salween District. Karen representatives, however, had not been signatories to the Panglong Agreement and the Karen National Union thus began its armed resistance to the Burmese government in 1948.

Although signatories to the Panglong Agreement believed they had signed in favour of general political principles that were of benefit to all ethnic minorities within what was to be the new Burmese state, the 1947 Constitution had to directly address issues such as the founding of Karen State and other ethnic minority interests that were not engaged with in the generalized statements of Panglong. Karenni State, for example, was expected in 1947 to re-orient its historical autonomy from a Burmese centre; no representatives from these areas had been signatories to the Panglong Agreement. One of the Karenni territories, the State of Mongpai, controversially became part of Shan State in 1947; prior to this an unsympathetic account of the Mongpai *saopha,* who was attending the Panglong Conference at the same time, is recorded by the Frontier Areas Committee of Enquiry, which was taking place concurrently.[17] The report of this Committee is nothing if not revealing of some of the complexities of ethnic relations within the Frontier Areas with respect to Ministerial Burma, and perceived ethnic minority interests in relation to the Dominion or other post-independence structures, which one gets no sense of from Panglong. Other communities, such as the Mons, had no separate, ethnically-framed territorial determinant in the 1947 Constitution, despite a consciousness on all sides of a distinct historical Mon presence as a non-Burman people in the Burman state (a territory which, at various points in history, they also ruled). The area which in 1974 was redesignated Mon State was in 1947 part of a wider Tenasserim Division, and once again, no Mon representative signed the Panglong Agreement. It was only in 1974 when, in the midst of some of the most serious internal conflicts experienced by the post-colonial Burmese state, the military regime amended the 1947 Constitution and progressed with its concerted nationalization programme, that some of these issues were 'resolved', albeit in an entirely negative sense.

Citizenship, Indigeneity and Ethnicity

The inverted historical view of U Saw and U Nu presented in Stevenson's document on Panglong, when seen from a 'non-central' perspective, is useful for refocusing on the immediate post-Independence years, when U Nu was Prime Minister. This is commonly referred to as the Parliamentary Era, the high watermark of democratic maturity in independent Burma. Yet the 1950s were from the outset challenging times for the new state as the Cold War and the war in Korea dominated international headlines in Rangoon, and awareness of the immediacy of a Kuomintang (KMT) counter-attack and the threat of Communist expansion were relayed not as international news but as issues that were embedded in domestic politics. This was because of the involvement of communist and KMT forces with insurgent groups in many areas of the country which were in active revolt following Independence, as well as discussions regarding the inclinations and political affiliations of Burma's extensive range of political factions. However, a continuing theme in the popular press also indicates some of the more xenophobic inclinations that lay just beneath the surface of post-colonial Burmese political and social life. Distrustful representations of Chinese residents domiciled in Burma and their multitudinous societies filled many newspaper columns, especially reports of Chinese intra-community muggings and assaults on the streets of Rangoon, which were often attributed with a political motivation and which seemed to bring the KMT and the communist onslaught on the Burmese state right to people's doorsteps.

A continuing theme in Burmese politics in these early years of independence was that of nationality and who should be given citizenship in the new state. The Union Citizenship Act of 1948 fleshed out the label 'indigenous' as used in the 1947 Constitution and stated that this was to be used in reference to the following groups:

> 3. (1) For the purposes of section 11 of the Constitution the expression "any of the indigenous races of Burma" shall mean the Arakanese, Burmese, Chin, Kachin, Karen, Kayah, Mon or Shan race and such racial group as has settled in any of the territories included within the Union as their permanent home from a period anterior to 1823 A. D. (1185 B.E.).

It is the 1982 Citizenship Act which is usually cited as a notorious act of ethnic discrimination, targeted at Moslem Rohingya immigrants in Rakhine State (in particular). However, it is important to remember that the complex and confused rendering of the relationship between notions of indigeneity, ethnicity, territoriality and rights within the modern Burmese nation's structures of governance existed in a nascent form even at the outset. 1823 was selected as the year according to which indigeneity was to be defined, for this was a moment prior to the concerted, military British colonial expansion that took place in Burma, commencing with the first Anglo-Burmese War of 1824–26. The colonial state is deemed by the present military regime, as well as by the norms of Burmese national history, to be the originator of a host of ethnographic perversions wrought upon Burma, which transformed its ethnic integrity. Thus, the claim of habitation prior to 1823 is deemed a minimum requirement of historical affiliation to the contemporary state — even though the Burmese state did not then exist as a structure of governance in many of the territories it today claims.

The arrival of the British, who extended their control over Burmese territory, its satellite areas and beyond through three wars (1824–26, 1852–53 and 1885), transformed the political organization of the state at an epistemological level by removing the monarchy and forcing most of the Burmese administrative and intellectual elite into exile.[18] This led to a large demographic and ethnographic shift in urban Burma due to immigration from India, particularly from the south, and from Sri Lanka, as immigrants entered the country to fill the administrative positions and economic niches left vacant. The reality and perception of Indian influence on Burma's political and economic life under colonialism led to violent anti-Indian riots in the 1930s, mass-scale Indian emigration from Burma in the 1950s, and an entrenched racial discourse against the influence of Indian economic self-interests in Burma (typified in an iconic way by the Chettiar moneylenders). Anti-Chinese riots were seen in the 1960s when China declared its open support for the BCP. While many Indian immigrants returned to India, a comparable option was not available to Chinese residents, many of whom would only consider moving to Taiwan, with whom non-aligned Burma had no diplomatic relations. This discourse against 'non-indigenous' residents was present during the U Nu period and was exacerbated over many decades by the particular hatreds of the military dictator General Ne Win.

Early Citizenship Acts writ the claims of peoples domiciled in the new state to citizenship fairly broadly, but the militarized state has modified these further. For example, the 1982 Citizenship Law states:

> 3. Nationals such as the Kachin, Kayah, Karen, Chin, Burman, Mon, Rakhine or Shan and ethnic groups as have settled in any of the territories included within the State as their permanent home from a period anterior to 1185 B.E., 1823 A.D. are Burma citizens.
> 4. The Council of State may decide whether any ethnic group is national or not.

It goes on to posit a three-fold classification of citizenship types, including a notion of 'Associate Citizenship', which was criticized as a contravention of the right to equality in citizenship by the UN Special Rapporteur on Human Rights in 1997.[19] A person's citizenship is colour-coded by one's identity card, and in 1990 these cards also started carrying details of one's ethnic origin and religion. Chinese people domiciled in Burma are refused rights to full citizenship and, as stated, amendments to the Citizenship Law have had particularly deleterious effects on the human rights of Rohingya people and, as a result, on their access to international aid in Myanmar. It is worth quoting the conclusions of this report in some detail, as the unstable arbitrariness of constitutional practice, once again pointing to a less than ideological framework for its development, becomes clear:

> 142. The 1982 citizenship law would in fact seem to be intended to prevent the Rakhine Muslims from being recognized as citizens, as the majority of the group settled in Myanmar after 1823. The law is, however, not always applied, and the Rohingya were permitted to vote and to form political parties during the 1990 elections, which must be seen as a de facto recognition of the status of the Rohingya by the Government — Conclusions — An analysis of the laws relating to citizenship and their effect on the exercise of civil and political rights raises serious questions of the consistency of those laws with generally accepted international norms, since those laws appear to be discriminatory on the basis of religion, ethnicity, equality before the law and special measures of protection to which children are entitled. In the short term this situation produces serious violations of the rights of both minorities and other persons living in the country as well as a sense of not belonging to Myanmar. In the long term, the situation is likely to encourage and exacerbate secessionist movements likely to be destructive of a multi-ethnic and multi-religious nation. Sheer repression following efforts at ceasefire agreements would not appear to be the answer.[20]

Again, it is not the ideological nature of such laws that is necessarily the biggest problem, rather their arbitrariness in relation to rights, which in turn makes everyone vulnerable to the vagaries of laws introduced merely to assert control over a particular 'ethnic issue' at any given time. Such laws have deep-seated prejudicial roots that defy ideological definition. These prejudices are not confined to state structures but also extend out from societal discrimination, although many ordinary Burman people may feel justifiably angered and frustrated at the unceasing pressure for increased militarized nationalism arising in large part from the need to fight those who are also part of same nation. Societal discrimination configures itself in many ways. For example, it is a common practice amongst some international donors today to require opposition groups from Rakhine (Arakan) State to make a statement of their own attitude towards the Rohingya problem before they can receive funds, so deep-rooted is the local antipathy to the Rohingya presence even amongst many groups who are opposed to the military regime.

This rendering of 'Citizenship' through a historically defined indigeneity has also engendered an ethnographic realpolitik amongst some of the main ethnic groups. Returning to the local context of Kachin State once more, this region has experienced large influxes of migrants, especially hill communities from China during the twentieth century as a result of nationalist and communist revolutions taking place across the border. It has been deemed essential by Kachin political leaders that these minority immigrant communities from China be identified as being historically kin with them (the Lisu, for example) as a means of ensuring their affiliation to the broader Kachin ethnic category within the state, and thus giving them their right of residence. By default this would also lead to the expansion of the ethnic Kachin demographic, which has struggled to assert its right to determine the future of Kachin State because of the large numbers of non-Kachin people who were incorporated in the territory at the time of its foundation. The criteria of citizenship has thus engendered a particular kind of ethnic pressure in relation to these large community labels, their claims to citizenship, rights and representation within the state.

Building Ethnic Categories and their Claims to Community Rights

The main beacon of hope in the newly independent Burmese state seemed to be, somewhat surprisingly, Kachin State. In June 1951 *The Nation* ran an editorial in which it lauded the Kachin administration as a model of development. It stated that the blame for Burma's problems could not in any way be levelled at Kachin State. Within a matter of weeks, however, even this image was shattered as the political tensions in the Kachin State government became public. In July 1951 reports slowly filtered to Rangoon of arguments between Council members, of resignations and serious fissures. A new editorial was written in *The Nation* in which U Nu was criticized for not revealing some of these difficulties, accusing him of misrepresenting the levels of progress and political harmony, and of putting forth what was clearly an idealized rather than accurate account of the situation. What is striking about the Burmese national press at this time is that it was in some ways forced to be so centred because of the degree of fragmentation being seen throughout the country, and the lack of information transmitted from the States to the centre. This contributed to disconnecting the peripheries from central purview and decision-making, adding to the lack of understanding of regional complexities in the central structures of government at a critical time.

The use of some of Burma's most well-known ethnic category terms, or, more specifically, those determined by the 1947 Constitution and the Nationalities Act of 1948 to refer to the main non-Burman 'indigenous races' of the country to identify new structures of government did not mean that these new States were homogeneous ethnic territories, for these categories were in themselves ethnographically complex entities 'on the ground'. Whilst the 1947 Constitution consolidated the political use of some of these terms as primary ethnic referents and gave them geopolitical boundaries, in doing so, it concealed ethnographic and geographical discontinuities. For example, in the 1947 Constitution (as with all others since) the term 'Kachin' was a constitutionally undifferentiated term, juxtaposed straightforwardly to 'non-Kachin' rather than being understood as a complex nexus comprised of diverse kin, language and culture groups. Paragraph 166 of the 1947 Constitution states that of the twelve seats in the Kachin State Council, six were to be reserved for 'Kachins' and the remaining six for 'non-Kachins'. The Minister for Kachin State was to be a 'Kachin', but half of his cabinet had to comprise 'non-Kachins'. Non-Kachin referred principally to Shan and Burmese communities; Indian, Chinese and Nepali origin groups not being considered indigenous races of Burma, whilst the Kachin community was a non-constitutionally defined catch-all category for the 'upland other'.

Kachin State was constructed from the two main colonial administrative districts of the Kachin Hills region, Myitkyina and Bhamo, with Myitkyina being made the new State capital. As a colonial ad-ministrative centre, Myitkyina was a complex demographic space incorporating both new and imperially-derived community networks and relationships along with older, social and mercantile ties. Large numbers of Indian, Chinese, Burmese and Nepali origin people, amongst others, settled and established this town, which, historically speaking, was not an ethnic Kachin stronghold. Satellite communities of Sino-Shan, Shan and others, including various Kachin sub-groups, also established themselves in relation to its various trading, educational and military establishments that emerged. Such satellite villages continue to develop in its environs as a result of displacement caused by contemporary conflicts and the oft-related impact of rice famines and poverty. Both the colonial authorities and the Burmese administration's attempt(ed) to manipulate population demographics in the environs of the town — sometimes by force — with the understanding that this would also have an impact on the wider system of governance in the Kachin region as a whole. Likewise, the administrative, military and cross-border trading centre of Bhamo was an ethnographically rich and diverse place being a historically important trading centre on the southern trade routes between India and China.

The relative vagueness of the term 'Kachin' and its longstanding use as a multi-group category meant that immediately following independence from the British, the term possessed a degree of political malleability within the new state in relation to its internal composition. Since colonial taxonomy of the Kachin ethnic category was neither wholly prescriptive nor wholly consistent, there was still much to be played for in terms of how the ethnic composition of this category ought to be defined. For example, in 1955, the new administrative unit of North Hukawng in Myitkyina District was created, and the Naga people living there were now to be referred to as 'Kachin-Nagas'. This would help the state to curb the authority of predominantly Jinghpaw interests in defining the political agenda of Kachin State, as well as allow it to separate these groups from other Naga communities, which were at this time declaring their support for an armed independence movement.[21] The appellation did not stick, but it does demonstrate the elasticity that ethnic categories were deemed to have in the political sphere. On the one hand, the creation of Kachin State in 1948 seemed to legitimate claims made by the Kachin nationalists concerning their 'possession' of this territory, if they could also consolidate the idea that it referred to the dominant ethno-political community of this region. This community would expect, in turn, to have a dominant role to play in its political determination. On the other hand, in being forced to accept the use of the term 'Kachin' on the broader political stage of Burma, tension was also partly created between the local understanding of identity, place, and cross-group relationships of the groups which came under this umbrella. Such tension might not have had much significance had the desired level of local political autonomy from the Burmese centre been established following independence in 1948. However, as the failure to establish a federal structure in Burma became apparent, and Kachin State was increasingly being considered as just the northernmost region of an expanded Burmese state, the problems inherent in the multiple referents of the term became apparent.

The Kachin nationalist movement, led by the KIO/KIA, has made considerable efforts to assert that the Kachin ethnic nationality should be understood as a composite of six principal sub-groups — the Jinghpaw, Lachik, Lawngwaw, Lisu, Zaiwa and Nung-Rawang. This latter sub-group is particularly problematic and the two labels have been used at times independently and at others one or the other has predominated, depending on the ability of either grouping to influence the local structures of power. In the 1950s, for example, Rawang elders were influential in the Kachin State Council and the term Rawang gained wider currency. It is no coincidence then that some of the main fissures that have taken place in the military structures of the Kachin nationalist movement often relate to, or are embedded in, local issues of sub-group representation and interests within the wider militarized governance of the Kachin region. In 1968, the New Democratic Army-Kachin (NDA-K), led by Zakhung Ting Ying, split from the KIO/KIA. Formed from the KIO/KIA's 3rd Brigade and BCP's Army Division No. 101 based on the Sino-Burmese border at Pangwah, the group drew much of its support from its Lachik dominated base. In 1990, the Kachin Defense Army (KDA), was formed by Mahtu Naw of the KIA's 4th Brigade in the north-eastern Shan State, reflecting local political and military concerns in this region and the influence of the drug economy in determining military governance across this area. In 2006, the Rebellion Resistance Force emerged in the Hkawnglang Hpu region of Putao District, Kachin State as a Rawang militia created with the support of the military commander Maj General Ohn Myint.

As the independent militarized state became a reality after 1960, defining the specific ethnic and geographical boundaries of the term 'Kachin' within the state became a pressing concern in the face of what were seen as Burmese nationalist Buddhification policies and the geographical redefinition of Kachin territory. Initially, Jinghpaw predominance prevailed in the broader Kachin identity, but following the outbreak of conflict between the KIA and the Burmese government in 1961, the need to create coherence within Kachin ethnic identity became a priority. It is no coincidence that with the onset of armed opposition to the Burmese government, vigorous attempts were made to re-articulate the term 'Kachin' through the local ethnonym '*Wunpawng*'.

This reification process was progressively consolidated through state symbolism. In particular, the impact of the development of a national ethnographic stage through the performance of Union Day festivals from 1953 onwards was important, especially as it was used to visualize the rhetoric of the Panglong Spirit, as discussed earlier. The principal communities deemed residents of the various sub-divisions of the Burmese States were represented on this stage in ways that consolidated markers of identity, such as costume and dance, into an essentializing ethno-cultural representation of the nation-state. However, the emphasis was not so much on the display of complex ethnic categories but the display of regional diversity through an expression of various 'types'. Ethnic nationalists then sought to lay claim to the ethnic relations of the particular groups that this stage privileged and codified.

The notion of six groups united as one became increasingly fixed as an internal nationalist construct within the KIO/KIA. The means by which *Wunpawng* was interpreted as a primordial ethnicity reflected the very typical strategies adopted by other nationalist ethnic groups in similar situations. A generic example of oral tradition was transformed from being a narrative of lineages, segments, clans and family lines, into a narrative of the common ancestry of the six sub-groups. The development of multi-group ethno-cultural symbolism was also seen during the years of conflict. Furthermore, from the 1970s onwards, when the indigenized Christian missions renewed their efforts across the Kachin region, Christian nationalism deemed there to have been a common multi-group historical experience, expressed through the Christian notion of redemption. This delineated the historical commonality of *Wunpawng* peoples' ethno-political relations with the Burmese state, as well as their aspirations towards modernity, development and progress. In this way, *Wunpawng* also became embedded in, rather than separated from, colonial models of Kachin, and by esteeming the arrival of Christian missionaries was woven into a historicist narrative of redemption. The various Christian churches in the State, although sometimes a cause for division and conflict, have also provided the main forum through which civil society organizations flourish and have been, therefore, very important in the maintenance of local languages among young urban people, facilitating access to the region by international donors and non-governmental organizations (NGOs).

The contemporary politics of ethnicity in the Kachin region is largely predicated on the issues delineated above and the need of the Kachin nationalist organizations to consolidate, in a time of armed ceasefire, a scenario of indigenized inter-ethnic relations that can continue to unite a disparate range of sub-groups. Community cutural rights in the post-ceasefire setting are very often expressed through distinct community-specific Cultural Committees. This has its origins in the requirement that all groups must have official approval for their activities, many of which have been able to arise only in a post-ceasefire setting, such as in large community festivals. Most of these Culture Committees are deeply embedded in local inter-group pol-itics, but they also have had some positive functions in terms of ensuring the continued negotiation of status between groups and in developing discourses on the relationship between modern identities and notions of 'tradition'. They also have a role in civil governance, as the Constitution of 1974 allowed both civil and criminal cases to be resolved according to customary laws in cases where both the defence and the prosecution agreed to their jurisdiction. Many opt for customary law, to be decided upon by members of the Cul-ture Committees that act as arbiters in such cases, and which are also considered the main interpretors and protectors of traditional practise. It is sometimes tempting to criticize these committees as potential sops to the military regime, but a closer analysis of them often reveals that they have a complex role in negotiating the pos-sibilities for community representation in ways that are sometimes, at least symbolically, challenging to the central regime and to local military structures of governance.

Military Governance and Border Development

The consolidation of ethnicity as a social fissure in contemporary Myanmar politics relates to the all-pervading reach of militarism: military governance is overlaid from the centre, and when it reaches the limits of its extension, militarism assumes other shapes through the authority of ethnic and other militarized forces, which have in turn consolidated their own systems of alternative governance in areas in conflict with the central regime. The agreement to a ceasefire in the Kachin State region has created new challenges for Kachin communities and how they express and claim their rights. Paradoxically, the period since the early 1990s, when most of the ceasefires were signed, has also seen the greatest extension of the

Burmese army, from 180,000 to 300–350,000, although some claims put the figure at 400,000 making it one of the ten largest armies in the world.[22]

The dual system of governance that existed in the Kachin region during the time of conflict has since 1994 been modified in its extent. The KIA, with its parallel civil organization — the KIO — had almost complete control of most of Kachin State for almost thirty years. The KIO was not originally, however, and struggles to be in the present, an organization with responsibilities for the development of civilian infrastructure in the region; its role was administrative, with the specific agenda of supporting the military functioning of the KIA. This was effected principally through the dual structures in which the five Brigade Areas of the KIA were paralleled by five Administrative Divisions of the KIO, whose Divisional Officer was of equivalent rank and/or status to the Brigade Commander. The divisions were divided into administrative layers, which were the *Kahtawng* (village), *Mare* (township), *Ninghtawng* (district) and *Ginwang* (division) and the main responsibility of KIO administrators in these respective units was to ensure that the taxes for the KIA's war fund (in kind or, in places like Myitkyina, in cash) were levied and passed on to the KIA. The hardships wrought by continued conflict and the nature of military governance in Kachin during this time of conflict meant that there was almost no infrastructural development at all. With the conclusion of a ceasefire in 1994, the KIO has rescinded its right to levy a war tax and the Burmese military has been able to move its bases into almost all areas of the Kachin region. The massive expansion of the national army as described earlier, however, often means that these remote Burmese battalions are largely left to fend for themselves, creating great pressures for the local people, and some serious criminal and human rights abuses have taken place committed by these soldiers, who are without an ideological cause and are left feeling somewhat adrift from a clear moral code of conduct.

The Burmese regime's response has been to enforce the integration of 'ethnic areas' through so-called Border Areas Development programmes, road building, and so forth, the main objective of which is security rather than the reconciliation of rights. The Development of Border Areas and National Races Law of 1993 has five objectives:

(a) to develop the economic and social works and roads and communications of the national races at the border areas, in accordance with the aims which are non-disintegration of the Union, non-disintegration

of the national solidarity and perpetuation of the sovereignty of the
State;
(b) to cherish and preserve the culture, literature and customs of the
national races;
(c) to strengthen the amity among the national races;
(d) to eradicate totally the cultivation of poppy plants by establishing
economic enterprises;
(e) to preserve and maintain the security, prevalence of law and order
and regional peace and tranquillity of the border areas.[23]

Curtis Lambrecht has written about the impact of these programmes on the development of Kachin State up to 2003,[24] and a host
of NGO reports have been produced recently, describing the social
and environmental impact of logging, mining and other forms of
environmental exploitation. The prevailing urban myth, which may
yet prove to be more than just that, is that more young men have died
in the ten years since the ceasefire from drug abuse, AIDS and malaria
than during the entire thirty-year conflict. The ceasefire was originally
seen as a strategy for the achievement of community rights for the
Kachin peoples and as providing a means of negotiating further with
the military regime. Few desire a return to conflict, but in the present
situation, with the massive increase and extension of Burmese military
involvement in the region, with international pressures being felt from
India and China for the 'opening up' of routes across this space in
the future, there are very real and realistic concerns that the present
constitutional 'discussions' and the orientation of the economic and
infrastructural development of the region are very far from securing
the rights of ordinary Kachin people towards a stable future. As
one senior KIO figure commented when I asked what difference it
would have made for the achievement of autonomous Kachin rights
if ceasefire negotiations had been successful in the 1980s rather than
the 1990, he replied simply by saying that now it is much harder.

Conclusion

It is standard of post-colonial thinking that ethnicity is a constructed
category, yet this acknowledgement ultimately leads us a very short
way down a very long road. Burma is a bafflingly complex nation
and the role of ethnicity in generating this complexity, as well as the
elusive 'something other' from which these constructed categories

take their epistemological origins, have yet to be fully understood. The emergence of communities with claims to rights within the state, and the longstanding difficulties that they have faced in achieving those rights is not easy to describe or to understand if one wants to penetrate below the surface of a straightforward analysis of ethnic politics. One of those difficulties is to understand the nature of the social fissure that has generated such an endemic conflictual relationship with the concept of ethnicity. This article has been an attempt to outline some of the issues involved; finding a resolution to these problems is a whole other challenge and will require many decades of reconstruction even if and when the present regime may be replaced.

Notes and References

1. The NLD won the 1990 elections and is therefore considered by many to be the rightful government which has been denied power by the military regime. For a detailed account of how this constitutional process functions, see Burma Lawyers Council, 'Burma: The Military and its Constitution', May 1999, http://www.blc-burma.org/pdf/Constitution/bmic.pdf (accessed 15 March 2008).
2. Burmese Ethnic Nationalities Council, 27 November 2007, http://www.encburma.org/enc/enc_info/November/Burmese%20Ethnic%20Nationalities%20Council.pdf (accessed 1 March 2008).
3. In this article, as in most other writings on this subject, the term 'Burman' has been used in relation to the majority ethnic group; 'Burmese' has been used either in relation to a distinct historical period prior to the change in the country's name, or to refer to structures that are perceived as being dominated by ethnic Burman people, with the necessary proviso that this oversimplifies both society and state structures in contemporary and historical Burma/Myanmar and the variety of ways in which the terms Bamar, Burman and Burmese can be used.
4. See, Mary Callahan, *Political Authority in Burma's Ethnic Minority States: Devolution, Occupation and Co-existence* (Singapore: Institute of Southeast Asian Studies, 2007) for a discussion of the difficulties that can arise from various uses of the term 'state' and 'State' in political discourse on Myanmar. In this article, State shall be used when referring to one of the administrative areas designated a State; state shall be used when referring to the national political structures, although I have tended mainly to use the term 'nation'.

5. Bertil Lintner, *The Rise and Fall of the Communist Party of Burma (CPB)* (Singapore: SEAP Publications, 1991).
6. Martin Smith, *State of Strife: The Dynamics of Ethnic Conflict in Burma* (Washington: East-West Center; Singapore: Institute of Southeast Asian Studies [ISEAS], 2007).
7. See, Ashley South, *Ethnic Politics in Burma: States of Conflict* (London: Routledge, 2008).
8. A new centre for ethnological research into the Central Highlands has recently been established, which seems to have been a direct response to the recent conflicts that have taken place in the region with regard to coffee plantations.
9. Mary P. Callahan, *Making Enemies: War and State Building in Burma* (Ithaca, NY: Cornell University Press, 2004).
10. http://www.tehelka.com/story-main36.asp?filename=wss241107Thant_interview.asp (accessed 25 February 2008).
11. Bénédicte Brac de la Perrière, 'Sibling Relationships in the *Nat* Stories of the Burmese Cult to the "Thirty-seven"', in *Moussons: Recherche en sciences humaines sur l'Asie du Sud-est*, 5 July 2002, p. 44.
12. Willem Van Schendel, 'A Politics of Nudity: Photographs of the "Naked Mru" of Bangladesh', *Modern Asian Studies* 36 (2), 2002, pp. 341–74.
13. Chao-Tzang Yawnghwe, 'The Pyidaungzu, Federalism and Burman Elites: A Brief Analysis', *Legal Issues on Burma Journal*, 3 May 1999.
14. M/4/2811, B/F&FA 3/46 (vii): Frontier Areas, relations between Frontier Areas and Ministerial Burma. Panglong Conference, 9 June 1945–14 May 1947: *Secret Report by Mr Stevenson, Director of Frontier Areas Administration, on the Sawbwa's Conference held at Panglong in March 1946.*
15. Ibid.
16. Hugh Tinker, *The Struggle for Independence 1944–1948*, Vol. II (London: HMSO, 1984).
17. M/4/2854, B/F&FA 3/46 (48a): Frontier Areas, Frontier Areas Committee of Enquiry – Report and Evidence, 16 April 1943–10 June 1947. Extract from Minutes of Frontier Areas Committee of Enquiry meeting held at the Old Secretariat, Maymyo, 14 April 1947, agenda item 3: Hearing of Karenni witnesses.
18. Thant Myint U, *The Making of Modern Burma* (Cambridge: Cambridge University Press, 2001).
19. United Nations, Fifty-second session Agenda item 112 (c), 'Human Rights Questions: Human Rights Situations and Reports of Special Rapporteurs and Representatives: Situation of Human Rights in Myanmar', 16 October 1997.

20. Ibid.
21. *The Nation,* 15 February 1955, Rangoon.
22. My thanks to Ashley South for his comments on this and other matters in this article.
23. The State Law and Order Restoration Council, *The Development of Border Areas and National Races Law (The State Law and Order Restoration Council Law No. 11/93),* The 11th Waning Day of Second Waso, 1355 N.E. (13 August 1993).
24. Curtis W. Lambrecht, 'Oxymoronic Development: The Military as Benefactor in the Border Regions of Burma', in C.R. Duncan (ed.), *Civilising the Margins* (Ithaca, NY: Cornell University Press, 2004).

9

Mapping Discourses of Community Rights in Northern Thailand, from the First National Economic and Social Development Plan to the Thaksin Era

Amnuayvit Thitibordin

Introduction

The Mae Ping is a very important river in Northern Thailand. Its source is in the northern mountains near Chiang Dao and its flows southward. It is the heart and soul of the Chiang Mai basin and was originally the major source of water for household agriculture. Till the nineteenth century, the Mae Ping had played a decisive role in communication and transportation between the northern principality of Chiang Mai and the central plains of Thailand. However, when the 'Bhumipol Dam' was constructed in 1953, the resulting environmental impact led to the decline of many of the traditional agricultural, not to mention sociocultural activities that were centered along the Mae Ping River.

During the course of the twentieth century, the urban areas of Chiang Mai greatly expanded. Municipal areas and commercial zones have taken over from the old floodplains that used to be a rice-growing area. One of the unforeseen results of this change is that, at the present time, large numbers of Chiang Mai locals suffer because of severe annual flooding during the monsoons. Many people long for the 'good old days' of Chiang Mai, when the 'rose of the north' was supposedly calm, quiet and peaceful. The people blame the development process for this and, more generally capitalism, which has penetrated Chiang Mai over the last thirty years. One of the major culprits for this is the tourism industry. The construction of resorts and hotels has led to the dumping of soil and other wastes into the Mae Ping, which is one for the causes for the river overflowing its banks. However, the Mae Ping is also at the centre of another, more intellectual controversy. Over the same period, the twin concepts referred to as 'community rights' (*sitthi chumchon*) and 'community culture' (*watthanatham chumchon*) have been developed by a number of academics and students in Chiang Mai. This discourse reached its zenith in the 1990s, and has played a significant role in local and national politics. This article will focus on Chiang Mai and discuss research on the subject of community rights and village community that has been undertaken by various Thai scholars. 'Mae Ping' has another, even more contemporary significance. Chiang Mai is the birthplace and electorate of the former democratically-elected Prime Minister of Thailand, Thaksin Shinawatra, whose government was overthrown in a royalist military coup on 19 September 2006. Both Thaksin and the policies his government introduced were seen to be a direct confrontation with the networks of scholars, NGOs and media commentators that have been active in promoting the discourse of community rights and community culture.

The other term in the title, 'Moonlight', refers to the romantic notion that the urbanized middle class (especially in Bangkok) has towards Thailand's rural villages. Those active in community rights discourses dream about an idyllic, rural utopia inhabited by pure, innocent villagers living in harmony with their fellows and with nature. Capitalism does not and certainly should not be allowed to infiltrate into such a society. When Thaksin was Prime Minister his private residence in Bangkok was named 'Jan Song La', which is a literary phrase meaning, 'moonlight that shines upon the world', but which also carried a second, more political connotation of the small clique of 'Thai Rak Thai' (TRT) party members, who were directly associated with Thaksin.[1]

In this article I have used the phrase 'Mae Ping Moonlight' to refer to the romantic notions in Thailand of 'community villages' and 'community rights', first introduced by Marxian academics in the 1970s and that have enjoyed enduring popularity amongst Thai academics, the media and the urban middle class over the last thirty years. These notions clashed with numerous government policies implemented by the TRT government, which tended to be viewed negatively by the middle class as a cynical form of 'populism'. Royalist forces, supported by the military, eventually took advantage of this wave of middle-class emotion and a resulting street protest movement, using them as a pretext to carry out the coup d'etat of 19 September 2006.

Northern Thailand and Discourses of Development

Northern Thailand is a borderland that comprises the native lands of numerous ethnic minorities including the Tais, Lahus, Karens and others. It is also well-known for the cultivation of narcotic crops. This article focuses on four distinct time periods in order to understand how discourses about community rights have been constructed and have established themselves in Northern Thailand in particular and in Thailand generally.

The first period dates from just prior to the implementation of the first five-year 'National Economic and Social Development Plan' in the early 1960s by the World Bank and the Thai government. Northern Thailand was perceived as an underdeveloped area and the homeland of various unruly ethnic groups. With this preconception, development organizations and government officials went into the field as if on a civilizing mission. During this period Thailand was also categorized as a high-risk country based on the Domino Theory following the outbreak of the first Indochina War in 1946. Many projects in Northern Thailand received substantial aid from US development funds to reduce the incidence of poverty in rural Thailand.

The second period can be said to begin with the historic student democracy protests of 14 October 1973, when scholars and the student movement began to debate and evaluate the effects of 'development' on villagers. The ideological polarization that took place during the Cold War between capitalist and socialist camps had a major influence on Thai academia. The eminent figure in Thai scholarship for the study of the village was Chatthip Nartsupha, who produced numerous socialist-inspired works on the economic and social conditions in Thai rural areas. It is also during this period that the concept of community rights received particular attention from the academics of Chiang Mai University. Chiang Mai later became a key centre for a nationwide network of academics, students, NGOs and village movements campaigning for community rights.

The third period follows the watershed May 1992 Democracy Protests. In this period, numerous academics from Chiang Mai University, such as Nidhi Eoseewong and Anan Ganjanapan, played important roles in popularizing the notion of community rights. The notion of community rights also received unprecedented legal support with the inclusion of numerous articles in the 1997 Constitution which formally recognized rights of villagers and minority groups over local resources as well as to preserve their own culture and identity.

The fourth period that I intend to look at is the 'Thaksin era' (from 2001–06) when 'revolutionary' changes took place both in approaches to and discourse about local community development. Thaksin's TRT government introduced numerous innovations, such as the village development fund, the One Tambol One Product scheme (OTOP), the thirty baht healthcare system, the 'converting assets to capital' policy and the legalization of illegal lotteries. This article will attempt to address the question why the academics, NGOs and other organizations that had been prominent in promoting community rights were so critical of the TRT government, which had received such unprecedented political support at the village level.

Origins of the 'Community' Discourse

The discourse on communities in Northern Thailand has its origins in the research on ethnic minority groups that was first carried out by Protestant missionaries around the end of nineteenth century.[2] Many works described/explained the diversity of minority groups and their folk culture and practices. However, the most prominent work on the minorities and their culture was written after the Second World War by Boonchuey Srisavasdi, a senator from Chiang Rai, who had published *30 Ethnic Groups in Chiang Rai* and *Hill-Tribes in Thailand* in 1950 and 1963 respectively. Both works were based on first-hand information. Boonchuey's place in the ethnography of minority groups in Northern Thailand is very important. Unlike the works produced by missionaries, Boonchuey's works were the first detailed accounts to be written in the Thai language, and thus had a much greater impact on Thai academic literature. His work is significant also for its consciousness of Northern Thailand's place in a changing world. Boonchuey's background was quite different from other people of his generation. He was born into a bourgeois family and his father sponsored his studies. Following graduation Boonchuey went to Japan for higher education in 1940.³ Boonchuey, therefore, differed from his contemporaries not only in terms of his economic background but also in his more educated, international worldview gained from his experience abroad. This background would shape his perceptions about the world and the people around him. His work on the hill-tribes of Thailand displays his concern for the condition of the highland peoples, who suffered from a lack of education and an adequate healthcare system.⁴

Boonchuey can thus be seen as a prototype of the well-educated Northern Thai elite and middle class, whose relationship with rural northern minority communities was informed by the self-conception of a civilized people who desired to help and protect another inferior people.

Coincidentally, it was also during this period that modern ideas about development were gaining influence in Thailand. In 1950, the 'Office of the National Economic and Social Development Board' (NESDB) was set up, in the same period as the supra-state organization, the World Bank. In 1961, under the Sarit military dictatorship, the NESDB launched its first National Social and Economic Development Plan, whose main objective was the building of basic infrastructure such as power plants, roads, and dams which would stimulate economic development in Thailand's regional hinterland.

Royal Patronage of Development in the North

The first period of modern development in northern Thailand received a strong boost in the form of patronage by the King and the Thai royal family. The King took a keen interest in development projects. Indeed, Northern Thailand's largest dam, located in Tak province was named after him — Bhumipol Dam. Originally named 'Yanhi Dam', construction on the Bhumipol Dam began in 1953 and was completed in 1964. The huge dam cuts across the Ping River, thus obstructing all river-bourne transportation and traffic between Northern Thailand and the central region. This dam personified and portrayed the idealized characteristics of the king as patron and protector of all the people — including both Thai and non-Thai populations — living within his realm. However, the role of the king in the development of Northern Thailand was not isolated but closely tied up with the expansion of the bureaucratic system in that region, which took place with the emergence of a 'bureaucratic polity'. The development plan was implemented by NESDB and was the first economic and social development plan, covering a time period of six years (1961–66).

Constructing the Community

With the expansion of economic development to the north and the disruptions it caused to local populations, these people began to come to the attention of social scientists. According to Anan Ganjanapan, the concept of 'community' came into being in around 1962.[5] Its entry into the discourse of Thai social scientists was a result of Western academic work. Originally, the Thai word *chumchon* differed from the word for village, *mu ban*. It began to be used increasingly frequently for research carried out on rural society. In the initial phrase many researchers portrayed a picture of lonely, isolated villages living separately from other villages.[6] Until 1970, many works on Northern Thailand sought to understand the complex relations between remote villages and the state. The understanding of community was influenced by an ideological framework in which the village and the state were in conflict and villagers were engaged in a struggle against the state and capitalism.[7] However, the academic debate about community and community rights did not have any significant impact on public opinion. This would develop later during the height of the Cold War period and the Vietnam War.

The Cold War and Development of Community Rights in Northern Thailand

Academic debate in Thailand was crucially influenced by the expansion of Marxist social critiques after the Second World War, the onset of the Cold War and the ideological conflict between the Soviet Union and the US, and especially the escalation of the Vietnam War. The Thai government, as a member of the free world camp, offered the US the use of military bases for the American war effort in Vietnam, including Sattaheep naval base and the military airport in Udon Thani, north-eastern Thailand. However, local armed conflict between the Communist Party of Thailand (CPT) and

186 ÷ AMNUAYVIT THITIBORDIN

the Thai government, such as that in Nan province located on the Laotian border, brought about a dramatic increase in infrastructure development in the north. This policy was based on the rationale that modernization would prevent villagers from joining the CPT. Some aspects of local development, for instance the construction of regional road networks, were part of the National Social and Economic Development Plans; otherwise, development was specifically designed to serve military needs, such as the military airport in Chiang Rai.

During the period of Marxist domination over schools of thought in Thai academia the most important thinker was Chatthip Nartsupha, who influenced many scholars and contributed a great deal to the discourse of 'community culture' (*watthanatham chumchon*). Chatthip's research dealt mainly with communal economy and village culture and focused on the development of capitalism in central Thailand and its role in changing the structure of the subsistence economy as well as communal production. In addition, he played a significant role as an editor, especially of a seminar book, *The History of Thai Economics* (1989), which contained two important articles on northern Thailand; the first one by Anan Ganjanapan, titled 'Laborers in Lanna Thai History'.

The principal thrust of the interest in 'community culture' during this period was to try and understand the socio-economic structure of the rural village in the past. Many academics, especially the pro-socialist and Marxist groups, shared the same idea that the process of economic change in Thailand originated from the world outside the village. This romantic idea, developed by these academics and which later influenced large sections of Thailand's middle class of colourful ethnic minorities and rural villagers disrupted by the intrusion of capitalist forces, became a more and more influential trope for academics and NGOs in the 1990s.

A challenge to Chatthip's argument about the outside origin of economic modernization in Thailand came from Nidhi Eeoseewong and his research on the social and economic history of the early Bangkok period. His seminal work, *Pak kai lae bai ruea (Pen and Sail)*, originally published in 1984, argued that capitalism and the money economy had already begun to transform Thai society well before Bowring signed his famous treaty with King Rama IV in 1855.[8] Another notable work edited by Chattip Nartsupha and Somphop Manarangsarn, *Thai Economic History until 1941*, was a large volume that dealt with the impact of the 1855 Bowring Treaty on

Thai society and rural economic conditions. This volume contains numerous articles concerned with many aspects of Thai society. Chusit Chuchat in his article on the 'The Subsistence Mode of Production in Feudal Society: A Case Study of the Village Level from Northern Thailand, 1851–1932', pointed to the decline of the subsistence economy, especially in Chiang Mai. After the construction of the railway line to Chiang Mai was completed in 1916, the north was physically linked much more closely with the Chao Phraya delta. The modern money economy could now access Northern Thailand with greater ease. Import of textile goods led to a decline in weaving activity at the household level because of the former's cheaper cost.[9] Later works by Chatthip continued to focus on the relationship between state and village, and socio-economic conditions of the villages, which were subordinated to the state. Atsushi Kitahara defined Chatthip's view on the village as 'anti-modernist' because he believed that the village had broken down and lost its traditional way of life as a result of state-led development.[10]

In 1980, the government of Prem Tinsulanonda (Prime Minister from 1980 to 1988) offered amnesty to all members of the CPT who surrendered to the government, through the issue of what was known as Order 66/23. This declaration of amnesty led to CPT's complete defeat by the Thai government by the end of the 1980s. As the social demonstrations led by students had begun to decrease, Prem switched to an export-led growth policy and supported private companies to invest in agrobusiness. In 1984, the government announced a devaluation of the Thai currency. Prem's economic policy stimulated the private sector to intensively exploit the country's natural resources, which sparked a new conflict between villagers and the government. The number of demonstrations related to natural resource issues increased sharply.[11] Research on the villages of Phayao province by Ariya Sawetamarn showed the decline of the community in the Prem period caused by the development of commercial plantations from 1982 and the growth of villager out-migration to search for employment in Bangkok.[12]

During the 1980s, academics at Chiang Mai University became more involved in promoting education about development. The Social Science Faculty offered a masters degree in Social Development in 1990. The programme was hosted by the Department of Anthropology and Sociology, and taught by various professors from the same department. From 1990 until 2005, the programme produced fifty masters degree holders. Most of the topics of their research dissertations were related to community rights, community and natural resources, ethnic minorities and their identity.[13]

After the 1997 financial crisis, Thailand's book market had indicated the alternative solution for the urban middle class. These books largely discuss the development and interaction of the Thai economic system and Thai rural society. Many of these books were simply reprints of books published in the 1980s that reflect the polarization between capitalism and socialism. A good example is Chatthip Nartsupha's *The Thai Village Economy in the Past*, first published as a monograph in 1982 and later reprinted as a book in 1984, 1985, 1990 and 1997. In 1999, Chris Baker and Pasuk Phongpaichit translated the book into English.[14]

Post-Cold War: New Social Movements and Middle-Class Politics

In May 1992, the military junta that had seized power in a coup the year before attempted to crush pro-democracy demonstrations. Thai middle-class protestors became known as the '*mob mue thue*' or the 'mobile-phone mob' — a term coined by political scientist Anek Laothammathat. The May 1992 demonstrations show us the appearance in Thai politics of a new social movement led by the middle class.[15]

The short period between 1992 and 2006 was a very important period of transformation. Thai society experienced rapid economic change. The new middle class had gained greater space in public opinion. The end of the May 1992 demonstrations signalled the start of the era of 'the new social movements' in Thailand. The role of the NGOs greatly increased in this period. They viewed themselves as a representative of civil society.[16] Mass communication also underwent dramatic changes. The mass media became more critical than at any previous time. Though many programmes were censored, few of them were taken off air.[17]

The Middle Class and Localism

In the previous period, 'community rights' had been a debate among social science academics, but in the post-1992 era, community rights discourse successfully claimed its place among the non-academic middle class. One outstanding example is Dr Prawet Wasi. Though trained in medicine, Prawet promoted a Buddhist fundamentalist view to building a peaceful and righteous community which he called *santiprachatham* and proclaimed his Buddhist political ideology of '*thammatipatai*', or the 'Sovereignty of Dhamma'.[18] Compared to previous scholars like Chatthip, Prawet was more moderate. Chatthip had called for the autonomous condition of the community. Prawet rejected the modern value system and materialism — especially materialism based on capitalism and 'Westernization' — and called for a new spiritualism based on Buddhism.[19]

Apart from public intellectuals like Prawet, the community rights discourse was largely merged with the concept of localism and further developed by non-state institutes. One such institute at the frontline was the Local Development Institute (LDI). A major NGO, the LDI played a crucial role in creating formal networks between NGOs, government organizations, and social activists.[20] In this period, the LDI was led by Saneh Chamrik, a high-profile human-rights activist and academic. Saneh differed from Chatthip and Prawet in that he accepted capitalism but found the problem of unbalanced economic growth unacceptable. According to his view, villages and villagers ought to be able to find a suitable economic model from their own culture and villagers should be encouraged to interact with the market. The accepted notion supported by the LDI was that community rights had been preserved in the rural areas of Thailand. In Northern Thailand, the LDI supported the concept of community rights for natural resource management based on local communities. By far the most important and controversial issue related to community rights was the debate over 'community forests' (*pa chumchon*). This concept promoted the principle that villagers should have the right to manage the natural resources in their community. The LDI under Saneh's presidency and editorship published a milestone series titled, 'Community Forestry: the Development Process in Thailand'. This series contained three substantial volumes; the second volume dealt solely with community forestry in Northern Thailand and was co-edited by an academic from Chiang Mai University.[21]

Development During the Thai Rak Thai Period

In 2001, Thaksin Shinawatra rose to power and became Prime Minister of Thailand following the TRT's landslide election victory.

Later it became the first party to govern without coalition partners. Thaksin's populist policies attracted the so-called 'poor people' to his campaign with the promotion of popular policies like a cheap healthcare system ('*30 baht raksa thuk rok*'), a village development fund, debt relief, the OTOP local product promotion scheme, and support for Small and Medium Enterprises (SMEs). Furthermore, TRT raised the issue of the economy, which was still in a state of recovery from the 1997 financial crisis, as the first problem that need to be overcome, in particular the poor conditions in the rural areas of Thailand.

Thaksin's policies were highly controversial and attracted much criticism from both conservative and 'progressive' forces in Thai society, especially academics, most of whom were middle class and were deeply sympathetic to the discourse of community culture and community rights.

Thaksin made sophisticated use of the media, including radio, television, the print media and the internet to promote his solutions to Thailand's problems. He encouraged people to read, and take notice of books that were related to business administration, modern management and economic globalization, that he thought might be necessary for his audience, and required his cabinet ministers to read the same books. 'The Prime Minister's Office' collected all the books recommended by Thaksin from 1999 to 2005, which came to a total of 109 books.[22] The books recommended by Thaksin help us understand his government's policies and administrative system. Sometimes he recommended a series of books written by the same author. One important author recommended by Thaksin was Hernando De Soto, a Peruvian economist and Minister of Finance in Fujimori's Peruvian government. He wrote two famous books dealing with development economics in the Third World — *The Mystery of Capital* and *The Other Path: The Invisible Revolution in the Third World* — which Thaksin believed provided lessons for Thailand's own development challenges.[23] The Prime Minister's Office divided the series of books recommended by Thaksin into five periods. The book by De Soto emerged in the first administrative year (2001) of his government. Thaksin himself realized that he was always talking about De Soto's concept about 'converting assets to capital'.[24] Thaksin showed his admiration for De Soto's theory by inviting him to give a lecture in Thailand between 7–9 November 2001.[25]

Thaksin promotes these books in every media and made them required reading for everyone in his party. Once, at a press conference, having eagerly described the short content of this book, Thaksin announced that he would apply the model from Latin America, especially from Peru. The core argument of this book was the importance of the role and productivity power of the informal-sector, business that can boost the economy as well. The book also dealt with the dual relationship between legal institutions and various kinds of businesses in the informal sector. These businesses are more lucrative and more adaptable than the formal sector, or in other words, state-approved businesses.

Thaksin's policy of converting 'assets to capital' and formalizing many informal sector activities like the illegal lottery and motorcycle-taxis was apparently derived from De Soto.[26] Many academics in Thailand argued against his policy. Given the continuing influence of Marxist thought from the 1960s–70s, Thaksin's policy of converting assets to capital could be compared to the Bowring Treaty of 1855. Following the Treaty, the money-economy system deeply penetrated rural society and transformed rural areas from individual units into a dependent economies tied to the urban area. However, the development of capitalism as a result of the Bowring Treaty for most people appears to be a story narrated by an old professor and recorded in books on dusty shelves. It could not be compared with the nightmare that haunted everybody from top to bottom in Thai society caused by the Thai Baht Crisis in 1997. The resulting economic crisis drove many businesses into bankruptcy, and some business people even committed suicide. It was following this crisis that there emerged another powerful discourse related to the earlier community rights and community culture: King Bhumibol's concept of the 'sufficient-economy', which was strongly opposed to foreign investment, multinational firms and the process of Westernization.[27]

The Subsistence Economy Boom

At the same time that Thaksin was promoting his policy in the rural areas, on the other side of Thai society, King Bhumibol invented his 'theory' of the 'subsistence economy'. Under the slogan 'living subsistence', a large number of state organizations and private firms have publicly accepted the 'sufficiency economy' idea and purport to apply it in their everyday life. Unsurprisingly, many middle-class people in Thailand, led by academics and NGOs opposed to Thaksin and his government's policy, have joined in expressing their support for the King's 'theory' of 'sufficient economy'. The state-controlled media, which closely monitors and heavily promotes the image of the monarchy, launched a campaign to promote the King's idea.

The telecommunications company DTAC, which was a competitor of AIS, formerly part of Thaksin's Shincorp group of companies, produced a TV advertisement based on 'sufficiency economy' to promote their product. The advertisement has been shot in a beautiful rural landscape. It is morning and the villagers are preparing themselves to go to the temple for a Buddhist ceremony. The theme of the advertisement is the harmonious relationship between the younger generation and the senior people of a community, who all live peacefully in a 'sufficiency economy'.[28] The advertisement ends with the logo of DTAC, a corporation that earns a huge income from the telecommunications business. What is a large, partly foreign-owned and managed corporation, specializing in a luxury service, thus presents itself with the King's rhetoric of a 'sufficiency economy'. DTAC also hosts a website about sufficiency economy named *Samnuek Rak Ban Koet* ('Love your Hometown') that hosts information about 'sufficiency economy' in text and video format.[29]

The important question to ask is, who is the audience for this advertisement — in other words, who is the audience for a 'sufficiency economy'? The image of villagers in remote areas portrayed in the advertisement as living contentedly without electricity in rural Thailand seems identical to the romantic idea of the rural village that is held by the Thai urban middle class, and has been nurtured by academics, media and the NGOs for almost thirty years.

The 'sufficiency economy' discourse also receives support from large corporate groups like the Charoen Pokphand Foods Public Company (CP) and the royal family's own investment company, the Crown Property Bureau.[30]

Furthermore, shared concepts about community rights and community culture were constructed among Thai academics. Chiang Mai University was transformed into a hub for Thailand's NGOs and academics who share the same worldview on community rights and community culture.

The idea of community culture and a sufficient economy share one common element: both concepts were constructed by the middle class and were also consumed by the middle class. Relying on the idea of anti-capitalism, both are concerned about the condition of rural society and both ideas try to prevent a rural society from being transformed by capitalism, especially by transnational or multi-national companies.

Chris Baker's report on the 2007 UNDP working paper (after the coup d'etat of 2006), optimistically supports the King's 'sufficient economy'. In his article, 'Sufficiency approach vital in globalised times', published in *The Nation*, he describes the 'sufficient economy' as 'an innovative approach to development designed for practical application over a wide range of problems and situations'.[31]

The Right of Ethnic Communities: Quest for Thai Citizenship

The result of rural development in Thailand has been like providing a certain material culture to the ethnic groups without giving them the basic right to be able to constitute their ethnic culture and practices. Instead, the middle class tried to freeze the idea and understanding of these ethnic minorities. This knowledge, constructed on the basis of middle-class perceptions, was based on differentiating between the Thais and the non-Thais on the basis of their language and everyday practices. The Thai government decided to use 'National Social and Economic Development Plans' to modernize Thailand and therefore followed the established discourse on the 'modern world'. To that end, Thai people, especially those residing in the central areas, tried to develop the ethnic groups to become the members of Thai society.

Although the processes of highland development or any other development projects were mostly intended to improve the basic infrastructure and living conditions — for example, providing basic education, electricity, health care and ensuring personal hygiene etc. — on this project, bureaucrats and many non-government offi-cials, as the agents of change, did not consider the ethnic people as Thai citizens but as the other(s) who was merely living in the realm of the Thai kingdom.

In the Cold War period, the Thai government and foreign secret agencies used these ethnic groups as proxy targets living between Thailand and areas under communist/socialist control. During this time, the Thai government's development project was to use the ethnic minorities to prevent any attack from the communist party.

The ethnic groups were quite passive as well. From the Thai perspective, most ethnic communities were considered non-Thai both by the government and by the Thai people, because based on socialization and modern education, the former's behaviour was deemed deviant[32] by the latter. Generally speaking, development projects often improved only the infrastructure and rarely educated the ethnic peoples about their right to preserve their culture and everyday practices.

In 1997, Thai society was hit by a financial crisis. Various old economic structures collapsed. Besides the emergence of a sufficient economy, the idea of 'Thai-ness' had penetrated every aspect of Thailand, due in most part to the influence of the Thai free media.

Ethnic minorities in Thailand never enjoyed any legal rights. In 1997 a constitution was promulgated, known as the 'People's Constitution'. There were at least three articles in this Constitution[33] that guaranteed the basic dignity of human beings. It protects, preserves, maintains their communities rights, culture and natural resources.

While the 1997 Constitution had guaranteed the basic rights for Thai citizens, in Northern Thailand, many dwellers in the borderlands and certain hill tribes still had problems related to their identities. With non-Thai people, many state agencies consider these ethnic groups as illegal migrants. In some cases, for example the Hmongs, state agencies associated ethnic Hmongs with opium production and drug dealing.[34]

The movement on citizenship was led by 'The Mirror Foundation', its headquarters located in Bangkok but operating mainly in Chiang Rai province.[35] They put pressure on Thaksin's government to evaluate the laws pertaining to nationality and the criteria for people who did have a basic right to become Thai citizens. At the level of cultural practice, many ethnic groups in Northern Thailand have multiple identities — between Thai and non-Thai — and they employ their identities interchangeably in their economic activities.[36]

The demand made by many ethnic groups and The Mirror Foundation received a quiet answer from the Thai government and the Thai middle class. The perception constructed by the middle class and Thai state strongly distinguished between Thai and non-Thai ethnic groups, and it is difficult to change the perception that established the law. In Thailand, after the 1997 financial crisis, foreign currency was required to secure it from the crisis. An image of the other(s), of the hill-tribes and the borderland dwellers, can fulfill the tourism industry, which served the economic needs and the romantic feelings of the Thai middle class.

The coup d'etat of 2006 halted all processes associated with the new regulation on nationality and citizenship. But the most difficult problem remained: how to change the Thai's people's perception of the ethnic minorities who lived alongside them and shared the same natural resources?

Conclusion

The emergence of the notion of community in Northern Thailand took place because modern development had penetrated rural society. The pioneers of this idea were middle-class intellectuals like Booncheuy, and the concept was further elaborated during the Cold War when academics, using a Marxist approach, began to view capitalism as fierce foreign evil penetrating Thai villages. From the Prem period, the government's export-oriented economic policies led to the exposure of Thai villages in every aspect, while simultaneously, the concept of community rights found a place in the formal education system, especially in the universities. The idea reached its zenith when the Thai middle class also planted it into the 'People's Constitution' in 1997. During the Thaksin period, two concepts were opposed to the TRT government's policies. Community rights and a sufficiency economy share the same premise, namely that in a capitalist economy, people in a village are lost and helpless, and should thus be protected from its evil influence. Yet, politically speaking,[37] the result of the vote in favour of the new Constitution promulgated on 19 August 2007 did not surprise the people even though the result hints at a direction opposite to that of community rights and a sufficient economy. The northern and north-eastern areas were opposed to the new Constitution pro-muglated by the military junta, both being well known as TRT strongholds, especially Northern Thailand or the Mae Ping river area — Thaksin's hometown. Ironically enough, the result of the vote for a new constitution was a satire of the idea of an academic who worked on community rights. During the entire Thaksin period, they criticized his various so-called 'populist' policies: his war on drugs, OTOP, etc. One of Thaksin's most trenchant critics was one of the foremost academics campaigning for community rights — the Chiang Mai-based academic, Nidhi Eeosiwong. A newspaper article he published on 24 February 2006 in the middle-class newspaper *Matichon Raiwan* (Matichon Daily), titled 'The culture of people like Thaksin', became very popular among various media. In this article Nidhi criticized Thaksin as being middle class of a neo-liberal type: to Eeosiwong, Thaksin represented the dark side of people of this type.[38] Ironically, some months later, the military junta used the same reason as the academics and middle class as their justification for carrying out a coup d'etat on 19 September 2006.

Notes and References

1. Many middle-class Thais blame rural villagers for using mobile phones, hi-fi stereos, refrigerators, etc., which upsets this preconceived romantic notion. This sentiment increased during the period of the Thaksin government, especially following the implementation of its 'village-fund' policy.
2. Daniel McGilvary, *A Half Century Among the Siamese and the Lao: An Autobiography* (New York: Fleming H. Revell, 1912).
3. Boonchuey Srisavasdi, *Chao Khao Nai Thai* [Hill Tribes of Thailand] (Bangkok: Matichon, 2002), pp. 20–21.
4. Ibid., p. 461.
5. Anan Ganjanapan, '*Kwam Pen Chumchon*' ['Living Communally'], in Anan Ganjanapan (ed.), *Kan Wichai Nai Miti Chumchon* [Research from a Community Perspective] (Chiang Mai: Chiang Mai University: 1999), pp. 66–67.
6. Ibid., p. 69.
7. Ibid., p. 75.
8. Nidhi Eeosiwong, *Pak kai lae bai ruea: ruam khwam riang wa duai wannakam lae prawatisat ton ratanakosin* (Bangkok: Amarin, 1984); see also the translation, Nidhi Eoseewong, *Pen and Sail: Literature and History in Early Bangkok*, edited by Chris Baker and Ben Anderson (Chiang Mai: Silkworm Books, 2006).
9. Chusit Chuchat, *Kan Palit Leang Ton Ang Nai Sangkhom Sakdina: Suksa Chaphor Kan Palit Radub Muban Nai Pak Nua Khong Prathet Thai Por Sor 1839–2475* [Subsistence Mode of Production in Feudal Society: A Case Study of Village Level from Northern Thailand, 1851–1932], in Chatthip Nartsupha and Somphop Manarangsarn (eds), *Prawattisart Setthakit Thai chon Thueng Por.Sor. 2484* [Thai Economic History until 1941] (Bangkok: The Social Science Association of Thailand, 1984), pp. 369–75.
10. Atsushi Kitahara, *The Thai Rural Community Reconsidered: Historical Community Formation and Contemporary Development Movements* (Bangkok: The Political Economy Centre, Faculty of Economics, Chulalongkorn University, 1996), pp. 78–79.

11. Praphat Pintoptaeng, *Kanmuang bon thong thanon: 99 wan samatcha khonchon lae prawattisat kan doen khabuan chumnum prathuang nai sangkhom Thai* [Politics on the Road: 99 Days by Assembly of the Poor, History of Demonstration in Thai Society] (Bangkok: Kroek Unversity, 1998), pp. 212–13.
12. Ariya Sawetamarn, *Phapa Khao: botsathon withikhit khong chumchon* [Phapa Khao: Reflection of Community's View] (Bangkok: Samnakngan Kongthun Sanapsanun Kanwichai, 1999), pp. 44–45.
13. The Faculty of Social Sciences, MA Thesis, abstracts from the 'Social Development Program', http://www.soc.cmu.ac.th/~socant/menu_thesis. html (accessed 15 October 2007).
14. Chattip Nartsupha, *The Thai Village Economy in the Past* (Chiang Mai: Silkworm Books, 1999).
15. Anek Laothammathat, *Mob Mue Thue: chon chan klang lae nakthurakit kap kanphatthana prachathipatai* [Mobile Phone Demonstrations: The Middle-Class, Businessmen and Democratic Development] (Bangkok: Matichon, 1993), pp. 91–95.
16. Chris Baker and Pasuk Phongpaichit, *Setthakit Kanmuang Thai Samai Krungthep* [Thailand: Economy and Politics] (Chiang Mai: Silkworm Books, 1996), p. 457.
17. Ibid., pp. 462–63.
18. Michael Kelly Connors, 'Democracy and the Mainstreaming of Localism in Thailand' in Francis Kok-Wah Loh and Ojendal Joakim (eds), *Southeast Asian Responses to Globalization: Restructuring Governance and Deepening Democracy* (Singapore: ISEAS, 2005), pp. 270–73.
19. Atsushi Kitahara, *The Thai Rural Community*, pp. 92–93.
20. Connors, pp. 274–75.
21. Chalardchai Ramitanon and Anan Ganjanapan (eds), *Pa Chumchon Phak Nuea* [Community Forestry in Northern Thailand] (Bangkok: Local Development Institute, 1993).
22. Ban Phitsanulok, *109 Nangsue Kwan Arn Jak Nayok Thaksin* [109 Books Recommended by Thaksin] (Bangkok: SE-ED, 2005), p. 90. The books on the list were all approved by Thaksin. The Office of the Prime Minister published the same list of books under a different title.
23. 'The Other Path' was translated into Thai in 1999.
24. Ban Phitsanulok, 109 Books Recommended, p. 90.
25. Ibid., pp. 90–91.
26. For details on Hernando De Soto see *Peru: Bon Senthang Sethakit Nok Rabob Kan Patiwat Thi Mong Mai Hen Nai Lok Thi Sam* [The Other Path: The Invisible Revolution in the Third World] (Bangkok: Kobfai, 1999).
27. King Bhumibol Adulyadej, speech on 23 December 1999, http://www. rakbankerd.com/goldenland/SufficiencyEconomy/se6.html (accessed 16 November 2007).

28. In the past ten years problems related to the elderly have gained more prominence in Thai society, especially the loneliness experienced by the elderly in the rural areas where the younger generation has migrated to urban areas seeking work. Every day on every TV channel there will be short programs devoted to stories about older people living alone or having been abandoned by their children. Gratitude is typically expressed for the elderly, interestingly they always blame the economic condition and those who leaving their native land and parents without hesitation and did not propose the way to solve the problem.

29. Rakbankerd Foundation, http://www.rakbankerd.com/rbk_foundation/ (accessed 16 November 2007).

30. In my opinion it is necessary to do an in-depth study of the relationship between those companies and Thaksin's government. Many business firms that publicly supported the 'sufficient economy' theory are opposed to or stand to lose their benefits from Thaksin's policy.

31. Chris Baker, 'Sufficiency approach vital in globalised times', http://www.nationmultimedia.com/2007/01/11/opinion/opinion_30023814.php. (accessed 1 October 2007).

32. Pinkaew Laungaramsri, 'Introduction', in Pinkaew Laungaramsri (ed.), *Attalak Chatphan lae Kwam Pen Chai khob* [Ethnic Identity and Marginalization] (Bangkok: Sirindorn Anthropology Centre, 2003), pp. 9–14.

33. Articles 45, 56, and 59.

34. Aranya Siriphon, *Phin kab khon Hmong: Attalak heang kwam laklai lae kwam sabson haeng attalak chai khob* [Opium and Hmong People: Multi-Identity and Confusion in Marginal Identity], in Pinkaew Laungaramsri (ed.), *Attalak Chatphan lae Kwam Pen Chai khob* [Ethnic Identity and Marginalization] (Bangkok: Sirindorn Anthropology Centre, 2003), pp. 27–80.

35. They also operated on the same issue in Southern Thailand with the sea nomad group.

36. Niti Pawkapan, 'Bang Klang Phen Khon Thai Bang Klang Mai Chai: Attalak Heang Tua Ton Thi Pan Plae Dai' ['Sometimes Thai, Sometimes Not: Self Identity and Its Changeable Characteristic'], *Journal of Political Science* 3(20), 1998: 215–51.

37. The total number of people who voted in the referendum was 25,978,954 (out of a total voting population of 45,093,033). Of these 14,727,306, or approximately 57 per cent approved the Constitution; 10,747,441 or 42 per cent rejected it; and 504,207 of the votes cast were illegal. See the proportions, numbers and maps showing how people voted at, http://votemap.longdo.com/ (accessed 15 November 2007).

38. Nidhi Eoseewong, *Watthanatham Khong Khon Bab Thaksin* [The Culture of People like Thaksin] (Bangkok: Matichon, 2007), pp. 11–18.

10

Governing Minority Rights?
The South and South-East Asian Scenario

Samir Kumar Das

Introduction: The Coming of a New Political Space

In the famous Girish Karnad play *Tughlaq*, written in 1964, Muhammad bin Tughlaq, Sultan of Delhi (1326–51), while deciding to shift the capital of his kingdom in 1327 to Daulatabad — about 700 miles away from Delhi, ordered his subjects to immediately settle in the new capital:

> Every living soul in Delhi will leave for Daulatabad within a fortnight. Everyone must leave. Not a light must be seen in the windows of Delhi, not a wisp of smoke must rise from its chimneys. Nothing but an empty graveyard will satisfy me.[1]

Although Tughlaq considered Daulatabad impregnable in terms of its defensibility and central in terms of its command over the whole of Hindustan compared to Delhi, which he thought was too close to the north-west and hence vulnerable to outside attacks organized mainly from that side, he readily understood that defence has no meaning without a kingdom that needs to be defended and a kingdom has no meaning without the subjects expressing their unwavering loyalty to the Sultan and therefore, it is logical that the shift of capital will have to be accompanied by a transfer of population. Thus began a saga of forced migration — perhaps the first of its kind in the region's history, sparked off and catalyzed at the instance of political masters with hardly anyone of Tughlaq's subjects, as the play informs us, willing to oblige him and shift voluntarily to the newly-established capital.

We therefore have traumatic and brutalizing stories of people — old and infirm, challenged and suffering, ailing women and little children physically unable to walk and move — tied firmly to the chariots and horse-carriages driven majestically by the royalty and the Sultan's men dressed in their full ceremonial regalia and dragged all the way to Daulatabad. Many of them lost their limbs or died on the way, yet the capital was established and Muhammad Bin Tughlaq ruled his kingdom from this newly established capital for about two years until he decided to return to Delhi once again, with those subjects who had been able to survive the ordeal of the first round of forced migration. At one level, both these rounds of migration — albeit cruel, traumatic and brutalizing even by medieval standards — helped in making a spectacle that was probably unprecedented in Indian history. While nomadism and human migration are phenomena as old as the formation of human groups, their transformation into a political spectacle — with rulers exercising power over their subjects by herding and organizing them, dividing them into neatly distinct and distinguishable categories, bodily transferable to places and areas suitable for their government — is of course a modern phenomenon.

At yet another level, Tughlaq was tragically modern: he was a modern ruler trying unsuccessfully to come to terms with his pre-modern times. He was perhaps ahead of his times, with rather modern thoughts about the technologies of government in his repertoire. Karnad's *Tughlaq* does not provide us with any comic relief, which most school textbooks that we read in our childhood and our children continue to read, from an otherwise very serious and somber his-tory of kings and battles, wars causing bloodshed and agony. *Tughlaq* aptly sums up the tragedy of a failed ruler, who failed not because he lacked ingenuity and innovativeness but because he was a bit too ingenuous and did not remain rooted in his time. Indeed, he is fed up with his constantly ingenuous self — the 'patient' in him as he puts it — and he finds it impossible to get rid of it without terminating his life. His own self becomes a problem for him. As he cries out:

I wish it was as easy as that. I have often thought of that myself — to give up this futile see-saw struggle and go to Mecca. Sit there by the Kaba and search there for the peace which Daulatabad hasn't given me. What bliss! But it isn't as easy as leaving the patient in the wilderness because there's no cure for his disease. Don't you see, this patient racked by fear and crazed by the fear of enveloping vultures, can't be separated from me? Don't you see that the only way I can abdicate is by killing myself? Could have done something if the vultures weren't so close. I could have crawled forward on my knees and elbows. But what can you do when every moment you expect a beak to dig into you and tear a muscle out? What can you do?[2]

When our political masters repeated the bizarre act, by acceding to the Partition of the subcontinent in 1947 (if not actually conniving to partition it) and getting their populations 'adjusted' and 'transferred', boxed and disciplined into neat and distinct categories of nations, they, unlike Tughlaq, are adored as our 'founding fathers' and celebrated as the great architects of our histories — this time, history in plural. While there *was* history in the past, there *are* histories now. One act of partition severed all our links with a common past history and has given unto us our histories, equally distinct from one another. All that was common will have to be forgotten. Nationalist histories make this act of collective forgetting an obligatory part of our history-writing. This did not happen in the case of Tughlaq. Why did the history of Delhi continue to haunt Tughlaq in Daulatabad such that he had to return and resettle his people there after two years? History continued to operate on two altogether divergent registers; he could not bridge the chasm. Why was Tughlaq unsuccessful in investing his people with a different history? Why did the constant cracking and splitting of political boundaries of kingdoms and empires in pre-modern societies not coincide with population adjustments and transfers? The reason is simple: his belief that he could create history in the manner he had intended turned out to be a self-deception, given that he lived at a time when people actively believed that history was divinely ordained.

There existed certain mechanisms in place in our societies that evidently helped in keeping social spaces relatively free and un-trammelled by the constant changes and upheavals that otherwise swept the political arena. Village life, we are informed, remained un-affected by the vicissitudes of regional kingdoms and central empires. Thus, even if people became parts of different political orders and dispensations — thanks to conquests and outside invasions — they could be sure that all this was happening within a vast yet continuous civilizational space where cultural differences appeared more as differences of degree within a wider mosaic than of kind with frag-ments that could not be pieced together. Besides, political orders and dispensations did not seek to inscribe any new history; they allowed themselves to be instruments of its inscription. Nehru was no Tughlaq — although Karnad's *Tughlaq,* written ironically in the same year in which Nehru breathed his last, according to some, makes an opaque reference to him and at times, caricatures him. While Tughlaq sounds enigmatic, Nehru does not. If the Partition of 1947 did not sound either bizarre or grotesque — 'Tughlaqi' in popular parlance — it was because the surgery was done in order to create a new political space in which the political is expected to coincide with the social and vice versa. The age of modern states has brought in a new political vocabulary in which it is considered neither absurd nor monstrous to talk about partition, followed inevitably by popula-tion transfers. It is only with the emergence of the modern state that each political space had to be culturally distinct and, to use Benedict Anderson's famous term, 'particularistic', required to give unto itself a cultural uniqueness, however fictive and unhistorical it might be.[3] The fiction is potent and modern states seek continuously to do the impossible — of actualizing the fiction in order to become what they want to. Modernity, as we know, is not so much a being as it is the art of becoming. But as partitions turn out to be 'messy' belying all our expectations of surgical precision from them,[4] the articulation of a political space seems to exist only as a chimera, a fiction, but a potent fiction constantly driving states to actualize it. Partition, accordingly, becomes the new means of building nations in a de-colonized world.

If the Partition of 1947 connotes the articulation of a new space — a terribly fragmented one with each fragment thriving and assert-ing its autonomy on the powerful fiction of the distinctiveness of its history and culture — it also encourages people to embrace, enact and further elaborate on the fiction. The articulation of a new political space creates a new form of power; one that (unlike the colonial power) does not inflict pain and thus stands in a certain opposition to it, but holds out the promise of liberating them even as they are turned into its objects. It evokes the pleasure of being at home in one's homeland. This is what the turn from the colonial to post-colonial forms of power signifies to us. Atin Bandyopadhyay's *Nilkantha Pakhir Khoje*[5] (In Search of the Nilkantha Bird) is a two-volume Bengali novel of epic magnitude, in which the *Karta,* the head of a Hindu joint family then living in East Pakistan, notwithstanding opposition from members of his family and most importantly his Muslim neighbours, finds it immoral, more than anything else, to remain there. The family was widely respected in the area and did not have to directly suffer the riots that broke out on the eve of the Partition. In spite of all their persuasions, he was adamant and clung to his decision, something he subsequently regretted insofar as the bubble of fiction did not take time to burst. Correspondingly, we know stories of many Muslims in Calcutta (now Kolkata) who refused to remain in West Bengal once East Pakistan was formed, on the ground that it was immoral on their part to remain in a state that was not theirs. In short, the burgeoning ethnographies on migrants from either side of the divide speak of the same thing: the arrival of a body of people who — unlike Tughlaq's recalcitrant subjects — are now willing to acquiesce to a new political authority with which they can identify themselves and in which they expect to be constituted as sovereign subjects and politically-empowered citizens. Their subjection to the newly-established political author-ity was also a means of subjectifying them — endowing them with the rights and freedoms that flow from it.

Elsewhere I have described this process as 'natural selection'.[6] The appearance of a modern post-colonial state — whether in South or in South-East Asia — is marked by the project of articulating political space in a manner that selects its own people. The Indian state overtly promised to retain its secular character. Mohammed Ali Jinnah assured the minorities that the state would do everything to make them feel safe in the newly created Pakistan. Nehru and Liquat Ali Khan signed the famous agreement in 1950 in which both leaders renewed their pledge to protect the respective minorities in their states. Yet, everyone knew that their pledges ran contrary to the way the two countries' political spaces were organized and articulated in the wake of the partition. Thus, in spite of their pledges, people moved — whether with the assurance of transfer as in the west, or without it as in the east. Not many paid heed to them by way of re-turning to their ancestral homes. Tughlaq's irony was that he had to operate within the political milieu of his time, which was not yet ready for his project. Political forces this time around were themselves maverick and clearly Tughlaqesque; if only history could provide a leader like Tughlaq to preside over them. It only made a Tughlaq out of Nehru — without the travails and irony implicit in the figure of the Sultan of Delhi. Nehru thus became a hero, while Tughlaq remained a much-maligned maverick. The mad rush for settling oneself on the right side of the newly-drawn international borders was evident in all post-partition migrations and population transfers.

This article proposes to review the recent rise in concern for minority rights. While the concern reflects a certain subordination of minorities and their rights to the imperatives of governance — thanks to the initiatives of such multilateral agencies as the World Bank and the International Monetary Fund, etc. — we also argue that the assertion of minority rights in recent years points to the articulation of a new political space, one located beyond the established order of nation-states. Minority rights today are contingent on the remapping of this space and this article makes a preliminary attempt at remapping the political space in which minority rights may become relevant.

Popular Sovereignty and Minorities

I have dwelt at length on the articulation of this new political space, for I consider it critical to our understanding of the state of minorities in South and South-East Asia. Each such space created its own people who were unique to it and this explains why there was a mad rush of people immediately before and after partition in South Asia, relocating themselves on what they considered as the right side of the border that encloses it. Few of us recognize today that the doctrine of popular sovereignty in Social and Political Theory is predicated on the emergence of the people as a unique and homogeneous body. The experience seems universal — only the historical routes are different. The constitution of an unwieldy and haphazard multitude into a well-knit, disciplined and homogeneous body of citizens — so eloquently shown in the historical researches of E.P. Thompson and in more recent times, of Sandro Mezzadra, took place in Europe in its 'highest time' between 1640 and 1660. In Europe, it happened without colonial mediation.

This historical experience gave everyone an opportunity to identify oneself *supposedly* with one's own people, whom one considers as one's own, one's nation, and with it, the nation-state. Thus, many Hindus of Pakistan decided to move to India, just as many Muslims of India decided to respond to the call of Pakistan and migrate to that country. While being free to identify with a nation of one's own choice — if we were to call it a choice at all, in view of the tumultuous days of partition and post-partition riots — one was also constrained with only a given menu of nations and nation-states. History offered a choice, but only a limited choice. The articulation of a political space and the people filling it was made possible by the serial repudiation of similar claims made by many others within society. 'India' and 'Pakistan' were just two of many such possibilities like 'United Bengal', 'Dalitsthan', 'Dravida Nadu' and 'Sikhistan', etc., available in history. I wonder whether there were any possibilities other than heading towards forming nations and nation-states. A lunatic in the unforgettable Manto story 'Toba Tek Singh' discovered after the Partition that he had hailed from a village that lay between the borders of India and Pakistan and was therefore 'no-man's land'. But as the two governments decided to exchange their lunatics, he was sought to be handed over to the Indian side. However, at the time of crossing, he stood motionless on the border for days and finally died lying prostrate there. Repudiation of the claims of such communities as the Nagas and Kashmiris, the Muhajirs and Baluchs, the Chakmas and Hajongs, the Tamils, Shans, Kachins and Karens, the Lhotsampas, the plainsmen of the terai, the Malaya Muslims, the Moros and the Acenese forms the basis of nationhood in India, Pakistan, Bangladesh, Sri Lanka, Burma/Myanmar, Bhutan, Nepal, the Philippines, Indonesia and Thailand, respectively.[7] Minorities are not produced through any act of our choice, for none of us wants to be in a minority. Minorities are produced through sovereign repudiation of their claims to peoplehood.

The works of Giorgio Agamben suggest that there is hardly any philosophical basis involved in the process of repudiation or, for that matter, vindication of a group's claim to peoplehood or nationhood. Popular sovereignty, he would argue, is not about people constituting them as sovereign, but about the power that first of all recognizes and privileges them as people and throws others into the scrapheap of history. People and minorities are determined by what he calls 'practical considerations' — the power of 'pure violence' as he illustrates it — a violence that only the sovereign can exercise without offering any philosophical or moral justification. The way modern states treat their minorities, some of which are named above, is reflective of this sovereign power. This is the power that can suspend all legal and constitutional provisions, keep rights and freedoms otherwise enshrined and guaranteed in the Constitution, the laws of the land and norms in limbo and arrogate to itself the license to expel and exterminate those who do not deserve to be known as 'people'.

Hence, they deserve to be ruled by 'exception' and summarily killed. They simply do not exist in the eyes of the state. As he says:

> In modern biopolitics, sovereign is he who decides on the value or the non-value of life as such. Life, which with the declaration of rights, had as such been invested with the principle of sovereignty — now itself becomes the place of a sovereign decision.[8]

While the people are invested with rights, minorities are left with their 'bare lives'. Sovereign power impinges on whatever they are left with — their 'bare lives'.

The point I am trying to emphasize is simple: violence against minorities is not to be confused with any ordinary kind of inter-communal violence. For, it is not violence that takes place as a result of any chance conflict between communities. Violence against minorities is committed as part of the exercise of sovereign power in order to create and maintain the purity of the 'people'. As such, it is a tribute to the doctrine of popular sovereignty. The 'flag of rights' can only be flown over the bare bodies of the minorities. Every single act of violence against minorities gives credence to — if not reinforces — the doctrine of popular sovereignty. I propose to come back to this theme in the next section. Let me now focus a little more on the dynamics of violence against the minorities. Violence against them has acquired a random character. Minorities are attacked today not because there is an elite emerging from within minority societies threatening to question the economic and political domination of the majorities as most of the analysts would have us believe — although the majority's perception of threat coming from them can only make the situation worse — but because they are minorities, pure and simple. Everyone outside the people defined by the sovereign authority is an enemy and a potential target of attack. The modern state seeks to realize the fiction of a 'people' in probably the most grotesque way. Besides, communal riots are increasingly taking on the character of pogroms organized and executed by the state authorities — most importantly by its security agencies. The Gujarat carnage of 2002 in India and post-election violence in Bangladesh in 2000 point out how organized violence against minorities has become the dominant mode of exercising sovereign power. The Sri Lankan case is interesting: it shows how a conflict initially emerging between the dominant Sinhala and the minority Tamils gradually transformed into a seesaw battle between the Tamils of the north and the east and the Sri Lankan state, centered mainly in Colombo.

Democracy's Secret Project of Nation-Building

That most states of South and South-East Asia can hardly be described as democracies, even in a very formal sense of the term, does not seem to make any difference to the nature of their responses to minorities. For democracies, as Agamben argues, are first of all constituted as modern states. His works draw our attention more to the mechanics of sovereign power in liberal–democratic states of Europe than in the so–called authoritarian ones. The mechanics of popular sovereignty escape the paraphernalia of democratic regimes. Apart from the minorities with a 'bare life' mentioned in the last section, democracies also create contingent minorities, produced through the ever-contingent outcomes of elections.

Insofar as a new political space comes into being with a body of people as its legitimate inhabitants, any further division between the majority and the minority *within* that space — that any representative democracy is bound to create under modern conditions — does not alter its basic character. Democracy, we often tend to forget, is not merely the name of a game; it also implies the reconstitution of the field in which the game is supposed to be played. Such terms as 'majorities' and 'minorities' make sense only within the field of a homogeneous body of people where minorities with a 'bare life', *as if* do not exist. The liberal project of bringing such a field into existence, blood-soaked and painful as the process is, always remains secret and unacknowledged. One has to deconstruct the great liberal texts in order to make sense of what the project stands for and what it augurs for the minorities. In our enthusiasm to play the game that democracy introduces, we often lose sight of the field that it reconstitutes in order for the game to be played on it.

In his *Two Treatises*, John Locke, widely considered as the father of classical liberalism — argues that the will of the majority passes on as that of the people.[9] Although this comes as a sudden and off-the-cuff remark without any reason being provided in support of it, the contention can be cited only if we envisage an organic connection between the majority and the people at large within whom the majority is one group. The minorities cannot be so defiant as to rule out the deep cultural consensus that binds them with the majority.

If Locke ever talks about minorities, it is about minorities of a very special kind — not the minorities with a 'bare life' who are far too adventurous and refuse to exercise their choice from within the historically steered menu of alternatives, therefore remaining docile and tame, and at the end of the day, deciding not to fracture the consensus of the people. John Stuart Mill warns that democratic institutions cannot function in a society 'made up of nationalities', for a society divided into different nationalities is too weak to put up a 'joint resistance' to the authoritarianism of the majority. He also lays down that 'it is in general a necessary condition of free institutions that the boundaries of governments should coincide in the main with those of nationalities'.[10] The political space will have to be adequately flattened in order that the electoral division between the majority and the minority does not turn out to be a cultural fault line too wide to be narrowed down to make them available for collective mobilization against the authoritarianism of the majority. Liberal democracies are unable to cross the fault lines of cultures and civilizations.

This minority, in other words, will have to be culturally vacuous in order to sustain our democracies. Unlike the minorities with a 'bare life', they are produced through the electoral and representative practices of a modern democratic state. The democratically constituted minority, as we have said, is a docile body firmly ensconced in a well-knit and homogeneous people. Nowhere has the importance of minority resistance to majority authoritarianism been more sharply focused than in Alexis de Tocqueville's two-volume magnum opus, *Democracy in America,*[11] a book that in spite of being written with aristocratic fervour, aptly summarizes the author's nagging anxiety that majority rule could act as the 'highest limitation' on justice. For him too, majorities and minorities are plotted along a horizontally laid out social matrix for they are part of what William Connolly calls the same 'national imaginary' insofar as they subscribe to Christianity, give up nomadism and are involved in settled cultivation.[12] By making the majorities and minorities an integral part of the same 'national imaginary' of America, de Tocqueville categorically rules out the claims of Indians and other indigenous tribes, who being neither Christian nor settled cultivators cannot be a part of the people of America. Thus, people as a body is brought into existence through a series of such repudiations and denials, and democracy, by way of constructing contingent minorities, takes no notice of them. Democracy is thus for those who secure the sovereign recognition of peoplehood — and not for the minorities with a 'bare life'. People are sovereign insofar as the sovereign power makes them so. Democracy does not harbour any obligation whatsoever to those who lie outside its ambit.

The distinction between 'bare life' minorities and minorities produced through the electoral and representative practices of modern democracies roughly though not exactly coincides with a distinction I made about a year back, between minorities as nations and national minorities.[13] Mohammad Ali Jinnah — the father of the Pakistani state — never considered Muslims of pre-partition India as minorities; he only considered them as nations entitled to form a sovereign state of their own. But I understand that the category of 'bare life' minorities seems to be wider than my category of minorities as nations. For the former opens itself to many of the non-national possibilities that history might offer to us. As I have said, the point needs further exploration. However, the modern state's treatment of these two kinds of minorities is also different. 'Bare life' minorities are ruled by suspending the constitution and the laws of the land — by way of making an exception to them. Thus, Gujarat 2002 sounds like a re-enactment of Auschwitz — the only distinction being that the victims did not have to be herded together inside any camp. The entire society instead was conveniently converted into a concentration camp. On the other hand, modern states find national minorities to be safe and sanitized, capable of being governed by laws: thus, we have special provisions for the preservation and protection of minority languages and cultures in India. At the same time, there was also the nagging fear expressed by most members of the Constituent Assembly that the Muslims might refuse to remain in India as national minorities — thanks to the horrid memories of Partition. While the Indian Constitution provided for the reservation of seats and posts for them in government-run educational institutions and legislative bodies, the same provisions were not extended to Muslims.[14]

The Age of Minorities and the Neo-Liberal Agenda of Governance

The separation of democratically constituted minorities from minorities with a 'bare life' was essential for our democracies to function, and modern democracies often make us forget that they are first and foremost, modern states. Our greatest illusion about democracies is that we see them as democracies without being states. In this part of the article, I focus on the crisis that democracies of South and South-East Asia have been facing say, during the last two and half decades.

While democracies everywhere thrive implicitly on the creation of a new political space that refuses to recognize any entity situated outside it and develops a consensus around it, we have to recognize that we live in what I prefer to call 'an age of minorities'. The popular consensus seems to show signs of a breakdown — not because of the return of 'bare life' minorities with a vengeance after so many years of de-colonization, but because the so-called 'people' find it difficult to survive any longer as a well-knit and homogeneous body. This is primarily thanks to globalization, labour migration (particularly that of cheap and unskilled labour migrating 'illegally' to foreign countries) growing crisis of livelihood and life-bearing resources, systematic persecution and human rights abuses and the rapidly changing demographic balance in most of these countries. The menace of women's trafficking cannot be understood without reference to the forces of labour migration. We have some sporadic reports on Kachin women in the brothels of Bangkok, the Bangladeshi and Nepali women being trafficked to Mumbai and other metros, Chin women serving as domestic helps in Mizoram, Bangladeshi rickshaw-pullers and umbrella repairers on the streets of Kolkata — migrants are everywhere, notwithstanding the fact that they are 'rejected' in their own land and 'unwanted' in the guest countries.[15] We live in a region where even the so-called 'people' are haunted by the nagging fear of being outnumbered by others and consequently losing their language, livelihood and culture. Their fear might have been misplaced, if not unfounded — but is powerful enough to stir up xenophobic reactions among them. The Assam movement (1979–85) in India provides a paradigmatic expression of these fears and anxieties. The demand for detection, disenfranchisement and deportation of 'foreigners' illegally settled in Assam is an expression of such fears and anxieties.

Besides, as globalization has loosened, in a certain sense, the grip of the fairly centralized national governments over the societies they are supposed to command — thanks to the growing influence of such multilateral agencies as the World Bank and the scruples of stricter minority, refugee and human rights auditing and environmental monitoring, governance today has become a much more disaggregated and multi-centered activity. Under the circumstances, the principle of 'one state, one nation and one people' does not seem to apply in the same way it used to, say immediately after de-colonization and during the emergence of national governments. The people are now called upon to prove their unity at every level of governance. Thus, who exercises control over the streets of Mumbai in India, Karachi in Pakistan or over land to be inundated with saline water for cultivation of exportable shrimp in Khulna, Bangladesh becomes as much, if not more, important than winning national elections in the respective countries.[16] The newly-resurgent gang wars for control over localities and *mohallas* are a sequel to globalization. The majority that rules the country from the Parliament of New Delhi in India finds it difficult to establish its unflinching authority over the streets of Mumbai or the *mohallas* of Gujarat. As the local has acquired a hitherto un-precedented importance for with nations and governments losing much of their primacy, the majority gets disaggregated and the minority conveniently finds a space to play its role.

The plea for minority rights today is part of the agenda of governance — more particularly, that of 'good governance'. To my mind, the Human Development Report prepared by UNDP in 2000 was probably the first to make an explicit reference to the minorities — and thankfully, to minorities based on ethnicity, language, religion and such factors, and underlined the importance of minority rights in guaranteeing 'good governance'. It noted with concern that in countries such as Germany and Sweden, minorities are unable to realize them. While the rights and freedoms are usually guaranteed for all in a democratic country, it pointed out that unless a 'systemic assessment of economic and institutional constraints to the realization of rights as well as of the resources and policies available to overcome them' is done, minorities would continue to be subjected to discrimination by the majority.[17] A justice mechanism, in other words, will have to be an enabling mechanism for the minorities. It indirectly talks about certain special provisions that would compensate for their inabilities and ensure their entitlement to rights and freedoms. The enabling mechanism, most importantly, will be subjected to further monitoring as the National Human Development Report (India), 2001 puts it, by 'empowered, autonomous and credible structures' and civil society groups. Civil society vigilantism has become the new lingo of minority rights.[18]

I, however, propose to read the plea for minority rights being made a part of 'good governance' as only a desperate attempt on the part of the neo-liberals at restoring the liberal popular consensus otherwise severely undermined in recent times. The plea is based not so much on the realization that the consensus around 'peoplehood' was only too impossible a fiction to be actualized, but on the realization that the fiction helped in privileging the cultural majorities in course of discriminating against the minorities. While liberals look upon the individual as the final and irreducible unit of their philosophical formulations, rights, according to them, pertain to the individuals rather than groups or communities. The right to education, viewed in this light, becomes an individual right. But when I witnessed a little tribal girl of 6 years in one of the remotest villages of Keonjhar in Orissa studying in a primary school run under the auspices of a programme viz. 'Education For All' supported by the Dutch Core Financing Agencies (which I was asked to evaluate about seven years back) I soon realized that this right is bound to discriminate against tribal children unless it is accompanied by their right to primary school education in their respective mother-tongues. While the right to education is an individual right, right to education in minority languages is a group or community right. The puzzled and bewildered look of the little girl was instantly suggestive of her complete inability to make sense of the world of education being through Oriya — the dominant language of the state. Individual rights, left to themselves, reinforce the pre-existing cultural differences and inequalities instead of bridging them. Group rights are the means of mitigating these differences and inequalities. The unequals — unless made equal through the conferment of these rights special to them — cannot be treated equally. This will have disastrous consequences for the minority cultures. As Will Kymlicka, perhaps the staunchest defender of minority rights in recent times from within the liberal camp, argues:

> This conception of equality gives no recognition to cultural membership; and if it operates in a culturally plural country, then it tends to produce a single culture for the whole of the political community, and the undesired assimilation of distinct minority cultural communities. The continued existence of such communities may require restrictions on choice and differentials in opportunity.[19]

The liberals and neo-liberals are also mindful of the threshold beyond which minority rights cannot be stretched. It is, as we have said, a means of mitigating cultural differences and inequalities till a point when they become part and parcel of the people as a homogeneous body. The inside of the 'people' is flat and horizontally laid out — occupied by individuals equal only in the eyes of law and does not recognize any hierarchy and inequality within it. Cultural rights are a preparatory ground for their assimilation into peoplehood. Governance — as the neo-liberals argue — will have to be geared to the objective of guaranteeing minority rights as a means of mitigating discrimination and nothing more. It only replicates the liberal project of making and taming a people, disciplining them into a peaceful and tranquil body of nation and citizens and thereby turning them into an object of governmentality.

What if minority rights encroach on individual rights? An example may be cited in this connection. About a year back, there was a story flashed in many of the regional newspapers of Kolkata. A Muslim man while deeply asleep muttered the word 'Talaq' (Muslim word for divorce) thrice without — as he subsequently admitted — being conscious of his act. As his wife heard it, she took it as a joke to be shared with her other friends and close neighbours, some of whom might have communicated it to the local clergy and the Muslim leaders. As the news spread, the couple had no control over it and the clergy sat in a customary court and asked the couple to solemnize what was uttered and remain separate. The woman never thought that the joke would prove to be so cruel for her and their little child. The judgment was: if they wanted to reunite, they would have to remarry and the remarriage would have to be intervened by the solemnization of their marriage with others. Unlike the tribal girl's case, here we seem to side with the couple and argue that minority rights should not be so stretched as to transgress their will to live together as husband and wife. Indeed, Rajeev Bhargava calls it, 'democratic multiculturalism', which, unlike liberal multiculturalism, does not allow the groups and communities to do whatever they want in the name of their culture, for example, practices such as female genital mutilation, *sati*, head-hunting and so on, but asks the state to censor those minority rights which flout the benchmark set by our basic human rights.[20] The liberal uneasiness points to the subservience of minority rights to basic human rights. The neo-liberal dependence on the state insofar as minority rights are concerned is evident in course of both the giving and taking away of these rights. Never before in their history have the minorities been so dependent on the state for the administration of their rights. Never before has the rights agenda been so much defined by the imperatives of governance. The accent on state leads them to make advocacies for building and reforming states in these countries.

Redefining Political Space: A Plea for Minority Rights

It is imperative that we push the agenda of minority rights beyond the neo-liberal agenda of re-integrating them into the people. The neo-liberals fail to realize that the agenda they are propagating and pursuing has lost its relevance at a time when the liberal popular consensus has taken a beating and the world is getting fragmented into minorities at multifarious levels and spaces without being articulated around any centre. The fragments lack the potential of being brought together around a focal point. 'People' today is no longer a homogeneous body but is visited and penetrated as it were by the so-called 'other' — the poor, the marginals, the minorities, the gays and the lesbians, etc. Etienne Balibar has been talking about the emergence of a new notion of sovereignty (especially in the changed European context) that he terms 'anti-strategic' sovereignty. It is anti-strategic because it refuses to remain part of any grand strategy that seeks to organize people into a body, and most importantly, a nation.

A new space has thus been created, as the popular space hitherto organizing and consolidating diverse bodies of people into a nation is getting eroded. A space in which 'bare life' minorities might get a chance to stage their return is thus slowly taking shape. The path that it will take is still unclear. But local overlords and factions, local gangsters, regional satraps and musclemen have become important in institutional politics, either by demystifying the early popular consensus or by forcing the central forces to enter into an alliance with them. All this was perhaps preceded by the collapse of Congress Party dominance in Indian politics since the early 1980s. Minority governments have been ruling India since then. Some states of South and South-East Asia seek to manage the crisis by resorting to military takeovers. The breakdown of a popular consensus has not been followed by any single strategy to cope with it. While minorities have reasons to feel empowered in such a dispensation, I do not know how long the states will take to appreciate the importance of sharing sovereignty with them without adding to the number of sovereign states. Minority rights today call for sharing of sovereignty. Minorities have started making claims to a share of sovereignty without breaking the states. The Naga demand for a 'special federal relationship with India' is just one such example.

Notes and References

1. www.tribuneindia.com/2003/20030817/spectrum/travel.htm (accessed 18 April 2009)
2. www.litarkay.tripod.com/tughlaq.htm (accessed 18 April 2009)
3. Benedict Anderson, *Imagined Communities: Reflections on the Origin and Spread of Nationalism* (London: Verso, 1991), p. 9.
4. Joya Chatterji, 'The Fashioning of the Frontier: The Radcliffe Line and Bengal's Border Landscape 1947–1952', *Modern Asian Studies* 33(1), February 1999.
5. Atin Bandyopadhyay, *Nilkantha Pakhir Khonje* [In search of the bird nilkantha], (Kolkata: Karuna, [1971] 2006).
6. Samir Kumar Das, 'Wars, Population Movements and the Formation of States in South Asia', in Ranabir Samaddar (ed.), *South Asian Peace Studies: Peace Studies: An Introduction to the Concept. Scope and Themes* (New Delhi: Sage, 2004).
7. Reports prepared by human rights organizations or various state and statutory agencies on each of these groups document in detail the atrocities routinely committed on them.
8. Girogio Agamben, *Homo Sacer: Sovereign Power and Bare Life*, trans. Daniel Heller-Roazen (Stanford: Stanford University Press, 1998), p. 142.
9. John Locke, 'An Essay Concerning the True Original, Extent and End of Civil Government', in Sir Ernest Barker (ed.), *Social Contract: Essays by Locke, Hume and Rousseau* (London: Oxford University Press, 1946), p. 82.
10. John Stuart Mill, 'Considerations on Representative Government', excerpted in Micheline R. Ishay (ed.), *The Human Rights Reader* (London: Routledge, 1997), p. 182.
11. Alexis de Tocqueville, *Democracy in America* (Chicago: University of Chicago Press, 2000).
12. William E. Connolly, 'The Liberal Image of the Nation', in Duncan Ivision, Paul Patton and Will Sanders (eds), *Political Theory and the Rights of the Indigenous Peoples* (Cambridge: Cambridge University Press, 2000), p. 184.
13. Samir Kumar Das, 'A Background Paper on Minority Conflicts in India's Northeast' (Washington, D.C.: East–West Center, 2005), mimeo.

14. I have discussed this in Samir Kumar Das, 'Social Justice in the Constitutional Mirror', in Ashok Aggarwal and Bharat Bhushan (eds), *Social Justice in India: The Constitutional and Legal Dimensions* (tentatively titled) (New Delhi: Sage Publications, forthcoming).

15. See, for example, Kachin Women's Association Thailand (KWAT), *Driven Away: Trafficking of Kachin Women on the China–Burma Border* (Bangkok: KWAT, 2005). Sanlap, Jabala and Action Aid have also brought out reports on the trafficking of the Bangladeshi and Nepali women, and women from such districts as Murshidabad and Malda in West Bengal, India. For the state of Chin refugees, see, J.H. Hre Mang, *Report on the Chin Refugees in the Mizoram State of India* (New Delhi: The Other Media Publications, 2000).

16. A good deal of literature is centered on these themes. See, Thomas Blom Hansen, *Urban Violence in India: Identity politics, 'Mumbai' and the Post-Colonial City* (New Delhi: Permanent Black, 2001). Malini Sur presented her findings at a workshop on 'Gender and Non-Traditional Formulations of Security in South Asia', organized by Women in Conflict Management, Security and Peace, in New Delhi on 24–25 September 2006.

17. UNDP, *Human Development Report* (London: Oxford University Press, 2000), p. 2.

18. Planning Commission, *National Human Development Report (India)* (New Delhi: Oxford University Press, 2001), p. 123.

19. Will Kymlicka, *Liberalism, Community and Culture* (Oxford: Clarendon Press, 1989), p. 152.

20. Rajeev Bhargava, 'Introducing Multiculturalism', in Rajeev Bhargava, Amiya Kumar Bagchi and R. Sudarshan (eds), *Multiculturalism, Liberalism and Democracy* (New Delhi: Oxford University Press, 1999).

Governance, Culture and
the Aspirations of Minorities

11

Contested Identity, Negotiated Rights: The Muslim Minority of South Thailand

Mala Rajo Sathian

You cannot integrate every element of our society just by a flag; we cannot win the trust and confidence of all elements and sectors of our society by just a language. They have to feel secure in the system with full respect under the law.

Surin Pitsuwan[1]

Introduction

Thailand's population is constituted predominantly of the Tai race, comprising Tai, Lao and Shan groups, whose ancestors migrated to the region from China. However, there are also many non-Tai groups inhabiting Thailand today such as the Mon, Khmer and Sino-Thai who, like the Tai, are Buddhists. There are also non-Buddhist communities, such as Muslims and highland groups such as Karen, Hmong and Lisu. The latter groups are the minorities of Thailand — demographically smaller and culturally distinct from the majority Tai-Buddhists.

In their attempts to consolidate power, Thai monarchs, from their capitals located in the central region, extended Tai-Buddhist hegemony over large parts of the upper (Lao) and southern (Mon-Khmer) territories adjoining the kingdome. For much of the early parts of twentieth century, the Thai kingdom faced dissent from the Lao (in the north and north-east). However, processes of accommodation and assimilation have managed to pacify the Lao who have been 'fairly' integrated into the Thai state, their common Buddhist faith being a contributing factor to the assimilation. Governing non-Buddhist minorities has been far more problematic, in particular the assimilation of Muslims into the Thai Buddhist polity. Since the beginning of the twentieth century, there have been long periods of crisis involving the Thai state and Muslim minorities. This, however, is a problem exclusive to the ethnic Malay Muslim community of Thailand, who are predominantly concentrated in the southern Malay cultural belt, comprising the provinces of Pattani,[2] Yala and Narathiwat. Muslims who are not Malays, namely those of South and West Asian origin, i.e., Indians, Pathans, Persians and Chinese of Haw descent, are concentrated in the central and northern parts of Thailand and, in contrast, are rather well assimilated into Thai society.

Why have Thai Muslims (who are not ethnic Malays) become better assimilated as compared to ethnic Malay Muslims in Thailand?[3] The answer to this question will partly explain the distinct problem of the assimilation of minority ethnic Malays, especially from the southernmost Thai provinces of Pattani, Yala and Narathiwat, into the Thai sociocultural domain.

Despite their long historical cultural and socio-economic presence, the Malay Muslims of south Thailand are today overtly vulnerable and their sociopolitical rights are often contested. In some cases, their survival and religious–cultural existence is threatened by the hegemonic nation-state. And while the state is seen as contesting the primordial/community rights of the minorities (e.g. their land, resources and cultural norms) and their place in the nation-state, the minorities contest the state's demands on the people and their encroachment into what is seen as a 'minority preserve' (e.g. Islamic religion, institutions and laws). This article will examine issues pertaining to the rights of Malay Muslim minorities by focusing on the present-day rights of the Malay Muslims of Thailand as seen from the peoples' perspective.

From Subjects of a Malay Sultanate to Citizens of Thailand

The provinces of Pattani, Yala and Narathiwat in south Thailand, bordering northern Malaysia, are home to Thailand's ethnic Malay Muslim community. While the Malays constitute the numerical majority in these provinces, in national statistics they constitute about 2.8 per cent of the Thai population.[4] Other Muslim groups, such as Indians, Pathans and Persians, are smaller in number and live mostly in the central and northern regions as opposed to the Malays, who are concentrated in the southern border provinces. In total, Muslims constitute about 5.5 per cent of Thailand's population.[5] Their geographical location in the southern borderlands of the Thai state conjures images of their peripheral position vis-à-vis the Thai nation-state which is centered in Bangkok.

Their 'border' status, however, is fairly recent. Historically, these provinces formed the 'heartland' of the former Kingdom or Sultanate known as the Kingdom of Patani (ca. fourteenth–nineteenth century). The Patani Kingdom was a prominent commercial and political centre in the isthmian region, reaching the heights of its glory in the mid-1600s. The kingdom was ruled by Malay Rajas, who established trade and diplomatic networks throughout the archipelago. In addition, they sought the patronage of the court of Ayutthaya (ca. fourteenth–eighteenth century), a powerful Siamese polity located to the north of Patani, to ensure the survival of the kingdom. Ayutthaya was a formidable regional power at the time and maintaining relations with Ayutthaya provided Patani protection from military attacks from rival states. In exchange for its protection, Patani paid annual tributes to the Ayutthayan court, retaining, however, its autonomy in administrative, fiscal and cultural matters of the Sultanate.[6]

Patron–client relations between Ayutthaya and Patani ceased with the fall of Ayutthaya in 1767. Patani became vulnerable to military attacks from the new King, Phya Taksin and his successor, Rama I. The attacks followed allegations that Patani had attempted to free itself from Thai patronage after the fall of Ayutthaya. Thus, during the rule of Rama I, who established the Chakri Dynasty, Patani lost its autonomy and began to be gradually incorporated into the Kingdom of Siam, a policy that was followed throughout the rule of successive Chakri kings. In 1809, in a move to prevent uprisings against Siam, Bangkok divided Patani into seven smaller states/provinces and administered the region through a trusted intermediary state located in the south. The provinces of Pattani, Yala and Narathiwat were three of the seven provinces. This period of Siamese 'indirect rule' lasted until about 1902, when the last Malay Raja of Patani, Tengku Abdul Kadir, was deposed and replaced with a Siamese Commissioner, while other Malay potentates from the remaining provinces gradually became salaried officials of the Bangkok government. By this time, the Malay Rajas had effectively lost their traditional source of income as well as their seat of power and support. Finally, through a Royal Decree (1901), Bangkok brought the provinces of the former Kingdom of Patani under its direct rule. The centralization of Patani's administration and finances through a centrally-controlled Revenue Department ended Patani's autonomous status and sparked the beginning of movements of resistance against direct Thai rule.

Initial reactions to Bangkok's incursion came largely from the Malay ruling elite and senior Muslim clerics who began organizing (informal) resistance movements. They objected to Bangkok's 'occupation' of their (Malay) territory in a mostly non-violent manner. A change in policy in the 1930s, particularly after the end of the absolute monarchy in 1932, saw Bangkok forcefully impose assimilation policies in an attempt to integrate the Malay Muslim provinces into the cultural realm of the Thai-Buddhist nation. This was a period when identity formation was very much shaped in the 'we versus them/aliens' paradigm, most obvious in the case of South-East Asian states on the eve of independence.

This process of assimilation led to state intervention in traditional Malay preserves, namely their culture, language and religion. The Malay community viewed Bangkok as encroaching on the primordial rights of the Malays, i.e. rights they had long held with little intrusion from the Thai state. These primordial community rights, which included both tangible and intangible rights, were central to the identity and history of the Malay community of the Patani region and therefore considered almost 'sacred and inalienable'. The need to defend these 'community' rights against the conqueror (Bangkok) became a prime factor for the subsequent decades of conflict and confrontation between the Thai state and the Malay Muslim minorities of south Thailand.

The Thai state, for its part, was reacting largely to the fear of colonial expansion in the region. To that end, Bangkok began to embark on wide administrative reforms based on Western ideals of a modern state, necessitating in the process, the need to forcefully consolidate its powers over all its subjects, especially those located away from the capital, in the northern and southern frontier regions.

To the Thai state, the need to remain an independent sovereign nation, given the growing Western colonial presence in the region, necessitated demands of loyalty from its subjects and the creation of a united nation with a strong sense of attachment and loyalty to the monarchy. This was needed essentially to ward off colonial incursions into its territories and, no less important, to prevent the peripheral territories from breaking away.

Contested (Community) Rights

Language–Culture–Religion

In its zeal to create a 'mono-ethnic' Thai state, Bangkok introduced numerous assimilation policies that, to a large extent, disregarded the 'inalienable' rights of the Malay Muslim population, such as the right to practise Islamic law and education.[7] The Malays viewed such policies as threats to their culture, in particular the Malay language and Malay *adat* (Malay customary laws), and their religion; in other words, the intangible rights of the community. For instance, the introduction of Thai laws to replace the *sharia* and *adat* and the implementation of compulsory education in Thai in place of Malay vernacular education through the Education Act of 1921 created strong resentment among the Malay Muslims towards the Thai state.

Whereas in the early part of the 1900s (after the sacking of Tengku Kadir), the conflict between the Malays and the Thai state was centred on a reactionary struggle to reclaim the autonomy and territorial sovereignty of the Patani kingdom, the period after the 1930s was marked by a zealous drive to preserve the distinct identity of the Muslim community. This feeling grew during the reign of Premier Marshall Phibun Songkhram (1938–45), who launched a policy of 'Thai-zation' of non-Thai minorities through his national policy called '*ratthaniyom*'. Under the *ratthaniyom*, the term *Malay Muslim/Islam* in reference to the Malays in southern Thailand was abolished; instead they were simply called 'Thai Islam', referring to their nationality rather than their ethnicity or religion.[8] The move was seen as a clear indication of Thai intentions to blur the connection between Muslim and Malay identities and the blatant disregard for Malay history and identity. This in turn prompted the emergence of Malay secessionist movements.

The rebellion of 1947–48, which took place under the leadership of renowned Muslim cleric Haji Sulong, is one such incident demonstrating the struggle by the Muslims of the southern provinces for an independent Patani. In a memorandum submitted to the Thai state, Haji Sulong listed seven main concerns for which the Muslims sought redress. These seven points indicate not only the mindset of the Malays at that time but, more importantly, it tells us clearly the main areas of concern, all of which are closely related to the issue of rights traditionally held by the Malay Muslims, both as individuals and as a community. These rights, as pointed out by Haji Sulong, are considered 'inalienable' by the Malay Muslims and remain as vital a concern today as it was back in the 1940s. To illustrate this point, I refer briefly to the seven demands.[9]

Two of the seven points refer to the status of the Malay language; that it should be elevated to the position of official language in the south and used as the main medium of instruction in primary schools. This is obviously a reaction to the compulsory use of Thai in the south as required by Bangkok. Language is closely entwined with the identity of the Malay people, therefore their right to use their native language cannot be compromised in favour of the national language. Of late, the Thai language has also become the official language of Islam in Thailand.[10] Thai translations of the Quran and a growing corpus of Islamic literature are now available in Thai. But in the Malay provinces of south Thailand, the language of Islam is Malay, written in Arabic script and called *Jawi*. Therefore, traditionally speaking, Malay (*Jawi*) is the language of Islam in the south and its use is reflective of the Malay identity of the people there. While the translation of works on Islam into Thai is encouraging and will allow for a larger readership and wider dissemination of Islamic knowledge, the right to studying Islam in *Jawi* cannot be taken away from the Malay Muslims. *Jawi* education in the Patani region is a significant part of the history and cultural heritage of the Malay community there. The *pondok* and *madrasah* institutions of learning had existed long before Siam incorporated Patani into its administration, and a threat to *Jawi* education is tantamount to threatening Patani Malay identity and history. In fact, the people of the Patani region refer to themselves as *Jawi*, rather than using the term Malay in everyday parlance.[11]

Up to the late nineteenth century, central Thai was spoken only by about 15 per cent of the people living within the borders of the Siamese Kingdom, while about 55 per cent spoke *kam muang* (northern Thai) and Lao, and about 9 per cent spoke *Melayu* (Malay).[12] As a result of the educational reforms, undertaken partly to fulfill Siam's modernization process, King Chulalongkorn promoted the use of the Thai language as the lingua franca in both religious and secular education. Through a decree in 1875, the King explained:

> The Thai language is of great benefit to the study of the *Tripitaka* which works to the support of Buddhism and, if one is a layman, to the utility of the government service, so that it is an advantage to be literate.[13]

The edict reflects the language policy of the kingdom, which promoted standard Thai as the language of education, religion as well as government. Despite a policy that attempted the 'homogenization' of multi-linguistic groups in Thailand, the Malays in the south continued to be able to speak their own language as compared to the Lao who have dropped their Lao and *kham muang* for Thai. The Malay language is deeply rooted in the historical kingdom of Patani and is inextricably linked to Islam, which in the southern three provinces is taught and learnt in Jawi, thus providing a historic continuity to the language spoken in these provinces.

Another demand closely associated with the identity of Malay Muslims in the south is their right to Islamic law practised through Islamic (or Sharia) courts. Apart from the practice of Malay customary law (*adat*), Malay Muslims are subject to Islamic law especially in matters concerning inheritance of property, marriage, birth and death. Two points in Haji Sulong's list of seven refer to Islam, i.e. the creation of an Islamic court and the establishment of an Islamic council to monitor the welfare of Muslims in Thailand. Requests were also made for the appointment of a *Tok Khadi* (Islamic Judge) to preside over matters brought to the Islamic Court.[14] Although *sharia* offices were established in the Muslim provinces in the south, both Islamic judges and Thai judges presided over these cases. Besides, Islamic law has only been partially implemented, in matters pertaining mainly to family, whereas other matters pertaining to Muslims are adjudicated under the Thai (civil) legal system. There has been, however, an attempt by the Thai government after the September 2006 coup under PM Surayud to consider the implementation of *sharia* law for the Muslims. In November 2006, Surayud was quoted as having said:

> They [the Muslims in southern Thailand] should have the Islamic law in practice — the Shariah,' Muslims in southern Thailand have different values from Buddhist Thais. You can live with your own rules, your own laws.[15]

While non-Malay Muslims in the central and northern regions of Thailand accept Islam as the religion of a minority community living in a Buddhist polity, to Malays in the Thai south, Islam is much more than a religion; it is in fact an integral part of the ethno-linguistic identity of the people and their ancestral land. Imtiyaz Yusuf argues that the ethnification of religion (i.e., Malay is a Muslim; Thai is a Buddhist) has led to identities being shaped by ethno-religious constructs.[16] The conflict between the Malays and the Thai state is largely a conflict between two ethno-religious identities — Thai Buddhism and Malay Islam. Just as Buddhism is central to the identity of a Thai, Islam is central to the identity of a Malay. It is in this regard that Malay Muslims in Thailand, more than their non-Malay co-religionists, have persisted in demanding (and defending) their rights associated with Malay and Islam. Apart from demanding for Islamic law, the Malays most notably have defended the *pondok,* or the Malay Islamic institution of learning in south Thailand and *Jawi,* the Malay language of Islam, for both these constitute an essential part of the ethno-religious identity of Malay-Islam in the south. This is also indicative of the localization of Islam in the region, taking into consideration its history as an Islamic kingdom and as a renowned centre of Islamic learning.

The remaining three points in Haji Sulong's list relate to the issue of autonomy in the administration and economy of the southern Malay provinces. Although the Thai state has practiced an affirmative policy over the past few decades with regard to enhancing Malay-Muslim participation in the state bureacracy (public service) and economy as well as opportunities for education in tertiary institutions, they have yet to win 'the hearts and minds' of the southern Muslim population.[17] In more recent times, the demand for autonomy has grown even louder especially in the aftermath of the escalating violence seen in south Thailand since 2004.

While having to deal with calls for autonomy and separatism in the south, the government must also remember that the issues of language, religion and Islamic law are central to the worldview and identity of the Malays of south Thailand. These aspects are the collective markers of a Malay identity; an identity based on ethnicity (Malay), religion (Islam) and a shared common history (descendents of the Muslim Sultanate of Patani).

Being a Thai national (based on one's citizenship) is only complementary and certainly much less central to the identity of a Malay Muslim of south Thailand. Any attempt to blur these markers of identity through forced assimilation and ultra-nationalist or culturally-chauvinist policies will only hamper any meaningful attempt at finding a peaceful solution to the southern crisis. However, it must also be pointed out that the Thai national identity has evolved from one based on a 'sense of belonging', i.e., loyal subjects of the King (1900–20s), to one driven by ultra-nationalism, and race/ethnicity-based preferences(1930–40s) This change has had a drastic impact on the ability of minorities like the Malays to express their ethnic identity, having brought about a huge divide between the majority and minority groups in Thailand and a greater consciousness of 'ethnic' over 'national' identity. It has taken a long time to undo the impact of the latter process of national identity formation in Thailand. In fact, the current turmoil is largely traceable to this phase. Malay Muslim identity formation in Thailand must be understood vis-à-vis the history of Thai nation-building.

Malays and the Evolution of National Identity in Thailand: 1900s to 1940s

Prince Damrong, King Chulalongkorn's trusted aide, outlined three core values expected of a Thai citizen. These were: (*i*) love for the nation's sovereignty, (*ii*) demonstrating fairness, and (*iii*) the ability to tolerate and compromise on differences of interest for the greater good of the nation.[18] To Damrong, inculcating these core values would in turn produce good citizens/subjects of the kingdom, irre-spective of ethnic considerations. This policy was rather inclusive, for it allowed all the ethnic groups in Thailand to become part of the citizenry, without too many demands being made or limitations being placed on the practice of their culture and religion. The pol-itically expedient policy was largely a reflection of the state of the monarchy and it was indeed a 'court construct'. The looming threat of Western encroachment on its territories and the possibility of frontier provinces seeking British help, as had happened with the displaced Malay Rajas of the south, forced Bangkok to reform its administration and consolidate its powers. Clearly, at this point, Thai national identity was defined primarily in terms of the people's loyalty to the Thai monarchy and, by extension, the court effectively extended its hegemony over much of the kingdom. As Thongchai Winnichakul has argued, in the case of Siam, the court was the prin-cipal actor in the construction of a national identity, departing from the Andersonian mode of thought which attributes national identity formation in South-East Asia largely to colonialism.[19]

The monarchy's absolutist survival was certainly put to test during the tumultous reign of King Watchirawut (1910–25), as nationalism reared its ugly head and began to assert itself as the de facto force in nation-building. It was Watchirawut who introduced notion of the Nation–Religion–King trinity (Thai: *chat–sassana–Phramahakasat*) that holds in Thailand even in the present time. The first two categories 'ethnicized' Thai identity; the nation, in this case, referred to Siam, with ethnic Thai as the dominant people and Buddhism as the religion of that nation. Both categories posed a threat to the identity and rights of Malay minorities. But the hardest blow to their survival as a distinct cultural and religious community came during the premiership of Phibun, whose infamous *ratthaniyom* policy began a new era of national identity formation; pursued zealously in order to create the ideal Thai citizen demonstrating 'Thainess' (e.g., speak Thai, dress Thai, adopt Thai ways). As mentioned earlier, a policy of forced assimilation followed, with the resultant impact of further alienating minorities such as the Malays from the Thai state. It was this period which saw an intense call for support for Patani's liberation from Thailand, and led to the subsequent growth of secessionist movements. Nationalism based on ethnocentrism intertwined with a Thai national identity was essentially exclusive and tended to marginalize the minorities. As Will Kymlica has pointed out, nowhere is this more evident than in 'governments by the majority', i.e., governments dominated by an ethnic majority, whose control of the state machinery tends to exclude minorities.

In this regard, the Patani Malay identity as it exists today can also be seen as resulting from a reaction to the Thai nation-state's 'construction' of a national identity over the last century, and to a lesser extent, shaped by colonial policies and the construction of identity in what was then British Malaya. The special position awarded in the Malayan constitution to the ethnic Malays or *Bumiputras* (sons of the soil) must have created both a sense of desire and regret on the part of Thai Malay Muslims to be or not to have been part of the Malayan state.

More recently, a global identity based on the Muslim *ummah* can also be seen as becoming an integral part of the Patani Malay identity, particularly since the era of Islamic revivalism in the 1980s.

The development of religiocentric identities among Thai Muslims cannot be overlooked by the Thai state for it can complicate domestic matters a great deal, especially given the violence taking place in the southern border region. It must be acknowledged that multiple identities held by a citizen by no means makes him/her any less patriotic and perhaps allowing the co-existence of both Thai and Malay identities within the Thai nation can provide long term peace in the region.

Tangible Rights

Land and Resources

Traditionally, the right to resources such as land and minerals belonged to the *raja* (king). In the Malay concept of *adat* (customary law), land belonged to the *raja*, whereas the earth (*bumi*) belonged to God. A similar concept is found among the Thais, in which case, land in the kingdom belonged to the king, and as such he is referred as *Chao Paendin* (Lord of the Land). The Thai King had absolute ownership rights over the land in his kingdom and the people who tilled the soil and farmed on the land were mere tenants. This similarity between the Thais and Malays, in fact, became the root of conflict. To the Malays, Patani land belonged to the Malay Sultanate and therefore had to be defended from incursion. To the Thais, on the other hand, the Sultanate of Patani was defeated and later incorporated into Siamese territory, therefore the Patani region is viewed as belonging to the Siamese kingdom.

Resources from the earth (*bumi*), for instance minerals such as tin and gold, belonged to the *raja* (or state). In the tin-rich south Thailand, with the advent of Chinese and western mining companies, the Thai state was forced to adopt modern methods of guarding its resource-rich areas. The state used legislation, such as the Mining Act of 1901 (*Phraratchabanyat*) to claim its right to these territories. Included within these tin-rich areas were the Malay provinces of Pattani, Yala and Narathiwat. As a result of the mining legislation, Bangkok not only terminated the right of the Malay *rajas* to earn from state land and minerals, it also made it extremely difficult for the local Malays to acquire mining rights in the 'Malay territories', preferring instead to offer mining concessions to Chinese companies, whom the Thai state perceived as useful economic allies.[20]

Meanwhile, the threat of British and French encroachment on Thai/ Malayan territories forced Siam to clearly demarcate its territories and land ownership. Thus, in 1901, the system of *chanod tidin* (land title deeds) was introduced. Private ownership of land began to be widely acknowledged with the certification of title deeds. Since the Malay lands belonged to the Sultanic regime, upon their sacking, these lands came to be owned by the Thai state. Unlike in Malaysia, where the Malay *bumiputras* had land gazetted as Malay Reserve Land, in Siam, there were no similar allocations to protect the rights of the '*orang asal*' (original people, i.e., the Malays). The situation was made worse through the *nikhom sangton* policy implemented in the 1960s, whereby Bangkok enticed rural north-eastern Thais to move to the south to work in rubber plantations through the grant of land ownership in the southern Muslim areas. This resulted in more Buddhists settling in what was a traditionally Muslim territory. This social engineering feat thus managed by the Thai state had the effect of further agitating and marginalizing the Malay population in the south.

In comparison, however, the Patani Malays tend to demonstrate greater affinity and give more importance to cultural rights based on language, religion and *adat*, as opposed to land rights. Whereas the indigenous or *pribumi* in Borneo and Peninsular Malaysia were primarily concerned over rights to (ancestral) land and the collective culture of the community therein, the Patani Malays were concerned first and foremost about the language and religion of its community and less for the ownership of land per se. The sense of importance associated with land goes beyond the spatial, rather it is driven more by a sense of nostalgia for a lost 'homeland', namely the Kingdom of Patani. After all, it must be emphasized that the Malay Muslims of Thailand are the *orang asal* of the Patani region, unlike their South Asian and Chinese co-religionists who migrated to Thailand from neighbouring countries for economic and political reasons.

Acknowledging this important difference is vital for the Thai government if it sincerely intends to find a peaceful solution to the conflict in south Thailand. Otherwise, methods adopted by Bangkok may only lead to failure, a case in point being the suggestion made by Thaksin in 2005, that the southern provinces could be turned around through aggressive economic development, so that the Malays living there would not be envious of the better living standards enjoyed by fellow Malays in Malaysia. Economic development, while no doubt important, can contribute only partly to addressing the grievances of the Malays in the south. As pointed out earlier, it is essential to acknowledge the high premium that the Malays place on their cultural values and their identity as ethnic Malays, which they jealously guard from extinction.

A New Kind of Right

Human Rights and Human Security

In light of the lawlessness that has re-emerged from drugs and arms-related crimes and the stand-off between separatist movements and state armies/police in south Thailand since 2004, there is an urgent need to recognize the right of the Thai Malay community to human security and their right to defend themselves through an independent judiciary.

Throughout the period of 2001–06 there were numerous cases of heavy-handed administration on the part of the Thai Army and Police. In particular, the excessive use of force, as in the case of the Krisek Mosque (April 2004) and Takbai incident (October 2004) resulting in the death of Malay youths alerted the Thai people and the international community to the state of lawlessness and insecurity prevalent in the south. The frequency of security searches and seizures increased, especially in the *pondoks* (religious schools), and became a serious cause for concern. Reports of arbitrary killings, kidnappings and the disappearance of insurgents suspected to be involved in the violence in the south have drawn the attention of many international agencies such as the Human Rights Watch. Similar reports of everyday incidents of killing, beheading, sniper shots, bomb blasts have raised doubts on the ability of the government to end the state of anarchy that exists in the southern region. Perhaps the two most prominent cases of human rights violations and use of heavy-handed tactics in the Thai south involved Muslim lawyer-turned-activist Somchai Neelapaichit, who was kidnapped and killed, followed by the case of Imam Yepa, who was beaten to death while in military custody in March 2008.[21]

Minorities such as the Malays, like the rest of the country, are Thai citizens; and in accordance with the rights of the people enshrined in the constitution, the state is obliged to provide security to its citizens.

Besides, the UN Charter (1945) promotes 'universal respect for, and observance of human rights and fundamental freedoms for all without distinction as to race, sex, language, or religion'.[22] In particular, the Universal Declaration of Human Rights (1948), to which Thailand is a signatory, clearly states that the right to freedom from torture, arbitrary arrest and systematic patterns of other gross violations are absolute and cannot be constrained.[23] This right, which legally binds all member states, has become a customary international law, yet it is subject to violations and lax implementation.

In the case of the renewed conflict in south Thailand since 2004, an apparent lack of justice for human rights abuses has turned into a major source of grievance. The officials responsible for the deaths of almost 2,000 Muslims in the Kru Se and Takbai incidents have yet to be prosecuted. Draconian laws, in the form of Martial and Emergency Laws, in place in the south since 2004 have served only to further empower the military over the people. Reports of abuse, particularly of being denied access to lawyers while in detention and other harsh measures prescribed under the martial law decree have, in some respects, become a 'license to kill'. Amnesty strategies, such as dropping legal charges on suspected insurgents should they agree to confess and undergo six months of re-education under military supervision, have also been challenged by human rights activists as entailing unlawful detention.[24] There are numerous other grouses as well, resulting from the indiscriminate detention of suspected insurgents and the manner in which they are 'coaxed' into confessing. Needless to say, these measures have to a large extent tampered with the rights of the individual to self-defense and ensuring one's security, although the latter, in particular, is an essential right in a conflict zone such as south Thailand.

In the following section, we will look at the forms of governance, representation and state control used in Thailand. Generally speaking, the Thai state and monarchy support the freedom of the Malays to practice their religion and culture. State concessions in this regard include the construction of state-maintained mosques, religious councils at the provincial and national levels, as well as institutions of Islamic learning. On the other hand, some of the methods of governance, as implemented through inept state bureaucrats, have tended to result in the intimidation and marginalization of ethnic minorities such as the Malays.

Governance and Representation: Malays in the Thai State

Religious and Cultural Patronage

Islam has had a long presence in Thailand; a Muslim community had been firmly established since the time of the earliest Thai (Tai) kingdom of Sukhotai (thirteenth century). Since then, Islam has received official patronage in Thailand, most evidently in the Ayutthuyan era (1350–1767) when Muslims of Persian origin exerted significant influence on Thai trade and commerce. Leading members of the Persian mercantile community became trusted confidantes of the Thai kings, serving as ministers in the court.[25] Their prominence in courtly circles declined with the arrival of Chinese in Siam. They retained, however, their commercial interests in the country and continued to operate their businesses. Some of these early traders made Thailand their home and presently co-exist with Thai Buddhists in the country, with little interference from the state.

Since the Ayutthayan era, the Thai state has managed Islamic affairs in the country through the office of the *Chularatchamontri* (*Shaikh al-Islam*) or State Adviser on Islamic affairs, who advises the Thai King on matters relating to Islam. The position has been occupied by fourteen individuals, whose appointments were sanctioned by the King.[26] Regrettably, however, none of the fourteen who have occupied this position to this day were from the southern Malay community.

Apart from this, in the post-Constitution era (i.e. after 1932), a national council, as well as provincial councils for Islamic affairs in every province with a Muslim majority population, were created, indicating that Islam had state sanction in Thailand.[27] More importantly though, it would appear that Bangkok was attempting to centralize religious affairs under its control. By enforcing a system of administering Islam parallel to the kind of reorganization of the Buddhist order that was implemented with the Sangha Act of 1902, Bangkok hoped to regulate the Muslim clergy. The reforms in this case, however, had a far smaller impact because, unlike Buddhism, Islam has no ecclesiastical hierarchy.[28]

Until 1932, Thai Kings were patrons exclusively of Buddhism, in their capacity as defenders and upholders of Buddhism. After the end of absolute monarchy, 'the [role of the] King was transformed to shoulder constitutionally the role of supporting every other religion in his realm adhered by his subjects'.[29] In this context, the King began to show overt support to all religions, including Islam, in Thailand. Through a royal decree on the patronage of Islam in 1945, the support of the King to the Muslims in the south was specifically mentioned and the role of the *Chularatchamontri* as a proxy for the Thai kings in the promotion of Islam was introduced. In 1948 amidst much political mayhem in Thailand, the *Chularatchamontri* was demoted to the position of advisor to the Department of Religious Affairs.

Thereafter, the government supported the construction of mosques and *suraos* (small prayer halls) in the country and more recently, *musalla* (prayer rooms) in strategic public places. In fact, state-funded central mosques have been built in the Malay provinces as well. As Omar Farouk points out, Islam is both a personal and communal religion.[30] The community of Muslims — the *ummah* — have common obligations and rights, namely to congregate and worship in the communal practice of Islam. There is, therefore, a need for communal spaces and the mosque/*surao* is a focal point of Muslim community life. Apart from religious purposes, mosques also provide space for conducting funeral services, Quranic classes and the solemnization of marriages. However, the construction of mosques using the Thai style of architecture, such as the central mosque in Yala which has a dome in the shape of a lotus bud, has led to accusations against the state for extending a subtle Buddhist hegemony through such acts of benevolence towards the Muslims.[30]

Two points emerge from the discussion above. First, Thailand is a country of religious plurality and the King is constitutionally obligated to protect and defend all religions. In this sense, Muslims are guaranteed freedom of faith and worship. Nonetheless, state support for Islam in Thailand is 'skewed' and the structural differences that exist between Buddhism and Islam elude Bangkok and its officials, which, in turn, tends to trigger conflict. In the meantime, any change to the religious status-quo in Thailand has the potential to turn into a major political issue. The more recent proposal to endorse Buddhism as the official religion of the state during the redrafting of the Constitution in 2007, although rejected on the surface, resulted in a subtle compromise between the state and the Buddhist clergy.[32] As Thanet Aphornsuvan observes, the Constitution of 2007 states that the state and government must provide financial assistance in support of Buddhism, Buddhist organizations and Buddhist activities.[33]

It may be useful also to recall the observation made by Thai political analyst Panitan Wattanayagorn, that attempts to declare Buddhism as the state religion would 'inflame the south', and as such Bangkok must tread carefully on the issue of promoting an official religion in Thailand.[34]

Legislature and Political Representation

The Malays, being the larger group of Muslims in Thailand, should be a vital voice in south Thai politics, especially in the border areas that they inhabit. However, it was not until the General Elections of December 2007 that the south mattered as much, to the point that 'for the first time all political parties, seem to be paying serious attention to the region'.[35] Violence and political conflict in the south, escalating since 2004 and having claimed almost 3,800 deaths (till January 2009) is the reason for this change.

Yet, in terms of political representation, ethnic Malays have been relatively well represented. The earliest presence of a Malay Muslim in the state legislature was in the post-constitutional era of 1932, when a new electoral system was established during the rule of the People's Party, led by Premier Pridi Panomyong. Each province elected a member to the People's Assembly and for the first time, Muslim representatives appeared in the Siamese legislature.

Between the 1970s and mid-1990s, the presence of Muslim parliamentarians from the south in the Thai Parliament increased progressively. The number of Malay parliamentarians was as follows: 6 in 1979; 7 in 1983; 7 in 1986; 7 in 1988; 13 in 1992; and 14 in 1995.[36] With almost a two-fold increase in 1992 and thereafter, the collective voice of Muslim representatives became more forceful. Omar Farouk claims that 'in the post-1992 period, Malay Muslim representation was not only more visible but also became more credible, referring to their presence at all levels of Thai political–legislative structures'.[37]

In the mid-1990s, Muslim representation in Thai politics recorded unprecedented success when two Malay Muslims became Deputy Ministers in the Thai cabinet and one was appointed President of the Thai National Assembly. These individuals namely, Surin Pitsuwan (Nakhon Sithammarat), Den Tohmeena (Pattani, son of slain cleric Haji Sulong) and Wan Muhamad Nor Matha (Yala) respectively represented the elite Malay Muslim leadership active in Thai politics. All three of them were from the Malay provinces in the south. In the post-Thaksin era (2006), Thai Muslim leadership extended beyond politics to include the military; a Bangkok-based Muslim, Army Chief General Sonthi Boonyaratglin, who led the coup of 19 September 2006, was made Chief of the National Security Council (NCR). Sonthi's upward climb to the post of Chief of the Thai Army, a position traditionally held by Thai Buddhist, can be viewed as an achievement for the Muslims and the country as a whole, because for the first time in Thai history a Muslim (although not a Malay from the south) was chief of the army, indicating that Thailand had embraced, to some extent, the spirit of cultural plurality.

The number of Malay parliamentarians indicates that the Malay leadership was well-represented, pointing to a high level of political integration of the Muslims within national politics. But increasing representation in Thai politics and the legislature does not necessarily correspond with equal representation or bargaining power in the sociocultural domain (what I would call 'community space'). Given their growing numbers, Muslim representation in Thai politics can no longer be considered nominal. However, their active role in defending Muslim rights or as a 'watch dog' for the welfare of the community has been lax.[38] During Thaksin's premiership (2001–06), there were at least eleven Members of Parliament (MP) representing the three southern provinces, with several occupying ministerial and other prominent parliamentary posts, yet they were not able to raise their voice against Thaksin's high-handed approach to quelling the insurgency in the south. While the international community openly condemned the killings of the Kru Se and Takbai incidents in 2004, there was in contrast 'a very mild reaction from (Muslim) government MPs', despite their 'wide local networks and strong credentials as defenders of religious beliefs'.[39] It is very likely that for their own self-interest and political expediency, the politicians could not have questioned their superior but they paled in comparison to the efforts made by nonpolitical leaders of the Muslim community and NGOs who offered suggestions and solutions to restoring peace in the south.

Admittedly, there is a lack of effective political leadership at the local level, but the situation is made worse as a result of factions within the small community of Muslim leaders. The Wahdah, a political faction created in 1988 of Malay-speaking politicians from the south, primarily addresses the grouses of the Malay-speaking community. It first aligned itself with the New Aspiration Party (1990) and later with Thaksin's Thai Rak Thai (TRT) Party and made significant gains in the general elections between 1992 and 2001. Following Thaksin's abrasive strategies in managing the southern conflict, Wahdah lost all their seats in the elections of 2005, which were won by Muslim politicians from the Democrat Party.[40] Splinter groups tend to further polarize politics among small minority groups, especially in the event that these minority groups are not represented by their own ethnic or faith-based political party. Even in the case of the formation of a Muslim political party, the odds of gaining support from fellow members of their ethnic and religious community is dependent upon the commitment and priorities of the politicians involved. Seen in this light, the cleric Haji Sulong, who put forth his seven-point demands to the government at a time of great political uncertainty (1947–48) is a visionary and an effective leader of par excellence of the Malay community.

In spite of the lack of strong political leadership, and the fact that the south matters little at the level of Thai national politics, the Malay population (as a community) have participated rather impressively in national politics. James Ockey notes that for the south, electoral and political processes since 1932 have held the potential for integration rather than disintegration. Through the electoral process, Malay Muslims have been able to express support or rejection for national policies and politicians. In other words, elections have allowed people in the south to achieve their demands within the system and in the context of the larger national politics. For example, in the General Elections of February 2005 (in the aftermath of the Kru Se and Tak Bai incidents of 2004), voter turnout in the Muslim south was greater than the national average, ranging between 73 to 76 per cent.[41] People turned up in large numbers to reject the policies and hardline government of Thaksin, which despite a landslide victory nationwide, failed to win a single seat in the lower south. As mentioned earlier, even the Wahdah — representing Malay interests but allied to the TRT — lost all their seats in the Malay provinces. Subsequently, in the constitutional referendum held in June 2007, almost 80 per cent of the Malay population voted in support of the draft. This indicates a high level of Malay Muslim participation in the Thai political/legislative realm and the fact that these minorities, although culturally Malay, are politically Thai.

As is the case with most unitary states, Thailand's central government has decisive control over all matters concerning the state, in other words, the central government is the only legitimate power with the right to administer. Delegation of responsibilities and functions to the provincial states or departments is at the convenience of the central government. More often than not, state bureaucrats are trained and dispatched from the capital city, Bangkok. Most of the officers sent from Bangkok lack adequate knowledge about the people of the south, particularly their culture. Accusations of insensitivity to local norms and heavy-handed tactics employed by government officials when dealing with the southerners is another oft-cited reason for Malay agitation against the Thai state. As a result, insurgents fighting for the separation of Patani from Thailand direct their attacks at 'state targets', namely, the police and armed forces, army posts, railway stations and schools. Lately, however, their targets have included civilians, particularly Buddhists and fellow Malay Muslims suspected of being state sympathizers. This latest development has led to a state of lawlessness and fear in the south.[42] Muslim insurgents refer to fellow Muslims suspected of being state informants as *munafiqs,* invoking religious sentiments in the process and this phenomenon has tended to be politically further divisive.

Identity Negotiation through Instruments of State Control

National (Thai) Identity: Core State Policy

A Thai citizen, in the context of the Thai nation-state, must be culturally Thai, in other words, he must demonstrate Thai values which includes the ability to speak Thai and demonstrate *kwam pen Thai* (the ways of a Thai). Although Buddhism is the religion of the majority of Thai citizens, non-Buddhist Thais are free to practice their respective faiths. Thus Muslims can practice Islam but speak Thai and demonstrate *niyom* Thai (Thai sociocultural ways). This in turn has encouraged efforts to teach Islam in Thai language and have Islamic religious books translated into Thai. The Thai state, in other words, endorses a Thai-based Islamic identity, which is today the officially sanctioned Islamic identity in Thailand. To assert this identity, policies advancing use of the national language and education have been steadfastly pursued by the Thai state.

Thai Education: A Tool for Nation-Building and Nationalism

Language has long been used as a tool in nation-building. In multi-ethnic societies, any language spoken by the predominant majority is chosen as the national language in order to foster unity. Over years of nation-building, language has become a sensitive political and, at times, emotional issue. This is particularly evident in South-East Asian countries ruled by a predominant ethnic group such as Malaysia, Singapore and Thailand.

Ironically, language policies in South-East Asian countries like Thailand tend to be mono-ethnic in character, despite the diverse composition of its people. Despite claims that the Malay children's elementary knowledge of the Thai language, gained from compulsory Thai education, had little practical use in the south where Malay remained the language of communication and commerce, the forceful imposition of the Thai language was greatly intensified. Education in the Thai language is associated with Buddhism because Thai is seen as the language of the Buddhists. When this policy was initially introduced, the Malay Muslim community resisted centralized Thai education through the maintenance and expansion of the *pondok* school system. The languages used in these schools include both Arabic and Malay, particularly the *jawi* script which is widely used in *pondoks* throughout the south. The *pondok* system enables and asserts the Muslim community's right to learning about Islam and acquiring Islamic knowledge in the language of the Quran i.e., Arabic. Attempts to regularize Islamic education through the imposition of rules such as teaching Islam in Thai and the use of translated versions of Arabic religious texts into Thai for use in the *pondoks* was met with great opposition. The forceful imposition of Thai language in teaching secular curricula in religious schools was also viewed initially as extending Buddhist hegemony over non-Buddhist citizenry, because Thai is the language of Buddhists in Thailand.[43] Although at present most Malays who attend Thai schools have become very fluent in Thai and speak relatively less Malay, the students who attend *pondoks*, on the other hand, use more Arabic and Malay.[44]

Over the past few decades, there has been greater integration in terms of language; whereby younger generations of Malay students are increasingly more comfortable speaking Thai. This is partly a result of the government's move to introduce Thai curricula into the *pondok* system. These schools, called Private Schools Teaching Islam (or PSTI), combine Islamic and secular education, with the latter being taught in Thai. The older generation of Malays continues to fear the possible erosion of Malay language among Malay youth. There have been repeated requests for Malay to be accepted as the official language, along with Thai, in the formal (public) sector of south Thailand, particularly in the Malay provinces. This request has been rejected by many because language is increasingly being seen from the lens of nationalism; in this case, predominantly ethnic Thai nationalism. The need to sustain and preserve Malay language and by extension Malay culture, is a core struggle of the Malay community, while for the Thai state the national language serves as a means to integrate the people. The rationale for a national language *over* vernacular languages, for the purpose of unity and as a tool of nation-building, may have run its course, given the increasing tendency to turn language into an issue of separatism. This is certainly evident in the conflict between the Thai state and the Malay minorities of the south, where language, among other things, has been a constant point of contention. In a study on the success of federalism and a multi-national state in India, Alfred Stepan explains how India managed the issue of Tamil language, associated with Dravidian Tamil nationalism in south India, from turning into a potential issue of separatism. The study found that India's model of federal government recognized the country's cultural and linguistic plurality; instead of promoting Hindi as the official language, India maintained English as a link language while recognizing the numerous regional languages that remained in use. This allowed for the common language, namely English, to become the language for administrative/political and career opportunities, particularly in the Indian public service and corporate sector, while, simultaneously, the people remained culturally (or regionally) distinct.[45] In sharp contrast, in Sri Lanka, 'Sinhalese politicians eliminated English as a link language for government posts, downgraded the language of the largest minority, the Tamils, insisted on maintaining a unitary state, and elevated Buddhism to the dominant and privileged religion of Sri Lanka'.[46] In the end, these decisions or choices turned what Stepan calls 'the non-issue of Tamil separatism' in Sri Lanka (in the 1940s) into one of the most protracted ethnic wars in the world today.

In Thailand, through its policies pertaining to education, the state has attempted to manage (or silence) the articulation of minority rights, particularly through a national language policy that privileges the language of the majority (i.e. the Thai language). Nonetheless, unlike the case of the Tamils in Sri Lanka, Bangkok has shown a reasonable level of tolerance for cultural and language diversity. For example, the state has allowed for the continuing tradition of *pondoks* in the south with some level of reform and supervision from Bangkok. Since 2004, the *pondoks* have come under strict surveillance from Bangkok as a result of allegations linking them with the teaching and dissemination of 'militant Islam'. This development will probably pave the way for more reforms in the traditional system of education or may, in fact, lead to the eventual demise of this institution of learning. Nation-building and its prerequisite of conforming to national ideals such as a national type of education is laudable. In fact, the move to privatize *pondoks* and *madrasahs* as private schools teaching Islam (PSTI) wasn't entirely rejected by the Malays in the Thai south, indicating their willingness to become 'national',[47] but the implementation of such policies shouldn't result in a dismissive attitude towards ethnic minority languages and traditions.

The Military

The Royal Thai Army has always enjoyed a position of political prominence in the government. Since 1932, it has staged at least eighteen coups, the latest being the one staged in September 2006. The military has also formed the government in Thailand numerous times. A prominent role for the military in state affairs is a major setback for the south for it empowers the military to act with excessive power and at times force.

After the January 2004 attack on a military base in Thailand, the government declared Martial Law and sent extra police to the southern region. The pattern of violence has not changed, on the contrary, the number of casualties and deaths — involving various groups of people including military and police personnel — have steadily increased. As reported, during January–November 2004 alone, there were 1,253 incidents of violence in the south.[48] Two major incidents in 2004, namely the Krisek mosque attack (April 2004) and Takbai incident (October 2004), resulted in the deaths of many young Muslim men. The army was responsible for these deaths; the use of excessive military force (Krisek) and the inhuman method of transporting suspected agitators to detention camps (Takbai) led to the large number of casualties. These incidents also earned the Thai state international condemnation. In an attempt to bring peace back to the southern provinces, Bangkok sent more troops to the south in peace-keeping missions. The area has become a 'war zone' with the presence of military check-points and personnel posted everywhere. Military officers have also become the target of insurgents, resulting in an ever-increasing numbers of casualties.

The stalemate between the state and the insurgents led to arrests, deportation, disappearance and 'bizarre' deaths of members suspected of being involved in the struggle or of their 'sympathizers'. Malay-Muslims too have become increasingly vulnerable to the spate of unrest in the south. Issues of lawlessness and human security have become the prime concerns.

As mentioned earlier, Muslim lawyer–activist, Somchai Neelapaijit, who accused the police of barbarically torturing arrested suspects, 'disappeared' in 2004. Subsequently, even as four police officers were arrested and accused of abducting him, Somchai never re-appeared and was later declared dead. The trend, of course, had started much before. The arrest and subsequent death of Haji Sulong illustrates the tradition of 'kidnapping and arbitrary judgments' that exists vis-à-vis the Thai south. The increasing numbers of casualties and state of anarchy in southern Thailand has forced the current government to review its policy or at least attempt to engage with the suspected insurgents. The military too has come under review. While the issue of autonomy has not been openly discussed by the government, attempts to negotiate or conduct a dialogue with various groups in the south continue.

Through the Thai bureaucracy, army, and education policies, the state has 'managed' to control the articulation of rights by minority communities, although their dissenting voices, often seen as muted, have now with growing international attention become too big to be ignored.

Conclusion

In Thailand today, Malay names can be used, and the wearing of the Muslim dress *hijab* is also allowed. Muslim prayer places in public spaces such as airports, railway stations, and congregations for Friday prayers have become common particularly in the south. But the recent violence would suggest that these 'concessions' are not enough.

In fact, I am inclined to believe that with greater democratization there is greater room for realizing struggles for inde-pendence and self-determination. If in the past only state symbols were targeted, today civilians, particularly Buddhists, have become targets. The BRN-Coordinate movement (Malay: Barisan Revolusi National-Koordinas) not only wants to create a separate entity for Malay Muslims in the south but also hopes to rid the area of Buddhists and instead have a Muslim-only region. In an interview, Sunai Phasuk, member of Human Rights Watch, Thailand claimed:

> BRN-Coordinate is the backbone of new wave of separatism in southern Thailand and the agenda is very clear, to separate southern border provinces as independent entity which will be governed by sharia, and will be the land for ethnic Malayu Muslim not the land for Buddhists, no co-existence, this is the current platform.[49]

The recent developments in the south are both alarming and indicative of a heightened sense of ethnic nationalism and radicaliza-tion of religion within a national environment of greater democracy. This may in fact provide greater space and opportunities for religion-based parties, as well as in the case of south Thailand, enhance the call for autonomy. The Thai government has initiated attempts to consider some level of autonomy for the Muslim provinces, but this has not been reciprocated by the BRN-Coordinate movement. On the contrary, this group strongly favours a separate independent state, as stated clearly by a Malay youth involved in the *Runda Kumpulan Kecil* (RKK), the militant wing of a separatist group in south Thailand that 'we want to take back our land'.[50] The process of indoctrinating young minds with the idea that Patani is 'Malay land' and the Thai state is the enemy, has been deeply entrenched mostly through *tadika* (pre-schools) and *pondok*s, and they have to first be dismantled before successful reconciliation can be achieved. Injust-ice and lawlessness caused by the state needs to stop and confidence-building measures must be taken. In the present context of unitary Thailand, there is a hyper-concentration of power (through the state military and bureaucracy) and weak representation of minorities, particularly with respect to sociocultural rights.

It may not be irrelevant to refer to Haji Sulong's seven points mentioned earlier in this paper. A close reading of his demands points to a suggestion for the division of power between the central and provincial/state governments, a sort of a 'federalist model', where minority rights and privileges are represented and the local government and its people have meaningful control over their own affairs, particularly in the spheres of culture, language and religion, as well as some level of autonomy in the local economy and in resource management. Unfortunately, the suggestion for a certain level of autonomy was associated with separatism, an expedient national-ist discourse for Thai politicians to prevent the realization of their (minority) political demands. Autonomy need not necessarily mean political separatism; an example from neighbouring Aceh (Indonesia) has proven that special recognition for local administration goes a long way towards ensuring sustained peace in a multi-ethnic and historically and culturally distinct region such as the province of Aceh. The similarities with the Patani case cannot be overstated. Perhaps in this vein, one could suggest that a political rather than military solution is needed to return peace to the Malay provinces of south Thailand.

Notes and References

1. Secretary General of ASEAN in his keynote address at an international seminar on Religion and Democracy in Thailand. See Imtiyaz Yusuf and Canan Atilgan (eds), *Religion and Democracy in Thailand* (Bangkok: Konrad-Adenauer-Stiftung, 2008), p. 11.
2. 'Pattani' refers to the Thai spelling of the province, whereas the term 'Patani' is based on the Malay spelling that refers to the old Kingdom/ Sultanate which was annexed by Siam. In this article, 'Pattani' refers to the Thai province while 'Patani' refers to the former Sultanate and the region it historically encompassed, namely the Malay provinces in present-day south Thailand.
3. The only exception, however, are the Malays of the province of Satun, located on the west coast of south Thailand, adjacent to the north Malaysian state of Kedah, where the majority of the population profess Islam but speak Thai as their first language and adhere to the Thai sociocultural way of life. See Kobkua Suwannathat- Pian, 'National Identity, the "Sam-Sams" of Satun, and the Thai Malay Muslims', in Michael J. Montesano and Patrick Jory (eds), *Thai South and Malay North: Ethnic Interactions on a Plural Peninsula* (Singapore: NUS Press, 2008), pp. 155–72.
4. Phuwadol Songprasert, 'Chronic Conflict in the Three Southern Border Provinces of Thailand', in Utai Dulyakasem and Lertchai Sirichai (eds), *Knowledge and Conflict Resolution, The Crisis of the Border Region of Southern Thailand* (Nakhon Sithammarat: School of Liberal Arts, Walailak University, 2005), p. 132.

5. Aurel Croissant, 'Unrest in South Thailand: Contours, Causes and Consequences Since 2001', *Strategic Insights* 4(2), Feb 2005, p. 1.

6. On the administrative history of Patani, see Kobkua Suwanathat-Pian, *Thai-Malay Relations: Traditional Intra-Regional Relations from the Seventeenth to the Early Twentieth Centuries* (Singapore: Oxford University Press, 1988).

7. On mono-ethnic states and assimilationist policy see David Brown, 'From Peripheral Communities to Ethnic Nations: Separatism in South-east Asia', *Pacific Affairs* 61(1), 1988, pp. 51–77.

8. Suria Saniwa, 'De-radicalization of Minority Dissent: A Case Study of the Malay-Muslim Movement in Southern Thailand, 1980–1994', in Miriam Coronel Ferrer (ed.), *Sama-sama: Facets of Ethnic Relations in South East Asia* (Quezon City: Third World Studies Center, University of the Philippines, 1999), p. 121.

9. On Haji Sulong and Patani, see Thanet Aphornsuvan, *Rebellion in Southern Thailand: Contending Histories* (Washington: East West Center, 2007).

10. Omar Farouk, 'Islam, Nationalism and the Thai State', in Wattana Sugunnasil (ed.), *Dynamic Diversity in Southern Thailand* (Pattani and Chiang Mai Prince of Songkhla University and Silkworm Books, 2005), p. 10.

11. For a detailed discussion on the term Jawi and identity in the Patani region see, Pierre Le Roux, 'To Be or Not to Be... The Cultural Identity of the Jawi (Thailand)', *Asian Folklore Studies* 57, 1998, pp. 223–55.

12. Gothom Arya, 'Local Patriotism and the Need for Sound Language and Education Policies in the Southern Border Province', in Imtiyaz Yusuf, Lars Peter Schmidt (ed.), *Understanding Conflict and Approaching Peace in Southern Thailand* (Bangkok: Konrad Adenauer Stiftung, 2006), p. 33.

13. D.K. Wyatt, 'Education and the Modernization of Thai Society', in D.K. Wyatt (ed.), *Studies in Thai History, Collected Articles* (Chiang Mai: Silkworm Books, 1994), p. 232.

14. Suria Saniwa, 'De-radicalisation of Minority Dissent', p. 124.

15. *International Herald Tribune*, 7 Nov 2006, http://www.iht.com/articles/2006/11/07/news/thai.php (accessed 19 December 2007).

16. Imtiyaz Yusuf, *Faces of Islam in Southern Thailand* (EWC Working Papers) (Washington: East West Center, 2007), p. 1.

17. Syed Serajul Islam, *The Politics of Identity in Southeast Asia* (Singapore: Thomson Learning, 2005), p. 90.

18. Kobkua, 'National Identity', p. 162.

19. Thongchai Winnichakul, *Siam Mapped, A History of the Geo-Body of a Nation* (Chiang Mai: Silkworm Books, 1994).

20. Mala Rajo Sathian, 'Economic Change in the Pattani Region c. 1880–1930: Tin and Cattle in the Era of Siam's Administrative Reforms', PhD dissertation, National University of Singapore, 2004. See Chapter Five.
21. For details see, International Court of Justice (ICJ). *Thailand: Political Turmoil and the Southern Insurgency*. Policy Briefing: International Crisis Group (ICG), Bangkok/Brussels, 28 August 2008.
22. UN Charter, 1945, Article 1[3], http://www.un.org/aboutun/charter/chapter1.shtml (accessed 7 May 2009).
23. See Vitit Muntarbhorn, 'Human Rights during Times of Turmoil', *Bangkok Post*, 10 December 2008.
24. International Court of Justice (ICJ). *Thailand: Political Turmoil and the Southern Insurgency*.
25. Omar Farouk, 'Islam, Nationalism and the Thai State', pp. 3–5.
26. Imtiyaz Yusuf, 'Islam and Democracy in Thailand: Reforming the Office of *Chularajmontri/Shaikh-al- Islam*', *Journal of Islamic Studies* 9(2), 1988, p. 284.
27. Clive J. Christie, *A Modern History of Southeast Asia: Decolonization, Nationalism and Separatism* (London and New York: I.B. Tauris, 1996), p. 182.
28. Yoneo Ishii, 'Thai Muslims and the Royal Patronage of Religion', *Law and Society Review* 28(3), Law and Society in Southeast Asia, 1994, p. 459.
29. Ibid., p. 456.
30. Omar Farouk, 'Islam, Nationalism and the Thai State', p. 8.
31. Wan Kadir Che Man, *Muslim Separatism: The Moros of Southern Philippines and the Malays of Southern Thailand* (Singapore: Oxford University Press, 1990), p. 166.
32. See Hannah Beech, 'Stupa and State', *Time,* 21 May 2007, p. 47.
33. Thanet Aphornsuvan, 'Buddhist Cosmology and the Genesis of Thai Political Discourse', in Imtiyaz Yusuf and Canan Atilgan (eds), *Religion and Democracy in Thailand* (Bangkok: Konrad-Adenauer-Stiftung, 2008), p. 32.
34. Hannah Beech, 'Stupa and State-monks', p. 47.
35. 'Deep South finally factors into poll campaigns', Opinion, *The Nation*, 18 December 2007.
36. Omar Farouk, 'Islam, Nationalism and the Thai State', p. 13.
37. Ibid., p. 11.
38. 'Deep South finally factors into poll campaigns', Opinion, *The Nation*, 18 December 2007.

39. Ibid.
40. Imtiyaz Yusuf, *Faces of Islam in Southern Thailand*, p. 16.
41. James Ockey, 'Elections and Political Integration in the Lower South of Thailand', in Michael J. Montesano and Patrick Jory (eds), *Thai South and Malay North* (Singapore: NUS Press, 2008), pp.146–53.
42. See Human Rights Watch, *No One Is Safe: Insurgent Attacks on Civilians in Thailand's Southern Border Provinces* 19(13C), August 2007, pp. 47–88.
43. See Uthai Dulyakasem, 'Education and Ethnic Nationalism: A Study of the Muslim-Malays in Southern Siam', PhD dissertation, Stanford University, 1981, pp. 83–84.
44. On education in religious schools in south Thailand see, Hasan Madmarn, *The Pondok and Madrasah in Patani* (Bangi: Universiti Kebangsaan Malaysia Press, 1999).
45. Alfred Stepan, 'Federalism, Multi-National States, and Democracy: A Theoretical Framework, the Indian Model and a Tamil Case Study', June 2003, http://www.columbia.edu/~as48/Stepan%20-%20Tamil%20Case20Study.pdf (accessed 2 February 2009).
46. Ibid.
47. Geof Eley and Ronald G. Suny, *Becoming National* (New York: Oxford University Press, 1996).
48. Chidchanok Rahimmula, 'Violence in Southern Thailand: A Crises Issue', in Utai Dulyakasem and Lertchai Sirichai (eds), *Knowledge and Conflict Resolution: The Crises of the Border Region of Southern Thailand* (Thailand: School of Liberal Arts, Walailak University, 2006), p. 32.
49. Sunai Phasuk, Human Rights Watch, Thailand, interview on Program 101East, Aljazeera News, Southern Thailand Special, 28 Sept 2007 (part 2), http://www.youtube.com/watch/v-ITU5OZOrCCc&NR=1 (accessed 17 December 2007).
50. Sunai Phasuk, Human Rights Watch, Thailand, interview on Program 101East, Aljazeera News, Southern Thailand Special, 28 September 2007 (part 1), http://www.youtube.com/watch/v-OnMBzbGsob4 (accessed 17 December 2007).

12

Minorities and Cultural Dominance in Malaysia: A Legacy of Co-optation and Capitulation

Sunil Kukreja

Introduction

On 3 September 2004, one day following his release from prison, Anwar Ibrahim opined about the need for Malaysia to become a more open and democratic society. Seemingly, his own ordeal, which in the eyes of many Malaysians and international observers was a fallout of his political rift with the former premier Mahathir Mohamad, had impressed upon him that Malaysia must undergo some fundamental political and social changes: 'What's the point of blaming the west and conspiracy of the Jews when you have the power but refuse to create reform in your country.'[1]

Perhaps Anwar might seem like a 'Johnny-come-lately' in this regard as there have been numerous others, especially in the Opposition parties, who for years have called for serious reforms, including the repeal of the Internal Security Act. Indeed, for years Anwar seemed to tow the government's line with respect to limitations on civil liberties, control of the press in the country and, in no small measure, the perpetuation of a pervasive ethno-religious state logic during his days as Mahathir's heir apparent. The assault on the judiciary by Mahathir in the late 1980s stands as another glaring misdeed of the very government Anwar was to condemn following his arrest and conviction. Yet, Anwar's relatively newfound voice — amid his emergence both as a victim personified and, to his enthusiast, the rightful Opposition leader in waiting — cannot do anything if not help rekindle the debate in Malaysia, not just for fundamental political reforms, but surely also the continuing dilemma of ethno-religious inequality and state sponsored discrimination. Nevertheless, this historical moment and the opportunities it presents for revisiting some of the more troubling facets of Malaysian society should not be confined to a narrowly defined set of issues. Quite simply, the ethno-religious divide is an issue that cries out for attention and — for all the progress that can be made on the civil and political liberties front — 'reform' in Malaysia will ring hollow indeed if there is no real effort to confront this divide which is in no small part perpetuated by the systematic marginalization of the non-Malay Muslim population through discriminatory policies.

Particularly since the early 1970s, Malaysians have been regularly reminded of the imperativeness of ethno-religious tolerance and the delicate political and economic compromises that will be necessary to achieve viable and lasting stability. Long indeed has been the shadow of 1969, the year that independent Malaysia lost its political innocence; with racial inequality and mistrust of the times being cast as the central culprits. A whole generation of Malaysians has since come of age, grown up without knowing of a Malaysia prior to the New Economic Policy (NEP) or the New Development Policy (NDP), and a Malaysia without a system of special rights, privileges and dis-crimination associated with the preceding. Picking up the pieces after the race riots of 1969 required a good bit of vision, a lot of credibility, and of course the means to put into motion an unprecedented process of societal reorganization; one that has in many intricate, but also in other straightforward ways, given us contemporary Malaysia. It was clear that the status quo, marked by a discernible economically marginal and poor Malay-Muslim population, was neither tolerable nor tenable; a new economy, a new social order was imperative. Yet, the form and process involved in re-creating Malaysian society was far less definitive, at least in the initial aftermath of the riots.

Malaysians are often, and perhaps rightfully so, reminded by academics and politicians alike of the many ways in which the country has persevered and has largely avoided the overt social rifts or conflicts that have dotted the social history of some of its neigh-bours. In this regard, some more recent notable examples of violent internal ethnic conflicts in the region stand in stark contrast to the comparatively serene state of ethnic relations in Malaysia. The fall of Suharto in Indonesia in 1998 coincided with a bloody and brutal assault on the country's Chinese population. Resentment of Chinese economic prowess amidst the overwhelming majority of Indonesians of the Malay ethnic stock has long been a point of friction in Indonesia. This coupled with other major internal rifts like the Aceh separatist/succession struggle. To the north, Malaysians continue to see a tense situation unfold in southern Thailand where ethnic Malays (and overwhelmingly Muslim) struggle to assert some autonomy and seek redress of its economic woes from Bangkok. These examples of unrest in the region resonate strongly in the Malaysian outlook and feed into a broader state logic about the tangible benefits of managing peace in a multiethnic scenario, and more importantly, inculcating a culture of co-optation and intimidation of the non-Muslim population to legitimize Malay Muslim hegemony. This outlook is one that has been methodically crafted and espoused by the dominant Malay nationalists, and for that matter by their non-Malay partners in the governing coalition dominated by the United Malays National Organisation (UMNO). The emergence of 'Malay ethnocrats', as they have been aptly referred to,[2] spearheaded a government-led process of social reorganization predicated on the centrality of asserting the rightful economic and political position of the Malay Muslims in the country.

To gauge the state of ethno-religious relations in Malaysia, or even the perspective of Malaysians on the state of ethnic relations especially between the Malay majority and non-Malay minorities in this post-1969 era is certain to be a process fraught with problems; in no small part due to the inherently sensitive nature of the subject. One might be inclined to put considerable weight on formal 'scientific' data such as the Civil Consciousness Index[3] that can be cited to suggest that Malaysians are highly receptive to the value of tolerance among the diverse groups.[4] Such findings certainly provide a valuable contribution to the overall understanding but it arguably is only a slice of the more complex interplay of a range of factors that shape and reshape Malay–non-Malay relations in the country. I cannot help but recall an occasion while travelling along a coastal road south-west of Kuala Lumpur, and we came by a town where many of the locals were out enjoying the late afternoon along the waterfront. We noticed a couple of soccer games going on in a nearby field. As we passed the kids playing, I turned to take a second look and was struck by the sight of essentially two soccer matches — one with Malays and the other among a group of Chinese kids — being played alongside one another. As I looked over to my

Malaysian counterpart, he said: 'Unfortunately, this is increasingly how the rest of the country operates. We seemed to have drifted apart, where though we may in many cases live alongside different races, we seem not to do things together or know one another'. The atmosphere in the car changed suddenly and it was as if some taboo had been broken. Then suddenly he continued, 'it's amazing how we have become so segregated'. By some measures, Malaysians seem more predisposed to embody the sentiment of tolerance and espouse the virtues of co-existence, while the Malay–non-Malay ethnic groups also seem noticeably removed and segmented from one another.[5] I wondered how racially segregated Malaysia, marred by the systematic discrimination of non-Malays that we see, reconciles with the optimistic interpretation of the pluralism that some[6] see as having emerged in the country.

Dominant Themes in Malaysian Racial Pluralism

Three general themes seem especially pervasive and widely articulated regarding the racial (majority–minority) arrangements in Malaysia. First, the country's racial division during the twentieth century can be traced to a racial ideology and the entrenched division of labour that accompanied British colonialism. As Charles Hirschman noted years ago, the conventional approach to interpreting racial and ethnic relations in Malaysia, which assumes the essentialist construction of racial groupings and all its concomitant assumptions about primordial ties, renders the racial divide in the country on the embededness and rigidity of the essentialist view about racial groupings and differences. Yet, as his own contribution and that of others has shown, the political economy of colonial domination not only corresponded closely with the '...spread of racial theory from Europe...'[7] but also gave rise to and legitimized institutional racism in the colonial context. In this context, the work of various others can be linked to Hirschman's critique of a peculiar form of racial division emerging from the consolidation of British domination in Colonial Malaya.[8] Others like A.B. Shamsul have advanced a theme consistent with the above assessment of the colonial role in imbuing a racialized character to Malaysia. Noting in particular the application of 'investigative modalities' such as historiography by the British, Shamsul argues that the colonial influence, coupled with the increasing presence of Chinese and Indians by the end of the nineteenth century did significantly contribute toward the consolidation of the notion of a Malay 'race'.[9]

Another common theme one encounters is associated not with the consolidation of racial categorizing in nineteenth and twentieth century Malaysia, but the basis for the relative absence of overt ethno-religious conflict between the dominant Malays and minorities in the country. The relative lack of such conflict, it is often noted, can be attributed to the ability of the state to deliver on the 'bread-and-butter' concerns, and to be able to placate the other ethnically-based political parties in the Barisan Nasional coalition. In this sense, Malaysia's relative racial harmony rests fundamentally on how well the major groups continue to fair and continue to believe in the ability of the Barisan Nasional coalition to deliver on the economic aspirations of the collective. Whether expressed through the notion of the 'inclusivist' politics of multiculturalism that has helped forge a stable order[10] or by means of co-optation and control of junior coalition parties in the coalition,[11] these views — implicitly or otherwise — acknowledge the theme of economic prosperity as a necessary determinant of relative racial harmony between the Malays and non-Malays. Some polling data seem to suggest that there is something to be said about this particular interpretation, and helps explain its continued appeal, if not popularity, in the discourse on majority–minority race relations in Malaysia. In one post-election survey in 2004, 42 per cent of respondents, cutting across ethnic lines, said Barisan Nasional's 'promise of continued develop-ment' was especially appealing.[12] Arguably, what was being reflected here again is the propensity of Malaysians to have faith in Barisan Nasional's ability, within the framework of a multicultural coalition, to ensure economic growth and development and thus minimizing the potential for ethno-religious strife. By extension, it is often argued that development has been good for ethnic relations as it helps contain the potential for conflict. Also apparent in this particular line of reasoning is of course that sustained economic failures and acute economic problems can potentially be a pretext for ethno-religious animosities to resurface. Notable here is the overlapping and inter-related impact of class relations on the ethno-religious matrix.

A relatively more recent theme to emerge emphasizes a widely ignored aspect of the historical construction (and critique) of ethnic relations in the country: its trans-ethnic dimension. Here we encounter, among others, the works of Sumit K. Mandal, who emphasizes the salience of exploring how 'trans-ethnic solidarities' have been and continue to be manifested in Malaysian society. Though relatively marginal, the discourse in this regard reflects not only an oft-overlooked dimension of the inter-ethnic dynamics in Malaysian society, and especially the 'cultural tendencies' where notable trans-ethnic solidarities are claimed to be most manifest, but this discourse also provides a notable critique of traditional race/ethnic analysis. For Mandal, trans-ethnic solidarities embody both the rejection of 'primordial notions of ethnicity' as well as accentuate the colour-blind cultural terrain in the society. In this perspective, while trans-ethnic solidarity is by no means new to Malaysian society, numerous historical (and contemporary) signifiers of this process have been largely discounted, minimized and ignored through the propensity toward racialization of Malaysia. One crucial part of this critique centers on the process by which scholarship on ethnic relations in Malaysia itself is fraught with a propensity for erroneous dichotomization of groups into false categories like 'indigenous' and 'non-indigenous'.[13]

It warrants noting that these three themes in the literature are by no means mutually exclusive or necessarily competing interpretations to the analysis of ethnic relations in Malaysia. These prevailing themes serve as a rich storehouse of material for understanding the legacy and dynamics of majority–minority relations in the country. Yet, these frameworks do little to account for the rise of a culture and politics of domination we see unfolding through the institutional marginalization of minorities (see below). What remains relatively marginalized in critical analyses and often unacknowledged in public circles are the 'hidden injuries' of what has emerged as a highly racially fragmented society. These 'hidden injuries'[14] essentially constitute the suppressed resentment, frustration and even resignation among many (especially non-Malay) Malaysians about the continued racialization of Malaysian society, perpetuated by a 'culture of Malay supremacy' that has been systematically fostered since the early 1970s. It is through examining key facets of the 'culture of Malay supremacy' that we can find vivid reminders of the damage, and the hidden injuries, created by the former. In a fundamental way, the two are flip sides of the same coin, although the hidden injuries are, in very real ways, products of the 'culture of supremacy' repeatedly impelled by the state. For all intents and purposes then, the continued self-espoused rhetoric of pluralism and tolerance so pervasive in the country is largely part of the façade that disguises these hidden injuries and the precariousness of the ethno-religious divide between the dominant Muslim Malays and non-Malay minorities.

Confronting Realities: The Divide

The interpretation I propose here challenges the prevailing orthodoxy of Malaysia's apparent success at forging a highly managed form of ethnic pluralism. I argue that despite all the trappings of 'co-existence', 'accommodation' and relative racial harmony, the post-*merdeka* (independence) compromise — a moderate, albeit arguably inadequate accommodation (largely) between the Malays and non-Malays was radically altered in the early 1970s with the intro-duction of the New Economic Policy (NEP). This sharp shift in the national project and agenda, primarily to explicitly and aggressively redistribute wealth toward the Malays and widely touted by the hardline Malay nationalists, set the path for a highly precarious raci-ally based program of institutionalized discrimination that has fueled socio-economic fragmentation, amplified the cultural divide among the dominant ethnic groups, and contributed to new challenges along ethnic–religious lines (see below).

Writing about the transformation of the Malay community, Shamsul has suggested that 'one could argue that the NEP...has not only gone a long way to achieving the ultimate aim of repossessing the country's wealth from foreigner's...[it] has also established a community which has complex internal divisions fractured by a host of economic, political and cultural factors'.[15] While this obser-vation aptly reflects the growing fragmentation characteristic of the emergent diversification *within* the Malay body politic, what has been overlooked are the systematic critiques of how the politics of race and a Malay Islamic agenda have also exacerbated an interracial national divide — one arguably more precarious and divisive.

As Shamsul and others rightly affirm, while the NEP has helped Malay Muslims claim, in a relatively short period, significant control of the public sector of the economy and substantial economic wealth, it is sociologically equally noteworthy that this process has been complemented by the parallel construction of the 'indigenization' of the notion of 'Malaysian'. In this context, the political and cultural constructions of Malay-ness, Islam and Malaysian have become increasingly interchangeable, hence intuitively (and often overtly) 'othering' the non-Malays and non-Muslim minorities. Much like Indonesia's adoption of the construct of a *pribumi* (native), Malaysia's reversion to the notion of *bumiputra* (son of the soil) as a designation for the Malays clearly embodies Benedict Anderson's idea of inventing an 'imagined community'.[16] This dichotomization of the Malaysian identity between the *bumi* and non-*bumi* is both a precipitant and an embodiment of the racial divide. As surely as this dichotomization — for all its justifications — circumscribed the institutionalization of a caste-like stratification, the fragmentation foretells a path that undermines the very construction of a sense of Malaysian-ness (*Bangsa* Malaysia). Lest there be any misunderstanding, this observation is not based on any working premise that '...all cases of cultural diversity necessarily lead to violence and break-up'.[17] However, it is equally prudent to consider the path travelled, and to recognize that the processes and means by which Malaysian pluralism of 'tolerance and accommodation of one another'[18] has had serious adverse repercussions as well. Indeed, it is very questionable whether Malaysia's narrative can be accurately characterized as 'tolerance and accommodation of one another'. Rather, what we have seen is the co-optation of the non-Malay political elite and the systematic intimidation of the non-Malay masses on the one hand, and the systematic privileging of Malay Muslim culture, privileges and political power on the other.

While supposedly having been a 'success story' of a racially plural society, or even in having led to 'a softening of the mistrust, suspicion, and sense of insecurity that was so evident in the late 1960s',[19] I posit that Malaysia's ethno-religious divide has become deep and ominous; disguised in large part by the relative economic success of recent decades, the rhetoric of pluralism and sustained by the continued co-optation of the Chinese and Indian Malaysian elite that has been mostly submissive to the Malay elite. As we now see, for example from the controversy surrounding the debate whether Malaysia is an Islamic state, serious ethno-religious challenges simmering below the surface must be understood within the context of the rise of Malay economic success and hegemony. 'And past trends have indicated a penchant for perpetuating ethnocentric demands, especially when the stability and sometimes even survival of partisan interests is at stake.'[20] However, the racial/ethic divide is arguably more palpable than ever, particularly given the added complexities of the undeniable process of Islamization that has consolidated alongside the capitulation and co-optation of elites within the minority (non-Muslim) communities.

A Legacy of Co-optation and Capitulation

I'm sad that we...feel the need to continuously emphasize power, authority and coercion to extract obedience.

— Zaid Ibrahim[21]

Though nation-building and economic development have been critical for the political legitimacy of the state, I agree with Vidhu Verma[22] that the significance of Islam, and by extension, 'its relation to the country's different communities are most salient' in colouring contemporary entho-religious relations between Malays and non-Malays. The state's role in exploiting the religious divide (i.e., Muslims vs. non-Muslims) has been central to its political legitimization efforts; a process that has ironically actually served not only to undermine the *democratic* state but also exacerbated majority–minority ethno-religious tensions.

Dominated by the UMNO's persistent political calculations to project itself, in contrast to the Pan-Malaysian Islamic Party (PAS), as the standard bearer of Islam, the state's perpetuation of the dichotomization of the *bumiputra–non-bumiputra* discourse, particularly through a propensity to privilege Islam — even above Malay ethnicity — and the impotence of minority coalition parties (especially the Malaysian Chinese Association [MCA] and Malaysian Indian Congress [MIC] and Gerakan) within the state has practically legitimized a culture of intimidation of minorities and curtailed the constitutional rights of the latter. Since the 1970s, there has been no bigger illustration of this process than when in 2001 (then) premier Mahathir Mohamad unilaterally proclaimed in his '929 Declaration' that Malaysia is an Islamic state. Whatever the political (or for that matter, non-political) motivations for the timing of this declaration, there was no shortage of public commentary in the country sparked by Mahathir's declaration. One can also only imagine how private and everyday conversations among Malaysians would have been dominated by this sudden affirmation on the part of Mahathir. Amazingly, amidst all the public discourse and controversy generated by this newly proclaimed and widely challenged declaration, little if anything emanated from the MIC or the MCA. As the opposition Democratic Action Party (DAP), other non-political entities and individual commentators sought to engage and challenge the prime minister on the legitimacy and merits or his declaration, the otherwise traditional (and often self-espoused) representatives of a vast cross-section of Malaysian-Chinese and Malaysian-Indians seemed, in comparison, to be mute and irrelevant to the national controversy.

In a fundamental way, however, this public non-engagement on the part of the MCA and MIC is at least consistent with their historical pattern of uncritically succumbing to the dictates of UMNO and the state. Far from raising crucial concerns about the merits of such a declaration, let alone its constitutional legitimacy, these entities have done what seems to define their modus operandi: silently acquiescing and ostensibly capitulating on ensuring and protecting the social contract established constitutionally for a legitimate multiethnic and multicultural Malaysia. It is ironic indeed that as the president of MIC, Samy Vellu had the impudence to chastise the Opposition DAP for 'making Malaysian-Indians out as third class citizens' for political purposes while he and other notable 'leaders' of the non-Malay minorities, in this and other instances, continue to preside over the erosion and marginalization of the non-Muslim identity. Though the approach of the MIC, MCA and Gerakan may be described as the 'politics of negotiation'[23] through their affiliation with the *Barisan* governing coalition, their legacy thus far might be more aptly characterized as one of capitulation, where the impact of the political leadership of the Malaysian-Indian and Malaysian-Chinese is unflattering and, in large measure, has heralded the current state of political impotence of the minority groups' leadership on issues impinging on the status of all minorities in the country.

Surely Malaysians deserved and were entitled to a meaningful public exchange on the legitimacy of Mahathir's proclamation. After all, given the constitutional implications associated with the proclamation, it would seem rather perplexing indeed that, not withstanding their history of capitulation, significant procedural and substantive concerns were not raised by the MIC or the MCA. Procedurally, it certainly seemed warranted that the Malaysian-Indian and Chinese political elite explore (if not challenge) the constitutionality of the premier's declaration. Beyond that, the absence of an engagement with the issue by the MIC and MCA exposed the level of impotence of these parties within the *Barisan* coalition and raised the specter of their legacy of capitulation to a new level altogether. This posture on the part of these dominant minority parties is not inconsistent with previous situations. Indeed, this recent example only adds to the cumulative evidence that these minority parties are far from being significant intermediaries and spokespersons of minority interests.

Note that the former premier and the UMNO's posturing on this issue has been to capture stewardship in defining and regulating Islam (a role that was historically, traditionally, and arguably, constitutionally, prescribed to the respective state sultanates), through institutional mechanisms. In this vein, it should come as no surprise that after years of evasive posturing, Mahathir's successor, Abdullah Badawi has essentially echoed Mahathir's unilateral proclamation of 2001 by asserting that Malaysia is a '*negara* Islam'.[24]

This process of politicizing Islam has not been without controversy and has its antecedents as far back as the split of UMNO in 1951 when a religious wing broke off to form the Pan-Malaysian Islamic Party, later to be known as Parti Islam Se-Malaysia (PAS). In subsequent years, the UMNO's propensity to placate the new religious wing of the party by, for example, agreeing to the establishment of religious organizations and departments in States and the establishment of Persatuan Ulama Se-Malaya — a body within UMNO to oversee political and social issues — personifies the privileging of Islam in the Malay body politic. Another related narrative is discernible in the co-optation of progressive urban-based Islamic movements. The co-optation of Angkatan Belia Islam Malaysia (ABIM) and its then leader, Anwar Ibrahim, provides the most vivid case-study in this respect. Beyond this, the process of Islamization of the state itself, for example among many other things, through the establishment to the Jabatan Kemajuan Islam Malaysia (JAKIM) for disseminating and propagating Islamic teachings, provides a case in point.[25]

Beyond these institution-based centralization efforts, the state has in more recent years found itself negotiating the controversy on religious conversion in the country. This issue of religious conversion has brought with it a further test of the state's dilemma in negotiating between affirming religious rights of minorities and serving as a advocate of what is seem as the supremacy of Islam. Lina Joy's situation was but a case in point. Known as Azlina Jailani at birth, Lina claimed her introduction to Christianity in 1990 changed her life for the better, and no longer wanted to be officially identified as a Muslim on her identity card. 'Her appeal to the federal court centers on whether she must go to a Sharia court to have her renunciation recognized before authorities strike the word "Islam" off her identity card'.[26] Similarly, the death of M. Moorthy in December 2005 sparked a related controversy when Muslims insisted that he should be buried as a Muslim (while rejecting his wife's and family's to claim his remains) on grounds that he had supposedly converted to Islam before his death. Other conversion cases, including that of Rayapan Anthony (who chose to no longer be a Muslim) have been marred by a pattern where an individual's right to religious freedom has been trumped by the rising influence of Shari'a bodies. The civil and secular judicial system has deferred to Shari'a based bodies to exert authority over determining and ruling on these individuals' religious options. Indeed, the country's civil courts have decided they have no jurisdiction on such matters.'[27]

Coinciding with this issue of religious conversion has been the controversy associated with the targeting and destruction of Hindu temples by the state. By 2006, the state was moving aggressively to destroy alleged unregistered Hindu temples across the country and, understandably, the issue generated considerable controversy and anger among the already marginalized Malaysian Indians (who are predominantly Hindu). Finding the MIC essentially incapable or unwilling to seriously challenge the state on halting the destruction of these temples, many Malaysian Indians turned to a coalition of NGOs in the country which had banded together to form the Hindu Rights Action Force (HINDRAF). Led by a handful of attorneys, HINDRAF actively protested against, among other things, the state's systematic campaign of destroying Hindu temples. In the process, HINDRAF's popularity among Malaysian Indians took a marked turn upwards while the MIC's leadership, in the eyes of the non-Malay population anyway, became increasingly exposed as too invested in the UMNO dominated state and incapable of protecting the Malaysian Indian minority when it mattered the most. By late 2007, several leaders of HINDRAF were arrested for sedition, and following a massive protest in November of the same year and the dismissal of these charges, they were released only to be arrested shortly after under the Internal Security Act (that permits the State to imprison individuals indefinitely without filing any charges or providing any legal due process). As the 8 March 2008 general elections drew nearer, it became evident that the MIC's reputation among

Indian Malaysians was increasingly being undermined. The campaign to destroy temples and the crackdown on any dissent against this policy only confirmed for many non-Malays how much the MIC had capitulated, and how co-opted Samy Vellu — who was also a member of prime minster Badawi's cabinet — had become.

This non-Malay minority frustration against a slew of racially discriminatory state policies and practices was also being felt in the area of higher education. When the UMNO-dominated state implemented the 55 per cent reserved quota for Malays in university admissions back in 1973, there was little indication that the practice would persist until now or that the percentage of seats set aside for Malays, would be raised to almost 70 per cent by 2003. On this front, the frustration felt by non-Malays, especially centered on the fact that merit as a criteria had become practically inconsequential in determining admission to public universities — especially highly desired fields such as medicine or natural sciences — while sheer opportunities even for highly qualified non-Malays in public universities had become practically negligible. Further complicating this systematic discrimination against non-Malay students is the reality that the performance of Malay students continues to lag behind that of the non-Malays. Figures given in Table 12.1 below, based on the experience at the University of Malaya, the country's pre-eminent public university, shows this problem rather vividly.

Table 12.1: Proportion of First-class Honours Degrees for Malay and Non-Malay Students, 1994–99[29]

Year	Malays	Per cent	Non-Malays	Per cent
1994	29	21.5	106	78.5
1995	34	22.4	118	77.6
1996	38	18.8	164	81.2
1997	46	19.5	190	80.5
1998	72	23.7	232	76.3
1999	96	27.0	259	73.0
Total	315	22.8	1069	77.2

Source: Antonio L. Rappa and Lionel Wee, *Language Policy and Modernity in Southeast Asia* (New York : Springer, 2006), p. 40.

In recent years, the frustration being felt by non-Malays against discriminatory educational policies being has reached new heights. Below is an excerpt indicative of this frustration and worth quoting at length, from a letter written by a parent of a non-Malay child which appeared on the *Malaysiakini* news website:[28]

> In the recent SPM examination, many of my students did very well, some scoring straight A's. We, teachers of all races, felt so very proud seeing the achievements of our students. We had '*Hari Anugerah Cemerlang*' in my school. Parents, regardless of race or religion were there to lend support for the programme and at the same time to motivate the children. One such student is my own daughter, who scored 12 A's, best student of the school. She used to wake as early as 4 o'clock in the morning to start preparing for her SPM.
>
> When I asked her why she has to take up 12 subjects and 'torture' herself, she told me, 'I am not a bumiputera like many of my friends.' So the need to take up two extra subjects (not offered in her school) in order to be on par with her Malay friends.
>
> She applied for the Progran Matrikulasi well before SPM itself. Yesterday was the day she was eagerly waiting since obtaining her SPM results because all the applicants will get their reply from the matriculation office. While I was in school, my handphone rang. It was a call from my daughter. When I answered the call she was already sobbing, and I am so silly to think that it was tears of joy.
>
> The sobs turn to cries after she heard my voice — she was devastated, depressed and very disappointed because she failed to get entry into this government-sponsored programme. She is the eldest in my family. I have another three school going children. May be I am to be blamed because it was me who asked her to study hard, get good results because being an ordinary teacher I can not afford to send her to private colleges.
>
> When I came back after school yesterday afternoon, again I saw tears in her eyes. She asked several questions. 'Is it wrong to get 12 A's in SPM? My Malay friends who got 2 A's and 3 A's got to do the matriculation programme, I am denied. What's wrong? You are also a teacher just like uncle, (my Malay colleague in school) — his son was offered a place although he scored only 5A's. Why?' I don't have answers.

There is no denying that the co-optation of and the pattern of capitulation by the non-Malay political establishment has been closely accompanied by a regular chorus of not-so-subtle reminders and admonitions from UMNO (explicitly directed at non-Malays) to refrain from questioning, in any way, the validity of privileging Malay citizenship over that of other Malaysians. Such periodic veiled threats from various quarters of UMNO's leadership, verge on the public intimidation of non-Malays. Some of the more notorious of these instances include Najib Razak's well-known and emphatic promise, made during a political rally in 1987, to bathe his *keris* (a traditional Malay sword) in the blood of Chinese Malaysians. This incident was followed by another controversial episode of *keris*-waving in 2005 by the UMNO youth-wing chief, Hishamuddin Hussein, at its general assembly. Laced with negative rhetoric and widely seen to be directed at Indians and Chinese, his and Najib Razak's provocative acts have come to symbolize for many the UMNO's arrogance and insensitivity towards, not to mention the downright intimidation of, non-Malays.

Taken together, these developments and trends, albeit far from being an exhaustive account of the marginalization of non-Malays, present a genuine conundrum for proponents of a sanguine pluralist interpretation of majority–minority relations in Malaysia.[29] On another level, by capitulating and not exerting its voice on behalf of non-Malay/Muslim minorities, the MCA, MIC and Gerakan, despite being 'coalition partners' with UMNO, have ostensibly be-come peripheral — if not inconsequential — to the real struggles of the minorities in the country, and reveal, in a most vivid sense, the thoroughness of the political capitulation carried out by the former political entities and the minority elites who dominate them. Indeed, these developments, in no small part, embody the very re-production of the ethno-religious controversies by the state (and UMNO). They are, in my opinion, products of the very process by which the state pursued a programme of blurring the lines between its secular constitution and its claims to being as the steward of Islam in the Malaysian polity.

Conclusion

> If this is the indicator after 50 years, I do not want to look forward to the next 50 years as the situation may become worse.
> — P. Ramaswamy[30]

For decades, one of the fundamental aspects of state rhetoric in Malaysia rested on ensuring popular purchase for the idea of multi-ethnic harmony as an imperative that the state, under the stewardship of UMNO, purported to ensure. Equally noteworthy has been the sentiment that the country's formula to ensure this relatively stable, if not harmonious, ethnic pluralism is rooted in a distinctly democratic polity. Shamsul's following characterization is a typical case in point: 'As it is presently, Malaysia has all the features of a modern democratic capitalist state. It has a Constitution, respects the rule of law and the concept of citizenship, recognizes and staunchly guards its territory, has a bona fide government, and conducts relatively free elections at regular intervals'.[31] Unfortunately, such representations seem to have become accepted wisdom in much of the theorizing about Malaysian ethnic relations. Ominously absent — and very telling — in the above 'features' of Malaysia's 'democracy' is a meaningful and free press and the freedom of speech, arguably, a most fundamental tenet of any 'modern democratic state'.

The co-optation and capitulation of the minority elite, and the relative lack of engagement in a meaningful political discourse on representation in the country is very much a mirror reflection of the lack of a truly democratic culture — one where the civic and political culture is defined by a fundamental respect for the aforementioned tenet of a legitimate modern state. As the erosion of secular, democratic, constitutional considerations continues, abetted by UMNO's undeniable trajectory towards an increased Islamization of the state and, by extension, the marginalization and systematic discrimination of non-Malays in 'democratic' Malaysia, we are witnessing the palpable and systematic deterioration of inter-faith and inter-racial relations in the country.

Notes and References

1. Arfa'eza A. Aziz, 'Assault was my worst moment, says Anwar', htth://www.malaysiakini.com/news/29721 (accessed 5 September 2004).
2. See Antonio Rappa, *Modernity and Consumption: Theory, Politics and the Public in Singapore and Malaysia* (Singapore: River Edga, 2002), p. 154.
3. See Saravanamuttu *et al.*, *Civil Society Project: Final Report* (Penang: Universiti Sains Malaysia, 1996).
4. The authors reported that 69.7 per cent of respondents reflected an orientation towards ethnic tolerance and interaction with others.
5. Farish Noor has similarly commented on this trend in his reflections on students during his tenure at the University of Malaya. See Farish Noor, *The Other Malaysia* (Kuala Lumpur: Silverfish, 2002), p. 245.

6. For instance, Abdul Rahman Embong, 'The Culture and Practice of Pluralism in Postcolonial Malaysia', in Robert Hefner (ed.), *The Politics of Multiculturalism: Pluralism and Citizenship in Malaysia, Singapore, and Indonesia* (Hawaii: University of Hawaii Press, 2001).

7. Charles Hirschman, 'The Making of Race in Colonial Malaya: Political Economy and Racial Ideology', *Sociological Forum* 1, p. 332.

8. For example, see Collin Abraham, 'Racial and Ethnic Manipulation in Colonial Malaya', *Ethnic and Racial Studies*, Vol. 6, pp. 18–32; Collin Abraham, *Divide and Rule: The Roots of Race Relations in Malaysia* (Kuala Lumpur: INSAN, 1997); Syed Hussein Alatas, *The Myth of the Lazy Native* (London: Frank Cass, 1977); Leon Comber, *13 May 1969: A Historical Survey of Sino-Malay Relations* (Kuala Lumpur: Heinemann Asia, 1983); and Michael Stenson, *Race, Class, and Colonialism in West Malaysia: The Case of Indians* (Vancouver: University of British Columbia, 1980).

9. A.B. Shamsul, 'Identity Contestation in Malaysia: A Comparative Commentary on "Malayness" and "Chineseness"', *Akademika 55*, pp. 17–37.

10. Cheah Boon Kheng, *Malaysia: The Making of a Nation* (Singapore: Institute of Southeast Asian Studies, 2002).

11. See R.S. Milne and Diane K. Mauzy, *Malaysian Politics under Mahathir* (London: Routledge, 1999).

12. Pauline Puah, 'Survey confirms 'Pak Lah factor' in BN polls victory', 18 September 2004, http://www2.malaysiakini.com/news/30129 (accessed 5 September 2007).

13. Sumit K. Mandal, 'Boundaries and Beyond: Wither the Cultural Bases for Political Community in Malaysia?', in Robert Hefner (ed.), *The Politics of Multiculturalism: Pluralism and Citizenship in Malaysia, Singapore, and Indonesia* (Hawaii: University of Hawaii Press, 2001), pp. 51, 60; see also Mandal, 'Transethnic Solidarities, Racialisation and Social Equality', in Edmund Terence Gomez (ed.), *The State of Malaysia* (London: RoutledgeCurzon, 2004).

14. I borrow this term from Richard Sennett and Jonathan Cobb (*The Hidden Injuries of Class* [New York: Norton, 1993]), who used it to refer to the personal and emotional impact on the working poor struggling at the lower end of the labour strata.

15. A.B. Shamsul, 'A History of an Identity, an Identity of a History: The Idea and Practice of "Malayness" in Malaysia Reconsidered', *Journal of Southeast Asian Studies* 32, 2001, pp. 355–66.

16. Benedict Anderson, *Imagined Communities: Reflections on the Origins and Spread of Nationalism* (London: Verso, 1983).

17. Abdul Rahman Embong, 'Malaysia as a Multicivilizational Society', in Ahmad I. Samatar (ed.), *Malaysia: Crossroads of Diversity in Southeast Asia* (St. Paul, MN: Macalester College, 2002), p. 37.

18. Ibid., p. 51.
19. Ibid.
20. Oo Yu Hock, *Ethnic Chameleon: Multiracial Politics in Malaysia* (Petaling Jaya, Malaysia: Pelanduk, 1991), p. 1.
21. 'At 50, Malaysia questions its identity', http://www.malaysiakini.com/news/71682 (accessed 5 September 2007). Zaid Ibrahim is an UMNO parliament member.
22. Vidhu Verma, *Malaysia: State and Civil Society in Transition* (Petaling Jaya, Malaysia: Strategic Information Research Development, 2004), p. 89.
23. Khoo Boo Teik, *Beyond Mahathir: Malaysian Politics and Its Discontent* (London: Zed Books, 2003), p. 135.
24. Yoges Palaniappan, 'PM: Yes, we ARE an Islamic State', http://www.malaysiakini.com/news/71676 (accessed 27 August 2007).
25. Kamarulnizam Abdullah, *The Politics of Islam in Contemporary Malaysia* (Bangi, Malaysia: Universiti Kebangsaan Malaysia, 2003).
26. Elisia Yeo, 'Muslim Malaysia faces crucial religious freedom test', http://metimes.com/storyview.php?StoryID=20070111-073511-3401r (accessed 16 January 2007).
27. Jonathan Kent, 'Malaysia seeks to avoid faith row', 7 December 2006, http://news.bbc.co.uk/2/hi/asia-pacific/6216294.stm (accessed 15 December 2006).
28. 'A daughter devastated, a mother with no answers', http://malaysiakini.com/letters/81505 (accessed 17 April 2008).
29. For further examples of the co-optation of the non-Malay elite, see Sunil Kukreja, 'Political Hegemony, Popular Legitimacy and the Reconstruction of the Ethnic Divide in Malaysia: Some Observations', *Crossroads: An Interdisciplinary Journal of Southeast Asian Studies* 16, 2002, pp. 19–48.
30. 'At 50, Malaysia questions its identity', http://www.malaysiakini.com/news/71682 (accessed 5 September 2007). Ramasamy is a political scientist.
31. A.B. Shamsul, 'Nations-of-Intent in Malaysia', in Stein Tonnesson and Hans Antlov (eds), *Asian Forms of the Nation* (Richmond, UK: Curzon Press, 1996), p. 331.

13

Wong Cilik and *Wong Gede*: Contesting over Nationalist Imaginations[1]

Aris Arif Mundayat

Introduction

The relationship between state and society, when considered from a structural perspective, is mostly understood as a relationship of power between the superior and the dominated. But the interaction between these two entities is not merely about domination, rather it demonstrates a form of dynamic contestation that destabilizes a state's nationalist project. Following this assumption, this article treats the interplay of state apparatuses (*wong gede*) and the commoners (*wong cilik*) as a terrain of political contestation. How each party imagines 'Indonesia-ness', during and after the authoritarian rule of Suharto's regime, and how they contest it in their everyday lives — are the issues being discussed here.

The emic category of '*wong cilik*', as used by the *wong cilik*, refers mainly to the poor, rural peasants, urban industrial workers, street dwellers, people living in slum areas, petty traders, street musicians, lower-ranking state functionaries and some petty clerical groups. All of these would, in a Javanese context, be seen as 'underclass' if we were to use conventional sociological categories. On the other hand, the emic category *wong gede*, as used by the *wong cilik*, includes wider and more diverse groups — all of them, in one way or another, exercising economic or political power. They include, for example, politicians, wealthy Indonesians, high-ranking military and police officials, high-ranking bureaucrats (or *priyayi,* Javanese for high social status) and state officials. Students in this social structure are seen as someone who is located somewhere in between, because they have been uprooted from the customary locales of these emic categories. If they must be categorized by the *wong cilik*, it is usually done with reference to the students's parents' emic categories.

This article focusses on a form of contestation that is found in texts produced by the *wong gede* (in this the *pejabat*, or high-ranking bureaucrat) that shows an attempt to dominate and by the *wong cilik* (common people) that shows an effort to resist the dominant discourse. The texts consist of *bahasa pejabat* (language used by high-ranking bureaucrat), official speeches made by the President, as well as songs and poems. It also examines the idea of democracy from the *wong cilik's* point of view and the ways in which their ideas are used to ridicule the authoritarian state. Second, it explores the state's nationalist projects and discusses how they are contested by the *wong cilik* using various textual manifestations. These writings reflect the *wong cilik's* nationalist imagination of Indonesia at the turn of the twenty-first century, as well as their discontent with the state-sanctioned nationalist project. This textual analysis is mostly based on cases that I encountered in urban areas where the urban sections of *wong cilik* are located. On the basis of these texts I will demonstrate that various desperate imaginings have given a distinct meaning to the nationalist imaginary, in which difference and contestation play a dynamic role. The important contradictions that emerge from the construction of a state-sponsored nationalist discourse can also be observed in the power relations that are active between the state and society in the specific arena of these encounters.

The State Nationalist Project vs a Vernacular Nationalist Imagination

This section explores popular contestation of the nationalist imagination — the cognitive dissonance between state-sponsored nationalist projects and the *wong cilik's* nationalist ideas. I will reveal the constant struggle involved in trying to give meaning to the so-called nation as an imagined political community.[2] The term 'nationalist imagination' should be broken down into at least two distinctive categories, i.e., a state nationalist imagination and a vernacular nationalist imagination. It is important to acknowledge that all nationalist imaginings are plural and contested. The differences between the two are mostly based on the technology of mediation that they employ. Capitalist print and electronic media have become the main instruments in disseminating the 'state nationalist imagination' as a core element of a state's discursive practices. A vernacular nationalist imagination, by contrast, is disseminated orally by the *wong cilik* in their everyday social relationships. This discursive practice also serves to advance and develop their consciousness, which might be used to subvert the dominant power. Within this, the *wong cilik* constructs a vernacular nationalist imagination which is mediated by their colloquial language, in marked contrast and at a substantial remove from the 'official' language used by the state. This vernacular nationalist imagination coexists with the state's nationalist imagination. These vernacular imaginings are expressed through songs, poems and other forms, as will be discussed in the following paragraphs.

The State Nationalist Project

Before Suharto's resignation, there was issued a national banknote (Rp 50,000) which carried pictures of Suharto and state projects such as the development of tollways, air planes, boats, urban areas, agriculture, education, industry, as well as depictions of the harmonious religious relationships that exist in the plural society of Indonesia (See Figure 13.1) All these developmentalist projects are thus 'miniaturized' onto a small piece of paper, which functions as Indonesian currency.[3] The *wong cilik* of Malioboro Street call this money 'Suharto *mesem*', a Javanese term meaning 'Smiling Suharto'. At the level of the *wong cilik*, '*Suharto mesem*' has a pejorative sense rather than being a positive or even a neutral term. This is because this money was often used to bribe police officers, for instance, to release any street kids captured on Malioboro Street or to bribe officers in order to get a driving license made.

When the *wong cilik* attributed additional meaning to this money they were focused more on the 'Smiling Suharto' picture, which could perhaps make someone else 'smile' too, than on the smaller background pictures showcasing 'development'. The picture presented Suharto as the central theme on the nation's currency, reminding us that the New Order government referred to him as *Bapak Pembangunan Indonesia* (the Father of Indonesia's Development), as stated under his picture. On this banknote there are also written the words '*25 Tahun Indonesia membangun*' ('25 Years Developing Indonesia'), celebrating how he had already

Figure 13.1: Smiling Suharto, the Rp 50, One Banknote

ruled Indonesia for twenty-five years, and how this had brought a swathe of development projects to Indonesia that sprang from Saharto's nationalist imagination (represented in miniature and surrounding his smiling face).

Suharto's role in development projects is depicted in a miniaturized scene of a meeting between 'the people' and himself, a favourite moment of Suharto's 'talk show ritual', the *'Temu Wicara'*, which commenced around the late 1980s and became a characteristic of the 'peers' made thereafter. As can be seen in the picture on the bank note, Suharto sits in front of the people and the audience behaves politely, as can be seen from their hands folded in front of them and the uniformity of their posture in the picture. One person in the audience is also standing politely, again with his hands folded, asking Suharto a question. In reality, this ritual is rehearsed and is organized by the *Sekretariat Negara* (State Secretariat), after which instructions are passed down the state hierarchy to the provincial *kabupaten* (district) and *kecamatan* (subdistrict), and to village-level state apparatuses. The talk show is prepared and rehearsed before Suharto arrives on stage, in order to ensure its success and, indeed, to make sure that Suharto leaves the stage satisfied. Even the number of people expected to be invited to sit in front of Suharto, the audience members who would ask Suharto questions that had been prepared and already agreed upon, was decided by the *Sekretariat Negara*. There was no doubt that it was all very well planned. The important symbolic elements of the performance were the stage and the placement of higher-ranking government functionaries. First, the stage had to be built around 1.5 meters above the floor. The audience was seated in front of Suharto, below the stage. The upper stage would be occupied by some of his ministers, the governor and invited the *Bupatis* (Heads of Regency), *Camats* (the Heads of Districts) of the place where the *temu wicara* was held.[4]

The idea of a *temu wicara* is very close to the ideal representation of Suharto as an enlightened ruler as pronounced in a book edited by his daughter Herdiyanti Rukmana and published in 1990, as we can see below:

> *Negara kuwat uga marga saka wadyabalane kuwat lan kawulane suyud. Negara kang kuwat iku kalebu kasinungan kanugrahan dening Kang Maha Kuwasa. Dene kang mengku negara kudu ndarbeni watak ber budi bawa leksana.*
>
> *Negara kang mung kuwat marga wadya balane, lan disuyudi dening kawulane, iku durung mesti kuwat salawase, jalaran kawula mau suyude mung marga wedi karo wadya-balane mau. Dene negara kuwat marga kawulane suyud kamangka wadya-balane kurang kuwat, ikut marga kasinungan dening Kang Mahakuwasa. Apa dene kang mengku mau darbe watak berbudi bawa leksana.[5]*

> (A country is strong because, among other things, its army is strong and its people faithful. A strong country enjoys the blessing of God Almighty. Meanwhile, the ruler of the country must have a noble mind and generous heart)
>
> (A country which is strong only owing to its army and its subdued people, may not be strong forever as the people are subdued out of fear of the army. However, if a country is strong because its people are subdued although the army is not very strong, this is due only to the blessing of God Almighty. It will be all the more so if the ruler has a noble mind and a generous heart)

The formulation regarding a *'negara kuwat'* (strong country) and a *'kawulane suyud'* (subdued people) as shown in the text above is followed by an idealized depiction of the country's leader. This presents the regime's construction of a nationalist imagination, which also consists of a desire to subjugate a particular type of mess, achievable through processes of disciplining. This is an attempt to emphasize state symbolism where the people's obedience is constructed as an aspect of their natural duty. Moreover, the disciplining process was conducted under this regime not only through particular rituals and commemorations of national days, such as independence day, the commemoration of heroes, youth pledges, the Monday flag-hoisting ceremony for all school children, government offices, etc, it was also evident in civic education as per the curriculum system that indoctrinates students and teachers, and in the implementation of *Pancasila* as the sole ideology of all social institutions. This kind of discipline was designed to reinforce the construction of a state-sponsored nationalist imagination, and much of it was condemned with the political reforms introduced in post-Suharto Indonesia (1999–2004). However, the dissemination of state ideology through educational curricula, from primary school to university degree, still exists and continues to participate in the construction of the state nationalist project.

The importance of state symbolism in supporting many kinds of state nationalist discursive practices seems to be connected to the threat discourse where by the state projects itself as a regime that has the right to interpret what the nationalist ideal should be. This was evident, for example, in a speech given by Suharto (as keynote speaker) to members of the Kopassandha (Komando Pasukan Sandhi Yudha, the elite special forces corps) during it's twenty-eighth celebration on 16 April 1980:[6]

'*Kemudian marga kedua: Kami Patriot Indonesia pendukung serta pembela Ideologi Negara yang bertanggung jawab dan tidak mengenal menyerah. Jadi dalam keadaan bagaimanapun juga bilamana Pancasila dasar negara itu terancam, maka kita digugah harus bangkit sebagai patriot untuk tidak hanya mendukungnya saja, akan tetapi harus membela dengan tidak kenal menyerah. Yang berarti kita harus menggunakan segala kemampuan yang ada pada kita untuk dapat mempertahankan Pancasila sebagai dasar ideologi negara itu. Ancaman kekuatan senjata harus kita hadapi dengan kekuatan senjata pula yang kita miliki.*[7]

(Then the second way: We, the supporters of Indonesian patriotism and guardians of state ideology, are responsible and don't know how to surrender. Thus, in any kind of situation when *Pancasila*, the state philosophy, is threatened, we are awakened to stand up as patriots not only to support it, but also to defend it without surrender. Which means we have to use any force necessary to protect *Pancasila* as a state ideology. The threat of armed force must be also addressed with our weaponry).

The first sentence above (derived from *Sapta Marga Prajurit*, Seven Principles for a Soldier)[8] embodies an ideal that reflects a syndrome of all militaristic powers. Possibly a universal phenomenon associated with militarism throughout the world. It was also tied to nationalist ideas, utilizing state ideology in order to create and popularised the spirit of the state's nationalist imagination and to satisfy Suharto's growing desire for power. Suharto argued that the nation-state was endangered, as shown in quotation below:

Akan tetapi kita mengetahui bahwa ancaman ideologi Pancasila tidak semata-mata dari kekuatan senjata, artinya dipaksa kita merubah, mengganti Pancasila dengan ideologi lain tidak semata-mata dengan kekuatan senjata akan tetapi juga bisa dengan kekuatan subversi, inflitrasi bahkan sampai menghalalkan segala cara untuk menghilangkan Pancasila dan memaksa mengganti Pancasila sebagai dasar daripada negara itu. Suatu misal saja jalan-jalan yang yang akhir-akhir ini ditempuh, bahkan selalu akan terjadi bilamana kita mendekati kepada pelaksanaan Pemilihan Umum, akan timbul isyu-isyu yang sebenarnya adalah tidak pada tempatnya lagi.[9]

(However, we recognize that threats toward the *Pancasila* ideology come not merely from armed powers, which would mean we would be forced to modify, to replace *Pancasila* with another ideology. However, such attempts are made not merely by force of weaponry but also by the use of subversive forces, infiltration, even any legitimate attempts to dismiss *Pancasila* and demand that *Pancasila* be replaced (by another state philosophy). For example, the recent tactics that [they] have been using, are always apparent close to the general elections, and the issues that emerge are misplaced.)

The image of an 'endangered' state is typical of the nationalist fantasy of the New Order that was disseminated by the state through discursive practices on numerous everyday occasions. This idea or understanding has become a locus of horror for the subjects framed within state–society power relations. This is because Suharto created an image of 'threat as a phantom' on the basis of a specific reading of history and glorified by the state in, for example, the annual ceremony to celebrate '*Kesaktian Pancasila*' (the Sacredness of Pancasila) every 1 October. A commemoration of the six army generals slain in the 1965 political turmoil called G30S/PKI (*Gerakan 30 September/Partai Komunis Indonesia* or 30 September Movement/Indonesian Communist Party). This day also become a commemoration of the fall of Indonesian Communist Party (PKI, Partai Komunis Indonesia). The commemoration aims not only to glorify the victory of the New Order regime over Sukarno's regime and the demise of the PKI, but also to entrench the 'true' state-sponsored nationalist discourse and consolidate its axiomatic standing through state–society power relations, in which the term '*Kesaktian Pancasila*' (the Sacredness of *Pancasila*) has become as much part of the discourse of threat as it is a celebration of national unity.[10] As Ariel Heryanto argues, the New Order regime constructed grand narratives that served to preserve Indonesia's bloody history as a deep social trauma and acted continuously to psycho-politically terrorize the populace. The 'grand narrative' of the coup of 30 September 1965, used as evidence of the urgency of defending '*Kesaktian Pancasila*', leads to its annual ritualization. The obligatory observance of these public rituals is aimed at, disciplining society under the hegemony of the New Order regime. Heryanto describes how, every year, children from various grades of school were compelled to watch the lavishly produced, state-sponsored produced movie (paying for it with their own money) about *Kesaktian Pancasila*, directed by Arifin C. Noor, entitled 'Penghianatan G 30 S PKI'.[11]

Moreover, Suharto, as President for the period of 1966–98, also tried to establish a connection between the nation and his family and even between state ideology and his family. In the late 1980s, it was rumoured that he had a love affair with movie star Rahayu Effendi. His wife was also said to be involved in underhanded relationships with businesspeople. These dealings are related in music group Bimbo's song entitled 'Tante Sun' (Aunty Sun).[12] Suharto's speech at the Kopasandha anniversary sought to counter such gossip:

> *Mereka menghalalkan segala cara untuk menimbulkan isyu untuk mencapai tujuannya. Tidak hanya sekedar mendiskreditkan pemerintah, Pejabat-pejabat, tetapi akhir-akhir ini pula bahkan kemarin saya bertemu dengan kolega saya Saudara Kusno, Utomo, juga telah mendengar isyu-isyu yang sebetulnya tidak pada tempat yang ditujukan kepada saya, Bu Harto. Selalu diisyukan bahwa isteri Suharto menerima komisi. Menentukan kemenangan tender dan komisi dan lain sebagainya. Yang sebenarnya tidak terjadi sama sekali keadaan demikian. Jangankan untuk memikirkan itu, waktu untuk memikirkan kegiatan-kegiatan sosial saja sudah tidak mencukupi. Dan bahkan akhir-akhir ini sampai juga ditujukan kepada saya yang sudah diisyukan di kalangan mahasiswa dan juga di kalangan ibu-ibu yang biasa mudah untuk sampai ke mana-mana: Satu isyu kalau saya ini katanya mempunyai 'selir', mempunyai simpanan salah satu dari*

bintang film yang terkenal yang dinamakan Rahayu Effendi. Ini sudah lama bahkan sekarang ini juga dibangkitkan hal itu kembali. Padahal kenal. Berjumpa saja tidak. Tapi sudah toh dilontarkan isyu itu.[13]

Apa ini semua maksudnya? Maksudnya adalah tidak lain karena mungkin mereka itu menilai kalau saya itu menjadi penghalang utama dari kegiatan politik mereka itu.karena itu harus ditiadakan. Mereka lupa, andaikata bisa meniadakan saya, lupa bahwasanya toh akhirnya akan timbul mungkin lebih daripada saya,warga negara prajurit-prajurit anggota ABRI termasuk pula dari Korps Kopassandha Baret Merah akan tetap menghalang-halangi kehendak politik mereka itu, lebih-lebih jelas bilamana ingin mengganti Pancasila dan Undang-Undang Dasar '45 itu.[14]

(They make every possible means legitimate in order to raise issues and thus to gain political goals. It is not merely discrediting the government, the high level state officials, but recently, even yesterday I met my colleagues Mr Kusno, and Utomo, who also heard about such issues which could not only be applied to me, but also to my wife, Bu Harto. As usual, there are rumours that Suharto's wife is accepting commissions, that she determines the winning of tenders, which creates the image that Cendana Street (the address of the Presidential palace) is the headquarters for winning tenders and commission etcetera. This absolutely never happens. Not even the thought of it Thinking about social activities does not even allow enough time any more. And even recently I was accused in one rumor that originated from the students' circle and circulated among the housewives who usually easily disseminate rumours widely. One issue said that I have a concubine (selir), that I have a mistress (*istri simpanan*) who is the famous film star, Rahayu Effendi. This is an old issue but at the moment it has been reawakened. However, I do not even know her, I have never met her. But it is already spoken of as an issue.

What does it all mean? It means, perhaps, they think that I am the main handicap for their political activities; therefore they have to dismiss me. They forget that if [they] evict me, there might be a person who is more than me, the soldier citizen of ABRI including the corps of Red Beret Kopassandha who will besiege their political desires, and even more so if they want to change Pancasila and Undang Undang Dasar '45 (1945 constitution).

This speech was published by most of the newspapers and by TVRI (the only state-owned TV station in the late 1980s). Print and electronic media became an important means for the New Order to disseminate their nationalist project throughout Indonesia. The interesting point in the above speech is that the New Order regime constituted power relations between itself and its subjects by convince them that there was no difference between the 'state' and the 'nation-state' or between the 'regime' and the 'country'. Accordingly, any act against the New Order regime constituted an act against the country. In the extreme, attempts against Suharto's family and himself also translated into acts against the country and against the army, which is what Suharto imagined them to be. In addition, the creation of the phantom of threats to 'national stability', in practice, served to suppress the people and warn them not to act against the state.[15]

All the factors explained above contributed to the regime's sustained project of creating an unchallengeable nationalist imagination among the people. It became a 'macro-interventionist discourse' — as I explained in the theoretical review — used by New Order regime to create a 'benchmark for political interpretation' based on that project. In constructing this national vision, the dominant forces put together a standard interpretation which accorded exactly with the regime's political interests. The project identified the kinds of interpretation that were permitted to be taken up by society, both discursively and materially, and appropriated the exclusive right to the only 'true' reading of Indonesian nationalism. In practice, therefore, it operated not only through discursive practices among state functionaries but also through the institutionalization of this discourse throughout society with the aim of deciding and defining the true nature of the nationalist imagination. The institutionalization of this regime can be seen in the existence of the BP7 (*Badan Pembinaan Pendidikan Pelaksanaan Pedoman Penghayatan Pengamalan Pancasila* or 'Coordination Body for the Education, Guidance, Crystallization and Implementation of Pancasila') and *Bakorstranas* (*Badan Koordinasi Pemantapan Stabilitas Nasional* or 'Coordinating Body for Establishing National Stability') which had become necessary for the establishment of the 'regime of interpretation'. This regime was not only institutionalized at the political level but also at the cultural level, in the form of hegemonization.

In the 1980s, the New Order state set up a military body called *Bakorstranas*. It was established to monitor all subversive political activities that, it was assumed, would endanger the country's stability; a task previously undertaken by a similar extra-judicial military body called *Kopkamtib*, whose leadership had fallen out with Suharto. The Bakorstranas had branches in every province, known as the

Bakorstrada (*Badan Koordinasi Pemantapan Stabilitas Daerah* or 'Coordination Body for Establishing Regional Stability').[16] At the level of academic curricula, university students must take a course titled '*Wawasan Nusantara*' 'Indonesian View' to indoctrinate them in the nationalist idea. This kind of course actually begins to be taught in primary schools with the PMP (*Pendidikan Moral Pancasila* or 'Education of Pancasila Morality'). The importance of national stability is thus reiterated by this system, in addition to political practices. State officials also stressed the concept of *jati diri* (self-identity), whereby every region was expected to assert their local identity as an expression of the nationalist idea. This is merely a politically constructed understanding of nationalism, defined by the state rather than the people's own expression of their 'imagined community'. However, the state-sponsored nationalist imagination has gained popularity among state functionaries. Within this political atmosphere, the official interpretation of nationalist ideas has been monopolized by the regime and constructed centrally and perhaps exclusively by the state. In practice, this doctrine is also emphasized through another type of state award known as the *Adipura* (a Sanskrit term meaning 'beautiful palace'). This award is given to the city that best meets criterion such as cleanliness, neatness, serenity and beauty. Whenever a city gets this award an elaborate ritual celebration takes place, as in Yogyakarta in 1993.[17] All national festivals, commemorating various historical events, are used by the state to construct and promote its vision of Indonesia-ness, to which end celebrations are carefully ritualized by the state.[18] In fact, the glorification of such events is an act of hegemonization and the construction of state symbolism, which can be referred to as — borrowing Widodo's terminology — 'the rites of hegemonization'.[19]

The dissemination of nationalist ideas through such rites can be defined as the discursive practice of 'state nationalism' to construct Indonesia-ness according to the state's perspective. The regime's political desire to construct Indonesia-ness through development has placed the state at the center and at the top of the hierarchized regimentation process. Bureaucratic corporatism and bureaucratic authoritarianism, as a chain of power in this case, took over control of the political machinery in New Order Indonesia under Suharto, and to some extent its residue still exists in the post-New Order regime, which continues to use the national day to construct a 'uniform' nationalist imagination. Culturally, this form of modern politics has been interwoven with the remnants of old Indonesian political cosmology that located the state as the axis of political orientation.[20] Within the political context of New Order Indonesia, as previously explained, the state's nationalist imagination was disseminated using state apparatuses within the circuit of bureaucratic corporatism. State rituals became the main arena or stage for the enactment and dissemination of this nationalist conception. Indeed, it permeated down to the grassroots level, and has influenced the grammar used to imagine and articulate their community. However, it will never be able to completely coopt the vernacular discourses, as I will discuss in the following pages.

Monthly rituals such as the one practiced on the seventeenth day of every month by civil servants, show how the capillaries of power extend downwards and attempt to transmit their meaning through the tradition of hierarchical social relations.[21] To a substantial extent, even 'positive' meanings of unity are clearly bound to messages of symbolic threat. This can be seen in the obedience displayed by civil servants for one, who allow themselves to be vehicles of the dominant figures of the regime.

Within the context of the state's nationalist project, the need to find 'authenticity' and '*jati diri*' has become crucial to attaining the so-called '*puncak-puncak kebudayaan*' ('peaks of civilization') as part of constructing Indonesia-ness. The Department of Culture and Education leads this project, and university and state research institutions have become its clients, conducting research on finding its '*puncak*' (peak) and explaining how it contributes to the nationalist state projects. This is a consequence of bureaucratic corporatism channelling this kind of state nationalist imagination, which then, to some degree, succeeded in creating an academic discourse of the state nationalist imagination. Research concerning *puncak-pucak kebudayaan* as reported in 1995 by Sunarti in a work titled *Wujud, Arti dan Fungsi Puncak-puncak Kebudayaan Lama dan Asli bagi Masyarakat Pendukungnya di Daerah Khusus Ibukota Jakarta: Sumbangan Kebudayaan Daerah Khusus Ibukota Jakarta terhadap Kebudayaan Nasional* (The Manifestation, Meaning and Function of Old and Original Cultural Peaks for People in the Special Region of Capital City Jakarta: Contributions of Local Culture for the Special Region of the Capital City Jakarta toward National Culture) is evidence of this discursive practice of the state nationalist imagination.[22] This identifies the authenticity of Jakarta culture based on remnants of Javanese ancient high culture that still exist in Indonesian society.

The nomenclature '*puncak-puncak kebudayaan*' and '*jati-diri*' are aspects of the state nationalist project that reflect the interesting sociopolitical fantasy prevalent among state officialdom about 'high culture'. In practice this kind of 'culture' relates to ideas regarding authenticity and identity.[23] Sociopolitically speaking, this discourse has the potential of being utilized to support the state nationalist project. To be effective, however, it must be publicly displayed. Under the New Order, for more than thirty years, the nationalist project has shaped power relations between state and society. The state (represented by the bureaucrats) had significant resources at their disposal to construct the dominant discourse on nationalism. Indeed, bureaucratic corporatism lubricated this project, as in the case of the research project concerning *puncak-puncak kebudayaan,* which used the Department of Education and Culture to channelize money to academics in universities throughout Indonesia. The state nationalist imagination thus became popular among the civil servants, the military, and other organizations which were prepared to ascribe 'truth' to it. However, in the real world there are already different imaginings of nationalist ideas that can be found at the level of everyday mundane life, sustained by vernacular nationalist imaginations. Through counter-discursive practices, people at the grass-roots express their nationalist visions in their everyday life praxis. These vernacular discourses of nationalism subversively act against the state's nationalist imagination.

Within this largely regulated context, the vernacular nationalist imagination cannot be entirely dominated by the state. Moreover, there is a contradiction in the state nationalist imagination. The idea of *puncak-puncak kebudayaan* often fails to satisfy the people since it is conceived in ways that satisfy state functionaries and rationalize their desires to control and exercise power. This is because the state's nationalist imagination, as reflected in the concept of *puncak-puncak kebudayaan,* is based on a set of beliefs that reflect a kind of Darwinian cultural evolutionism. The category of *puncak* (the top or the peak) indicates that the subsidiary levels are merely stages of cultural evolution. Their idea reflects a devaluation and even a fear of the 'lower cultures' that flourish among the *wong cilik* or *rakyat* (people). These cultures are placed on the opposite end of *puncak kebudayaan* (high culture), and become objects of suspicion, denigration and fear.

This fear fuels the state's desire to marginalize lower cultures, which retain a degree of autonomy from the centre of the regime's power. In addition, it also reflects the state's fear of alternative ideas that originate among the *rakyat*, vernacular nationalist imaginings, and their ability to jeopardize the state's symbolic power. As a result of this, the state's nationalist imagination, that is popular among state functionaries, has become very elitist. In fact, this project reveals a contradiction between the state's fantasies of popularizing the state nationalist imagination, while at the same time trying to maintain their elitism through a hierarchy that is essential to their political cosmology. Accordingly, we can see that Suharto's regime presented a nationalist vision that was flawed in its claim to be speaking for the nation, whose people it neither trusted nor valued on its own terms. In turn, counter-discourses stemming from the vernacular language of the *wong cilik* have a substantial potential to corrode the state-promoted visions of the nation.

Wong Cilik and the Vernacular Nationalist Imagination: Subverting the State Nationalist Project

At 10.00 pm on 11 April 1998, around a month before the resignation of Suharto as the president of Indonesia, some street musicians sung '*Indonesiaku*' ('My Indonesia') loudly on the sidewalk where the street traders, *becak* (pedicab) drivers, and customers of Pak Yanto's *Warung angkringan* sat near the intersection of Malioboro and Sosrowijayan Streets. They were not singing to get money at that time, they were just playing the guitar as a jam session with friends, to kill time and to improve their guitar-playing abilities. The song 'My Indonesia' was created by Papa T Bob, a famous producer of children's songs. This song was first sung by Enno Lerian on TV and has been recorded on cassettes and CDs. She was one of the famous child singers of the early 1990s. When I listened to the street musicians sing the song, I noticed that the lyrics were totally different from the sung by Enno Lerian. The differences are apparent if we compare the lyrics of the two songs:

'*Indonesiaku*' ('My Indonesia'): Two Versions

Indonesiaku 'My Indonesia' by Papa T Bob (original version)	Kita tinggal menikmati (We just enjoy it.)
Batik Solo, empek-empek Palembang, peuyem Bandung (Batik cloth from solo, traditional food from Palembang, fermented cassava from Bandung)	*Mau makan nasi Gudeg Jogja,bukan berarti harus ke Jogja* (Want to eat Gudeg Jogja, it does not mean [we] have to go to Jogja.)
Kalian kesana juga tidak apa-apa, Indonesia kaya kok ada 27 propinsi mau berlibur mau tamasya lengkap deh. (All of you going there, It is alright, Indonesia is rich, [we] have 27 Provinces, [if] you want to go for a holiday it is very complete)	*Cukup ada disini dekat kita sendiri* (It is close enough to us,)
	Kita tinggal menikmati (we just enjoy it.)
	Hai Indonesiaku...hai Indonesiaku (Hi my Indonesia...my Indonesia,)
	Tanah subur rakyat makmur (Fertile soil, wealthy people.)
Mau makan buah pisang ambon (Want to eat Ambon Banana)	*Hai Indonesiaku...hai Indonesiaku* (Hi my Indonesia...my Indonesia,)
bukan berarti harus ke ambon (It does not mean [we] have to go to Ambon.)	*Aku sayang kepadamu*(I care for you.)
cukup ada disini dekat kita sendiri (It is close enough to us,)	*Tanam salak tumbuh salak* (Plant salak, grow salak.)
kita tinggal menikmati (we just enjoy it.)	*Tanam duren tumbuh duren* (Plant durian, grow durian.)
mau makan buah jeruk Bali (Want to eat Bali orange,)	*Tanam padi tumbuh padi* (Plant rice, grow rice.)
bukan berarti harus ke bali (It does not mean [we] have to go to Bali.)	*Hai Indonesiaku ...hai Indonesiaku* (Hi my Indonesia... hi my Indonesia,)
cukup ada disini dekat kita sendiri(It is close enough to us,)	*tanah subur rakyat makmur*(Fertile soil, wealthy people.)
kita tinggal menikmati. (we just enjoy it.)	*hai...Indonesiaku...hai Indonesiaku..*(Hi my Indonesia...hi my Indonesia,)
Mau makan direstoran Padang,bukan berarti harus ke Padang (Want to eat in Padang Restaurant, it does not mean [we] have to go to Padang.)	*Eno cinta kepadamu*(Eno love you.)
Cukup ada disini dekat kita sendiri (It is close enough to us.)	*tanam jagung tumbuh jagung* (Plant corn, grow corn.)
	tanam singkong tumbuh singkong (Plant cassava, grow cassava.)

'*Indonesiaku*' ('My Indonesia')

Lyrics: street musicians' version	E... *Indonesiaku*(Hey...my Indonesia,)
Ingin makan uang rakyat...banyak (Want to eat people's money...a lot,)	*Tanah subur rakyat ngangur* (the soil is fertile, the people are jobless.)
Bukan berarti harus memaksa (it does not mean you must force them.)	E...*Indonesiaku* (hey...my Indonesia)
Cukup dengan korupsi semua terpenuhi (Just through corruption, it will be fulfilled,)	*Sawah rakyat kamu gusur* (You displace people from their rice fields.)
Kamu tinggal menikmati(you just enjoy it.)	*Tanam padi tumbuh pabrik* (Planting rice, growing factories)
Ingin gusur tanah rakyat...desa (Want to displace people from their land... village,)	*Tanam jagung tumbuh gedung* (Planting corns, growing buildings.)
Bukan berarti harus ke desa (it does not mean you have to go to the village.)	*Tanam modal di korupsi* (Planting capital, being corrupted.)
Cukup dengan kolusi semua terpenuhi (Just through collusion, it will be fulfilled,)	
Kamu tinggal menikmati (you just enjoy it.)	

Papa T Bob's version of 'My Indonesia' is categorized by the street musicians as a song for the rich or *wong gede*. According to them, it needed to be subverted in a different direction matching the conditions they were actually familiar with and is now suitable for the poor. When I asked them who created the new lyrics for that song they said that the song's lyric had already been long recognized by the street musicians of Malioboro street and that it belongs to these street musicians. However, one of them said that these lyrics might have been created by members of the SPI (*Serekat Pengamen Indonesia* or The Indonesian Street Musician Union).[24] When I discussed this song with SPI members they said they had created these lyrics. When I then asked them about plagiarism, they made an interesting argument, as quoted below:

Menjiplak irama musik tidak masalah, siapa yang mau menuntut orang miskin macam kita ini, yang penting adalah ide untuk membalik lirik asli ke arti yang berlawanan dan kemudian dinyayikan untuk umum. Ini penting karena lagu asli ditujukan untuk anak orang kaya, dan ini kan mempromosikan Indonesia yang ideal. Faktanya, kenyataan yang ada justru berbalik dengan kondisi sosial yang nyata yang ada di Indonesia di bawah pemerintahan Suharto. Jadi penting untuk membalik arti dari lirik asli, dengan cara ini anak-anak miskin dikampung tahu bahwa yang indah-indah dari orang kaya itu tidak selalu benar. Kalau lagu ini dinyanyikan untuk orang kaya yang makan di warung lesehan Malioboro mereka juga akan merasakan bahwa ada orang miskin yang menderita.

(Plagiarizing the rhythm of music is not a problem for us. Who will sue poor people like us? The important thing is the idea of turning the original lyrics into the opposite meaning and sing that song publicly. The original song is for rich children, and it promotes an ideal image of Indonesia. In fact, the situation [described in the song] is the opposite of the actual social conditions which exist in Indonesia under Suharto's regime. So it is important to turn the meaning of the original lyrics into its opposite. This is the way the poor kids in *kampongs* will understand that the beautiful things the rich [talk about] are not always correct. If this song is sung in front of the rich who eat in the foot stall on the side walk of Malioboro street, they would feel that there are some poor who are suffering.)

From the idea of subverting the lyrics of the song, we can see that this is a conscious attempt to encourage poor children into becoming more politically critical towards the state. Moreover, not claiming that they created the lyrics can be seen as an assertion that this song belongs to everyone, which would imply that all *wong cilik* share the same problem. By using music which is already familiar to the audience, it is easy for them to follow the new lyrics created by SPI members. Their political agenda is obviously to subvert the state by creating an alternative discourse addressed to the *wong cilik*. The musicians want to encourage children to sing the new lyrics whilst using the original music that is so familiar and easy to remember. The street musicians sing this song in the *kampongs*, on buses, on the sidewalks and the streets, so that people will be just as familiar with the subversive rendering of the song as they are with the original.

Through the sharp contrasts they introduce between the two sets of lyrics, the street musicians and some *wong cilik* have devised simple means of dramatizing the social and economic disparities around them. The song is then reproduced by many other street musicians who sing it in the numerous places where the poor live in Yogyakarta. The original song of Papa T Bob is self-congratulatory, showing how easy it is for the *wong gede* to live in Indonesia, because everything is so easily available, just waiting to be enjoyed. For the street musicians, who are economically marginalized, living in Indonesia is not easy at all. From their point of view, what the original song indicates is that everything is already in the supermarket. According to them:

Membeli makanan yang asalnya dari tempat lain kita tidak perlu pergi ke asal makanan itu, karena semuanya sudah ada di supermarket disekliling kita. Ya supermarket Malioboro Mall ada didepan kita tetapi kita tidak mampu membelinya. Kita hanya mampu beli makanan dari warung angkringan Pak Yanto atau Pak Man. Orang macam kita ini beli beras dan baju dari pasar Beringharjo bukan dari Malioboro Mall yang punya beras dan baju import dari luar negeri. Semuanya sudah ada di super marke, memang. Tapi kita tidak bisa beli, dan karena itu kita harus mencintai Indonesia? Indonesia yang macam apa? Kalau lagunya Eno itu kan Indonesianya orang kaya dan dipengaruhi Orde Baru banget. Kalau orang macam kita, indonesianya ya seperti lagu itu tadi.[25]

(Buying local food from another place, we don't have to go to the place where the food originated, because it is already in supermarket near us. Yes the Malioboro Mall supermarket is in front of us but we cannot afford it. We can buy foods only from food stalls from Pak Yanto or Pak Man. People like us buy rice and cloth from Beringharjo market not from the Maliboro Mall, which provides imported rice and clothes. Everything is already in the supermarket, indeed. But we cannot afford it and because of this we have to love Indonesia? What kind of Indonesia? Eno's song shows what Indonesia is like for the rich, and is highly influenced by the New Order. As for people like us, our Indonesia is the one in the song.)

From the above we can see how their critical consciousness has developed as part of their craft and is disseminated through the spaces where they hang out in their everyday lives, as well as the streets, *warungs*, buses and *kampongs* where they struggle to earn a living. This is their space, and they draw their political ideas from it, letting them crystallize spontaneously into an oppositional discourse. Papa T Bob's song is categorized as belonging to the dominant groups, the rich or *wong gede*, and it is 'highly influenced by the New Order'. For the *wong cilik*, the state and its discourses have become objects that must be subverted through any available means of contestation until they lose their efficacy and their meanings are problematized. This is how they work against the state; by providing an alternative mode of imagining Indonesia to reject the state's nationalist imagination.

Nationalist imaginings found among/originated from the *wong cilik* are distinct from the state's nationalist imagination. The state's ideas issue ceaselessly from the vast means of communication commanded through bureaucratic corporatism. In contrast, *wong cilik* vernacular nationalist ideas utilize vernacular languages and oral communication, and are disseminated through innumerable, localized, interpersonal exchanges in everyday life. This vernacular identity can be gauged to some extent on the basis of vocabulary and grammar. It also employs certain expressions that may be a bi-lingual mixture of the mother tongue and Bahasa Indonesia, or a vernacularized Indonesian. The boundaries are vague and hazy because the schooling system already adjusts grammar and voca-bularies to incorporate many popular usages into the official Indonesian language. People use this still-evolving, blended national language (Indonesian), but also continue to speak in their local mother tongues as well.[26] Street language is also influenced by the fact that street musicians are not drawn from anyone ethnic group but from the several ethnic groups from all across Indonesia. Their language is a blend, constantly evolving in a dynamic relationship with people's lived experiences — a process clearly beyond the pre-scriptive reach of the state.

Opportunities for the construction of a vernacular nationalist im-agination, involving street musicians and other 'organic intellectuals', and merging with the blend of spectators surrounding the *warung*, readily and naturally develop as a ritual arena for the *wong cilik* to synthesize their own imaginings of their identity. Their sense of '*keindonesiaan*' ('Indonesia-ness') goes in a direction opposite to the design of the state nationalist project. The way the *wong cilik* give meaning to 'Indonesia' is based on their actual experiences, which especially include experiences of facing the police and the army. Such experiences have already been expressed in the form of a song entitled '*Mengadu pada Indonesia*' ('Complaining to Indonesia'),written by Joko Nugroho.[27]

These lyrics originates from their experience of state violence — either directly or indirectly, as witnesses. These are experiences that they share with each other. They then reflect on them as the collective

Mengadu Pada Indonesia	Complaining to Indonesia (Translation)
Oleh: Joko Nugroho	by Joko Nugroho
Hari ini sengaja aku mengadu padamu Indonesia	Today I intend to complain to you Indonesia
Tentang sistem Orde Baru yang menyiksaku, O.. tentu kamu tahu	About the New Order system that tortures me, O...you know about that
Bayangkan ulah mereka	Imagine their act
Mereka sok berkuasa	They are really over-acting
Mereka suka menyiksa	They like to torture
Bahkan membunuh sudah biasa	They even get used in killing
Aku melihat tindakan aparat	I witness the apparatuses act
Pukul sana, pukul sini sampai rumah sakit	Hit [someone] over there, hit [someone] over here until hospitalized
Aku melihat kekejaman aparat	I witness the cruelty of the apparatuses
Tendang sana, tendang sini sampai ke akhirat	Kick [someone] over there, kick [someone] over here to death
Sialan-sialan	Damn, damn
Aparat kayak preman	The apparatuses are like preman (lit: freeman, negative connotations meaning 'criminal')
Rakyat kecil dijadikan bahan percobaan	The lower class people are for exercise
Sialan-sialan	Damn, damn
Aparat kurang ajar	The impolite apparatuses ('*kurang ajar*' literally means less educated)
Kuasanya melebihi kuasanya Tuhan	Its power is more powerful than God

experience of those they call the *rakyat kecil* ('the little people' or the *wong cilik*). This song is performed in front of *warung* customers, in buses, in their jam sessions and also in university discussions especially when invited by student activists. The arena used by street musicians is not restricted to the street. There are a range of venues where they perform and their music goes beyond even those spaces. The language they employ in this song's lyrics includes colloquial swearing. SPI members often face difficulties when they sing this song in the *warung*, because this is also a space where the *preman* hang out. The *preman* ask them to stay away when they are spending time in the *warung*.

One interesting point about the song's title, *Mengadu Pada Indonesia*, is that it imaginatively addresses Indonesia as '*ibu pertiwi*' (mother nature). They explain that this expresses their complaint to their *ibu* (mother) because they are abused by the *bapak* (father) — here represented by the police, army, and *preman*. This also reflects the experience of street dwellers, abused mostly by their fathers rather than their mothers.[28] In this case, the allegory of the regime is imagined as a *jagoan bapak* figure rather than as the mother. From this perspective, complaints about the regime's brutal behaviour towards the people show that this imagining of Indonesia runs parallel to ideas regarding the proper relationship between a mother and her children rather than one between a father and his children. The song stresses on children's complaints to their mother, expressing their sadness and anger that their father always abuses them, while their mother cannot do anything but witness the abuse take place. Other factors that might also influence this situation are their experiences of life before they left their home and their family.[29] The way they perceive the regime is affected by their own personal experiences of facing the police or other state functionaries, who are invariably configured as a male (father). In contrast, they imagine their nation as being female (motherland) . This is similar to the concept of '*ibu pertiwi*' (lit: Mother Nature, meaning mother country, or specifically the nation).

Linguistically speaking, this verse is in total opposition to the state's nationalist imagination because the latter refers to patriotism originating from a male militaristic perspective: the discourses of *bapakisme* (fatherism) and *jagoanisme* (machismo) are embedded in the state, as I explained earlier. From this we can note that the state's nationalist imagination tends to unify the state and the nation as a single entity that cannot be split and which has a 'male-centric' image. On the other hand, a vernacular nationalist imagination stems from the idea of *ibuism* (matrifocality), which reflects a non-violent symbolic power and tends to construct a 'mother/children-centric' image. In this case, we can see the attempts of the *wong cilik* to connect the nation with the figures of mother/children, rather than father, and they position themselves as *rakyat* or the people.

The idea of 'mother/children-centrism' in the vernacular nationalist imagination stems from *wong cilik's* propensity to draw on their own experience in giving meaning to Indonesian nationhood rather than summoning up images of an exotic classical past to construct their nationalist discourse. Their experience of violence from state functionaries or from their own fathers, contributes to this 'mother/ children-centrism' and has become quite the opposite to the state's nationalist project. The *wong cilik's* experience of traumatic violence, for example, can be seen in the text and picture below:[30]

> *Bongkok: Kenapa kamu bisa masuk penjara?* (How can you be jailed?)
> *Ji'i: Pertama-tama saya masuk penjara itu ya gara-gara saya itu membela teman. Yang di bela teman dekat saya. Dia ada masalah, dia bilang sama saya. Terus saya belain, saya itu kok tau-tau terus langsung di tangkap gitu, ditangkap polisi. Saya masuk kantor polisi. Di sana saya di gebukin, digebukin polisi saya. Saya disuruh mengakui dimana teman-teman yang lain, saya bilang saya tidak tahu karena sama-sama anak jalanan. Abis itu saya juga dimasukin ke LP Wirogunan itu.*
>
> (First of all, I was jailed because I helped a friend. He is my closest friend. He told me that he had a problem. Then I helped him, but suddenly the police arrested me. When I entered the police station, I was bashed up, hit by the police. I had to say where my other friends were, I said that I did not know because they are street kids as well. After that I was jailed in Wirogunan prison house.
>
> Bongkok: *Digebukin pakai apa aja itu...*(Bashed up with what ...?)
> Ji'i: *Ya..., pakai shock breker, pakai shock breker. Sampai dua minggu ngga bisa jalan. Abis itu proses udah selesai saya di bawa ke LP Wirogunan. Setelah saya sampai sana itu....*
>
> (Ya..., with a shock breaker, with a shock breaker. For two weeks, I couldn't walk. After that was over, I was brought to Wirogunan prison house).

The absence of a mother figure in their real life and the existence of a dominant 'father' figure (who may appear as the police, the military or *preman*) who violently preys on them has become the contrast in figuring out their nationalist imagination. The image of *ibu* (mother) is an important figure, as drawn in Figure 13.2, by a street kid from Malioboro Street. He misses his mother and his home, but he does not want to go home for fear of his father. This picture shows the figure of a mother (*ibu*), the kid, whose name is Peri, a house with an Indonesian flag on the roof, a TV and stereo — electronic devices he cannot afford — and a bus as his space (shared with other street kids). All of these display the street kid's imagination

Figure 13.2: Peri's Sketch: Mother's World and the World of the Street

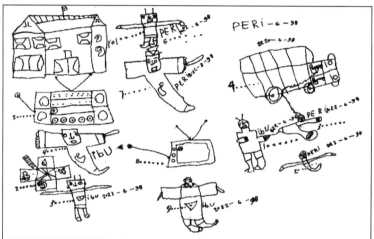

Source: *Jejal* 6, May 1998. The size of the picture has been reduced by 50 per cent from the original.

about home, street, and his mother as the ones he misses most. In imagining their homes and mothers, the street kids often behave strangely during the month of *Ramadhan* (Islamic month of fasting) and *Idul Fitri* (marking the end of the fasting period of Ramadhan) by travelling to their hometown in order to try and find their mothers. They rarely find them, and they grieve over their loss. Moreover, they too wish to lead a settled life. Accordingly, we can say that this picture simply reflects a kind of fantasy world that they miss, the world of 'mother' or the world without a father figure, who is clearly absent from the picture. This also means a denial or rejection of the father figure, for most children who become street dwellers have experienced abuse from their fathers, which is what made them run away from home.

Our examination of the state's nationalist discursive project under Suharto's regime reveals that it tended to connect Indonesia with ideas of militarism and a classical past. In addition, the project tends to promote something ideal, that can engender public pride, justify the use of authority and is compatible with the idea of '*negara kuwat*' (a strong state) and a leader who has '*berbudi bawa leksana*' (wisdom and charisma). The classical past in the nationalist idea is reflected in the slogan *Butir-butir Budaya Jawa* (The Points of Javanese culture) used by Suharto to expose the idea of militarism, and also to invoke 'the blessings of God', as I explained previously. This also shows how he connected himself and his family with the nation through state ideology and the importance of maintaining national stability. Suharto's ideas, which served as the blueprint for many prominent power-holders in society, seek to juxtapose 'family' and 'country' in order to stress the primacy of the goal of preserving unity. This functions as a means to unify the nation and to avoid disobedience against the regime.

Street musicians also utilize the concept of 'family' but not in harmonious terms, rather they invoke the trauma of broken homes, dysfunctional families where the father abuses other family members, and where those who suffer are the mother and children (the *rakyat*). This understanding has become a source of oppositional discourses that have emerged against the state.

Hatred against the father is expressed in Kirik Ertanto's paper entitled '*Ora ono bapak-bapakan kabeh bapak bajingan*' ('There is no father, all fathers are bastards').[31] When this seminar was held, and he finished making his presentation, one person in the audience emotionally said, '*jika semua bapak-bapak bajingan, maka bapak pembangunan juga bajingan*' ('if all fathers are bastards, then the father of development is also a bastard'). This response referred to Suharto, who had been nominated as the '*Bapak Pembangunan*' (Father of Development). The hatred for *pemimpin* (leaders) or *pejabat* (high-ranking bureaucrats) among the *wong cilik* living on the sidewalks of Malioboro is often expressed through mockery. For example:

'*Pemimpin awake dewe ki parah ra iso di arepke, kelakuanne malah koyo celeng mangkane pas Suharto arep lewat Malioboro, cah-cah ngomonge: 'celeng arep lewat ayo minggir-minggir.'*

('Our leaders are terribly hopeless, the way they act is just like swines, so when Suharto was passing Malioboro street, they said: 'a swine will pass by here, come away from there').[32]

Wong cilik in Malioboro street characterized Suharto as a swine based on an understanding of the character of swines, as greedy animals who destroy farmers' crops. When local officials asked street dwellers and traders not to conduct any activities on the sidewalk, they felt they had lost their income for the day because Suharto had passed through Malioboro street. It was just like a swine destroying a farmer's crops. Concepts like *pejabat* (high-ranking bureaucrats), *wong gede*, *bapak*, *ibu* and *rakyat*, from the *wong cilik's* point of view are not only representations of the family as a miniature version of the state, but also an invocation of morality. For the *wong cilik*, a good *pejabat* or *wong gede* is one who does not practice violence and does not act like a swine. The use of a colloquialized and vernacularized language, such as '*ora ono bapak-bapakan, kabeh bapak bajingan*' and *celeng* (swine) are not only a matter of opposing the dominant groups, but also a strong assertion of alternative ideas that define morality, truth and the nationalist idea itself, beyond official interpretations provided by the regime. The idea of '*ora ono bapak-bapakan, kabeh bapak bajingan*', in this case, can be viewed as breaking the hierarchical order established by Suharto's regime, a hierarchy both of power and moral authority, in which the figure of *bapak* (father) is located at the apex.

The statements uttered by street dwellers are actually instances of attempts by the underprivileged class which is marginalized by the regime to gain some power through the arenas of contestation that they have created. Through this space — which is not only located in concrete territories but also in imaginative spaces — they subversively manufacture their own social world, opposed to the dominant regime. Vernacular languages, which are already equipped with alternative ideas that come from a plurality of sources, subvert the *wong gede* creatively and continually through all kinds of opportunities that lend themselves to public performance or to the construction of meanings among members of their groups.[33] This situation not only reflects the condition of subjection but also the sophisticated process of consciousness-formation whereby, through their choice and interpretation of social categories (such as *bapak, jagoan, celeng*), street dwellers are able to identify who is the suppressor, the target that must be subverted.

The creativity of the urban *wong cilik* in expressing these ideas and in challenging the *wong gede* is manifested in many ways. It highlights the process of continual marginalization of the *wong cilik* in urban areas which has, to a significant extent, made them more reliant on their own resources — it has made them more self-sufficient, more independent and more resourceful in relation to their own struggle. This is in direct opposition to the condition of the dependent middle class, who rely on the state and on related socio-political and normative bonds that result in their dependence on the state.[34] The degree of independence and the resultant feeling of freedom has made people like street musicians, street children, *becak* drivers, taxi drivers and street vendors draw on their creativity and develop their own robust political consciousness which lies beyond the state's designs.

Official Language, Democracy and the *Wong Cilik*: Subverting the Official Language

The experience of the *wong cilik* constructing a subaltern space of their own through language is an interesting phenomenon. This is a space where the *wong cilik's* existence takes shape as an outcome of the dynamics of social differentiation. The example below, of satirical short fiction published by the *Jawa Pos* newspaper in January 1999, demonstrates the cynical stance adopted towards state symbolism. It was published amidst the political euphoria following the collapse of the New Order regime, also seen as marking the beginning of '*Era Reformasi*' (the Era of Reformation).

> *Kini, baju-baju safari itu begitu menakutkan dan membuatnya sedih. Ia masih ingat kejadian yang menimpanya seminggu lalu, ketika Pak Syafri dan beberapa orang teman sesama anggota dewan terkepung oleh ribuan mahasiswa yang tiba-tiba bagaikan lebah buncah menyerbu kantornya ditingkah oleh yel-yel yang mengerikan. Pakaian safarinya yang berwarna gelap dilengkapi oleh emblem lambang daerah tanda anggota dewan itu begitu mencolok dan gampang dideteksi para demonstran itu. 'Ini dia satu lagi, pengisap uang rakyat. Berani-beraninya menyatakan diri sebagai wakil rakyat. Rakyat yang mana?'*[35]

(Now, the safari uniforms seem frightening and make him sad. He still remembers the incident he faced a week ago, when Pak Syafri and some other friends of the members of parliament, were surrounded by thousands of students who came suddenly like angry bees buzzing around his office while shouting in a frightening way. His dark-coloured safari uniform, complete with the emblems of local parliament, was easily detected by the demonstrators. 'This is the one, sucker of people's money. How dare [you] declare yourself as a representative of the people. Which people?')

This fictional tale expresses the popular feeling of resentment against the New Order state's symbols and the rapid loss of its efficacy, as in the failure of the uniform of the members of parliament to command protection anymore. It describes how the people reclaimed their political rights as citizens of Indonesia by demonstrating outside the local parliament building. The uniform, in fact, had become a signifier for the students to identify the person as being a symbol of the state, one who could be blamed for Indonesia's crisis. For the Member of Parliament on the other hand, that uniform became a phantom that ought to have been banished if he was to avoid those who were running amok against state symbolism. The cynical evaluation of state symbols, which had been used excessively during the New Order regime, was actually not new. They had been widely disseminated since the 1980s. This becomes evident in Wiji Thukul's poem entitled *Peringatan* (Warning). Thukul used to read this poem to factory labourers in his town, Solo (Central Java) during their break time. He also worked in a factory. Wiji Thukul's lyrics bring to light an interesting counter discourse against an apparently omnipresent and omnipotent state.[36] The poem does not simply oppose the state, but also encourages listeners/readers to beware of state suppression. He uses the word '*kita*'[37] ('we') in this poem to urge listeners through this linguistic strategy that 'we' all have to be aware of the ruling class.[38]

Peringatan (Warning)
by Wiji Thukul

Jika rakyat pergi (If the people go away,)
Ketika penguasa pidato (when the ruling class give a speech,)
Kita harus hati-hati (we have to be careful,)
Barangkali mereka putus asa (perhaps they have given up.)
Kalau rakyat sembunyi (If the people hide)
Dan berbisik-bisik (and whisper)
Ketika membicarakan masalahnya sendiri (when they are talking about their own problems,)
Penguasa harus waspada dan belajar mendengar (the ruling class have to be aware and learn to listen.)
Bila rakyat tidak berani mengeluh (If the people do not dare to complain,)
Itu artinya sudah gawat (it means the conditions are already critical.)
Dan bila omongan penguasa (And if the speech of the ruling class)
Tidak boleh dibantah (cannot be debated,)
Kebenaran pasti terancam (the truth must be in jeopardy.)
Apabila usul ditolak tanpa ditimbang (If aspiration is refused without consideration,)
Suara dibungkam kirtik dilarang tanpa alasan (voices are silenced, criticism is banned without reason,)

Dituduh subversi dan menggangu keamanan (accused of subverting
and disturbing security,)
Maka hanya ada satu kata:lawan! (then, there is only one word:
resist!)

Wiji Thukul's poem encouraged the *wong cilik* to distinguish
between *bahasa pejabat* (the language of high-ranking bureaucrats)
and *bahasa rakyat* (people's language) or *bahasa wong gede* (the
language of big men) and *bahasa wong cilik* (the language of little
people). By recognizing the 'ruling class' speech (*penguasa pidato*),
this poem tells the audience that the 'ruling class' have the privilege
of giving speeches whereas the labourers do not. To emphasize this
contrast, the poem states: 'if the people hide and whisper when they
are talking about their own problems the ruling class have to be aware
and learn to listen'. The idea here is to contrast the verbal character
of the *wong cilik* and the *wong gede*. It is a shared meaning, ideas
which in this case Wiji Thukul shared with the labourers during lunch
time at a factory in Solo. Sharing meaning through discursive practice
in everyday life, as Wiji Thukul did, has given the *wong cilik* the
ability to distinguish the language of the *wong cilik* from that of the
wong gede, and also to mock *bahasa pejabat*. The idea of separating
out *bahasa pejabat* is not only accepted by the labourers who heard
Wiji Tukul poem, this idea can also be found in the utterances of the
wong cilik in informal locations too. For example, the owner of a
warung angkringan (food stall) in Yogyakarta, Pak Man, described
bahasa pejabat as follows:

*Bahasa pejabat itu kan bahasanya pegawai negeri golongan atas
yang dipidatokan dan yang dipakai untuk pertemuan antara pejabat
dengan rakyat seperti temu wicara antara Suharto dan rakyat yang
telah diseleksi seperti yang ditelevisikan di jaman Suharto. Itu juga
ada di pernyataan pejabat yang dipublikasikan di koran-koran, TV,
radio dan pidato kenegaraan. Biasanya yang selalu disebut di jaman
suharto kan kata-kata pembangunan, tapi kenyataannya korupsi, jadi
kan bahasa pejabat itu kan bahasa omong kosong namanya. Waktu
dijaman Suharto, Menteri Penerangan Harmoko itu kan disebut Hari-
hari omong kosong. Dia kan orang yang kasih nama Suharto Bapak
Pembangunan, nah untuk kita itu ya jadi bapak perngacengan karena
tiap pagi burung kita bangun. Ha...ha...*

(*Bahasa pejabat* is a language spoken by high-ranking civil servants
on ceremonial occasions and during official encounters between the

pejabat and *rakyat* on such occasions as the *temu wicara* [talk show] between Suharto and certain chosen people, as shown on TV during the Suharto era. It can be found used in bureaucrats' statements published by newspapers, TV, radio and official speeches. The term which is usually mentioned is *pembangunan* [development], but in fact they were corrupt, so the language of the high-ranking bureaucrat is the 'language of nothing' (*bahasa omong kosong*). During the Suharto era, Harmoko, the Minister of Information of the New Order regime, was also known as *Hari-hari Omong Kosong* [an acronym of Harmoko which means 'days of talking nothing'], and he gave Suharto the name *Bapak Pembangunan* [the father of development], which to people like us became *bapak perngacengan* [the father of erections] because every morning our 'bird' [penis] wakes up. Ha..ha...)

The recognition of *bahasa pejabat* or *bahasa wong gede* stimulated the *wong cilik* to celebrate and creatively adopt and use their casual colloquial language, *bahasa rakyat* or *bahasa wong cilik,* used by ordinary people, in everyday life. The differences between these languages are not based so much on vocabulary or grammatical structure (though those are present) but rely more on the image or connotative meaning of the characteristic expressions uttered by high-ranking bureaucrats. These bureaucratic neologisms are different from the vocabulary and semantics of *bahasa rakyat*. For example, the term *pembangunan* (development), was used in the title *Bapak Pembangunan* (Father of Development), formally awarded by the parliament to Suharto in the early 1980s. It was used incessantly by high-ranking bureaucrats, and signalled the central value of state power under the regime. '*Bapak pembangunan*' was, however, turned into colloquial Javanese by the *wong cilik* in a way that changed the connotative meaning to the 'father of erection'.

The *wong cilik's* techniques of mocking the distinguishing expressions of *bahasa pejabat* shows their ability to objectify it as a target for ridicule, done according to the context. For example, in the context of the economy, the preference of bureaucrats for the term '*penyesuaian harga*' (the adjustment of prices) over '*kenaikan harga*' (price increases) was advertised extensively through the media to explain the economic crisis. It was recognised as a 'fake language' that failed to explain inflation. To a *warung* owner in Yogyakarta (Pak Yanto, who owns *warung angkringan* near Sosrowijayan Street) it is a fake language (referred to in Javanese language as '*basa ngapusi*') because the *wong cilik* knew that the prices were in fact increasing and not merely 'adjusting'. This meant that the government had lied to the people. For him, '*pemerintah kuwi ra entuk ngapusi rakyat, sebab nek ngapusi berarti ono sing ora bener nang deweke*' ('governments are not allowed to lie to the people because if they lie to the people there must be something wrong with them'). Moreover, he added, '*Rakyat ki pinter kok diapusi, aku ki nek dodol panganan ya bingung kudu njawab opo nek langganan takon kenopo regane mundak terus, paling aku mung njawab regone pancen gonta ganti sebabe nggone aku kulakan ya ganti rego terus, sing ora ganti sing dodolan, pemerintahe yo ora ganti-ganti.*' ('People are smart, why do they have to be tricked? When I trade my foods, I also become confused. What answer will I give when my customers ask me why prices are increasing? I just answer that the price is changing because the grocers from where I bought food stuff also always hike up their price. The one who never changes is the seller, and the government also has not changed yet'). This was common during the economic crisis in early 1998 when Suharto was still in power. This statement of the *warung* owner explains how the customer shifts from an economic explanation ('the one who never changes is the seller') to a political one by saying that '*pemerintahe yo ora ganti-ganti*' ('the government also has not changed yet'). It is a technique used by the *warung* owner to create a discussion with customers, which functions to transfer the blame for price increase onto the government.

According to the expressions cited above, the *wong cilik* clearly senses that the idea of neutralizing the import of language originates from within state apparatuses which shows the weightlessness or emptiness of *bahasa pejabat*. The ability to recognize *bahasa pejabat* as empty speech should be understood within the context of the feeling of freedom that is secured in spaces such as *warungs* and the street, where people like Pak Yanto and his customers play around with language, exposing 'the adjustment of prices' as a political farce. In this situation, of intersecting relationships between classes in social spaces where the feeling of freedom is relatively high, we observe that the discursive practices that are shaped by the intersecting worlds begin to free themselves from the state's hegemonizing project. As these discursive freedoms are secured, *bahasa pejabat* gradually loses its cultural significance and with that the authoritarian regime's effectiveness is also diminished.

A telling example of a counter discourse against the authoritarian regime is the much celebrated nationalist declaration of 1928, the *Sumpah Mahasiswa*, (Oath of Youth)[39]:

> *Kami Mahasiswa Indonesia mengaku bertanah air satu, tanah air tanpa penindasan*
> *Kami Mahasiswa Indonesia mengaku berbangsa satu, bangsa yang gandrung akan keadilan*[40]
> *Kami Mahasiswa Indonesia mengaku berbahasa satu, bahasa kebenaran.*[41]

(We Indonesian students declare that we have one homeland, a homeland free of oppression.
We Indonesian students declare that we are one nation, a nation madly in love with justice.
We Indonesian students declare that we have one language, the language of truth.)[42]

The students' version of the original youth pledge can be read as a kind of 'language battle', a confrontation between the language of the people and *bahasa pejabat*. *Bahasa pejabat*, as seen in the governor's speech and some other state texts, is here characterized as injustice, untruth and oppression, as can be seen in Figure 13.3 below:

Figure 13.3: Satire, Linguistic Inversion and Counter-Discourse

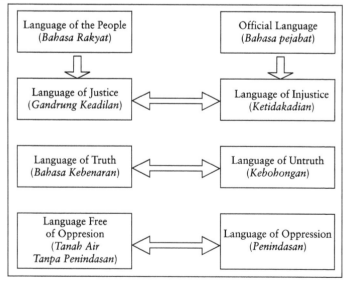

The idea of a counter-discourse, as seen in the flowchart above, functions by simply contradicting the official language as a form of communication used by the dominant official class. *Tanpa penindasan* (free of oppression), *gandrung akan keadilan* (devoted to justice), and *bahasa kebenaran* (language of truth) are characteristic of the language of the people, invoked by the students to subvert *bahasa pejabat* and the *sumpah pemuda* (youth pledge) that was orchestrated by the New Order state annually without fail.[43] Students in this case recognized that *bahasa pejabat* always consists of *penindasan* (oppression), *ketidakadilan* (injustice), and *kebohongan* (untruth). Therefore, they have to challenge the state by utilizing the youth pledge already taken by the state in an inverted way so as to make more people aware. Moreover, the language used by students in this pledge gives the sense of *jiwa kerakyatan* (the spirit of the people) and deliberately choses terms from vernacular languages rather than the language of the *pejabat*. For example, the word *gandrung* is originally a *ngoko* (a lower Javanese language) expression. It is a symbol of the people. For the students this type of tactic is important because by providing simple contradictory language they display an idea that publicly subverts the dominant language. It then functions to undermine the nationalist *Sumpah Pemuda* remembrance that had been monopolized by the New Order state at a time when the people had no opportunity to glorify it, even though historically it did originate from the people. The reproduction and dissemination of this kind of idea through the aesthetic and connotative aspects of discursive practice, challenges the dominant discourse of the regime and has become the modus operandi of their project of subversion.

Like the students, street musicians and intellectuals, and the *wong cilik* devised many linguistic responses to counter authoritarian rule. What Wiji Thukul was doing with the labourers was to try and create a subaltern space in which workers could develop their class consciousness. For example, the cynicism towards *bahasa pejabat* and the distrust of being deemed meaningful political participation is also expressed by Wiji Thukul through the lyrics of a song entitled '*Aku Lebih Suka Dagelan*' ('I Prefer Joking'):

Aku Lebih Suka Dagelan (I Prefer Joking)[44]
by Wiji Thukul
Di radio aku mendengar berita (From the radio I can listen to the news)

katanya partisipasi politik rakyat kita (our people's political participation)
sangat menggembirakan (is delightful)
tapi kudengar dari mulut seorang kawanku (but I hear from my friend's mouth)
dia diintereoggasi dipanggil gurunya (that he was interrogated, called by his/her teacher)
karena ikut kampanye pdi (for being involved in a pdi campaign)[45]
dan di kampungku ibu RT (and in my kampung, the RT's wife)
tak mau menegor sapa warganya (does not want to ask the people)
hanya karena ia golkar (just because she/he votes for golkar)
ada juga yang saling bertengkar (some of them quarrel)
padahal rumah mereka bersebelahan (whereas they are next-door neighbours)
penyebabnya hanya mereka berbeda ([quarrels] caused only by their differences)
tanda gambar (over signs)
ada juga kontestant yang nyogok (there are also contestants who bribe)
tukang-tukang becak (the pedicab drivers)
akibatnya dalam kampanye banyak (consequently many people in the campaign)
yang mencak-mencak (are grumbling)
di radio aku mendengar berita-berita (from the radio I hear the news)
tapi aku jadi muak karena isinya (but, I am sick and tired because of the content)
kebohongan yang tak mengatakan kenyataan (lying and not relating the facts)
untunglah warta berita segera bubar (fortunately the news will finish soon)
acara yang kutunggu-tunggu datang:dagelan (the program I have been waiting for:
humour)

These lyrics seem more like daily notes than a poem. They are easy for labourers to understand, but they also reflect what is wrong with the language of 'news' broadcasts, which usually use only the official language. This kind of news is stamped by people as '*corong pemerintah*' ('government voice') because all media under the New Order regime was controlled by the Department of Information (*Departemen Penerangan*). Thukul's lyrics claim that this department is always telling lies (*kebohongan yang tak mengatakan kenyataan*) to the people. Wiji Thukul in this case is simply criticizing bogus participation in politics, such as the practice of giving money to the *wong cilik* at election time to campaign for the political parties. These paid retrieval performances are not the kind of participation that people have been waiting for. They want something more democratic, reflecting *bahasa rakyat* (language of the people), and emancipating people as it happens in the *dagelan* (humour), a form of traditional Javanese theatre which involves the audience and the actors interactively, and reflects a form of popular participation and emancipation, allowing people to access politics through their own language rather than through *bahasa pejabat*. This is the way the *wong cilik* formulate democracy, using their own meanings and references. I will explain some of these in the next section.

Wong Cilik and Democracy: Decentring the State

The idea of democracy that has been disseminated at the grass-roots level has, to a great extent, the potential to decentre the authoritarian state in people's minds. It provides alternative ideas and creates counter-discourses that corrode the dominant discourse. For example, the lyrics of songs written by street musicians. The song cited below, shows a plurality of ideas used in understanding Indonesia-ness.

Demokrasi Kita (Our Democracy)
by Buthel & Serikat Pengamen Indonesia[46]

Kita sadari (We realize)
kita hayati (We internalize)
negara itu milik siapa (Who owns the country)
Dari mulut penguasa (From the mouth of the ruling class)
yang terus ngomongkan pembangunan (who always talk about development)
untuk menduduki kursi jabatan (in order to occupy high-ranking positions)
sehingga rakyat jadi korban (so that the people are victimized)
Kita mengerti, kita pahami (We conceive, we understand)
ternyata politik milik siapa (who actually owns politics)
Jika hanya milik penguasa (if only owned by ruling class)
lebih baik bubarkan saja (its better to dismiss it)
sehingga rakyat damai (so that people live in peace)
dan tenang hidupnya (and have a serene life)

Satu nusa beribu pulau kita (we are in one area with thousands of Islands)
Satu bangsa berjuta rakyat kita (we are one nation with millions of people)
Akankah terus jadi tumbal sejarah (would they be victims of history?)
untuk berdirinya demokrasi (to give rise to democracy?)
Indonesia satu kata berjuta maknanya (Indonesia, one word, million meanings)
Satu teriak belum tentu bangkit semuanya (one [person] screaming might not be followed by all)
Mari kita hapuskan omong kosong belaka (let us sweep away talking about nothing)
Sehingga rakyat tak jadi korban (so, the people will not be the victims)

This song's lyrics were created by street musicians using vernacular Indonesian language. This is less formal, blunt in meaning and less strict in the use of grammar. Because of this, some sentences used are grammatically confusing and incorrect. However, the meaning and its message can be easily grasped by the *wong cilik*. This song was created in 1997, and is usually sung on city buses in Jakarta, or on the sidewalk of Yogyakarta's Malioboro street.

An important aspect of this song is its process of creation. Street musicians usually have their own communal contemplation and jam sessions when they compose lyrics. They usually congregate while drinking coffee or tea and smoking cigarettes on the sidewalk or in a *warung* until late at the night. Their creativity is palpable in the way they play guitars and various other instruments while singing various different kinds of songs extempore. Most songs relate to the experience of living amid uncertainty. This is their performance arena, where they give expression anti-establishment discourses. It is also a space that creates solidarity among street musicians. The creation of songs depends merely on the creativity of those present. If they all agree that one of the spontaneously written songs is fun, but has a critical edge, and yet is easy to understand and good to listen to, then they play it many times over until it has been memorized. Most of the lyrics created in this way are unlikely to be written. Only after some people ask about the lyrics will they dictate them in order to be written down.

This song is addressed not only to the common people but also to themselves. It is expected that the song will be heard or at least people will realize that something is going wrong in New Order Indonesia.[47] The latter is a fantasy, because if a song is sung in a city bus in Jakarta, where the climate is hot and humid and the bus is speeding, the engine is very noisy, and people are in a rush, then perhaps the passengers will not be listening to it. Even though this song specifically criticizes the *wong gede* or *pejabat negara* (high-ranking bureaucrats), who victimize people in order to advance their own career, perhaps it will elicit different responses from listeners. As some street musicians said '*Indonesia satu kata berjuta maknanya. Satu teriak belum tentu bangkit semuanya*' ('In Indonesia one word has a million meanings. It is uncertain that one cry will awaken all of them'). Bus passengers might have similar experiences of suffering under the authoritarian regime, but it does not mean that they support the views expressed by the musicians. Some of the responses would be '*masuk telinga kanan keluar telinga kiri*' ('enter through the right ear, come out of the left').[48] It is understandable if the passengers were to simply give money to the street musicians, and then the interaction is over. Even so, counter-discursive expressions would have been disseminated and will perhaps be reproduced by other people in different ways. The responses are different when they sing among themselves in their jam sessions near the *warungs*. The *warung* customers will listen and some of them will even memorize some of the street musicians' songs. In this situation, the audience at least has ample opportunity to internalize it.

Perhaps the most interesting expression is about the dismissal of the state, '*Kita mengerti kita pahami ternyata politik milik siapa. Jika hanya milik penguasa lebih baik bubarkan saja sehingga rakyat damai dan tenang hidupnya*' ('We conceive, we understand who actually owns politics. If politics only belongs to the ruler it is better dismissed, so that people are peaceful and have a serene life'). This reveals their fantasies, expressing a feeling of freedom rather than the conviction that things will be different. This phantasmagoria, a representation of the mind in the form of an image, here expresses a passionate aspiration for an egalitarian rather than a hierarchical relationship. The concept of *penguasa* (power-holder, ruler or ruling class) in this case is viewed as a hierarchical barrier that prevents the people from gaining access to politics. The people believe that once the power-holder is ousted, hierarchies will be minimized and people will have the opportunity to access the state, and the state would no longer be exclusive and impersonal. From this perspective, we can see the endeavour of vernacular language usage as attempting to corrode hierarchy and to make society more egalitarian.

To a significant extent this kind of fantasy is based on pictures of everyday life rather than on abstract ideals of universal democracy. It also arises from their internal relationships or at least those found within the same social class. These are relatively more egalitarian. The term 'democracy', which was mostly used by students and some other 'agencies', was just another trendy term that would be appropriated by street musicians not only because it is fashionable but also in order to show that they can make the idea of democracy easy to understand for the uneducated *wong cilik*.[49] Furthermore, an important sentiment reflected in such lyrics is the feeling of freedom. This exists among the *wong cilik*. In this social environment, the attempt is to construct shared liberties rather than freedom in a liberal sense. Accordingly, the construct of freedom is located here in the people's imagination, where they feel relatively free from state control, or at least where they imagine that they are safe and beyond state-structured hierarchies. This is important for them, because in this they have found an arena where they can develop counter-discursive practices, and in the process work to corrode the influence of authoritarian state power.

The language contest between the *wong cilik* and the high-ranking bureaucrats explained above shows that the semantic efficiency of the authoritarian regime loses its force within the diurnal subaltern space of the *wong cilik*. The language of bureaucrats here is reduced to a meaningless or empty chatter (*omong kosong*). However, it is not only the vacuity of the administrative obfuscations of *bahasa pejabat* that they ridicule. The discourses of the *wong cilik* also erode a deeper, if more abstract, foundation of the regime's legitimacy, its claim to being the sole interpretor of the meaning of the Indonesian nationalist project; a project that is more abstract than *bahasa pejabat*.

Conclusion

The contest between the state and the *wong cilik* and their contrasting constructions of the nationalist imagination is a political phenomenon in which the state, which is considered a manifestation of the dominant regime, could not succeed in imposing its project over the entire Indonesian society. The state's project is only fully realized within the state's circuit, but is deflected and resisted by the common people such as the *wong cilik* at the grass-roots level, who even ridicule such state projects. The state's attempt to use its nationalist imagination in order to unify the state and the nation as an inseparable political unit also faces some failures when it is elaborated publicly, because it contains certain logical and normative contradictions, and because the *wong cilik* have the ability to detect this and to deconstruct the project in such a way as to yield different and perhaps even oppositional meanings. This shows that in these contests there are no truly 'dominant discourses', rather only 'contingent discourses'. They are contingent because all parties involved in this contest struggle to give meaning to public symbols and there are many ways in which the discourses of the powerful can be disputed. The dominant social elements lose the efficacy of their discourse, yet the *wong cilik* texts also do not dominate this contest. But the situation does allow subaltern spaces to take shape and challenge dominant ideas. It allows the subaltern actors, here the *wong cilik*, to show their inventiveness in rejecting the *wong gede*, the state and their projects of domination.

The state regime has attempted to construct nationalist projects based on the perceived authenticity that is associated with the classical pre-colonial past. These constructs utilize a symbolization of the state, which embodies 'male-centric' ideas that they insist should be honoured by people. Moreover, this state of inherited nobility is glorified through public rituals. In everyday life practices, this was shown to involve discursive practices within bureaucratic apparatuses. In this environment, the *pejabat tinggi* (high-ranking bureaucrats) and the low-ranking bureaucrats reflect distinctions amongst themselves as well as vis-à-vis the people. This discourse has been widely reproduced and disseminated through the practice of bureaucratic corporatism and its rituals. Furthermore, it was supported by the military stronghold in politics wherein it created a pervasive aura of authoritarianism, state terrorism and threat. In this environment, the vernacular discourse led a more or less subaltern existence. However, the *wong cilik* have been able to construct their own cultural productions, which they disseminate in the exchanges of mundane life, thereby opening discourse formation to processes of dynamic contestation. The evidence, as we discussed above, showed that when the two textual constellations contest each other, as between the state nationalist project and vernacular nationalist ideas, the dominant codes lose much of their efficacy and their meanings are rendered contingent rather than being axiomatic. When or meaning is contingent, the *wong cilik* has the opportunity to extend their subaltern space and to continuously produce counter-discursive ideas.

The techniques used by the state are deliberately ingrained in the dominant bureaucratic circuits. It is disseminated through state rituals in order to construct a social blueprint of the state nationalist imagination. The subaltern code uses a 'mother/children' nationalist fantasy based on such things as street kids' cultural experiences. The *wong cilik* have used their network through their spaces, such as *warungs*, sidewalks, jam sessions, and other subaltern spaces to disseminate their ideas and thus counter the dominant discourses. The role of vernacular language here has enhanced the *wong cilik's* creative capacity to subvert dominant projects, and to fashion their own vernacular nationalist ideas. The meaning of Indonesia as a political society is sited in a contested terrain in which the state and the *rakyat* both possess significant potency in terms of cultural production and the means to construct their own nationalist imaginings through dynamic discursive practices.

Notes and References

1. This article has been excerpted from Chapters One and Six of my PhD thesis. Aris Arif Mundayat, 'Ritual and Politics in New Order Indonesia: A Study of Discourse and Counter Discourse in Indonesia', School of Social and Life Sciences, Swinburne University of Technology, February 2005.
2. In this section I am using Anderson's concept of an 'imagined community'. 'It is imagined because the members of even the smallest nation will never know most of their fellow-members, meet them, or even hear of them, yet in the minds of each lives the image of their communion'. See Benedict Anderson, *Imagined Communities: Reflections on the Origin and Spread of Nationalism* (London: Verso, 1991), pp. 5–7.
3. This money was issued in 1993, on the occasion of the twenty-seventh anniversary of Suharto's presidency, and became a commemoration of '27 Tahun Indonesia Membangun' (27 Years Developing Indonesia), as can noted in the right corner of Figure 13.1. This currency was no longer valid just a few months after his resignation.

4. This account is based on information I gathered from local state apparatuses in Wonogiri in the early 1990s, just a month before Suharto's *temu wicara* was held there.

5. This quote has been taken from Suharto's, *Butir-Butir Budaya Jawa, Hanggayuh Kasampurnaning Hurip Berbudi Bawaleksana Ngudi Sejatining Becik*, edited by H. Rukmana, Herdiyanti (Jakarta: Yayasan Purna Bhakti Pertiwi, 1990), pp. 116–17. Before it was published, Suharto explained its content at the Javanese Language Congress in 1987. This book also mentions that most of the sources used in *Butir-Butir Budaya Jawa* originate from ancient Javanese classical literature. An interesting aspect of this book is that two languages — Indonesian and English — have been used to translate from the original — Javanese. One could argue that this was an attempt to locate this idea in a national and international context, albeit linguistically. It was also written in two scripts — Javanese and Roman — where the Javanese script reflects the idea of authenticity, claiming to bind itself with the ancient Javanese regime.

6. The text quoted here is from the newspaper *Merdeka*, 4 August 1980, but the celebrations were held on 16 April 1980. Indonesia's biggest newspaper company, Kompas, published an incomplete version of the speech and a report on the Kopassandha's 28th anniversary celebrations on 17 April 1980, as did some other newspapers. Suharto's speech became a source of dispute between Petisi 50 and Suharto. Indeed, it then involved DPR (presumably) members because Petisi 50 asked the DPR to request that Suharto be held responsible for that speech. Petisi 50 argued that Suharto's personal problems should not be mixed up with state ideology and constitution (*Pancasila* and UUD 1945), because any disturbance to Suharto's political position might also mean disrupting *Pancasila* and UUD 1945. The dispute was not concluded by the time Suharto resigned in 1998. That was why Merdeka newspaper published the full text four months after Suharto delivered it.

7. 'Sambutan Presiden pada HUT Kopassandha', *Merdeka*, 4 August 1980. This paragraph has been taken from the *Sapta Marga* (Seven Ways) of ABRI (the Indonesian Armed Forces).

8. '*Sapta Marga Prajurit*' is a Sanskrit name used by ABRI in order to maintain their hierarchical system and the unity of corps.

9. 'Sambutan Presiden pada HUT Kopassandha', *Merdeka*, 4 August 1980. This paragraph comes from the *Sapta Marga* (Seven Ways) of ABRI (the Indonesian Armed Forces). Suharto's language in this speech was grammatically incorrect.

10. From late March until May 2000, Abdurahman Wahid proposed to review the MPR decree concerning the banning of the communist party in Indonesia. See 'MUI Tolak Tap MPRS XXV/1966 dicabut. Komunisme

akan Merobohkan Indonesia', *Media Indonesia*, 3 March 2000. See also 'Pencabutan Tap MPRS No.XXV/1966 Terus Ditentang. Demo Antikomunis Makin Marak', *Media Indonesia*, 8 April 2000. Whether or not its abolition is warranted is still in dispute.

11. 'Ariel Heryanto, Discourse and State Terrorism: A Case Study of Political Trials in New Order Indonesia 1989–1990', PhD Thesis, Monash University, 1993.

12. In the late 1980s, the music group Bimbo wrote a song entitled 'Tante Sun' ('Aunty Sun') that described how 'Aunty' was involved in almost all the large projects in Indonesia and took large amounts of money from the *cukong* (Chinese entrepreneurs) and *tauke* (Chinese business proprietor). One example of these cynical-sounding lyrics mentions how businesspeople were under the control of Suharto's wife was: '*Cukong-cukong dan tauke, direktur dan makelar, tekuk lutut di bahah tante Sun*' ('Bourgeois capital-owners, directors and brokers, knelt before Aunty Sun').

13. See, 'Sambutan Presiden pada HUT Kopassandha', *Merdeka*, 4 August 1980. Kopassandha's name has now been changed to *Kopasus* (*Komando Pasukan Khusus*).

14. Ibid.

15. Analyses of labour conditions in Indonesia by Vedi Hadiz (1997) and Sri Kusyuniati (1998) show that systematic corporatism politically suppressed the labour force. For further details, see Vedi R. Hadiz, *Workers and the State in New Order Indonesia* (London: Routledge, 1997) and Sri Kusyuniati, 'Strikes from 1990 to 1996: An Evaluation of the Dynamics of the Indonesian Labour Movement', PhD Dissertation, Swinburne University of Technology, 1998.

16. According to the news article entitled 'Bakorstranas Resmi Bubar 10 April' at Tempo Online, http://www.tempo.co.id/harian/include/index. asp?file+542000-919 (accessed 5 April 2000), Bakorstanas was to be dismantled by President Abdurahman Wahid through a presidential decree (keppress No. 38/Tahun 2000) on 10 April 2000. On that day, the institution was officially dismissed. As a result of this, its branches, (Bakorstrada), Litsus (Penelitian Khusus or Special Investigation) and Posko Kewaspadaan (Alert Task forces) in every Kodim (Komando Distrik Militer or Military District Commando) were also to be dismantled. Historically, this body was set up to replace Kopkamtib (Komando Pemulihan Keamanan dan Ketertiban or the Command for Safety, Recovery and Order) through presidential decree (Keppres No. 29/1988) by President Suharto. Due to dissatisfaction with the previous general (General Sumitro), who had failed to prevent the Malari incident (15 January 1974), Suharto appointed General Ali Murtopo in his place. Four years later another decree was issued (Keppres No. 253/1988) to expand its functions. This decree appointed General Try Soetrisno as the

chairperson of Bakorstanas. This institution is structured by Bakorstanas according to a letter of statement coded: Kep/01/Stanas/XI/1988, dated 4 November 1988. This letter was authorized by another letter of statement from the highest commander in ABRI, No. Skep/962/XII/1988, dated 9 December 1988.

17. See Aris Arif Mundayat and Kunharibowo, 'Ritual Adipura: Sebuah Kontradiksi antara Demokrasi dan Hierarki', *Bernas*, 14 June 1993. This article discussed the performance of state-led ritual practices by the provincial government in trying to express the idea of the state as a 'centre' through notions of hierarchy. In this ritual, state officials, especially those from local government had to wear traditional Javanese dress. They rode in a traditional horse-drawn chariot and would be part of a parade across the city ending at the governor's office in Malioboro street. This ritual was designed to show to the people that the city had won an award from the central government in Jakarta.

18. According to the information I gathered, people feel that since the mid-1970s, the celebration of Indonesian Independence every August 17 has been completely taken over by the government. Almost all activities, such as sports, painting fences, cleaning up streets and alleyways, and *selamatan* (Javanese communal feasts) that take place around that time are organized and executed by the state rather than the people. Prior to this period, people felt involved in the preparations for the celebration, but now people feel they have lost their right to fully participate in the celebration of Indonesia's Independence Day.

19. Amrih Widodo (1995) has an interesting argument concerning the Tayuban dance in Blora. He shows that the Department of Education and Culture provides *pembinaan* (guidance) for the participants before the performance, *penataran* (training courses) for the dancers and issues them with an annual license. This state involvement transforms the ritualized and 'officialized' dance into a participatory event where the participants become spectators. This kind of *penataran* shows them how to dance in a way which is not considered immoral and which reflects the *jatidiri* (self identity) of Indonesianess. See Amrih Widodo, 'Stages of the State: Arts of the People and Rites of Hegemonization', *Review of Indonesian and Malaysian Affairs* 29, Winter and Summer 1995. I was visiting Amrih Widodo when he conducting his research in Blora in 1991 and I was involved in (the official rather than ritual) Tayuban dancing at the village level. In the official dance I was just a spectator. At the village level the Tayuban dancing is quite different to the official one, even though the dancer also carries a license to perform it — to some degree the participants not only become spectators but they are also actively involved in the dancing.

20. For further discussion concerning state–society relations and the position of the traditional state see Soemarsaid Martono, *State and Statecraft in*

Old Java: A Study of the Later Mataram Period, 16th to 19th Century (Ithaca: Cornell Modern Indonesia Project, Monograph series, 1963). See also Clifford Geertz, *Negara: The Theater State in Nineteenth Century Bali* (Princeton, NJ: Princeton University Press, 1990).

21. In Gadjah Mada University this ceremony was discarded a few weeks after Suharto resigned from power, but it is still practiced in some other state institutions.

22. One examples of a state project to find the 'puncak-puncak kebudayaan' through research funded by the New Order government is Sunarti *et al.* (1995), *Wujud, Arti dan Fungsi Puncak-puncak kebudayaan Lama dan Asli Bagi Masyarakat Pendukungnya di Daerah Khusus Ibukota Jakarta: Sumbangan Kebudayaan Daerah Khusus Ibukota Jakarta terhadap Kebudayaan Nasional* (Jakarta: Departmen Pendidikan dan Kebudayaan, Bagian Proyek pengkajian dan Pembinaan Nilai-Nilai Budaya Daerah Khusus Ibukota Jakarta). This kind of long title signifies a national research project to explore the *puncak puncak kebudayaan*, and can be found in research and publications on different subjects in Indonesia. The differences lie only in the name of the research location, the name of province.

23. John Pemberton demonstrates the significance of *keaslian* (authenticity) in cultural practices in Java. This idea is not only invoked by common people but also by politicians in their efforts to claim that every political practice shows authenticity. See John Pemberton, *On the Subject of 'Java'* (Ithaca, NY: Cornell University Press, 1994).

24. SPI (Serikat Pengamen Indonesia or The Indonesian Street Musicians Union) was formed in Jogjakarta in the early 1990s by the street musicians of Malioboro Street. In the beginning, the number of SPI member s was only six, and it seems the numbers never grew beyond this. In fact, this has become the name of a group, more than a union. Joko, a member of this group, is the lyricist and composer. The group was among the several street musicians who were actively involved in students' discussions and political activism, creating political lyrics against the New Order government. In the post-Suharto political reform period (2001–04), they were often invited by students' movements to sing songs in discussions or seminars. They remain critical even towards the post-authoritarian government.

25. This account is based on my observations. It was around 11 at night, and I was involved in discussion with street musicians sitting on the Malioboro street sidewalk. It was in the *warung pak* Yanto, and the situation was very informal. People hanging out together and listening as the street musicians argued about the meaning of Indonesia for the *wong cilik*. Some people present at the warung were actively engaged in the discussions.

26. In the Indonesian dictionary published by Department of Education and Culture many of the words come from vernacular languages without the

dictionary indicating whether they are colloquial or not. It only mentions their place of origin. However, Indonesian vernacular languages have not lost their popularity and spirit. This dictionary, however, tends to officialize many of the vernacular expressions. See Pusat Pembinaan dan Pengembangan Bahasa, *Kamus Besar Bahasa Indonesia* (Jakarta: Departemen Pendidikan dan Kebudayaan, Balai Pustaka, 1991).

27. The author of 'Mengadu pada Indonesia' is Djoko Nugroho, a member of Serikat Pengamen Indonesia, he wrote these lyrics in 1994.

28. The stories of everyday violence that takes place among the street dwellers have been described by Heri Bongkok. His account is based on personal experience, and shows how the people on the street endure struggle and suppression and how they have to suppress each other in order to survive. Heri Bongkok is illiterate. This personal story is transferred into a book through the help of recording technology provided by Girli NGO members. See Heri Bongkok, *Perjuangan dan Penindasan* (Yogyakarta: YLPS Humana, 1995).

29. For a detailed discussion on the experiences of street dwellers, see Kirik Ertanto, 'Ora Ono Bapak-Bapakan Kabeh Bapak Bajingan', paper presented at a seminar on *Keluarga, kekerasan dan Perubahan Sosial di Indonesia* ('Family, Violence and Social Change in Indonesia') Yogyakarta, 3 December 1994. Kirik Ertanto's real name is Bambang Ertanto Cahyo Dewo, he works for Girli, an NGO in Yogyakarta. Ertanto used this expression, which originated from the street children who experienced domestic violence, in this seminar paper. When Ertanto finished his presentation, a person in the audience emotionally said *'jika semua bapak-bapak bajingan, maka bapak pembangunan juga bajingan'* ('if all fathers are bastards, then the father of development is also a bastard'). This expression referred to Suharto, who was nominated by a sycophant parliament as *'Bapak Pembangunan'* ('the father of development').

30. This is an interview between Bongkok and Ji'i. It is interesting that Bongkok assumed that Ji'i was bashed up even before Ji'i told him. This assumption is a product of Bongkok's experiences, who has faced a similar situation many times. Quoted from 'Disana saya digebukin digebukin Polisi saya', *Jejal* 6, May 1998 (Yogyakarta: YLPS Humana).

31. Kirik Ertanto (1994), 'Ora Ono Bapak-Bapakan Kabeh Bapak Bajingan'. Kirik Ertanto's NGO, Girli, works on empowering street kids. His paper explains how street kids experience violence at the hands of their fathers, and this breeds hatred against father. I would like to thank Kirik Ertanto, who allowed me to interpret his data from a different point of view. My interpretation of his statement is based on the context of the seminar and I accept sole responsibility for it.

32. This occurred when President Suharto and his ministers participated in a parade through Malioboro Street in the late 1990s. The local government had asked that the side walk of Malioboro Street be cleared of street

traders, street children and becak drivers who were usually crowded around there. This account is based on the information from Pendekar. Pendekar is the pseudonym of one of the street dwellers in Malioboro. He is one of the older street children in that area. He also told me that the street children of Malioboro's sidewalks do not like academics researching them, but they would cooperate it if they establish good relationships with them. For them, these relationships were of greater importance rather than any interview.

33. Most of the street musicians are educated at least up to high school. Also, the everyday interaction between students and people at the grass-roots level influences their ideas. The stores which display televisions and keep newspapers also disseminate information to street dwellers. Some street musicians and street children often try to send their works of art (song lyrics, or poetry) to the newspapers. Some street dwellers in Jakarta for example, were offered free health checks in the clinic by the 'Angkatan 66 exponen' (the exponent of 66). In 1995, Golkar, through KUKMI (Kerukunan Usaha Menengah Indonesia or the Association of Middle Entrepreneurs of Indonesia) also approached them for its own political purposes but they refused to co-operate because they would have to wear a yellow t-shirt and carry yellow equipment provided by Golkar.

34. K.R. Young, 'Middle Peasant, Middle Bureaucrats: Middle Class?' in Richard Tanter and Kenneth Young (eds), *The Politics of Middle Class Indonesia* (Melbourne: Monash University, Centre of Southeast Asian Studies, 1990). Young analyzes this type of middle class in which the majority depend on connections with state apparatuses, that have made them middle class.

35. *Jawa Pos* published a cynical short story about safari uniforms. See 'Baju Safari Pak Syafri' by Harris Effendi Thahar, published in *Jawa Pos*, 3 January 1999, which tells us about the symbols used by the state apparatuses (in this case, members of a local legislative body) to show that the person who utilizes them becomes more powerful, but when the students demonstration acquired popular power that cut state power down to size and forced the state to introduce reforms, all forms of state symbolism lost their efficacy and people couldn't utilize them either.

36. Wiji Thukul was a political activist, a member of PRD (Partai Rakyat Demokratik or People's Democratic Party) from Surakarta (Solo, Central Java). In early 19998, during Suharto's regime, he was kidnapped and declared missing, and was never found. He was very active in labour circles and encouraged the workers to develp a political consciousness. As a labourer living in an industrial area he would often read his poems to his friends during break time or even in *kampong* alleyways near the factory. Before he was kidnapped he had been physically tortured by

the military and that police, such that one of his eyes had become half-blind. His lyrics quoted here are still remembered as one of the most significant expressions of resistance that contributed to the toppling of Suharto.

37. 'We' in the inclusive sense, unlike *kami*, which also means 'we' but excludes the person(s) being addressed.

38. This stanza is taken from his poem 'Peringatan' ('Warning') which he wrote in Solo in 1986. The words '...maka hanya ada satu kata: lawan!' ('...then there is only one word: resist!') was very popular among members of the PRD when they were involved in demonstrating for Suharto to resign from his presidency in May 1998. For further reading on his works of art, see Wiji Thukul, *Mencari Tanah Lapang* (Leiden: Manus Amici, 1994).

39. This 'student oath' deliberately invokes and subverts the original text of youth pledge which is usually celebrated by the New Order state as a means of remembrance, of the unification of the youth of Indonesia in colonial period to resist and oppose the imperialist regime. The original version of Youth Pledge is:

> Kami putra putri Indonesia mengaku bertanah air satu tanah air Indonesia
> Kami putra putri Indonesia mengaku berbangsasatu, bangsa Indonesia
> Kami putra putri Indonesia mengaku bahasa satu bahasa Indonesia
> (We Indonesian youths declare that we have one homeland, the homeland Indonesia.
> We Indonesian youths declare that we are one nation, the nation of Indonesia.
> We Indonesian youths declare that we have one language, the language of Indonesia)

40. The word '*gandrung*' is drawn from colloquial Javanese language and is used to express the feeling of being 'madly in love'. The standard term for *gandrung* in Indonesian language is '*cinta*' (love) which originate from Melayu language.

41. This student pledge has also been analyzed by Keith Foulcher, 'Sumpah Pemuda: The Making and Meaning of a Symbol of Indonesian Nationhood', paper presented at a seminar in Monash University, 1999. He explains that a student pledge is a form of counter-discourse against the official Sumpah Pemuda. I would like to analyze it differently. My quote from Sumpah Mahasiswa is based on my experience, when the students of Gadjah Mada University took the pledge in 1995. It also can be found in Foulcher's work. According to Foulcher, this 'counter Youth Pledge',

known as the *Sumpah Mahasiswa* ('Student Pledge') was taken for the first time by the students movement in Jogjakarta on 28 October 1988. It became well known after the commemoration of the Youth Pledge in 1988. In 1995, it was declared once again on 28 October, in order to challenge the glorification of the fiftieth anniversary of Indonesian independence. This day was celebrated every year till the 'Reformasi' era (Reformation) of 1998. It was also printed on t-shirts, which were widely worn by students.

42. This translation is similar Keith Foulcher's. However, in the second pledge I have translated the word of *gandrung* as 'being madly in love'. Keith Foulcher had translated *gandrung* as 'devoted'. See Keith Foulcher, 'Sumpah Pemuda: The Making and Meaning of a Symbol of Indonesian Nationhood', seminar paper presented at Monash University, 1999.

43. To a great extent, the glorification of *Sumpah Pemuda* during the New Order regime has made the *Sumpah Pemuda* a part of state symbolism.

44. Wiji Thukul, *Mencari Tanah Lapang*, p. 8.

45. The word of 'pdi' in small case letters as I quoted from his work, is the same as PDI (Partai Demokrasi Indonesia or Indonesian Democracy Party) before it split into PDI-P (led by Megawati) and PDI (led by Suryadi and subservient to the regime).

46. Serikat Pengamen Indonesia (Indonesian Street Musicians Association) is an independent association meant to unite street musicians who live on the street. This group has good relationships with the student movement affiliated with the PRD. The author of this song did not record it the year it was created, he just knows that this song was created in early 1997. It is commonplace for street musicians not to put the years of production because what is important to them is the context. The context of this song is provided by the themes of development and democracy around the 1990s.

47. This argument is based on my discussion with various street musicians of Yogyakarta.

48. This account is based on interviews conducted by me in November 1998 in Jakarta. The expression '*masuk telinga kiri keluar telinga kanan*' was uttered by a passenger of the city bus in Jakarta. While doing my research in Surabaya, I was travelling from Tunjungan Plaza to Kampong Dinoyo. A poem was recited on that city bus. Before he read his poem, the poet stated that he was not begging for money, he only wanted to read about himself. Then he read a story about his suffering, economic and social, living in the city of Surabaya. He was talking about social inequality based on his experience of living in urban areas. The story was somewhat long, because of which he lost the passengers attention, however, some people listened carefully to what he said. After he finished, while some people gave him money, some of them not.

49. During my interviews with the street musicians it became apparent that they do not like to admit that they appropriate the language and ideas of students. They claim, in fact, that all the ideas expressed in their songs are a product of their intellectual capacities. They explain that the fact that they have a relationship with the students does not mean that the latter are their idols, because from their point of view, students and intellectuals are mostly engaged in analyses that are complicated and therefore difficult to understand for the people at large. In contrast, their lyrics are simple and are easy to understand. This kind of claim suggests that they have a strong sense of identity and they do not want to be seen as just copying students. Nor do they want to be seen as trying to use the name of the people to criticize the regime in the manner that NGOs do. In their opinion, they are the people.

14

The Politics of Perception and Chinese–Philippine Writings

Lily Rose Tope

Introduction

Philippine politics has always been coloured by the politics of perception, which I ascribe to a situation where people make political decisions based on perception. This perception is usually a surface recognition of things, and often unsupported by empirical data, it creates prejudice. It is based not so much on knowledge or education, but on media, folklore, hearsay and uninformed experiences which often lead to a negative opinion on any given subject. It would have been easy to dismiss this phenomenon as one of those interesting and amusing social realities, except that in the Philippines, it has shaped a large part of the country's political life, created/destroyed political leaderships, and threatened the security of business and commercial sectors and minority communities. This article is interested in how the politics of perception is constituted, how it can grow from a simple misconception into violent actions taken against a community. It will deal with the effects of the politics of perception on a minority community — the Chinese Filipinos — especially in light of this community's social significance as an economic force in Philippine national life. Specifically, it will deal with the recent phenomenon of the kidnapping of Chinese Filipinos as a result of the politics of perception.

The Chinese comprise 1.2 per cent of the Philippine population, but control a significantly larger proportion of Filipino wealth.[1] They are involved in manufacturing, retail, and the basic industries. In the early 1990s, their perceived wealth triggered a series of kidnappings.

Between 1991 and 1992, there were 140 kidnappings.[2] The number would peak in the mid- and late 1990s.

> In the first 11 months of this year (2000), police say there are 135 kidnappings nationwide, involving 204 victims and $8.2 million paid in ransom. While the number of cases is slightly down from last year, the ransom figure is nearly three times the 1996 tally. And crime groups say that the actual number of kidnappings is up to four times the reported cases.[3]

The kidnappings have tapered off in this decade but have not stopped completely. While the Philippine state and the Filipino public are seemingly complicit in these crimes, with the slowness and neglect of the former and the relative indifference of the latter, it may have become a lucrative activity for criminals to target this ethnic minority because they do not fight back. As a silent and silenced minority, the Chinese community finds that the national treatment of these kidnappings is one of insulation. Thus, articulations on the subject tend to be cautious and relegated to the 'safer' sites of the creative and imaginative. Literary texts combine empirical truth and subjective renditions. As a means of creating, receiving and disseminating perceptions, this creative medium is just as much responsible for the tribulations of the Chinese Filipinos as it is their medium of redress.

I thought about the phrase 'politics of perception' (and I can be wrong in its use) while searching for a name that would suggest a type of imagining that is not necessarily based on empirical reality and in fact continues to persist despite empirical reality. It has a notion of prejudice embedded in it (minus the violence, although it can also lead to violence), propagated not so much by education as by media and casual observation. The conscious mind may disavow it but the subconscious demonstrates it.

Denotatively, perception is the act or faculty of apprehending with the mind or through one of the senses.[4] This definition suggests a close connection between materiality and concept. An observed reality can often be construed as empirical and can easily result in a conclusion with some measure of credibility. But an observed reality can also be highly mediated; the meaning that results from it and the perception formed out of the constructed meaning would be heavily dependent on the social and psychological conditioning of the observer. A half-withered plant in the desert can mean the waning of life and bring about despair to one who is in the desert for the first time, but it may mean the presence of life and hope to one who has lived there for a long time.

It is difficult to defend the objectivity of an observed reality when the meaning derived from it goes through a process of interpretation. The materiality of an observed reality is generally easy to assess but the meaning constructed from it can be unpredictable and intractable. In sum, because perception is a product of interpretation, its factuality is not entirely reliable.

Perceptions, moreover, cannot be monolithic. In fact, they exist in layers, formed according to age, gender or differences among communities. One's perception of an observed reality at the age of forty may be different from the one he had at the age of twenty. A person with no initial knowledge of the observed reality will have no perceptions of it. But exposure to it will inevitably lead to the formation of perceptions. When is a perception real or imagined? There is a thin line between what is real and what is imagined, some may argue there is no boundary at all. If we define imagination as an interpretive process that creates meaning, then all perceptions can be said to be imagined.

Perceptions are part of our quotidian life and most of them are dictated not only by our overt preferences but also by our unintentional and often hidden biases. They are responses to things that immediately affect us. There are certain spheres, however, that are particularly susceptible to perceptions. Most of these spheres involve matters of choice, commitment, resistance and judgement. One such area is politics. And since politics involves some form of belief, it too is a site for the construction of meaning, of perception. 'Politics is about perception, real or imagined.'[5]

In the Philippines, the politics of perception is very influential in determining political life. A woman without initial political skills and experience was elected Philippine president because she was the widow of a slain martyr. Another president was an action star who saved the poor and the oppressed in many of his films and whose popularity rested crucially on the common people's seeming inability to separate reel life from real life.

The perception most relevant to this study is that which promotes suspicion and fear. In his explanation of the endogenous nature of the dynamic of suspicion and fear, Talbot Imlay claims that it is 'not only capable of fuelling itself but also imposing its distorted image of events on the outside world'. As the 'observer necessarily mediates and thus distorts what he observes', a 'wide gap between perception and reality' is created.[6]

A more pernicious form of this perception has been seen in the recent crimes committed against the Chinese Filipinos. As mentioned earlier, a series of kidnappings alarmed the nation in the 1990s.[7] Chinese Filipinos, some of them children, were being abducted at gunpoint and ransoms, in millions of pesos, were being demanded. The abductions were usually precise operations that hinted at the extent and sophistication of intelligence work done by the perpetrators. Sometimes they even knew the amounts the family or business had in the bank, in what currency and in which banks they were deposited. Denials of assets just worsened the situation. It was not surprising that the Chinese were targeted. After all, they have become synonymous with business and wealth.

Historical data proves that the Chinese have a long history in the Philippines. They had been trading with the Filipinos long before the Spanish colonizers came. They were tolerated by the Spanish and American colonizers for the commerce they brought. Some intermarried and were easily assimilated. But a large number also kept to themselves, and their attempt at ethnic isolation was seen by the native Filipinos as an assertion of cultural superiority. They were also used by the Spaniards and Americans as *caciques* or compradors, agents of oppression and exploitation in the Filipino mind. They were allegedly corrupt and practised bribery liberally. What is not commonly said is that the attempt at isolation was for self preservation as they were harassed and massacred by the Spanish. The Chinese were just as oppressed as the Filipinos and their lack of political choice made it imperative for them to make themselves indispensable to the Spaniards and the Americans:

> The hostile environment drove them to communalism. Any minor infraction of the law could mean persecution, harassment or outright deportation. Hence, early in history, they learned their lesson well—that it is useless to fight because one can get hurt more; that it is easier and cheaper to buy your way out of a predicament.[8]

History and expediency have forced the Chinese to close ranks so that they may protect themselves against external threat and social iniquities as well as other hazards faced by a migrant people. This has brought about the racial tension that has driven a wedge between the Filipinos and the Chinese.

Due to their tenacity and capacity for hard work, the Chinese Filipinos prospered and today, they control 50–60 per cent of the Philippine economy by becoming the main players in various industries, especially in retail and manufacturing. They enjoy a lifestyle that has become the envy of the ordinary Filipino who has generally remained poor and dispossessed. 'They have not only moved out of the ethnic enclaves and into Filipino middle class residential neighborhoods but have also taken up membership at the village golf club.'[9] Since the Chinese owned a huge number of businesses, they came to be seen as 'The Capitalists'. In fact, one the strongest stereotypes of the Chinese Filipino is that of the unscrupulous, ruthless factory-owner. Popular literature and the movies showed the cruel Chinese capitalist exploiting the hapless Filipino labourers; while the former enjoyed his money, the Filipino starved.

The public display of wealth and the social mobility they enjoy have led to the creation of perceptions regarding the true motive and allegiance of the Chinese Filipinos. Do they see themselves as Filipinos? Are they rich Filipinos or rich Chinese? There is a big difference between the two. In fact, the Social Weather Station found in one of its surveys that lower Filipino classes are the least sympathetic to the Chinese. As labourers and employees of Chinese businesses, they have had close encounters with Chinese bosses who may have demonstrated traits based on the stereotype. As avid consumers of movies and popular literature, they have formed negative perceptions of the Chinese.

While it can be proven through statistics that many Chinese own businesses in the Philippines, it would be difficult to prove that many, if not all, are cruel and exploitative. In the Philippine politics of perception, wealth is not associated with kindness or fairness, therefore, the Chinese have to be cruel and exploitative by virtue of their wealth. Chinese wealth is an observed reality and the Philippine interpretation of it has led to a constructed meaning detrimental to the community. 'The politics of perception lies not on explicit connections but on implicit associations.'[10]

Ironically, only a few Chinese are rich. Most of them are just middle class. Chinese wealth pales in comparison to Spanish Filipino wealth.[11] 'Even while recent research on the top 100 corporations in the Philippines points out that the largest businesses are still held by the mestizo elites, the extent to which the ethnic Chinese in the

Philippines hold economic power is remarkable.'[12] For instance, huge shopping malls, commonly associated with Chinese wealth, dot the city skylines. But what is not perceived is the Spanish Filipino ownership of the land on which the malls stand or of the city of which the land is a part. The scope of perception does not include what cannot be seen or what can be found only in legal documents.

This visibility has made the Chinese perfect targets for kidnappings. They are perceived as having overflowing wealth that came from Filipino labour. If they do not want to share it, then it will be taken from them through other ways. Even during colonial times, they have been the 'whipping boy and milking cow' of the state.[13] They did not know the language, they kept to themselves, they did not fight back, they did not want trouble. In contemporary times, they are asked for election money (protection money for their businesses), for catastrophe relief, or even for neighbourhood basketball tournaments or a poor man's funeral expenses. They are regarded as a bottomless pool of funds.

It also does not help that they suffer from a negative image. In Philippine literature, for instance, they are portrayed as self-aggrandizing and unscrupulous, oversexed, uncouth and ignorant, pathetic and despicable in their addiction to opium, and more often than not, the butt of jokes.[14] This negative image makes the kidnapping easier. A community that is superior in every way will not make an easy prey. There is also the perception that Chinese allegiance does not lie with its adoptive country. The Chinese seem to continue the lives they led in China, albeit in a different land. National participation and interest are therefore lacking, indicating an absence of citizenship.[15]

While kidnapping, by most legal standards is a crime, kidnapping in the Philippines acquires a new meaning when seen through the politics of perception. One rarely articulated perception regarding kidnapping is that it is an economic leveller. What the Chinese capitalist has taken must be given back to the Filipinos. Never mind that the recipients are criminals or rogues. They belong to the Filipino masses, don't they? Since Philippine politics is always connected with class, criminals have become the articulators and perhaps champions of the exploited. As Chinese Filipino writer Clinton Palanca observes, kidnapping is a concept that empowers the Filipino masses, that lessens their passivity in the face of what they see as a monolithic and dominating entity.[16]

When mainstream Filipino writers such as journalist Teodoro Locsin Jr. write of Chinese Filipinos selfishly perpetuating corruption to further their businesses[17] or fictionist F. Sionil Jose accuses the Chinese of disloyalty to the Philippines, saying, 'If to be pro-Filipino is to be anti-Chinese, I am proudly, vociferously and vehemently anti-Chinese',[18] then it becomes easy to link this nationalism with the imagining at the heart of all Filipino struggles against colonizers and oppressors. The Filipino imagining sees the Chinese as an adversary, a threat to the Filipino's national well-being. The Chinese therefore cannot be part of the Filipino national community, and such a notion has led to the perception that a 'form of nationalism' is at work in the kidnapping of the Chinese.[19] When seen in this light, it seems that crime can have a nationalistic face and nationalism can have a criminal face.

On the morning of 7 January 1993, a fifteen-year-old Chinese Filipino girl, Charlene Sy, boarded the family van that would take her to school. The van had not gone far when men with high-powered weapons blocked the van and kidnapped Charlene. Everything happened within a few minutes, it was timed with frightening precision. As the convoy sped towards a busy city intersection, pursuing policemen caught up with it. A fierce gun battle ensued. Two policemen were injured, five people died. The dead included four of the abductors and Charlene herself.[20]

What makes Charlene Sy's case extraordinary, although not unique, is the fact that she was killed, not by her abductors' bullets but by those of her rescuers. The police claimed that they did not know she was in the car. On the surface, this explanation could be simply attributed to police incompetence, but cases of mistaken bodies, disappearing bodies, bungled surveillance have been too rampant. The politics of perception does not see police ineptness or the possibility of an accident as having resulted in the death of Charlene. What is seen is complete disregard for a young Chinese girl's life and the unmistakable semiotics of the state's disclosed position toward its beleaguered citizens of Chinese descent a position that is theoretically neutral but now seemingly partial against them.

Complicity on the part of the state can also be seen in the involvement of policemen and military men in such crimes. Officially, the government has declared war on the kidnappers, creating various task forces whose sole function is to solve cases of kidnapping. The most astonishing discovery however is the inordinate number of police and military men on active duty acting as masterminds and members of kidnap gangs.[21]

To my mind, this suggests two things: first, there is the actual use of state apparatus and resources in tracking down victims. The high-powered guns were sourced from the state. I am not suggesting here that the state has authorized the kidnappings but that the politics of perception has shaped the mentality of agents of the state and their participation in the crimes seems to imply their lack of recognition for Chinese Filipino citizens' rights. Consequently, many victims refuse to cooperate with the police since cooperation has sometimes led to a second kidnapping in the family. Second, the state involvement in these crimes presents an unofficial but persistent element in state structures of Chinese exclusion despite laws that decree otherwise. This renders the entire Chinese community vulnerable to state power as well as underscores the uncertainty of their inclusion in the Filipino nation.

While there is no legal structure that excludes the Chinese Filipino community, there can be no clearer statement of othering than to be targets of crime. Unlike hate crimes, the kidnapping of Chinese Filipinos has an economic and political rationale to it. Their perceived untouchability due to their economic clout, has resulted in the Chinese Filipinos being subjected to the illegal demands of crime — a forceful imposition of unsanctioned power over a community that is perceived to legally exercise power over the poor majority. Not only is the surfeit of kidnapping incidents seen as a form of distribution of what is perceived as unjust wealth, it is also a wresting back of power given to an immigrant community by virtue of economic achievement, a power unrightfully placed given that their allegiances are allegedly questionable.

Clearly, it is not genocide or ethnic cleansing that is the aim of these kidnappings. While many Chinese Filipinos consequently migrated or sent their families abroad or to safer places, the spate of crimes were not enough to force the majority to leave. While there have been deaths as a result of the kidnapping, it is still not in the proportion that annihilates a community, definitely a far cry from the massacres of the Spanish times. But these crimes have affected the community's psyche. First, the community realizes its vulnerability despite the assurances of legislation and a measure of state and police support. Second, it made them see the salience of ethnicity within a nationality. Even a Philippine passport does not automatically guarantee acceptance by the native population. Moreover, it must have been a shocking realization for the Chinese that the 'more inherently "open" and "adaptive"' Filipinos actually resented them.[22] Third, it must make itself viable as a community by entering mainstream Filipino life, working beyond marginality and connecting with Philippine realities. Conversely, the limelight has brought them to the attention of the greater Filipino public, who generally know little about them and have little or no understanding of Chinese culture. All things Chinese became interesting, soon the topic of several creative endeavors such as films and literature.

Literature has always been the repository of articulations by marginalized or suppressed discourses. While indignation can be articulated in public, sorrow and resentment are usually reserved for private, subjective expressions. Literature is then an appropriate venue for a Chinese response to the Filipino perception of them, already given lethal dimensions in the kidnappings. And surely the kidnappings caused enough tragedy to warrant a response. I made a cursory inspection of the literary pages of newspapers expecting it to be full of Chinese outpourings due to the kidnappings, but to my surprise, I found only a short story by Charlson Ong and several poems by students. The other writers used the feature and critical essay to deal with the matter and my conjecture is that the issue is more difficult to emotionalize but easier to intellectualize. This is not unexpected since the Chinese Filipino writer is usually a second or third generation Chinese who has been fully integrated into Filipino society. To be reminded of his/her ethnicity in such a brutal way forces him/her to interrogate assumptions regarding national affiliation and identity.

For the purpose of this study, I shall cite two articles and a short story to gauge Chinese reactions to the kidnappings. The first article, 'Chinatown: State of Siege' is written by Charlson Ong, who is considered as the most important literary voice in the Chinese-Filipino community. In this article, Ong provides images of terrorism and war, suggesting that the community is being assaulted by forces that are ironically its own. The perception of war is highlighted by images of parents fearing for their children, making them change school routes, giving the children cellphones so they can check on them every hour, employing bodyguards, of the children's unnatural silence in school, their parents' palpable fear which makes them pack the family into flights to safer countries.[23]

But the majority, although shaken by fear, cleave to their locations while struggling to keep faith in the larger Filipino nation. Born, raised and educated in the Philippines, they know no other country. The Chinese Filipino imagining thus contains a denial of the ethnic motivations of the kidnapping.

The second article, 'The Chinese Connection' by Clinton Palanca says that they are criminal acts and everybody's problem, not just of the Chinese Filipinos:

> It is very much the vogue these days to cry out 'Racism' at the slightest whiff. There is a temptation to apply the term here, to view the situation primarily as an ethnic problem: not, as I believe it is, a problem which, while it has an ethnic slant is primarily a criminal problem but which has been construed as an ethnic problem.[24]

While it is true that Filipinos and other nationalities have also been kidnapped, a hefty 80 per cent of the victims are Chinese.[25] Clinton Palanca's denial of the ethnic motive clearly suggests that young Chinese Filipinos like himself have never doubted their inclusion in the nation. KAISA, an organization of Chinese Filipinos working towards integration, articulates the basis of their belief in inclusion in its credo: 'Our blood may be Chinese but our roots grow deep in Filipino soil, our bonds are with the Filipino people.'[26] Those who recognize the ethnic nature of the kidnappings often react 'with panic and frustration mixed oddly with a sense of betrayal and confusion.'[27] This denial and/or sense of betrayal stems from the fact that young Chinese Filipinos know no other country, know no other kind of Chineseness except the Chinese Filipino one, even if they continually confront and accept the liminality of their identity. They usually do not see any contradiction in being Chinese and Filipino at the same time, although practical experience, time and again, has proven otherwise.

It has not always been that way. An older community was more attuned to and accepted exclusion. Prominent first-generation leaders, exemplified by the Federation of Chinese Chamber of Commerce, considered the events as unfortunate but not wholly unexpected. Thus their reaction has been one of silence, of quiet payments of ransoms, of diasporic survival attitudes rather than the struggle for rights of citizenship.

The most searing portrayal of the Chinese response can be found in Charlson Ong's short story, 'Mismanagement of Grief.'[28] Here, two imaginings — contentious but simultaneous — characterize responses to the politics of perception and the real threat that results from it. The confrontation of these imaginings is dramatized in the story. A young Chinese Filipino named Richard goes to the wake of his cousin who suffered a fate similar to that of Charlene Sy. Sophie is killed during the rescue operation which was bungled by a lack of coordination among the police. The incident has all the elements that induce fear and suspicion of the state, what Daniel Beland calls the 'politics of insecurity'. Insecurity is defined as 'the state of fear or anxiety stemming from a concrete or alleged lack of protection'.[29] Whether or not the Chinese are really assured of state protection is immaterial here, what is important is the perception that there is none, and this promotes a collective feeling of vulnerability. Beland also mentions the idea of a 'threat infrastructure' which somehow measures the readiness of the state to deal with a crisis. The bungled rescue indicates that there is none in place. The politics of perception and now the politics of insecurity increases the threshold of risk awareness, which according to Giddens 'is the ability of citizens to place their confidence in experts and civil servants (whom they rarely know personally) to fight environmental threats that seem overwhelming to them'.[30] The kidnapping and death of Sophie is the ultimate fulfillment of the fear — the vulnerability, the absence of state protection, and even if there were, the possibility of being collateral damage.

The community tries to protect itself. 'Ever since being informed by police intelligence that the family might be a target of kidnap gangs, Uncle Juanito had mapped out complex routes for each family member's itinerary.'[31] But the enemy is faceless and the protectors complicit.

The death of Sophie brings on a political dilemma for the characters. During the wake, Richard's father, distraught and threatened by his niece's death, decides to immigrate to Canada. Richard refuses to go and this infuriates his father.

'What do you really want?' he shouts into my face, losing control, and my stomach rumbles in victory for an instant. Fact is, I don't have a half-way sensible answer for him. 'What do you want to stay in this godforsaken country for? Hasn't it hurt us enough?' We are both silent awhile before he whispers —'Listen to me this once, son. We're not wanted anymore. It's time to go.' I wrack my brains for a reply but realize this is all quite futile. 'I want to be president,' I say. Father searches my face for a clue and shakes his head: 'I don't have time *for this.*' 'This is the only place in the world where I can become president', I say and I am strangely imbued with new power.[32]

The confrontation between Richard and his father is a confrontation between two generations — one cuts its ties with an ungrateful, hostile, adoptive country, the other stays because it knows no other; one seeks physical security, the other cultural certainty.

While the former survives by relocating, the latter survives by reinventing his location and empowering himself ('I want to be president.'). The former is a nation of immigrants, the latter of citizens.

I read in Richard's speech a new form of Chinese Filipino nationalism — articulated, born of pain as well as necessity. As the older generation continues with its pragmatic muteness, the younger generation asserts its willingness to earn a sense of belonging. Although besieged, it asserts its covenant with its adoptive country, the act of staying and keeping faith is a seal of national commitment.[33]

Charlson Ong, as a Chinese Filipino writer, thereby contests the constructed perceptions Filipinos have of their Chinese compatriots. Richard's father and the Chinese of his generation are *hua qiao*, travellers, people who pass through, enjoying the opportunities given by their chosen country but not committed to it. Richard, in contrast, proves that the Chinese Filipino can commit to one's chosen country. And it is Richard's generation who have thrown in their lot with a nation that sometimes misjudges them. It is Richard's political choice to stay.

I conclude by quoting the last stanza of a poem written by a non-Chinese Filipino whose sentiments, I would like to think, are shared by the greater Filipino nation. This poem, 'The Confession of Bones', chronicles the travails of a kidnap victim's family as they wait for word, for salvation, or if none, for bodies and evidence. It chronicles their encounters with deception and feelings of confusion as wrong bodies are given to them, making them go through their loved one's death repeatedly.

6. Nov. 23. Dy's family, noting the disappearance of witnesses And the NBI's puzzling ways, launch their own private probe. Even corpses

326 ÷ LILY ROSE TOPE

tire from having to rise too much. There comes a time when, armed only with names, You must begin to dig, handful of dead soil after Handful of dead soil, out of this nightmare cocoon And into the light of a fanged moon.[34]

The poem was written by Ruel S. de Vera. His pain is my pain, our pain is Chinese Filipino pain.

Notes and References

1. 'Kidnappings on the Rise, say Philippine Chinese', 5 May 2001, htpp://www.cnn.com/2001/WORLD/asiapcf/southeast/05/04/Philippines.kidnap (accessed 17 March 2009).
2. Philip Shenon, 'Abductions "Traumatize" Chinese in the Philippines', *The New York Times*, 18 October 1992, query.nytimes.com/gst/fullpage/html (accessed 17 March 2009).
3. Antonio Lopez, 'When Will They Ever End. Deadly Kidnappings Put Pressure on Ramos', ASIANOW, 30 November 2000, www.cgi.cnn.com/ASIANOW/asiaweek/97/1219/naT1C.html (accessed 17 March 2009).
4. *The Oxford Dictionary of Current English* (New York: Oxford University Press, 1984).
5. Paul Temple, 'The Politics of Perception', *The Badgerherald*, 2 December 2003, www.badgerherald.com/oped/2003/12/04/the-politics-of-perc.php (accessed 15 September 2008).
6. Talbot Imlay, 'Mind the Gap: The Perception and Reality of the Communist Sabotage of French War Production During the Phoney War 1939–1940', *Past & Present* 189, 2005, pp. 16–17.
7. The kidnappings continue to this day, with varying frequency.
8. Teresita Ang See, 'The Bamboo Bends, But How Much Longer?', *Sunday Inquirer Magazine*, 25 October 1992, p. 11.
9. Clinton Palanca, 'Beyond Binondo and Ma Ling', *Tulay*, 19 February 2008, p. 12.
10. Michael Blitzer, Review of *Here's Where I Stand*, a memoir of US senator Jesse Holms, *The Salisbury Post*, www.catawba.edu/academic/historypolitics/memoir_review.htm (accessed 15 September 2008).
11. R. Kwan Laurel, 'Interview of Teresita Ang See', *Midweek*, 24 April 1991, pp. 20–21, 46.
12. Palanca, 'Beyond Binondo', p. 12.
13. Teresita Ang See, 'Tsinoys: Responding to Change and Challenge', *Philippine Graphic*, 10 June 1994, pp. 18–32.
14. Joaquin Sy, 'Ang Larawan ng Tsino sa Panitikang Pilipinas' ('The Image of the Chinese in Philippine Literature'), *Tulay*, October 1987, pp. 86–87.

15. A study of Chinese Americans also shows a lack of Chinese participation in US politics and a greater concern for events in the homeland. Pei-te-Lien, 'Transnational Homeland Concerns and Participation in US Politics: A Comparison among Immigrants from China, Taiwan and Hong Kong', *Journal of Chinese Overseas* 2(1), 2006, pp. 56–78.

16. Clinton Palanca, 'The Chinese Connection', *Sunday Inquirer Magazine*, 31 January 1993, p. 19.

17. Teodoro Locsin Jr., 'Hopia Logic', *Philippines Free Press*, 23 January 1993, p. 20.

18. F. Sionil Jose, 'Stanley Ho and Some Anti-Filipino Chinese', *Today*, 5 February 2000, p. 9.

19. Caroline Hau, 'Afterword to Intsik: An Anthology of Chinese Filipino Literature', in Priscelina Patajo-Legasto (ed.) *Filipiniana Reader: A Companion Anthology of Filipiniana Online* (Quezon City: University of the Philippines, 1998), p. 198.

20. Michael Duenas, 'The PNP Purge', *Philippines Free Press*, 23 January 1993, p. 7.

21. *Tulay* (i.e., 'bridge'), the Chinese–Filipino digest, has a segment called 'Kidnap Watch' which records kidnapping incidents in the Philippines. The victims reported are both Chinese and non-Chinese. A sample of the reports shows the involvement of men in uniform. An officer and three policemen were arrested for kidnapping two persons (*Tulay*, 7 November 2006). A National Bureau of Investigation agent was charged with the kidnapping of a Chinese doctor (*Tulay*, 6 March 2007). Three policemen are arrested for kidnapping a Chinese businesswoman (*Tulay*, 23 October 2007). The worst case is the capture of a syndicate headed by a Senior Police Inspector of the anti-drug unit of the Philippine National Police. His nine cohorts are also policemen from the same unit ('Kidnap Watch: Summing Up for 2006', *Tulay*, 9 January 2007).

22. Palanca, 'Beyond Binondo', p. 12.

23. Charlson Ong, 'Chinatown: State of Siege', *Philippine Graphic*, 8 February 1993, pp. 15–16.

24. Palanca, 'Chinese Connection', p. 9.

25. Comparative Kidnapping Statistics (1996–2006) show that in 1997 around 150 persons were kidnapped. Kidnapping dissipated somewhat due to the efforts of law enforcement agencies but it did not end (*Tulay*, 9 January 2007). In 2007, around 70 persons were kidnapped. According to the latest tally, the number of Filipino victims has overtaken that of the Chinese with a ratio of 36:13 (*Tulay*, 22 January 2008).

26. Laurel, 'Interview of Teresita Ang See', p. 20.

27. Ong, 'Chinatown: State of Siege', p. 16.

28. Charlson Ong, 'Mismanagement of Grief', in *Conversions and Other Fictions* (Pasig City, Philippines: Anvil, 1996), pp. 35–48.

29. Daniel Beland, 'Insecurity and Politics: A Framework', *The Canadian Journal of Sociology* 32(3), Summer 2007, p. 320.

30. Giddens 1990. Cited in Beland, 2007.
31. Ong, 'Mismanagement of Grief', p. 37.
32. Ong, 'Mismanagement of Grief', pp. 44–45.
33. Lily Rose Tope, 'The Shifting Nation of the Chinese-Filipino Writer', in Chitra Sankaram *et al.* (eds), *Complicities: Connections and Divisions* (Bern: Peter Lang, 2003).
34. Ruel de Vera, 'The Confession of Bones', *Sunday Inquirer Magazine*, 31 January 1998, p. 8.

Afterword

Asghar Ali Engineer

Governance in a modern democracy faces numerous challenges in view of increasing awareness among different sections of population about their rights and also about the injustices being done to them by being deprived of these rights and a just share in political power and economic development. No modern democratic country has a homogeneous population. Had it been so governance would have been somewhat easier. Thanks to migrations, that can be triggered by political, economic or cultural reasons, even some historically homogeneous societies are fast becoming highly heterogeneous.

There have been few societies which were historically homogeneous and South and South-East Asian societies in particular have been known to be historically multi-religious and multicultural. As long as there were feudal monarchies, governance was never as challenging — after all, as subjects, people had no concept of 'rights'. Everything depended on the pleasure of the ruler, not on the rights of people.

But a modern democracy, even when it is controlled, depends on the concept of rights, and everyone, irrespective of religion, caste, ethnic origin or culture, is treated as a citizen and citizens enjoy certain fundamental rights. However, ensuring this is easier said than done. Any community that happens to be in majority can hardly be expected to refrain from asserting its 'majoritarianism'. In modern competitive economies majoritarianism acquires a much more aggravated form, as a whole political discourse replete with 'we' and 'they' is created and becomes a great challenge to providing just, non-discriminatory governance.

Often a section of the majority with a preference for 'right-wing' politics, assumes aggressive postures towards religious, linguistic, ethnic or cultural minorities and its entire political discourse assumes intimidatory tones as well, often resulting in the eruption of violence. Thus, various parts of South and South-East Asia too have been witness to violence between different religious and ethnic communities.

This book, edited by Dr Lipi Ghosh, who has done much work on the problem of governance in South and South-East Asian societies, is a most welcome publication. It covers almost all the countries of the region under discussion, including the Philippines, Malaysia, Thailand, Sri Lanka, India, Pakistan, Bangladesh, Nepal, etc. All these countries are quite diverse in terms of their demographic make-up and some bewilderingly so, like India.

It is crucial to gain an insight into the working of these complex societies through field studies, so as to make proper governance possible. Democratic governance, as stated earlier, faces challenges from different sections of society in view of their recent awareness of rights. Despite possessing the theoretical foundations of an egalitarian democratic discourse, minorities invariably suffer in all diverse societies.

India is a richly diverse country and has not only multiple religious but also cultural, ethnic and linguistic communities. Today, every region of India is faced with bloody conflicts: communal conflicts between Hindus and Muslims; ethnic conflict all across the North-East; linguistic conflict between Maharashtrians and non-Maharashtrians and an ongoing armed conflict in Kashmir, as well as the conflict between Kannadigas and Tamils, and so on. The Muslim minority, tribespeople and other ethnic minorities have serious grievances which are not being addressed, as a result of which large sections of these minorities continue to suffer.

This situation is not peculiar to India. Majoritarianism exists in all democratic societies, including Western democracies. In the Philippines, an armed struggle has been going on in Mindanao since 1971. Muslims are fighting for autonomy, for Midanao, once under Muslim rule, has now been reduced to a Muslim-minority area. There is no honourable solution in sight and a lot of people have already died in this conflict.

In Thailand, Muslim-majority districts of the South are faced with a similar situation. An armed struggle for 'independence' has been met by severe repression and has resulted in killings on both sides. Malaysia, once thought to be a good model for integration, is now facing a revolt from its minority Hindu community. The Hindus of Malaysia feel discriminated against and are now embroiled in a struggle demanding better treatment. In Pakistsan, Hindus and

Christians, and other small minorities, face numerous problems, even threats to the security of life.

Bangladesh is no exception. Hindus, the largest religious minority in Bangladesh, are victims of Muslim majoritariansm and often, in reaction to what happens in India, and even otherwise, are forced to suffer violence. Thus, even though there are many linguistic and cultural commonalities between the Muslims and Hindus of Bangladesh, the Hindu minority community does not feel safe and secure. Even those Bangladeshi Muslims who are secular in their orientation, face persecution when they stand by the Hindus.

Sri Lanka, a small island state located the south of India, has suffered much loss of life because of the Tamil separatist movement and the bloody battles that have followed between the Sinhalas and the Tamils. Had Tamil language been granted constitutional status in the 1960s when the Sri Lankan constitution was enforced, so much violence, loss of life and dislocation would not have taken place. Now, as the LTTE fights a bloody battle for independence, no acceptable solution seems to be in sight.

In Myanmar too ethnic and communal conflict, apart from the fight for democracy, is causing much turmoil. Myanmar is ethnically very diverse and it is claimed that almost 30–40 per cent of the country's population consists of ethnic minorities. Thousands of Rohingya Muslims have had to flee Myanmar and are today living as refugees in the border areas of Bangladesh. In Myanmar, even a democracy may not be able to bring an easy solution to these conflicts.

Indonesia, a Muslim-majority country with the largest population of Muslims in the world, also faces numerous ethnic and religious conflicts, particularly between the Christians and Muslims, and even after separation of East Timur. Violence between Muslims and Christians often erupts in certain parts of Indonesia where there is a sizeable Christian population.

Thus we see that minority-related problems pose a great challenge throughout South and South-East Asia to smooth and peaceful governance, and it seems that this region will continue to be dogged by such conflicts for a long time to come.

One feels, after reading this book, that even democracies provide no ready solutions for equitable governance, as majorities are not always ready to concede democratic rights to minorities and continue to assert their hegemony over such ethnic, religious and cultural minorities. No book can come up with viable alternative solutions as such, but can at least make us realize the complexities that exist in issues related to governance in modern societies. The academic studies such as are included in this book, must therefore be read by policy-makers so that they can realize the gravity and the complex nature of these issues.

About the Editor

Lipi Ghosh is Director of the Centre for South & Southeast Asian Studies and teaches History in the Department of South and Southeast Asian Studies and in the Department of History, University of Calcutta. She is also the former Head of Department, South & Southeast Asian Studies, University of Calcutta. Her areas of research interest are ethnicity, minority and cultural studies in the context of South and South-East Asia. She is especially interested in the history of inter-Asian connections. Her published works include *Burma*: *Myth of French Intrigue* (1994); *Prostitution in Thailand: Myth and Reality* (2002); *Indian Diaspora in the Asian & Pacific Regions* (2004); *Women Across Asia: Issues of Identity* (2005); and *Connectivity* and *Beyond: Indo-Thai Relations through Ages* (2009). She is also the co-editor of *Religious Minorities in South Asia: Selected Essays on Post-Colonial Situation* (2002) and *Ethnicity, Nations, Minorities: The South Asian Scenario* (2003). She was a Ford-Asia Fellow in Chulalongkorn University, Bangkok, in 2002. She was also a Charles Wallace Visiting Scholar to SOAS in 2004, Visiting Scholar to the Centre for Women Studies & Gender Relations, University of British Columbia, Canada in 2005 and Visiting Professor to Maison des Sciences de l'Homme, Paris in 2006, 2007 and 2009.

Notes on Contributors

Paula Banerjee is a Reader in the Department of South and Southeast Asian Studies, University of Calcutta. She specializes in diplomatic history and has worked on American foreign policy in South Asia. Her areas of interests include border studies, conflict and peace processes, displacement and gender issues in South Asia. Her published works include *Women and Peace Politics* (2008); *Autonomy: Beyond Kant and Hermeneutics* (2007, co-edited); *Internal Displacement in South Asia* (2005, co-edited); *When Ambitions Clash: Indo-US Relations 1947–1974* (2003); *Girls in the Twilight Zone: South and Southeast Asian Scenario* (2003, co-edited); and *Women in Politics and Society in France: 1945–1995* (1997).

Lok Raj Baral is Professor and Executive Chairman of Nepal Centre for Contemporary Studies (NCCS), Kathmandu. He was Professor and Chairman of the Political Science Department in Tribhuvan University in 1976–89. He has authored and edited numerous books as well as articles and chapters published in academic journals, edited volumes and monographs, and is perhaps best known for his pioneering work on oppositional politics in Nepal. His articles feature regularly in national and foreign dailies and weeklies. He is the editor of *Journal of Contemporary Studies* published by the NCCS, and has been invited as Professor and Reserch fellow to many universities abroad. He was the Ambassador to India in 1996–97.

Anasua Basu Ray Chaudhury is Research Associate at the Centre for South and Southeast Asian Studies, University of Calcutta. Her specialism includes regional co-operation, energy politics, partition refugees and women, and conflict situations in South Asia. In 1998–99 she received the Kodikara Award from the Regional Centre for Strategic Studies (RCSS), Colombo for her work 'The Energy Crisis and Sub-regional Cooperation in South Asia' (published as Policy Studies 13 by the RCSS in 2000). Her publications include

SAARC at Crossroads: The Fate of Regional Cooperation in South Asia (2006) and *Parbotyo Chattogram: Simanter Rajniti o Sangram* (Chittagong Hill Tracts: Politics and Struggle of the Frontier) (1996, co-authored). She is also the co-author of a Report prepared by the Calcutta Research Group entitled *Voices of the Internally Displaced in South Asia* (2006).

Samir Kumar Das is Professor of Political Science at the University of Calcutta, and President, Calcutta Research Group (CRG). A Post-Doctoral Fellow at the Social Science Research Council (South Asia Program), he is also the Deputy Co-ordinator of UGC–DRS Programme on 'Democratic Governance in Indian States'. He specializes in studies pertaining to ethnicity, security, migration, rights and justice. His recent publications include *Conflict and Peace in India's Northeast* (2008); *Ethnicity, Nation and Security: Essays on Northeastern India* (2004); *Blisters on their Feet: Tales of Internally Displaced Persons in India's North East* (2008, edited); and *Autonomy: Beyond Kant and Hermeneutics* (2008, co-edited).

Partha S. Ghosh is Professor of South Asian Studies at the School of International Studies, Jawaharlal Nehru University, New Delhi. His areas of interest are South Asian politics, ethnicity and the domestic politics–foreign policy interface. His books include *Politics of Personal Law in South Asia* (2007); *Unwanted and Uprooted: A Political Study of Refugees, Migrants, Stateless and Displaced in South Asia* (2004); *Ethnicity versus Nationalism: The Devolution Discourse in Sri Lanka* (2003); and *BJP and the Evolution of Hindu Nationalism* (2000). His forthcoming book is an edited volume *India's North-East and Beyond: Cross-National Perspectives.*

Sunil Kukreja is Professor and former Chair of the Department of Comparative Sociology at the University of Puget Sound. He is also a member of the Asian Studies Program, and contributor to the International Political Economy Program at the university. His areas of research interest include race relations, international political economy, South-East Asia and South Asia. His current research focuses on race and inequality in Malaysia. He has co-edited several books such as, *Discourses on the Beautiful Game* (2007) and *Nationalism in South Asia* (2009, co-edited), and contributed to distinguished journals.

Aris Arif Mundayat is Director, Center for Southeast Asian Social Studies, Co-ordinator of the Graduate Program in Human Rights and Democracy in Southeast Asia and Senior Lecturer at the Department of Antropology, Faculty of Culture, at Gadjah Mada University, Indonesia. He received a Doctorate in Social Studies from Swinburne University of Technology, Australia. A political anthropologist, he has worked on a range of subjects pertaining to Indonesian society and culture, including gender and sexuality, consumerism, Islam and social change, political cultures, peasant movements and militarism, human rights and democracy.

Atiur Rahman, is Professor of Development Studies at Dhaka University. An economist with multidisciplinary interests, he specializes in studies related to economic and human development, with special interest in peasant studies, public finance, poverty analysis, gender, environment and governance studies. He has published extensively on peasant differentiation, extreme poverty and participatory budgeting, and is perhaps best known for his seminal book *Peasants and Classes* (1986). He has also edited a number of volumes of *People's Report on Environment*. Previously associated with the Bangladesh Institute of Development Studies, he has also been the head of a think-tank called Unnayan Shamannay for more than a decade.

Mandy Sadan is Lecturer in the History of South East Asia at the *School of Oriental and African Studies* (SOAS), London University. Her areas of interest include the southern, south-eastern and eastern borderlands of Burma, the eastern Himalayas and the south-east Asian massif, especially issues relating to ethnicity and marginalization; material, ritual, oral and visual cultures; and comparative histories of state formation. She has written a number of articles on the cultural politics of identity formation among Kachin communities of Burma and has co-edited a volume with Dr Francois Robinne, *Social Dynamics in the Highlands of South East Asia* (2007), which critically reassesses the significance of the work of Edmund Leach in relation to highland societies.

Mala Rajo Sathian is Lecturer at the Department of Southeast Asian Studies, University of Malaya, Kuala Lumpur, where she teaches courses on Southeast Asian cultures and society, as well as on ethnic minority politics and conflicts. Her area of research is Thailand — its politics, society and history, with special focus on the southern border region of Thailand where she has conducted her research since 2001. Her recent writings include 'Thai-Malaysia Relations: Celebrating 50 Years of Friendship and Alliance', in Ministry of Foreign Affairs, Thailand, in *Rajaphruek and Bunga Raya: Fifty Years of Everlasting Friendship between Thailand and Malaysia* (2007) and '*Malayu* and Military in Pattani: An Analysis of the Political Crisis in Southern Thailand', in Hanizah Idris (ed.), *Asia Tenggara Kontemporari* (2006).

Amnuayvit Thitibordin is Lecturer, Regional Studies Program (Southeast Asian Studies), Institute of Liberal Arts, Walailak University, Thailand. His areas of interest include contemporary politics, political integration and economic issues in Southeast Asia, and he has written on the Association of Southeast Asian Nations (ASEAN), the Chinese overseas community and politico-economic developments in modern South-East Asia. He was awarded the Asian Research Scholarship from Asia Research Institute, National University of Singapore in 2005. Most of his Thai writings are related to region formerly known as Indochina. Recently, he reviewed Philip Taylor's *Cham Muslims of Mekong Delta: Place and Mobility in the Cosmopolitan Periphery,* published in the *Journal of Siam Society,* Vol. 97, 2009.

Maneesha Tikekar is Reader in Politics and Head of the Department of Politics, SIES College of Arts, Science and Commerce, University of Mumbai. Her work focuses issues related to identity politics, democracy and culture, and interstate relations in South Asia. She has received several international fellowships/grants, including the Fulbright Post-Doctoral Fellowship. Her published works include *Across the Wagah: An Indian's Sojourn in Pakistan* (2004); *Islamising a Muslim Nation: Politics of Identity, Legitimacy, and Security in Pakistan* (2005); and *Indian Socialism: Past and Present* (1985, co-edited), and a number of research papers and articles on the countries of the South Asian region. She is a member of the International Advisory Board, Regional Studies, Islamabad.

Lily Rose Tope is Professor at the Department of English and Comparative Literature, University of the Philippines. Her areas

of interest include South-East Asian literature, post-colonial literature, ethnicity and Filipino-Chinese writings. She is the author of
*(Un)Framing Southeast Asia: Nationalism and the Post Colonial Text
in English in Singapore, Malaysia and the Philippines* (1998). She
is the author of several articles, including 'Negotiating Language:
Postcolonialism and Nationalism in Philippine Literature in English',
in Ma Lourdes (ed.), *Philippine English: Linguistic and Literary
Perspectives* (2008) and 'Negotiating Postcoloniality: The Case of
Philippine Literature in English', in Michael Kenneally and Wolfgang
Zach (eds), *Literatures in English: Priorities of Research. SECL
Studies in English and Comparative Literature* (2008).

Index